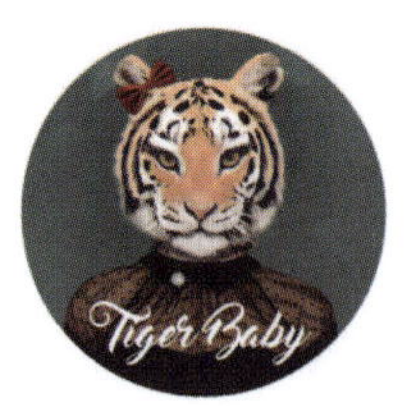

Thank you Tiger Baby
for generously supporting this book

STILL BOMBAY

MAYUR TEKCHANDANEY

For Ettan and Zreh

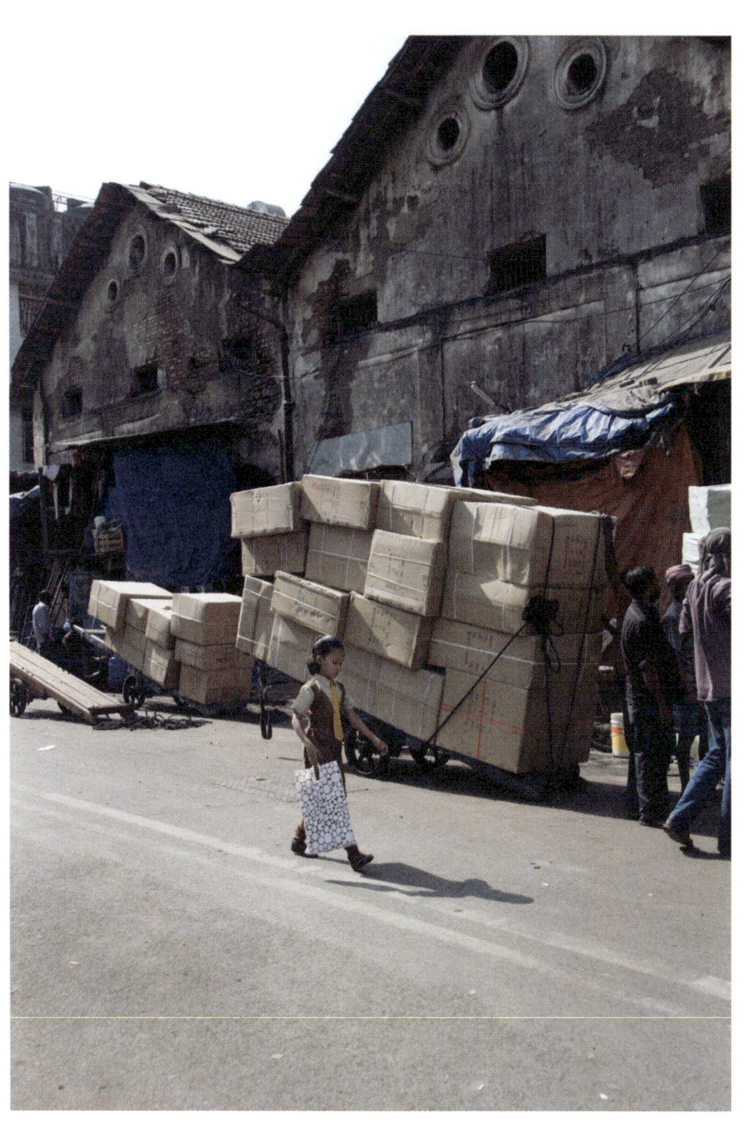

In our minds, we need movement; we need new
ideas; we need new experiences.

§

Movement

Movement is essential to human life. Everything in our body moves: our hearts, lungs, limbs, blood. We may not be nomadic like our hunter-gatherer ancestors. We may be more rooted in our homes, cities, cultures and ideologies, but we are not trees. In our minds, we need movement; we need new ideas, experiences. Otherwise, we get claustrophobic. I've been a Bombayite, a Bombaiya, a Bombaywallah, a Mumbaikar all my life, but for me, Mumbai is not just a place. It is an idea, made up of its people, structures and spaces, its history and its future, an idea that is not static, but in constant flux.

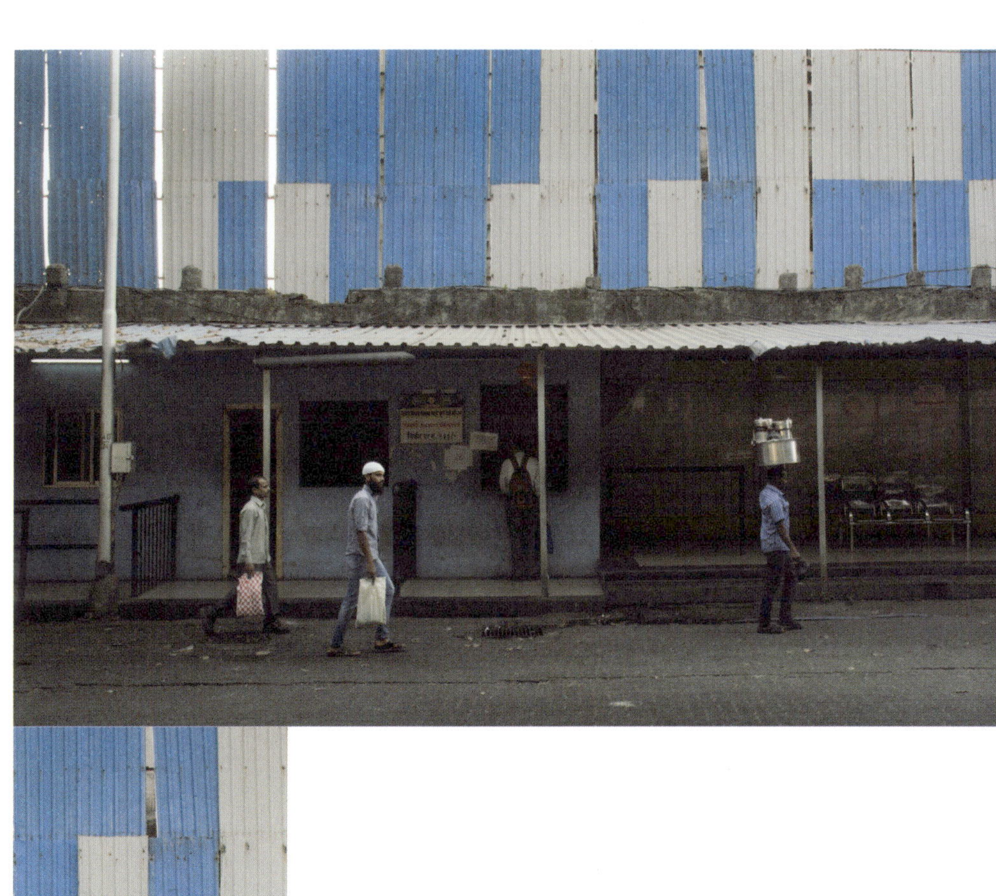

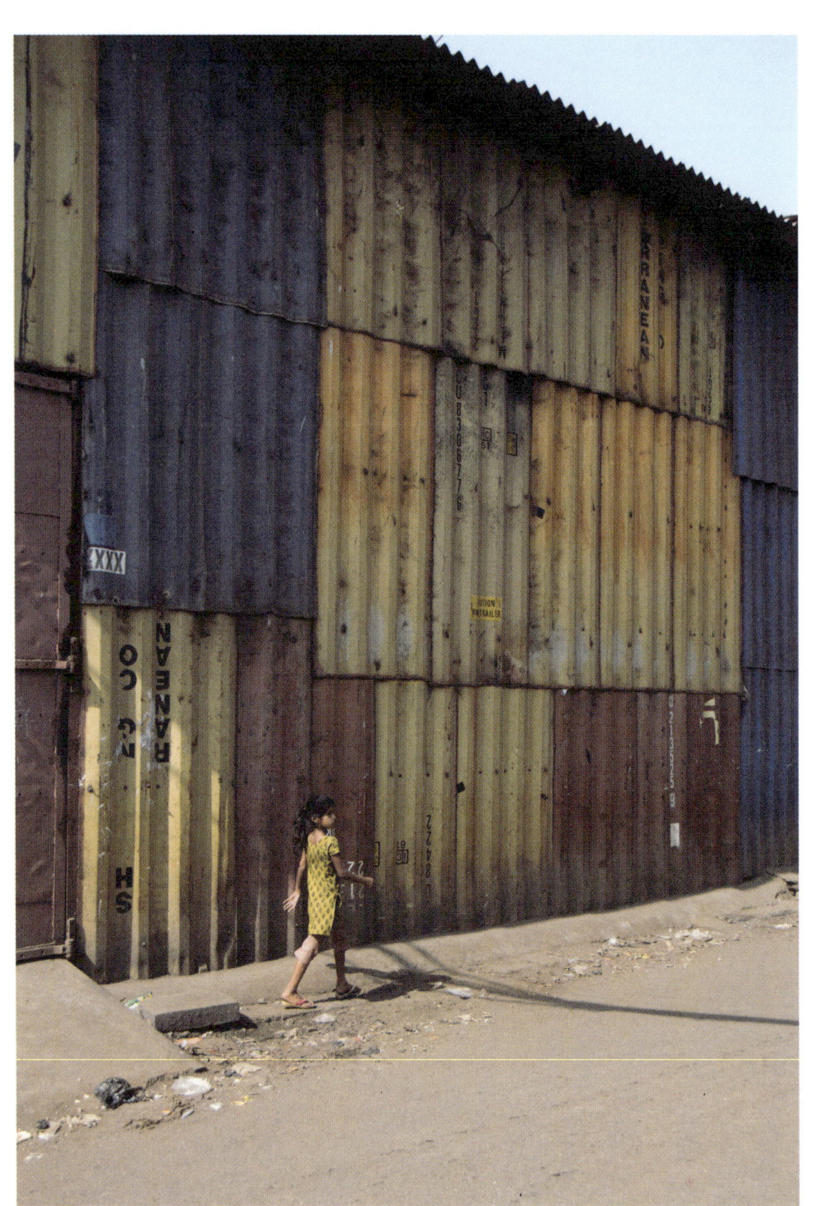

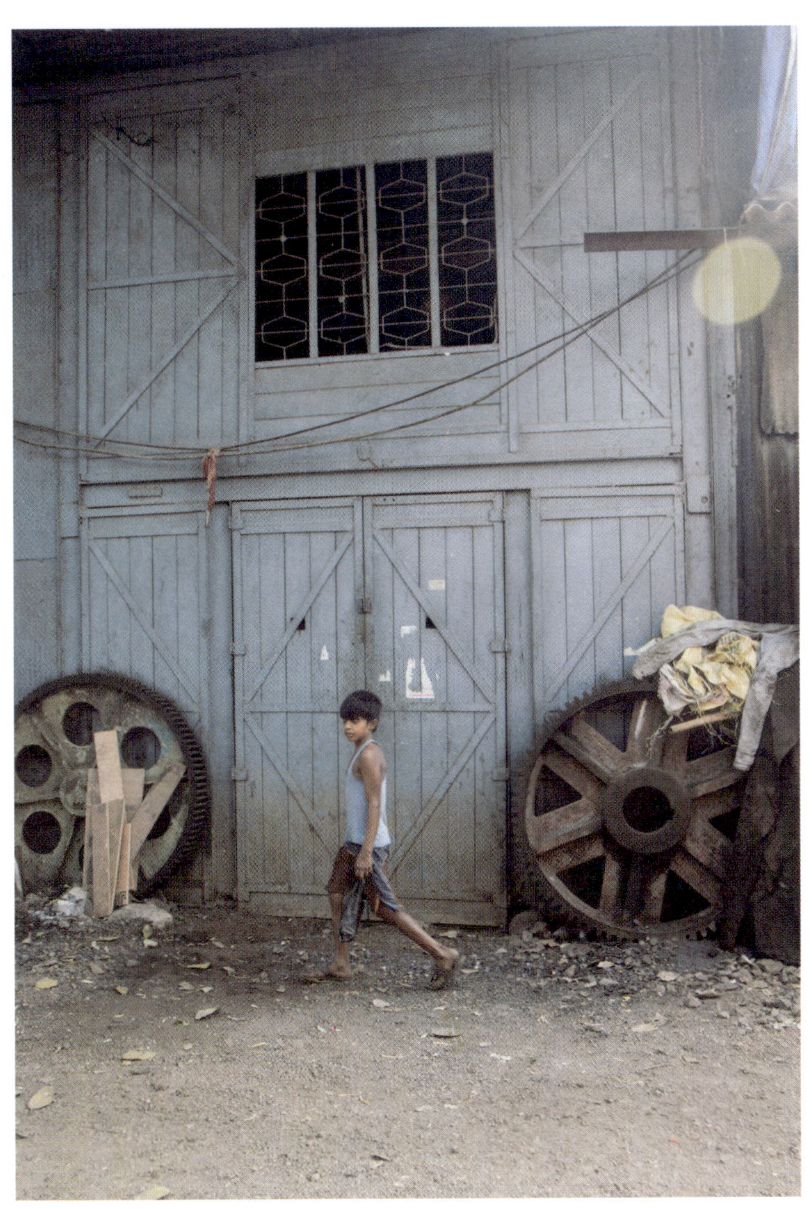

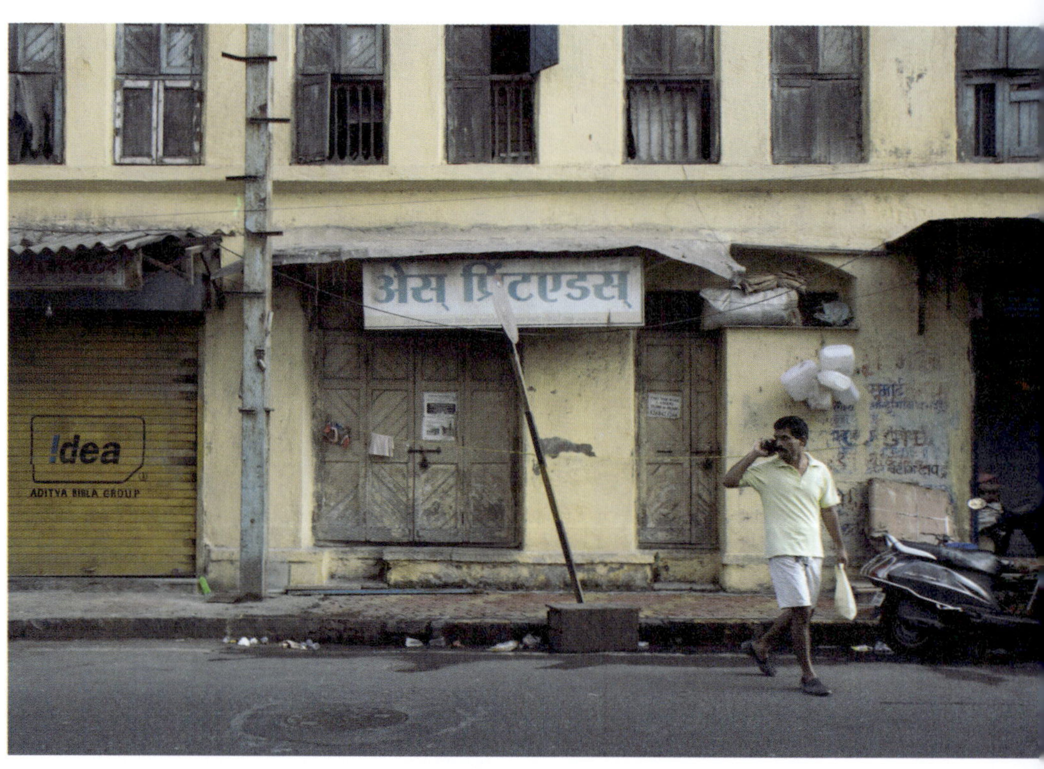

ऐस प्रिंटएडस
!dea
ADITYA BIRLA GROUP

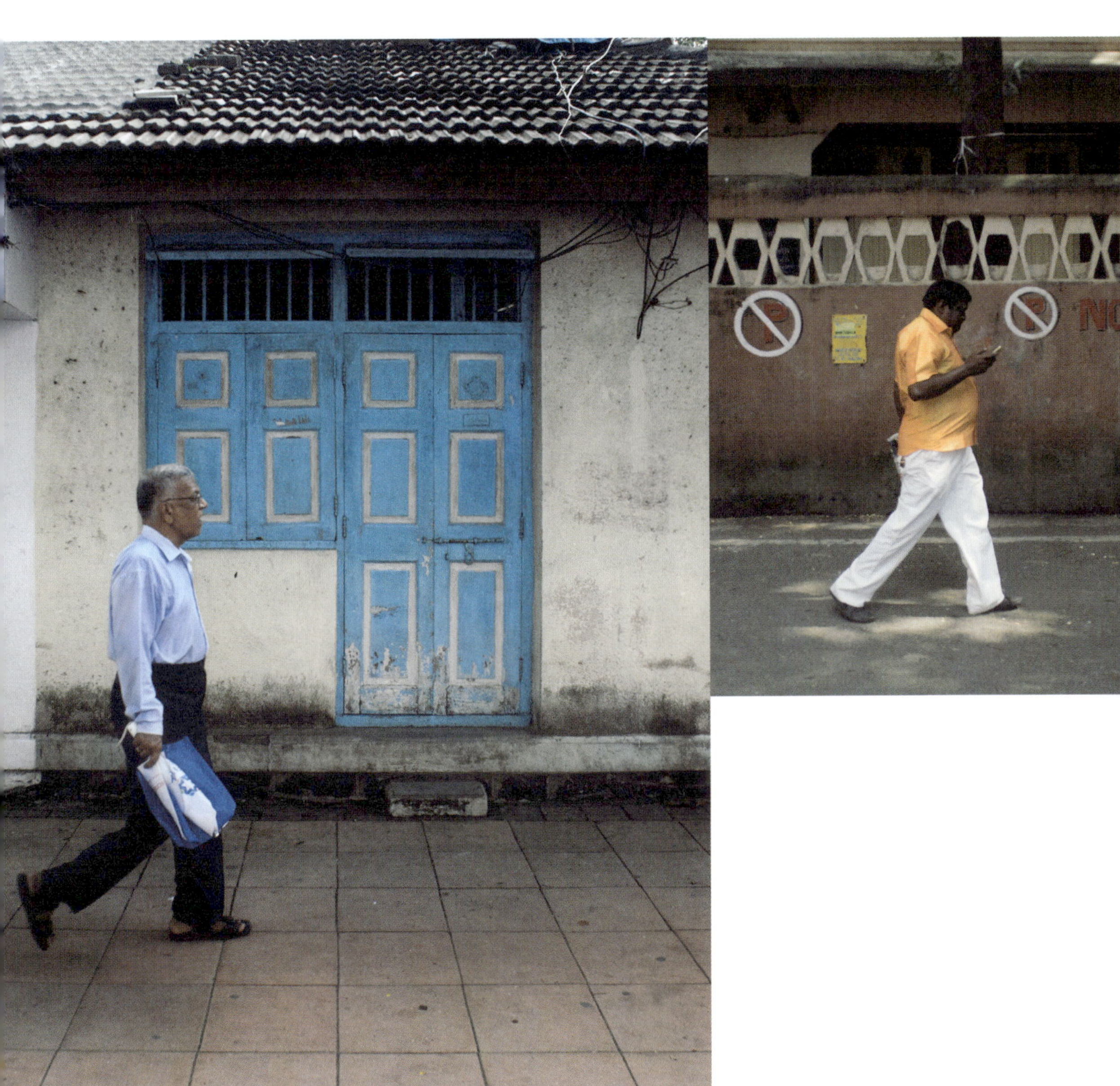

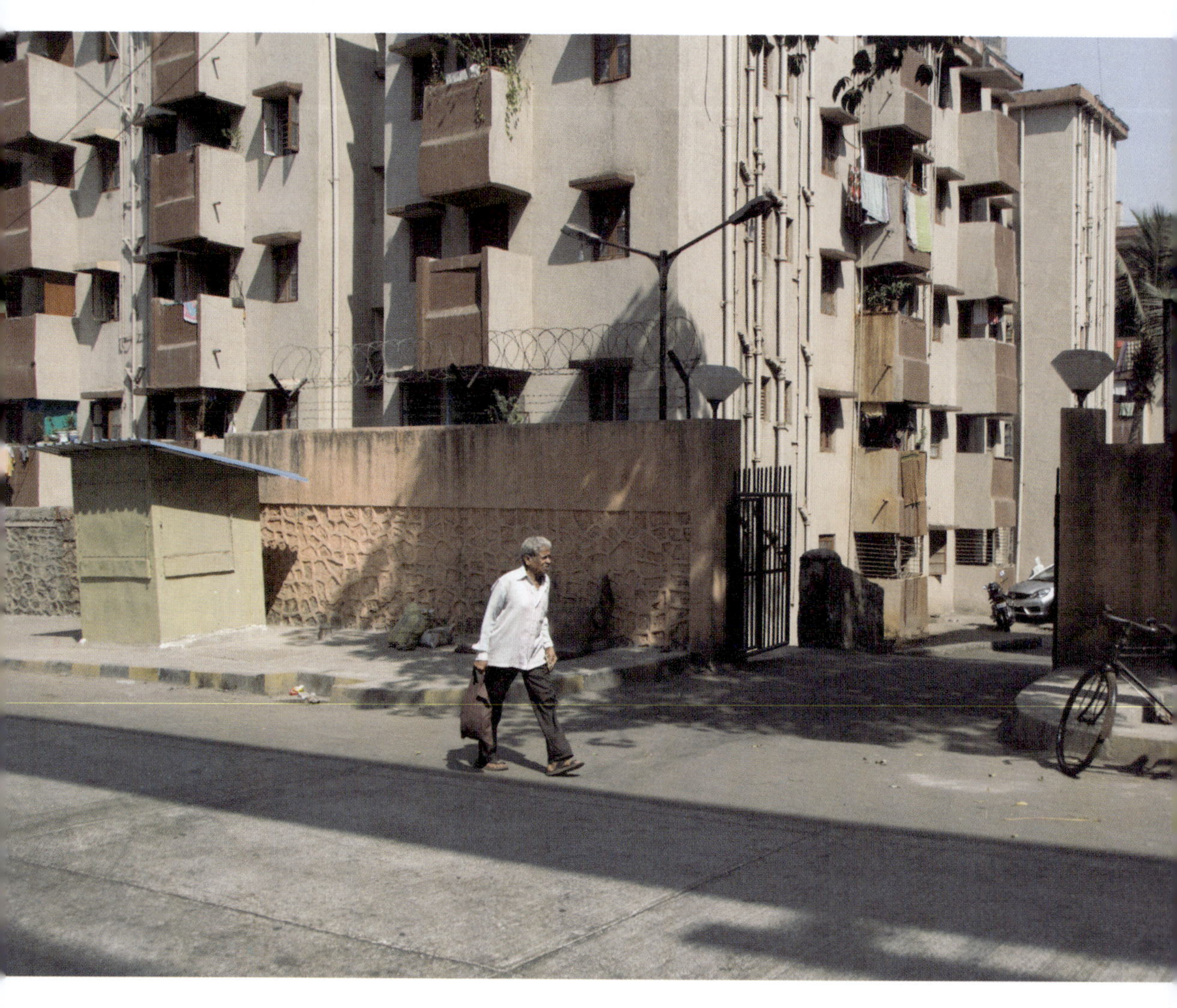

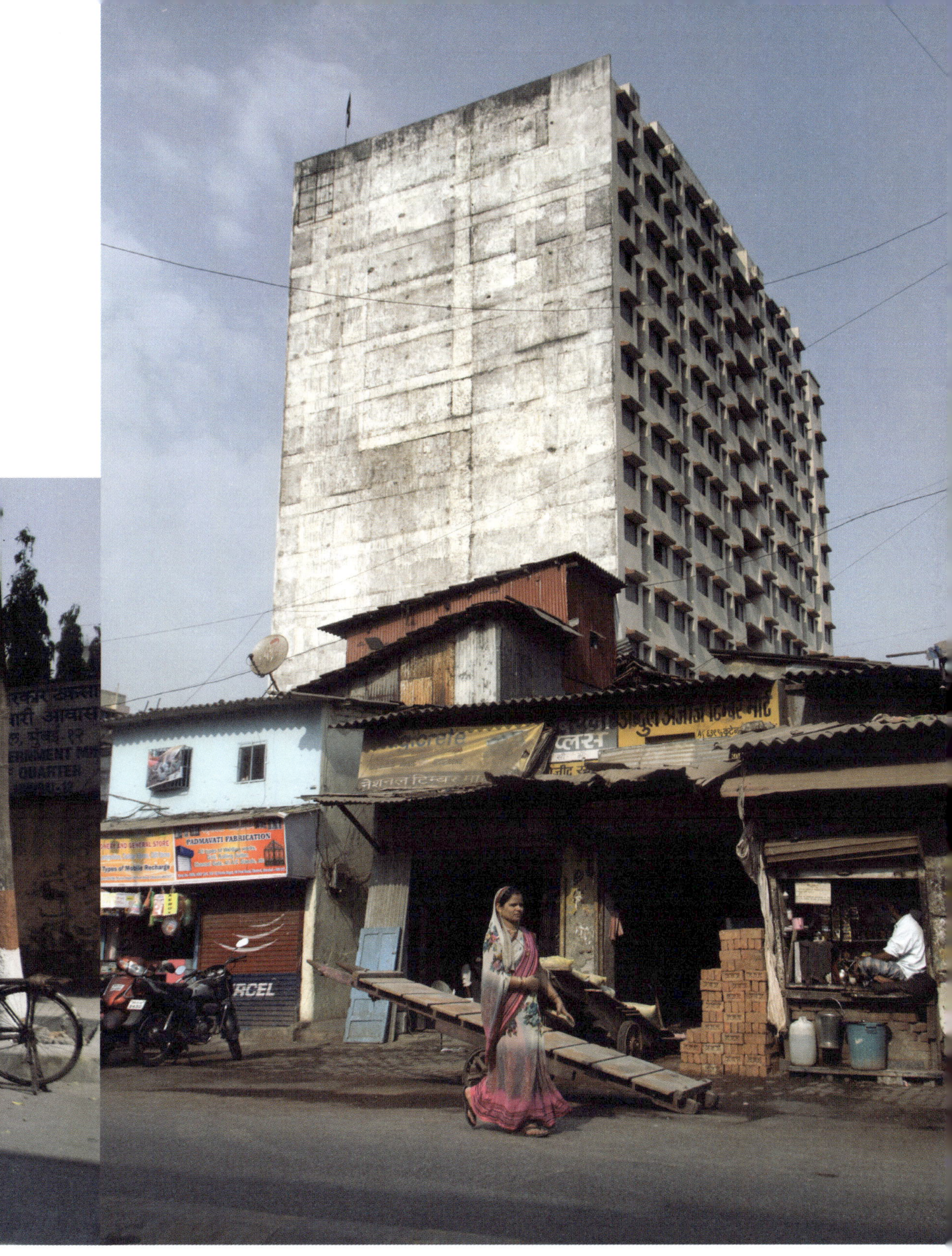
PADMAVATI FABRICATION
AND GENERAL STORE
Types of Mobile Recharge
CEL

CONVERSATIONS WITH A CITY

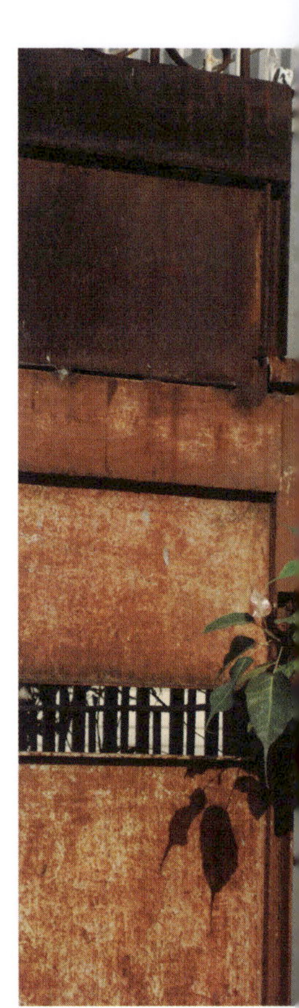

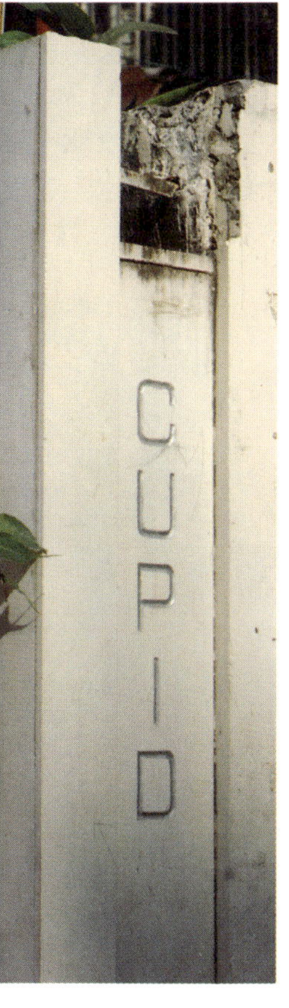

This book came to me quite by chance. Its shape and form changed several times, before evolving into what you see here.

A few years ago, I was in Delhi for a wedding. Having had a few too
many, I fell off the stage and embarrassingly broke my leg. The break
wasn't too bad, a torn ligament, but it still took a couple of months
for my leg to recover. As part of the recovery process, I started taking
short walks in and around my neighbourhood. On one of these walks,
I decided to take an old camera along.

Other than a brief stint in New York, I've lived in Mumbai for most
of my life. And in Mumbai, since I was four, I've stayed in a charming
coastal suburb called Bandra. Of late, I had been observing that a lot of
the older buildings in my area under redevelopment had new names –
the redevelopers had replaced their old names with new ones. Names
like 'Gorwani Excellenza', 'Pallazo Opulence', 'Kamla Presidente'
had replaced 'Rendezvous', 'Shantivan' or 'Cuz-Inn Apartments'.
I wondered if this rebranding indicated some significant change in the
neighbourhood's character. To explore this, I decided to walk the entire
suburb. Over time, the walking became a daily routine, I would pick
an area and zigzag my way through it looking for interesting building
names. But, while documenting the area, looking for these contrasts in
the names, I chanced upon an entirely different kind of image.

I started seeing these happy coincidences of colour. I would
find different objects of the same colour unintentionally arranged
together. For example, I would take a picture of stacks of old cardboard
boxes, in hues of pink, piled next to a rusted bicycle placed in front
of a weathered peach wall. Sometimes it would be a portrait of
a shopkeeper wearing a yellow shirt standing in front of a yellow
storefront. The simplicity of the compositions brought out the everyday
beauty of Mumbai. Just like the idea of documenting building names,
these pictures too became comments on a changing city.

Once the project picked up momentum, the morning was the
most convenient time I could give to it. Back then, my children were
small. Both my wife and I were working. The kids would get on their
school bus by 7.00 in the morning, and between then and 10.00,
which is when I got into work, I had some free time. In addition to
convenience, for artistic reasons too, Mumbai in the mornings worked
out best for me. The soft light, the quiet streets gave me a meditative,
reflective image, helping me paint a more flattering picture of the
city. With a renewed sense of my creative purpose and a rekindled
love for Mumbai, I decided to walk as many streets, bylanes and gallis
(alleyways) as possible, in the hope that I could reconcile my nostalgic
idea of Bombay, with the physical reality of Mumbai.

On reflection, it appears that my motivation for this project, other than mending my broken foot, was a search for mental solace. When the project first started, I was coming out of a tough period, in which my ailing father lost mobility, at which point the responsibility for the family's affairs fell squarely on me. Managing these, along with work, and being a new parent, proved to be overwhelming. It meant giving up my career as a film director and shutting down my production house. Subsequently, I refocused on graphic design, opening a small design studio, which I felt would be more manageable.

All through my career, along with my professional practice, be it design or film, I've tried to maintain an artistic practice. The medium of the work varies from painting to collage, to an occasional comic book. Whatever the output, the underlying creative approach has been a philosophical one. When I began photographing the city, I was exploring the concept of 'fairness'. Did the fact that Bandra was gentrifying mean that we had accepted inequality as the new norm? What did it mean, that in a city where half the population lives in slums, one family lived in one of the most expensive houses in the world?

These questions and others like them inform my art. And in much of what I do, Mumbai is an essential character. This obsession goes back to when I was a fresher in art school. Even when I was studying at Parsons in New York, my artworks were about Mumbai. I remember one painting, an abstract cityscape inspired by the minimal work of the Russian artist Kazimir Malevich. The piece was a stark black and white painting with angular geometry done on textured canvas. The idea was to demarcate the haves of the city from the have-nots. After art school, I returned to India and started working as a director and Mumbai featured as the 'city of dreams' in a lot of the ad films I made.

A consistent theme of all my past work had been a sense of nostalgia, a yearning for the Bombay of my childhood. This present exercise too began that way: the colour-coordinated photos of the city's unassuming details, its architecture and its people reminded me of the beauty of the city. A beauty I had stopped appreciating. So, when I started walking after my injury, photographing areas I had never been to earlier, venturing into parts that were out of my comfort zone, I felt that I'd chanced upon a format that enabled me to have the most comprehensive conversation I'd ever had with my city.

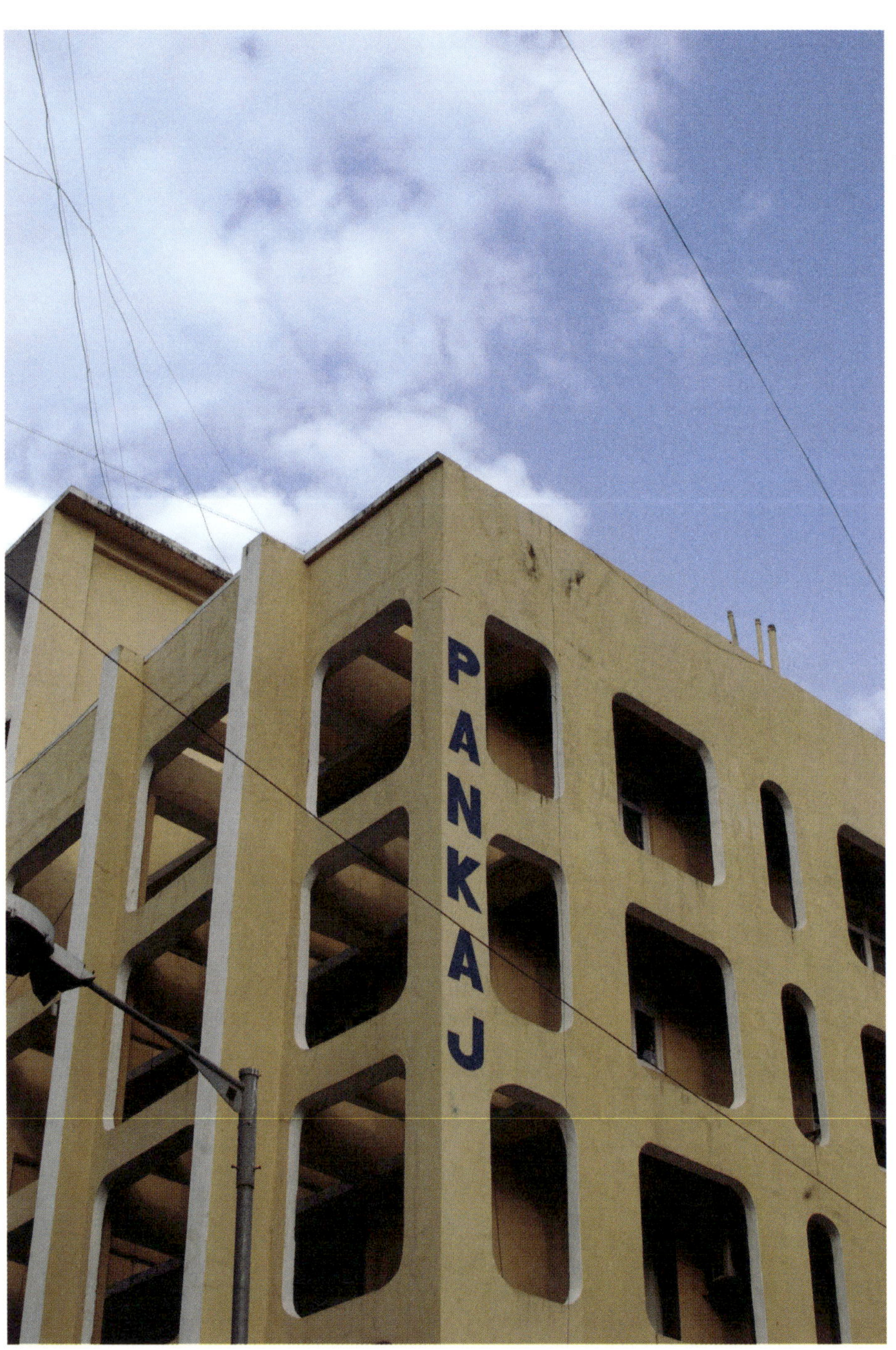

PANKAJ

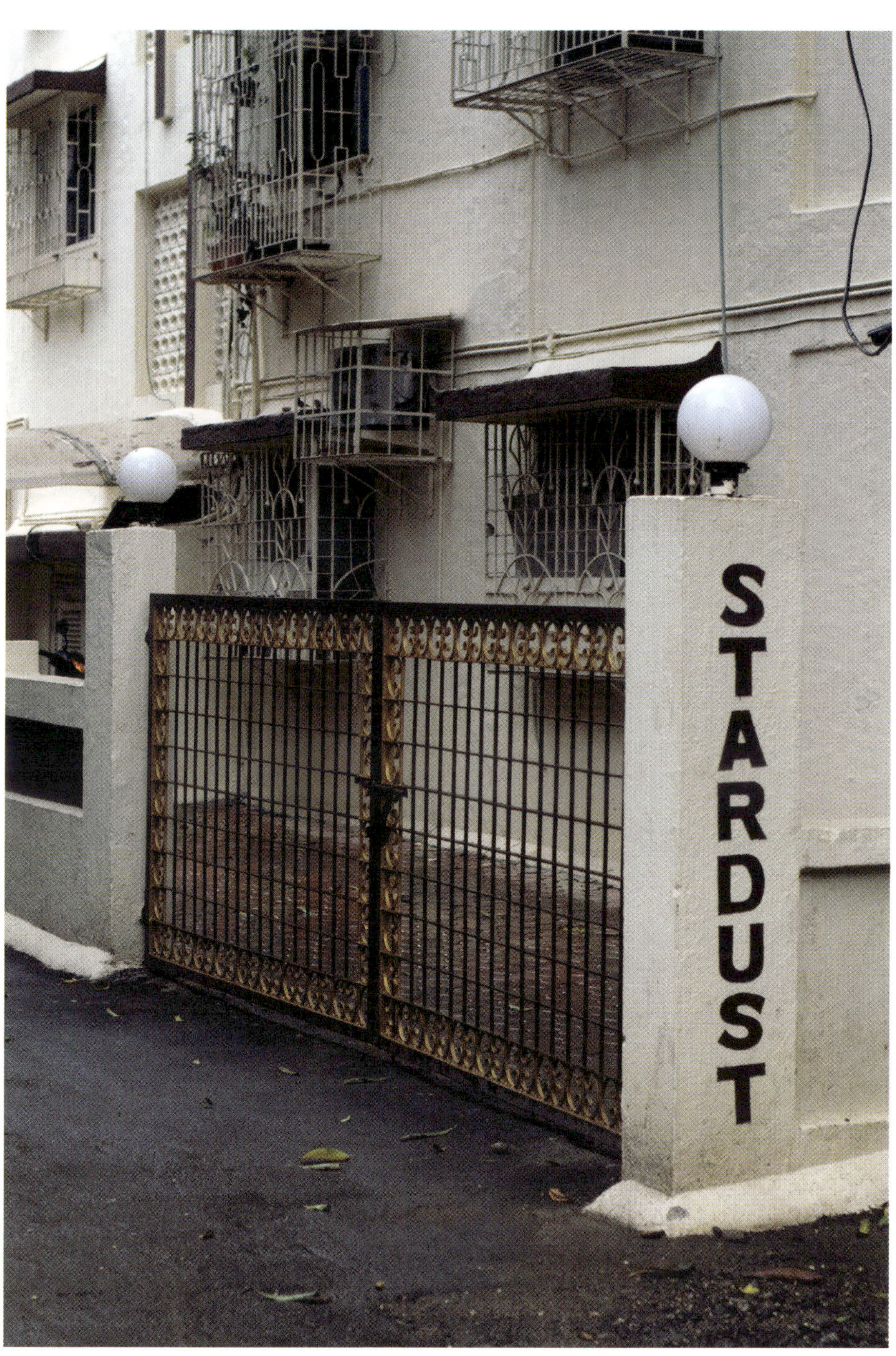

STARDUST

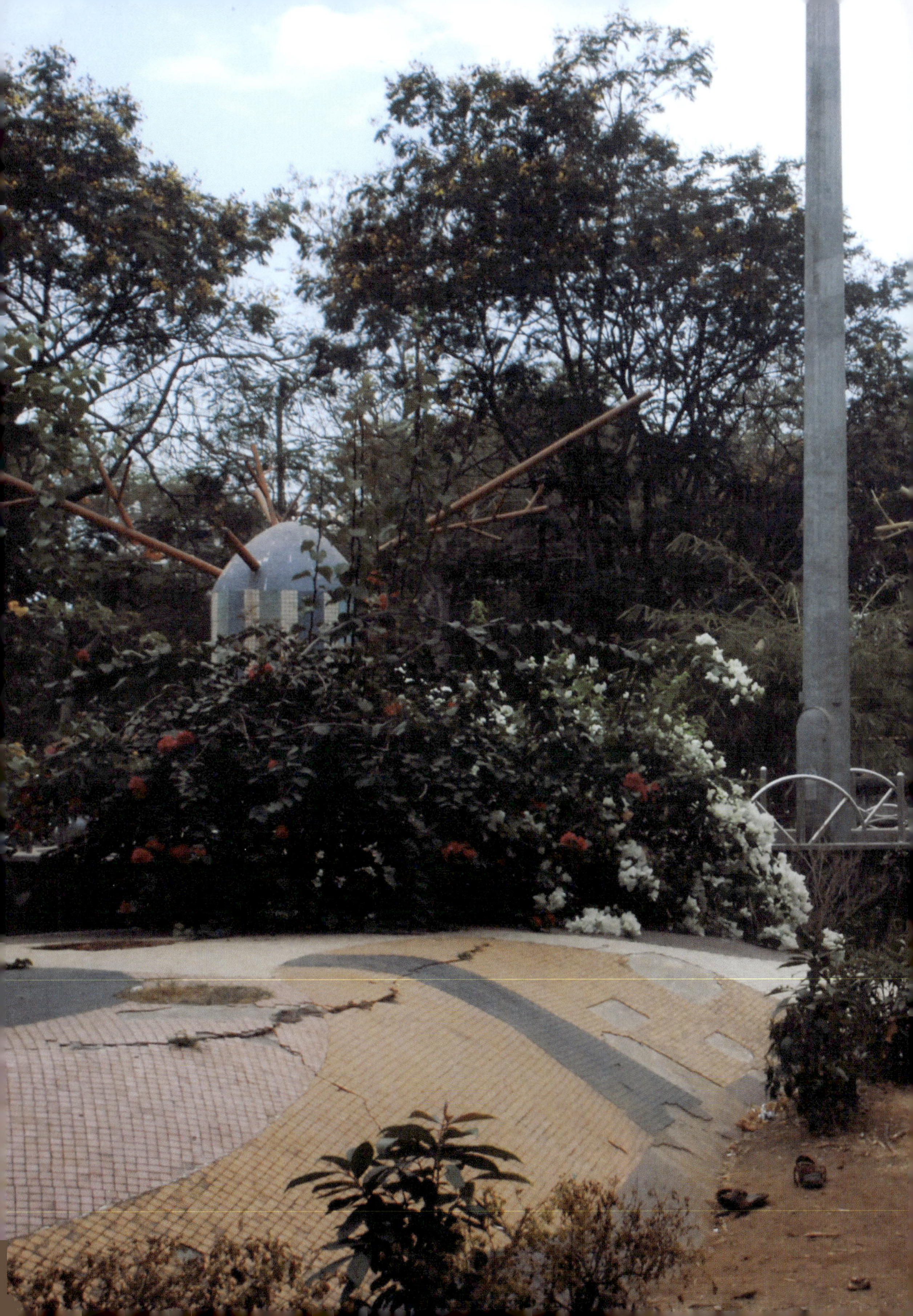

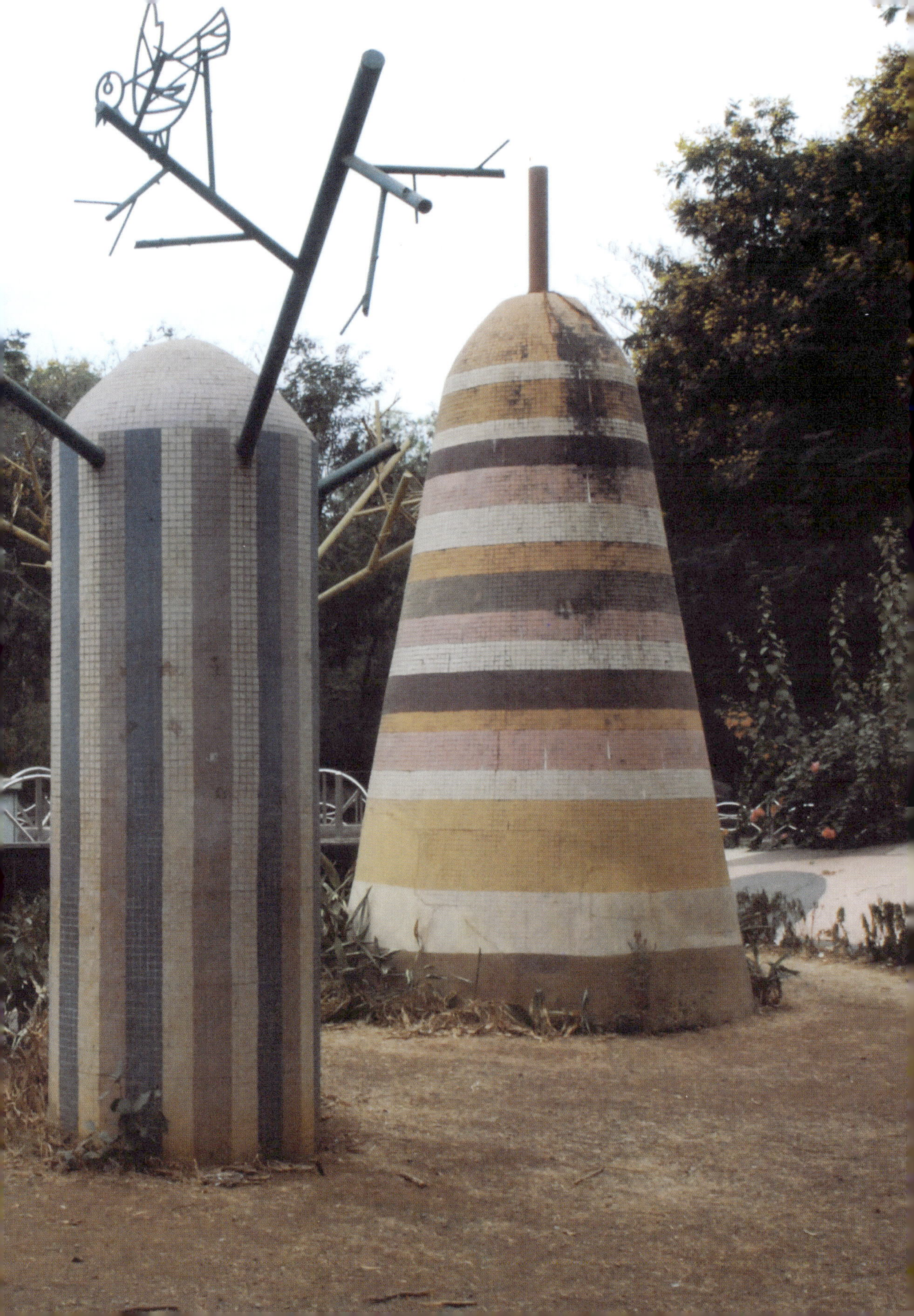

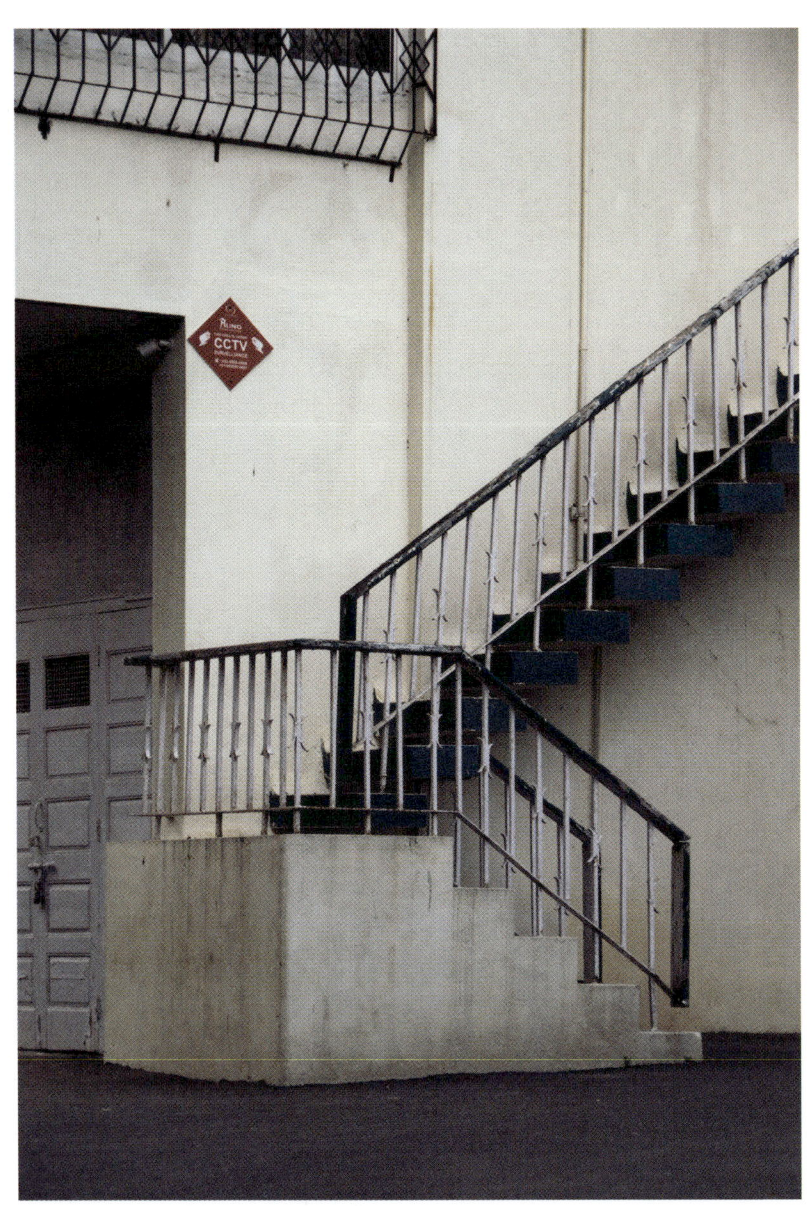
RINO
CCTV
SURVEILLANCE

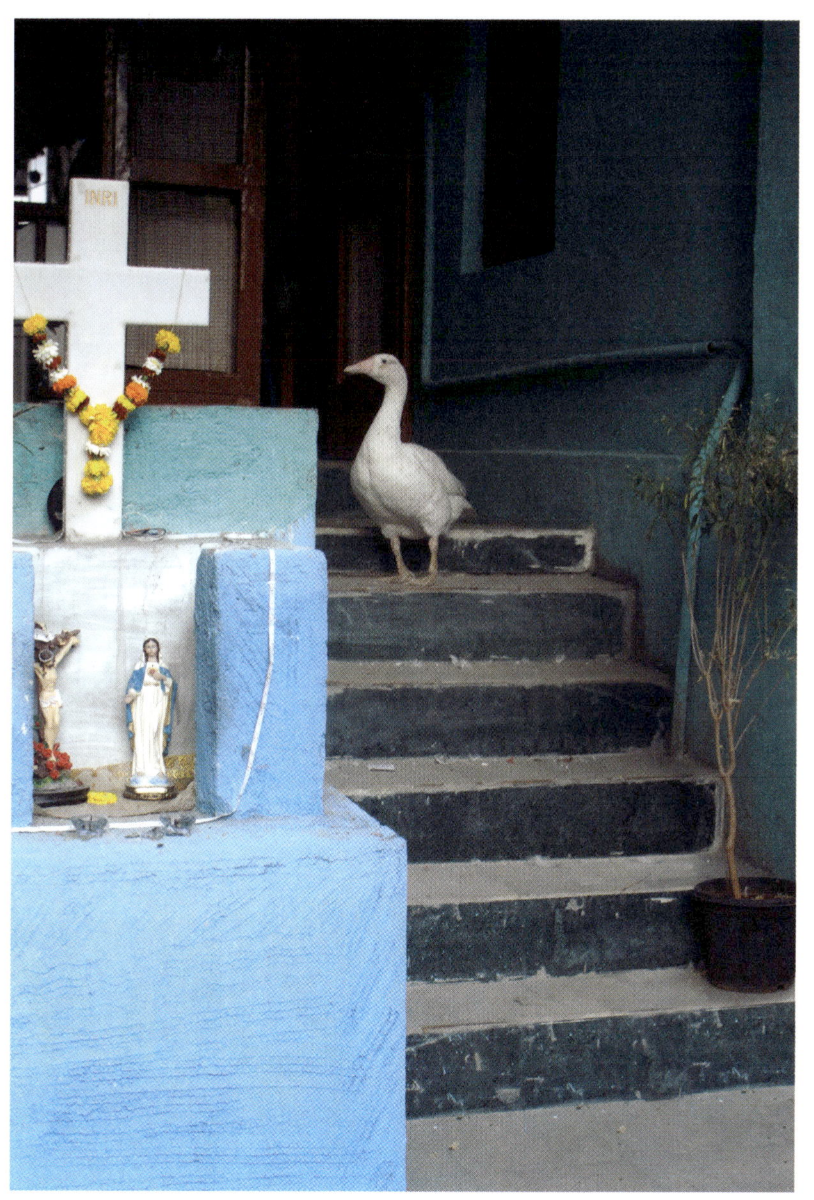

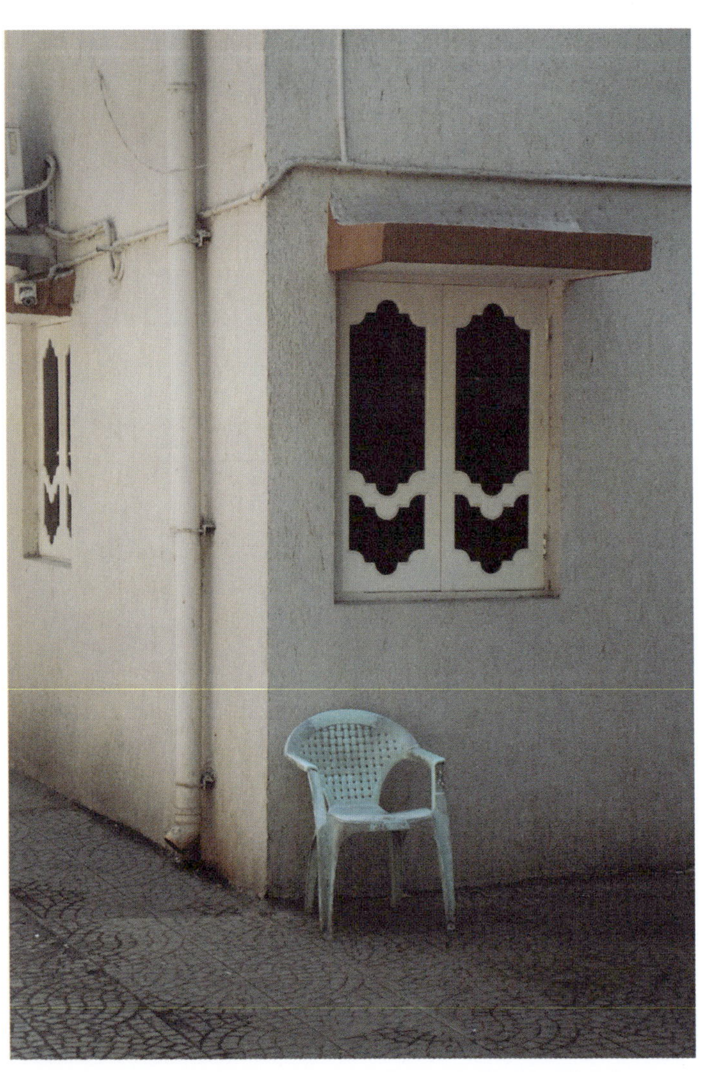

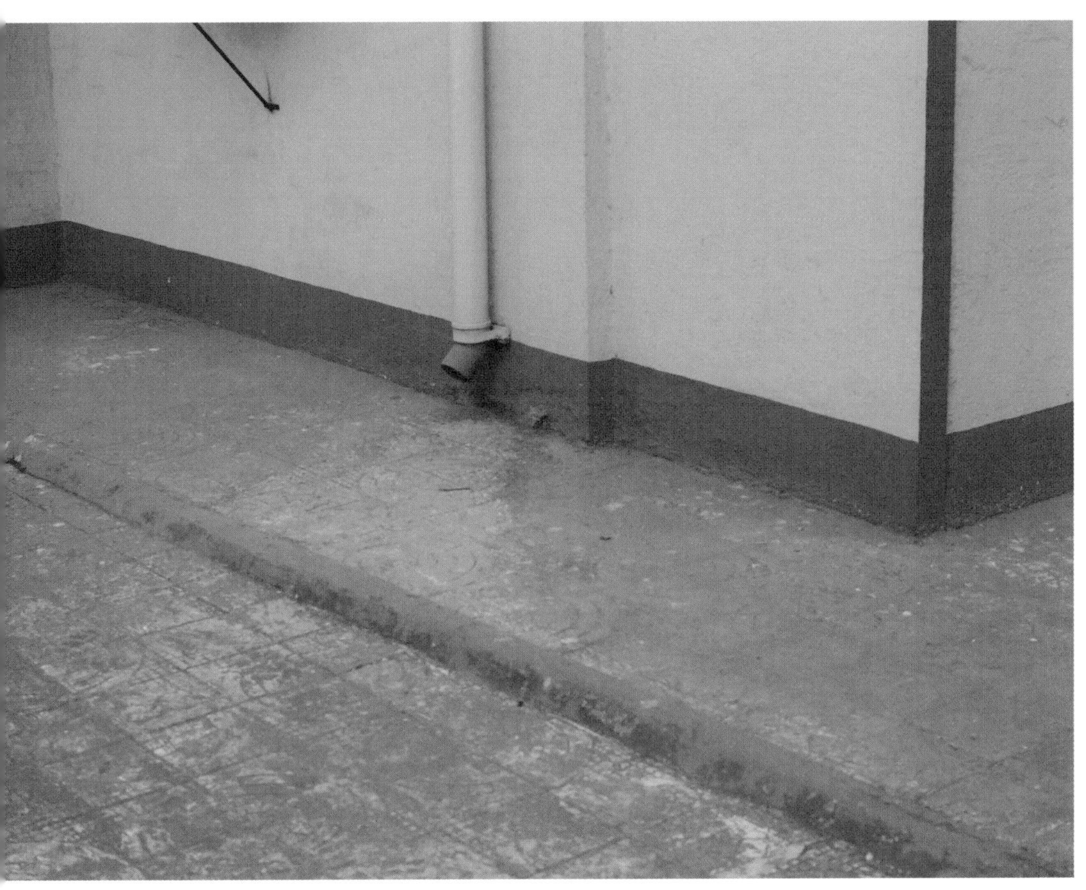

PHOTOGRAPHING FROM MEMORY

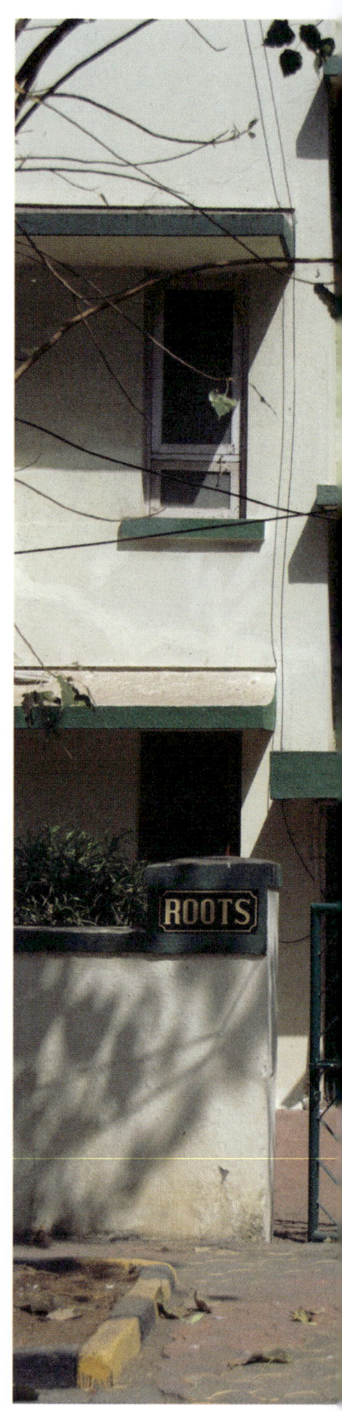

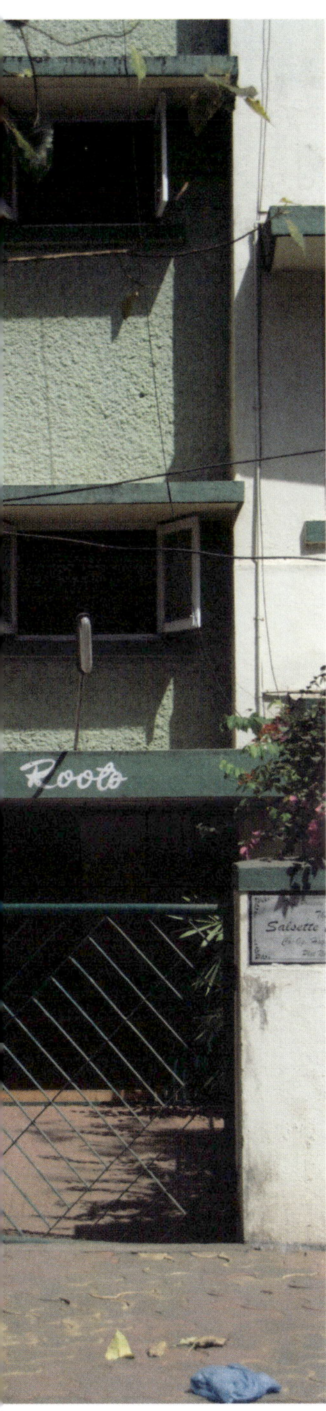

My family moved to Bandra when I was four. We stayed on the edge of one of the Bandra villages in a small cosmopolitan building called 'Casa Maria'.

Bandra is the first suburb beyond Bombay's old city lines, and it lies along the city's picturesque western coast. The suburb has an old world charm as it retains many of its old Gaothans, which are essentially village-like settlements, comprising single-family homes connected by small pedestrian bylanes. The original inhabitants of Bombay, the Kolis, associated with fishing, still live in these Gaothans (also known as Koliwadas [Koli neighbourhood]). In Bandra there are seven surviving Gaothans, more than in any other part of Bombay.

The Portuguese were the first amongst the European colonists to arrive on Bombay's shores. At that time, a lot of the local residents converted to Christianity. To this day, Bandra retains its Portugese-Christian flavor. I myself went to a Catholic school. But as Bandra joined the expanding megapolis of Bombay, it became a very cosmopolitan place. Growing up, my friends were Catholic, Muslim, Parsi, and every type of Hindu.

The Gaothans of Bandra hug its coastline, and back in the day as you went inland from the coast the dense villages gave way to small parcels of farmland. Over time these small farm plots got redeveloped as entrepreneurial families bought them over and built bungalows on them. I grew up in one of these bungalows – my family didn't live in one, but my best friend, Stafford Pereira, did and it seemed like I did too. Theirs was a beautiful single-storey bungalow called 'Desirée'. It had a driveway on one side and a lovely garden wrapped around the rest of it. In the back of the house, they had an avla tree. Come October, we would climb the tree and eat the fruit straight off its branches. I spent a lot of my childhood at the Pereira home, and bungalow life was a big part of my experience of growing up in the city.

I met Stafford Pereira in St. Stanislaus High School. Stafford was the oldest of five brothers, Bradley, Croyden, Christian and Rhys being the others. In the third grade, I was in the same class as Stafford, and since we lived one lane away from each other, we became friends. Since there were five of them, I didn't need many more friends. Between us we could play any game. We could set up a cricket match, football, play hide and seek… Other kids from the locality joined in, but we were the core group.

I would go over to their place around 5.30 in the evening, and by 7.00 sharp we would wrap up whatever it is we were doing. For, after that they would be called to bathe, after which they sat for dinner, followed by an hour of lessons, prayers and then bed. All this was quite a contrast to my home life. I would loiter outside their house past their evening deadline and cycle past their home, checking in on where they were in their routine. As the bungalow had windows all around, you could see what they were up to. Stafford would often have to shoo me away lest I got him into trouble.

My home life was less controlled, dinner at my place was at 9 o'clock. Even the scents in our two houses were different. Their house had stronger, more pungent aromas – vinegar, 'goa' sausage… my home had softer smells of, mostly, vegetarian Sindhi cooking. They lived in a bungalow and I, in a flat.

I never ceased being a Bandra boy. It is where I returned to, after finishing art school in New York. When I left my job at MTV India, this is where I set up my own office. The company was called ChingumChiclet and we rented a room on the ground floor of a house in Ranwar, one of the Gaothans of Bandra.

As redevelopment began to gentrify Bandra, the Gaothans remained its saving grace. Property values did not skyrocket here nearly as much, as these villages are not navigable by car. This small inconvenience created a creative renaissance in these villages, which then spread to the rest of the suburb. Young creative people from all over India and expatriate Indians have made the Gaothans their home. Cafés, niche boutiques, design studios and experimental art spaces have cropped up in these villages.

I am aware that boutiques and art spaces can be taken as a sign of gentrification as well. For that reason, I want to qualify this point a little further. Gentrification is a type of change and change, movement, is inevitable. If gentrification in some form is unavoidable, then I would choose the kind that brings niche cafés, and design boutiques that reconnect people to local crafts and produce versus the mass-produced brand-hyped consumption of high street malls.

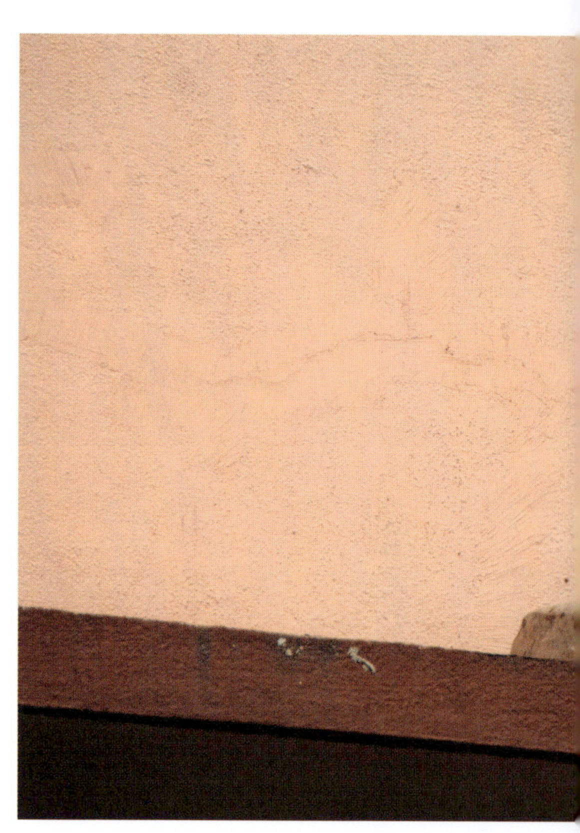

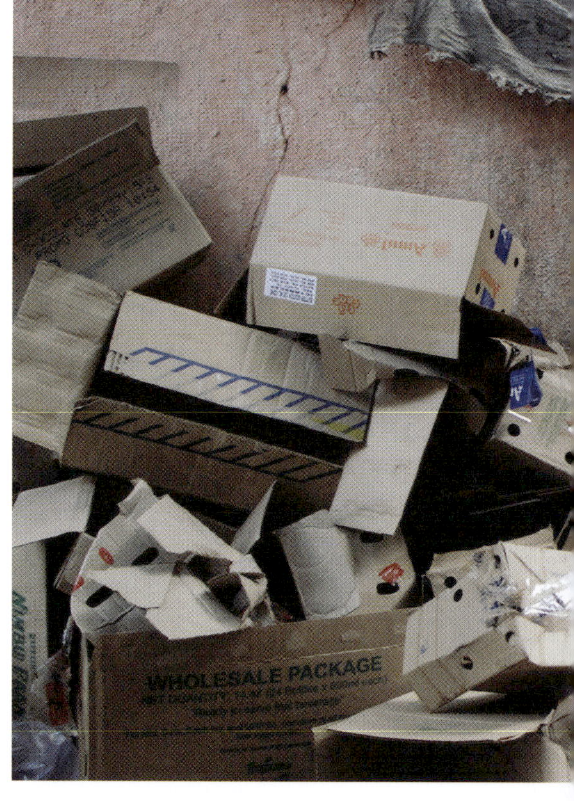
Amul
WHOLESALE PACKAGE

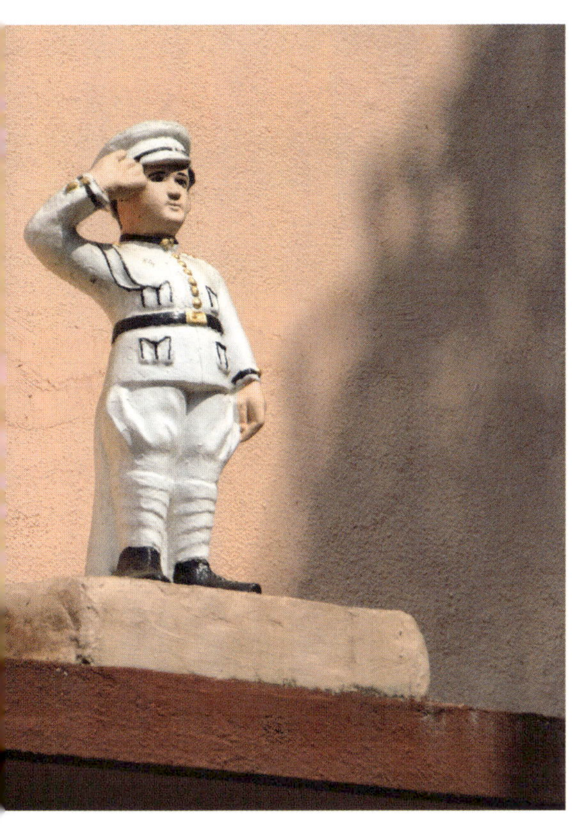

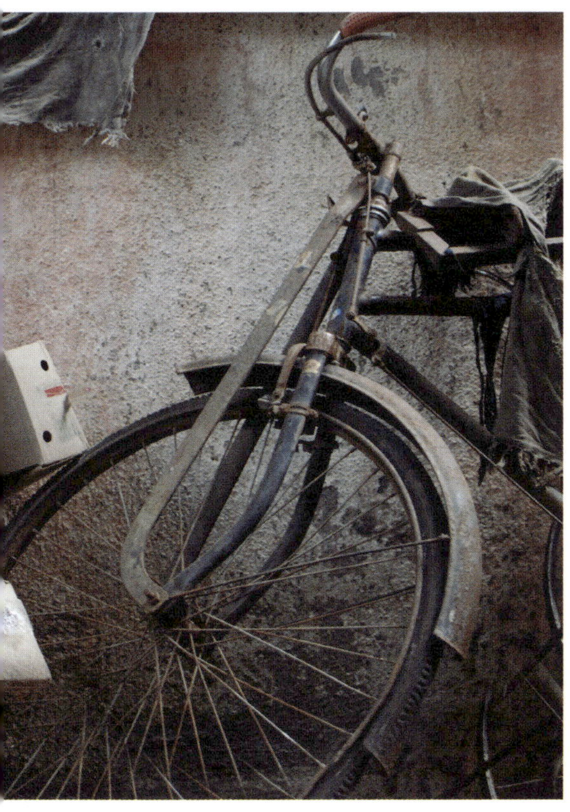

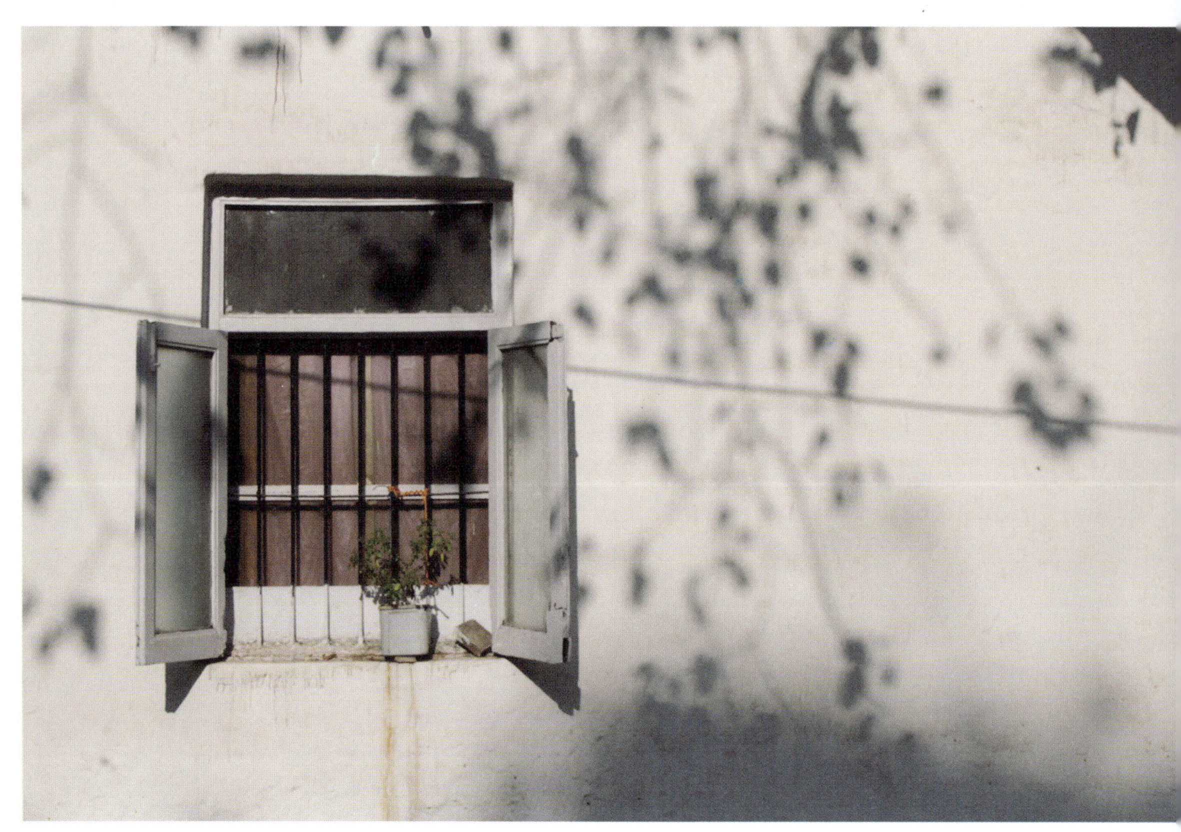

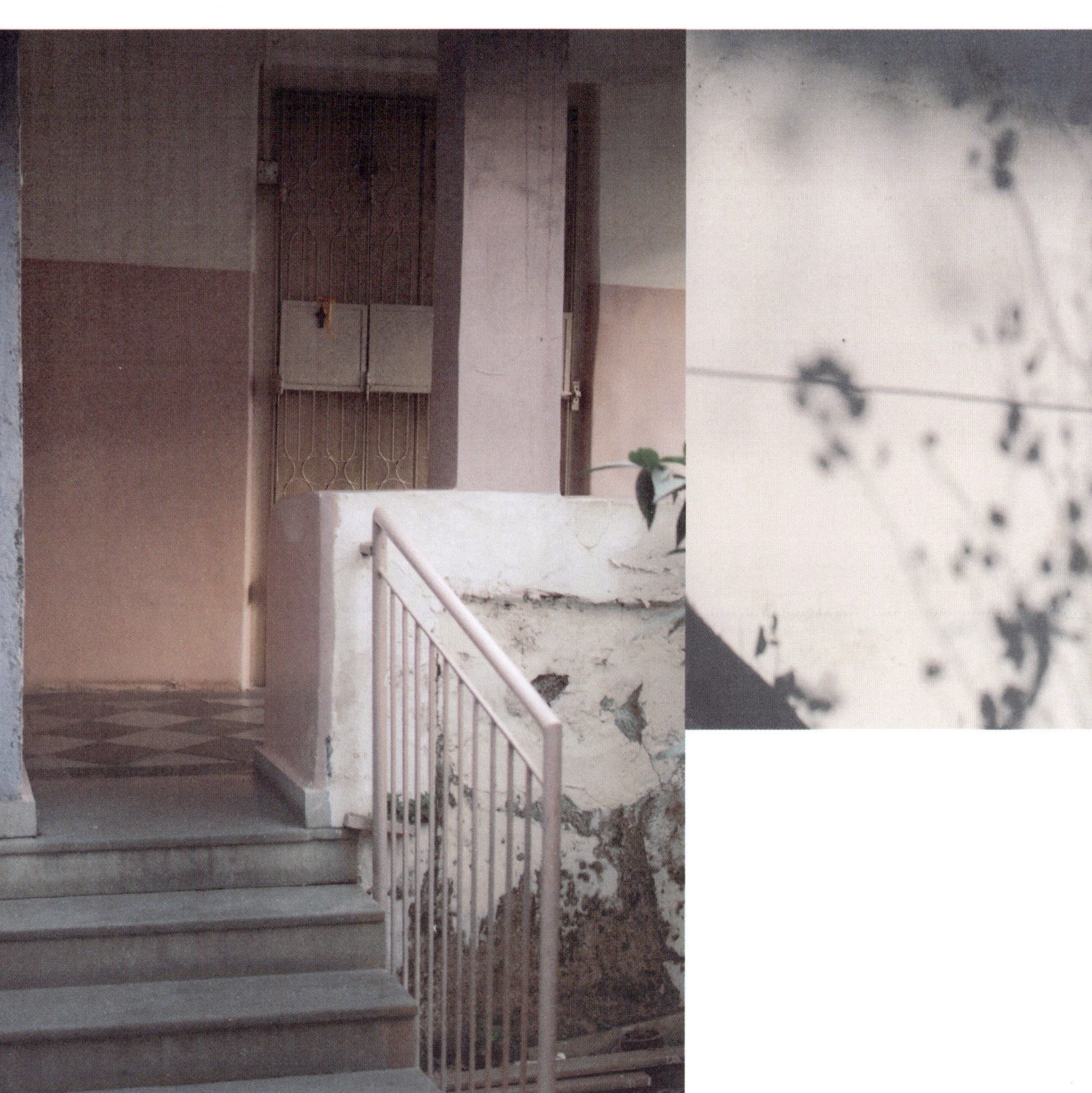

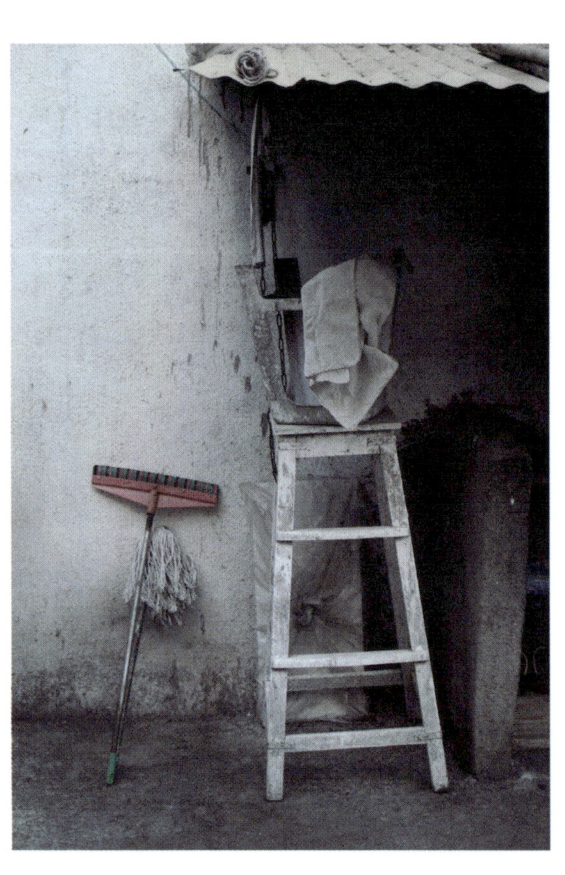

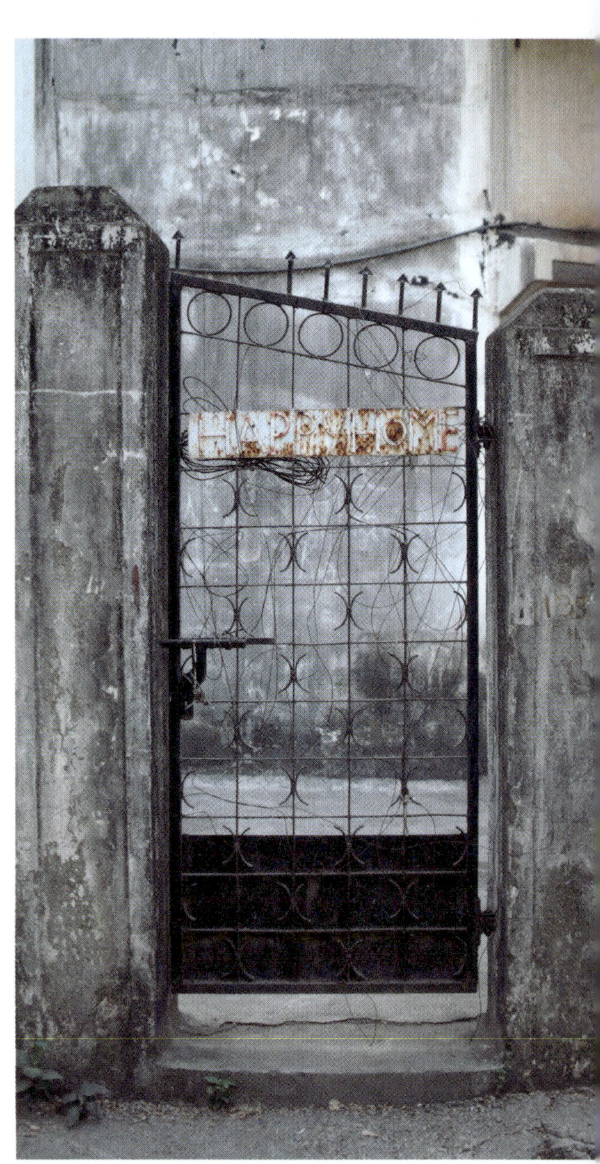
HAPPY HOME

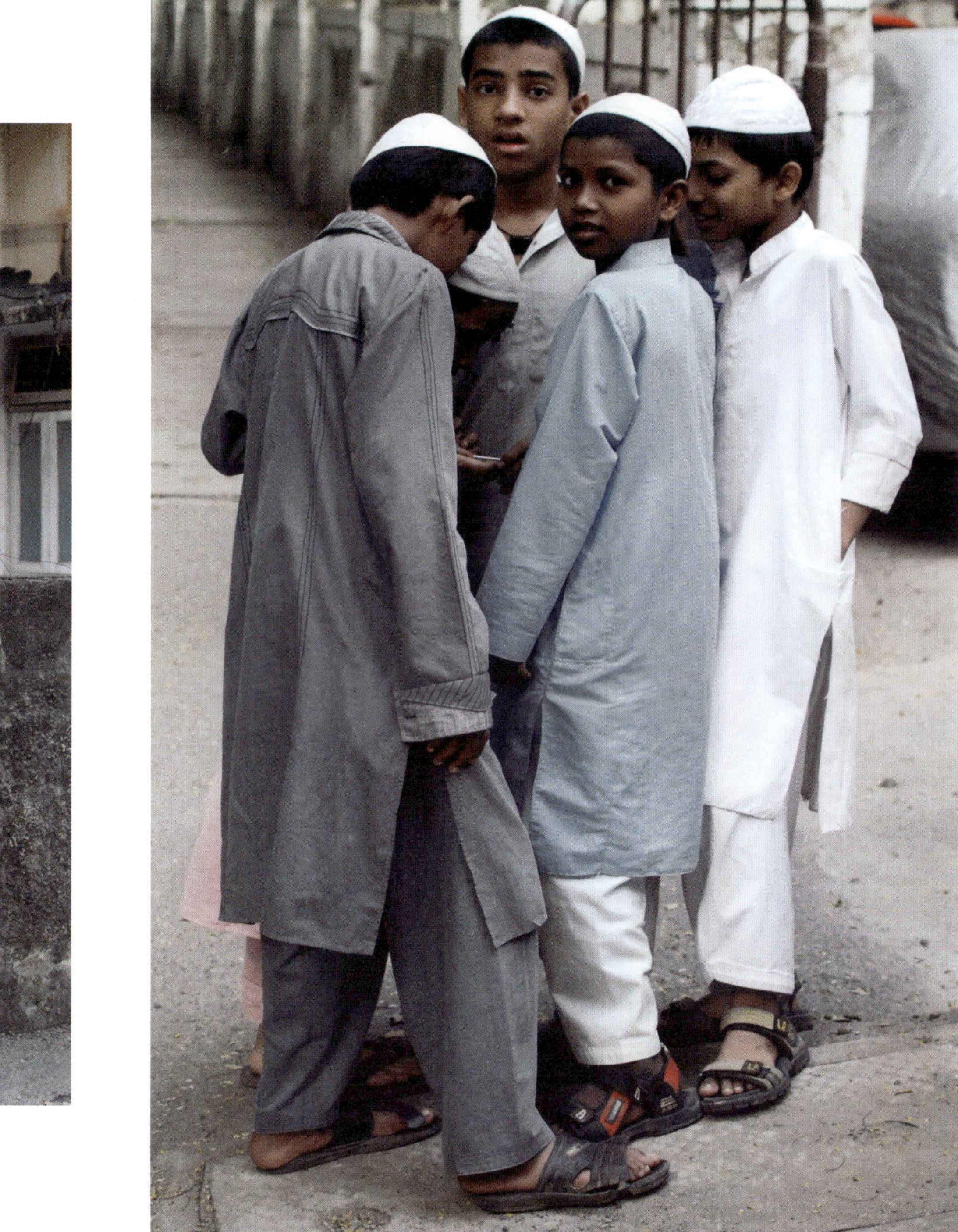

MAPPING MUMBAI

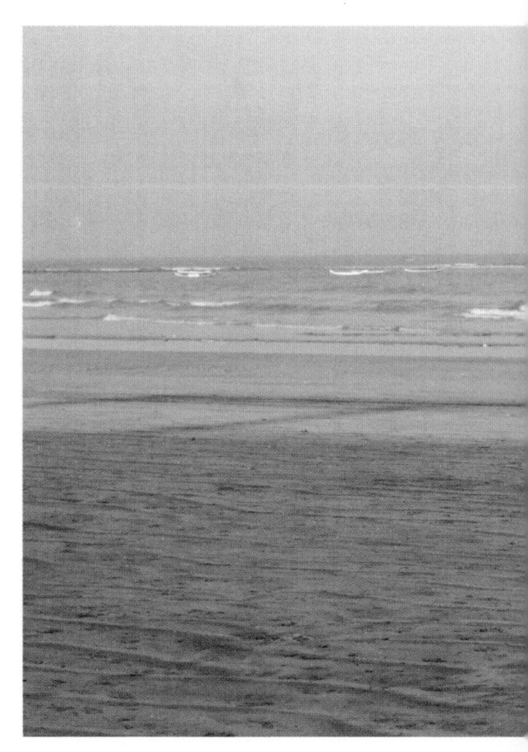

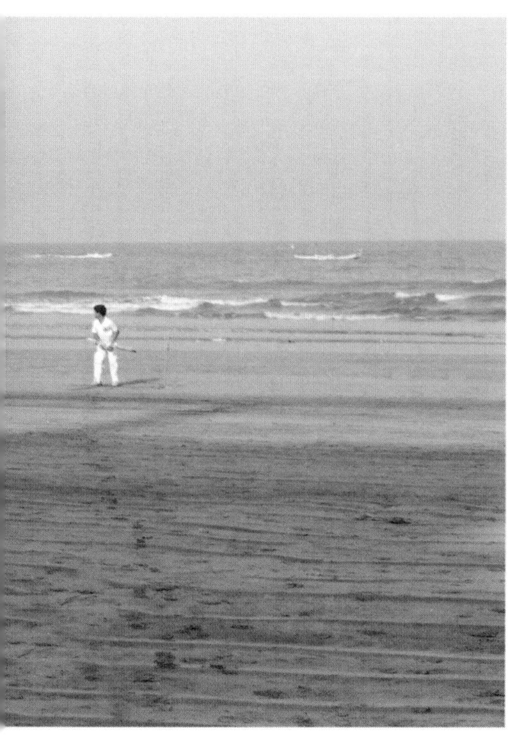

It took me around three years to take
the pictures you see in this book.

In this time, I walked that part of the 'Island city', which runs from Sion in the north of Mumbai to Colaba in the south. The suburbs of Mumbai come under 'Mumbai Suburban District', and here I walked all of Bandra, Khar, Santa Cruz and Juhu. The total road length I covered, including the many inner gallis of the city's slums, would come up to nearly a thousand kilometres.

It was quite a meticulous exercise, physically tracing the city, street by street. On occasion it felt tedious to commute to where I started to walk, but once the walk began it was a lot of fun because there was so much to discover, and I was playing tourist in my own city.

While I have spent most of my adult life in Bandra, when I was growing up, I did spend a lot of time in other parts of the city. Both my parents come from large families and because of this I have a lot of cousins. During my school vacations, I would go and live with them. I had cousins in Shivaji Park, Ghatkopar, Ulhasnagar, Thane, Sion, Andheri East, Lokhandwala and extended family in Colaba, Bandra and Mahim. We would move in small gangs of three or four from one house to another. Sometimes I would go directly from one cousin's house in Andheri to another in Ghatkopar. From there I would call my parents saying I'd be coming home later than expected. Because of my sleepover relays all over the city, my mum would call me 'rolu', which means vagabond in Sindhi.

Other than the bond I shared with my cousins, the neighbour-hoods they stayed in attracted me. In Colaba, the family lived opposite Cusrow Baug, which I found fascinating for its sheer scale, with large apartment buildings and vast open spaces, all encompassed within a giant gated wall. My Nana (grandfather) lived in Shivaji Park. Its low buildings with low boundary walls were like a jungle gym for us kids. We scaled those buildings like monkeys, racing across housing societies to the chagrin of the old aunties and security guards. Adjacent to my Nana's house was a fire brigade. It was unique as it was laid out almost like a residence. In between the two wings of the building was a parking space massive enough to hold two shiny fire trucks. Every time we heard the fire alarm, we made a beeline for the street to flag off our heroes.

In Mahim, right on the water's edge, lived one of my dad's closest friends. Though the children in that house, both older girls, weren't technically my cousins, I still called them Didis (elder sisters). They loved having me over and fussed over me, and I always stayed beyond my welcome. Eventually, I'd run out of fresh clothes and end up wearing their oversized girly tees. They probably got a laugh out of it, but it was a small price to pay. At night you could hear the ocean from their room. During high tide, the water would splash against their compound wall and the sea spray would reach their bedroom balcony on the second floor. We thus experienced every day what Mumbai's newcomers do, on weekends, when they throng Worli Sea Face, a popular tourist destination.

In Andheri, my cousins lived on the highway, opposite the road that leads to the international airport. Their building was called 'Viman Darshan', and that was precisely one of my favourite things about the place. From the terrace, you could see planes take off and land. Back then I'd never been on a flight and for us, pre-satellite TV kids, all this was a huge deal.

When school vacations ended, I would come back home just in time for the beginning of the school routine – the buying of textbooks, the covering of notebooks and sticking labels onto the new books. Barely into my first week of school, I'd dream of my next school holidays. My home life was good, comfortable, but the freedom, the more significant possibilities of the city beyond my home were always too compelling to ignore.

I've always been quite an introvert, pretty much a wallflower. The opportunity to explore the city from within the safety of my extended family worked beautifully for me, and I think it sowed the seeds of my love affair with it. I have been physically and conceptually mapping Mumbai since I can remember. So when I chanced upon the idea to walk all its streets, I immediately got obsessed with it and just kept walking.

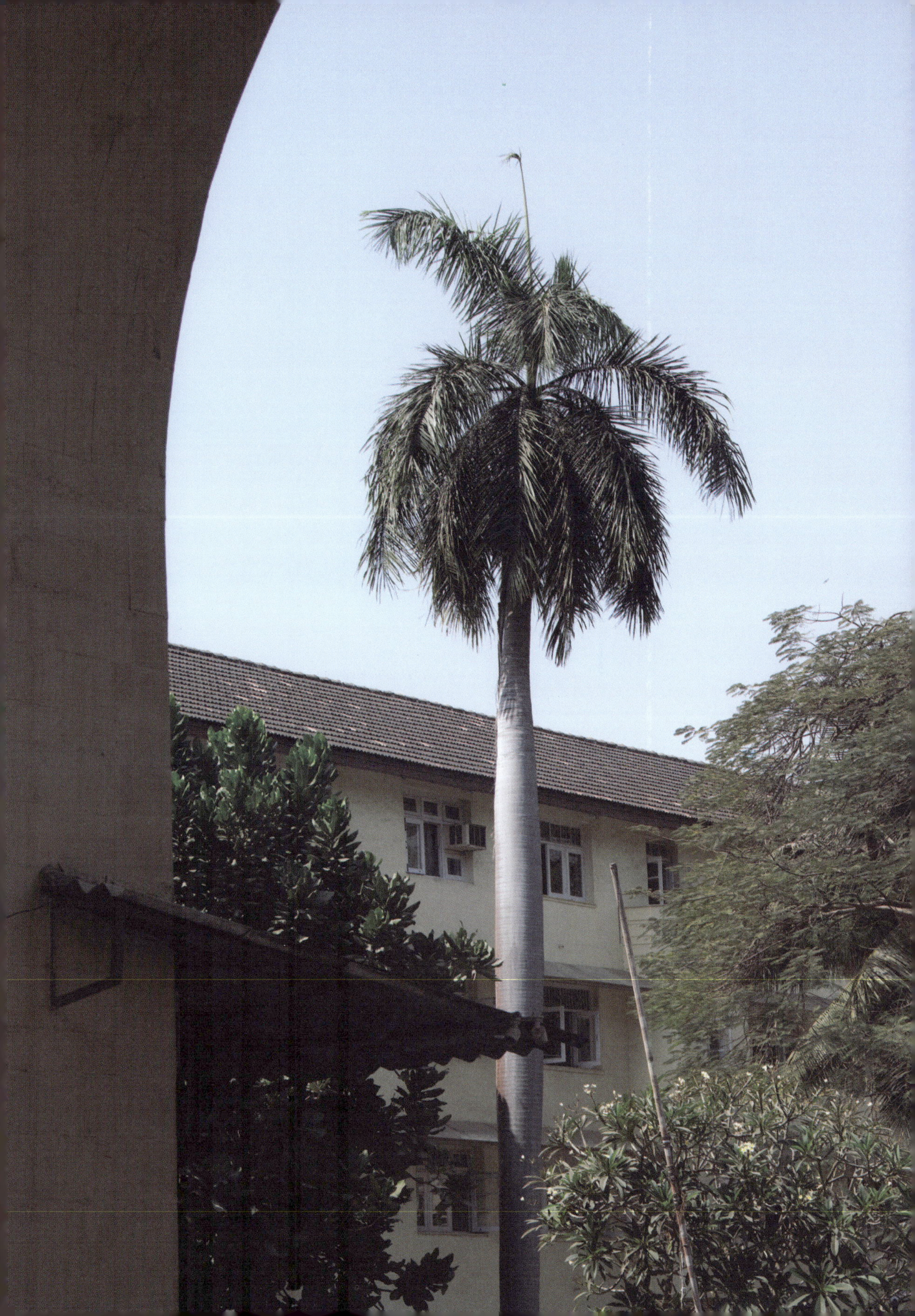

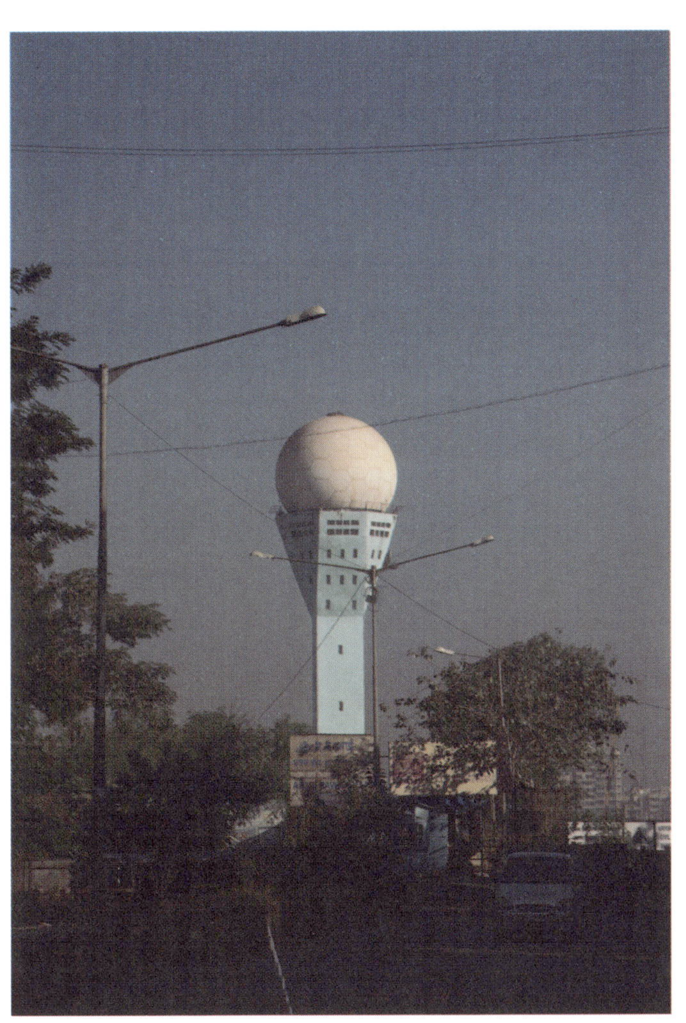

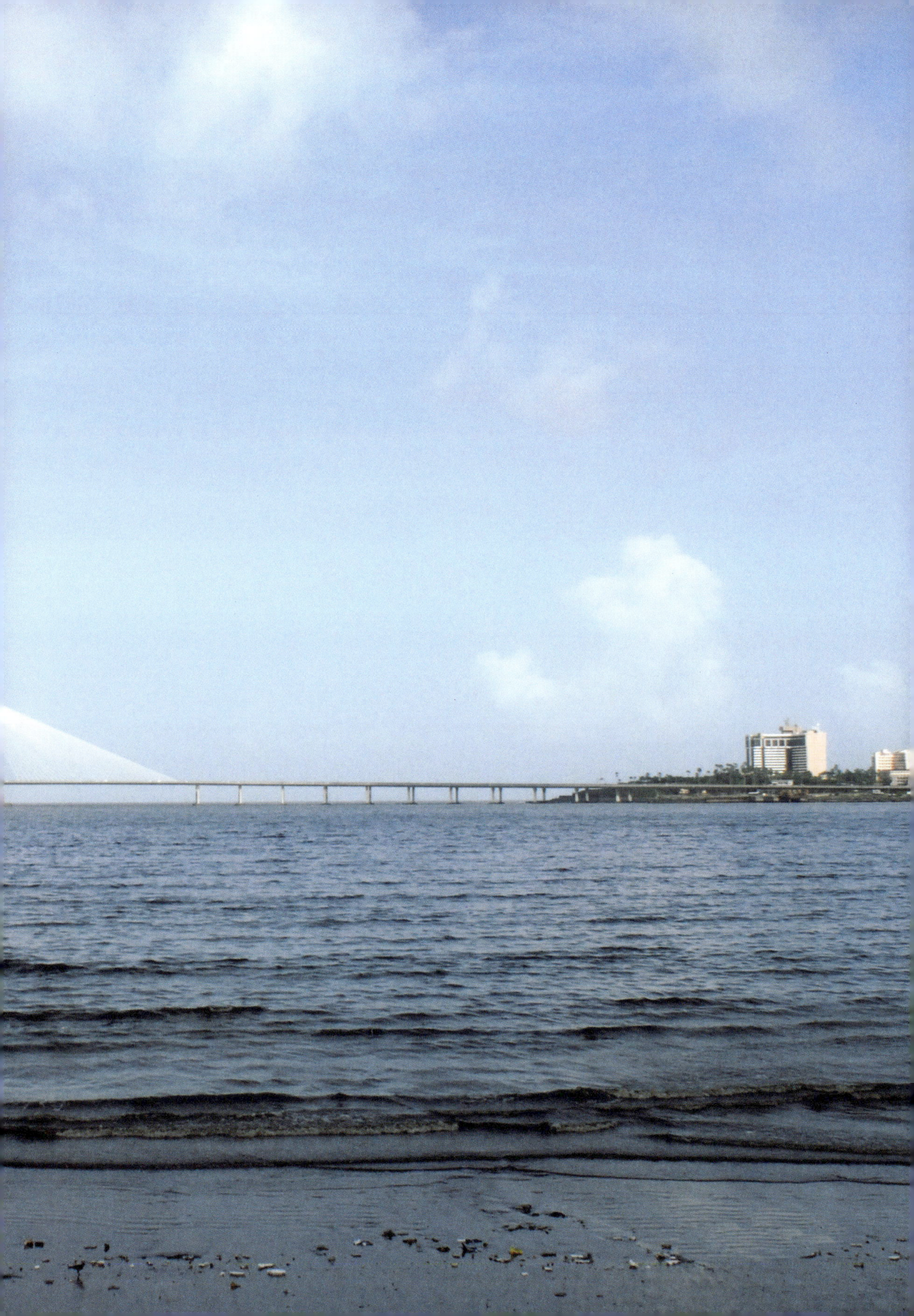

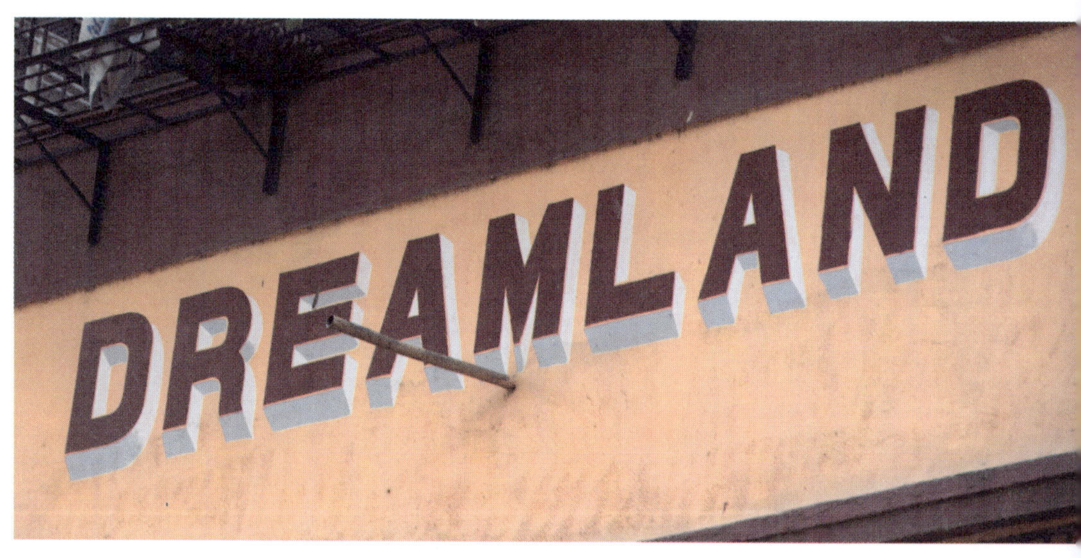
DREAMLAND

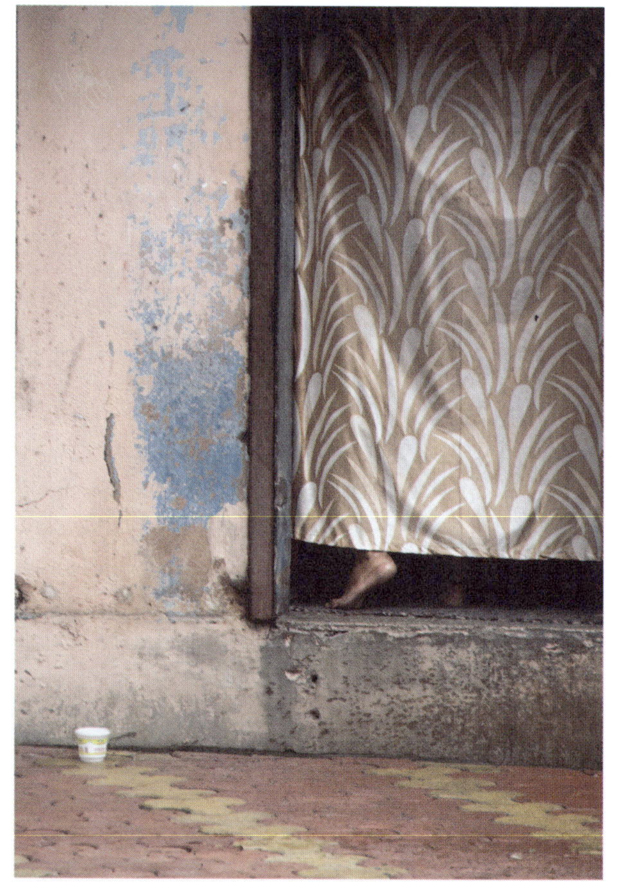

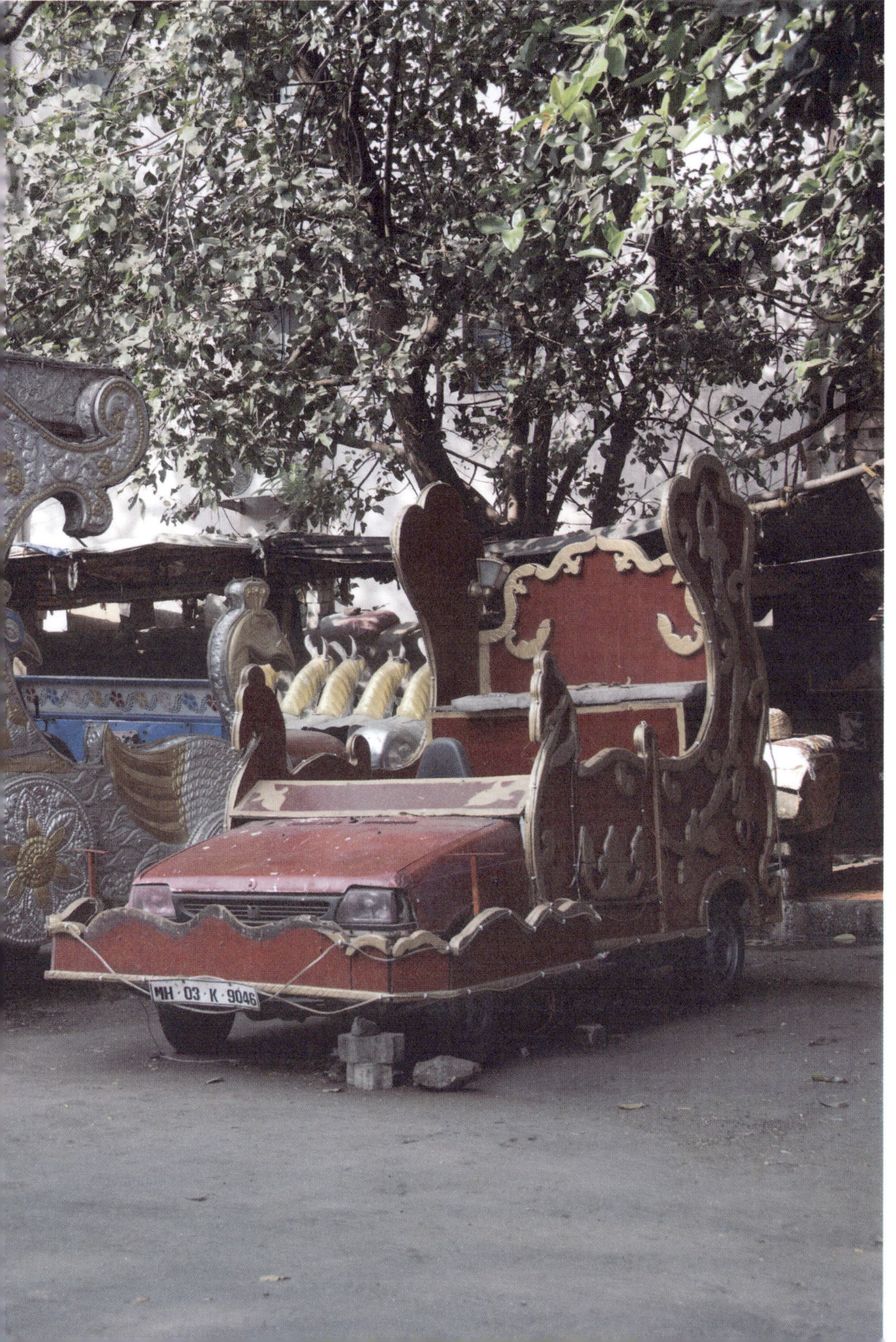
MH · 03 · K · 9046

§

Moving Out

My father came to Bombay as a child from
Karachi during the partition of India. He
earned a law degree from KC College and
eventually became the company secretary
of Siemens India. He paid for me to study
design in New York, and on my return to
India provided me with a house close to his
in Bandra. When I set up my studio, that
too in Bandra, I created a little bubble of
privilege as it were in this quaint suburb
of Mumbai.

About three months into the project,
I had walked and photographed all of
Bandra, Khar and Juhu. Charm and nostalgia
filled these pictures as these were the
parts of Mumbai in which I was the most
comfortable. But I soon realised that if
I had to do justice to my goal of creating
a portrait of the city, I would have to step
out of my comfort zone and venture into
the grit of Mumbai. Coincidentally, there
is a physical bridge that separates the
tranquillity of Bandra from the rest of the
city. This bridge goes over Mahim Creek.
Once, the Mithi River flowed here. But over
time, the river became a giant sewer. As it
happens, the physical act of crossing the
stinky Mahim Creek, leaving the comfort
of my home, became a metaphor for me
leaving my bubble and seeking adventure
in the megacity that is Mumbai.

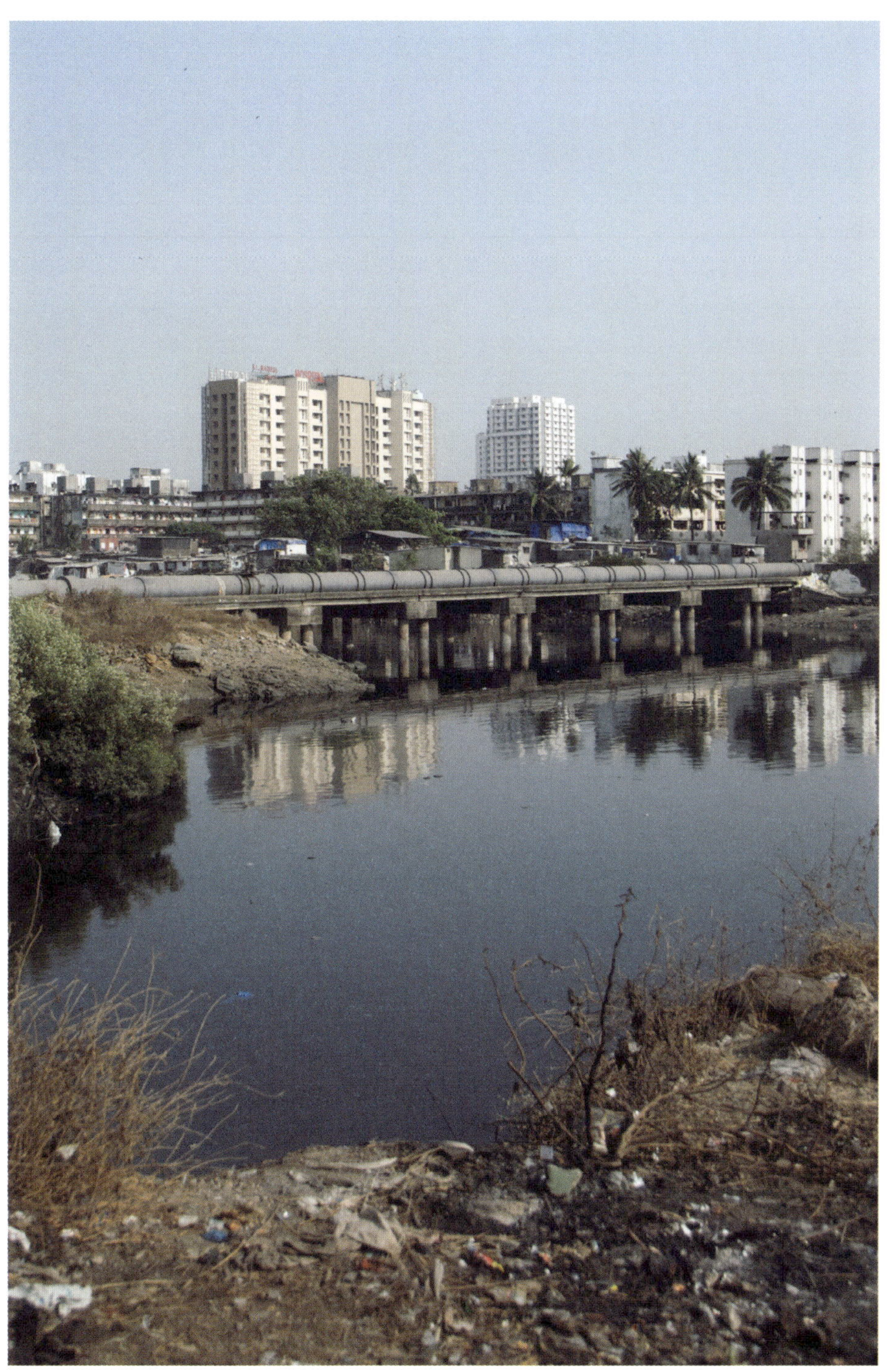

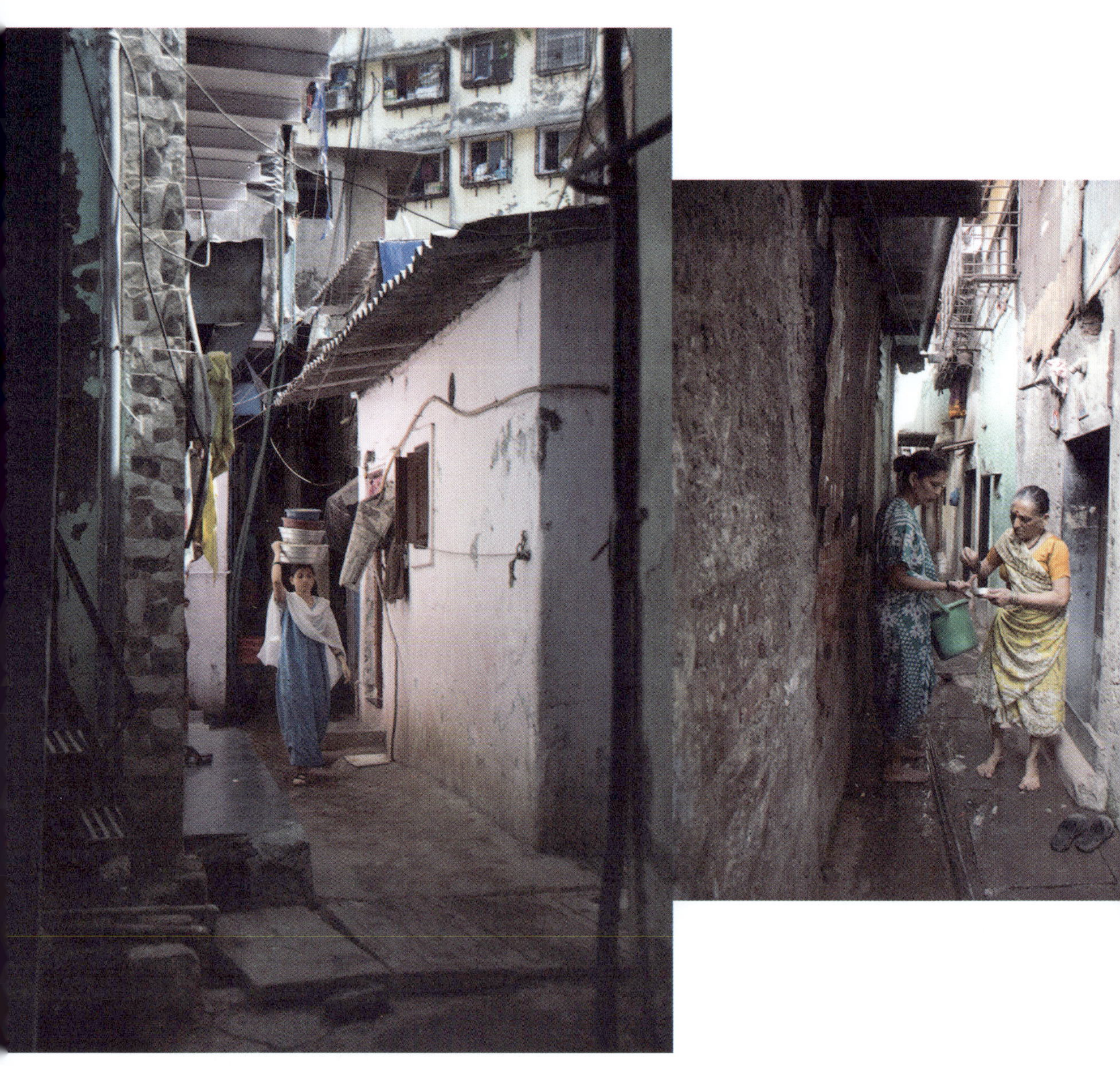

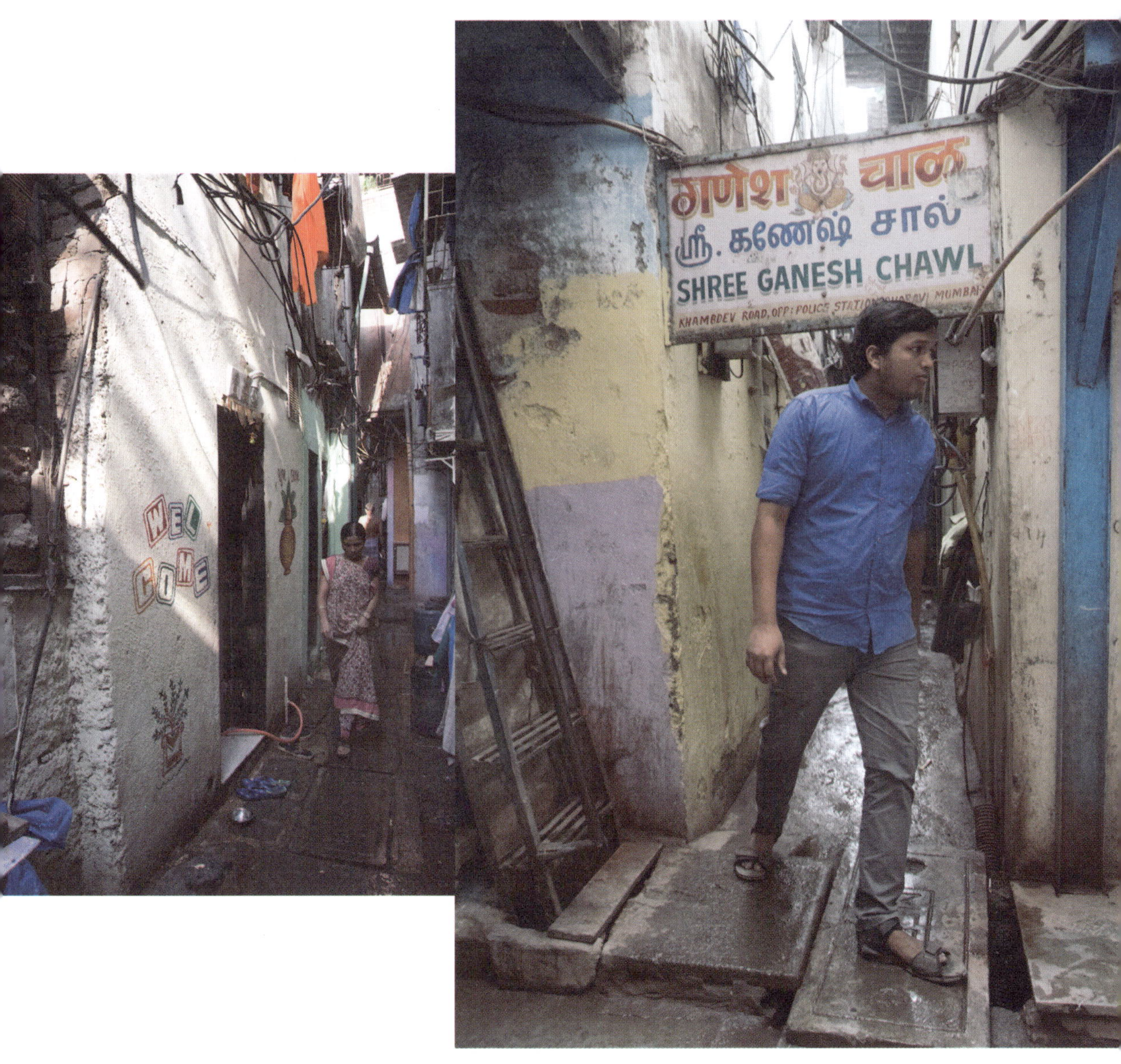

गणेश चाल
श्री. கணேஷ் சால்
SHREE GANESH CHAWL
KHAMBDEV ROAD, OPP. POLICE STATION DHARAVI MUMBAI
WELCOME

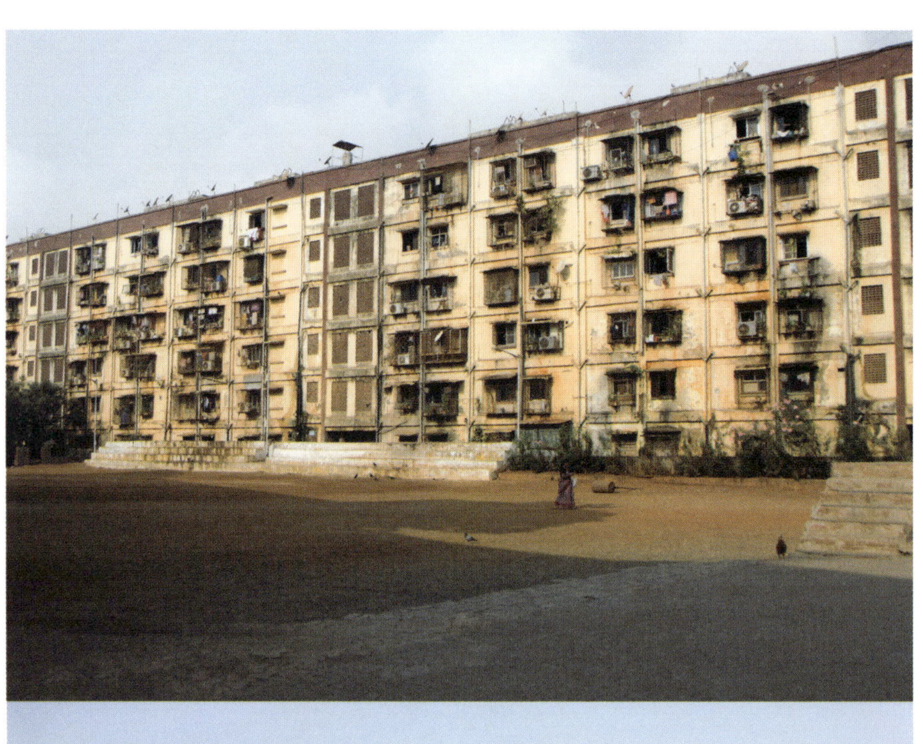

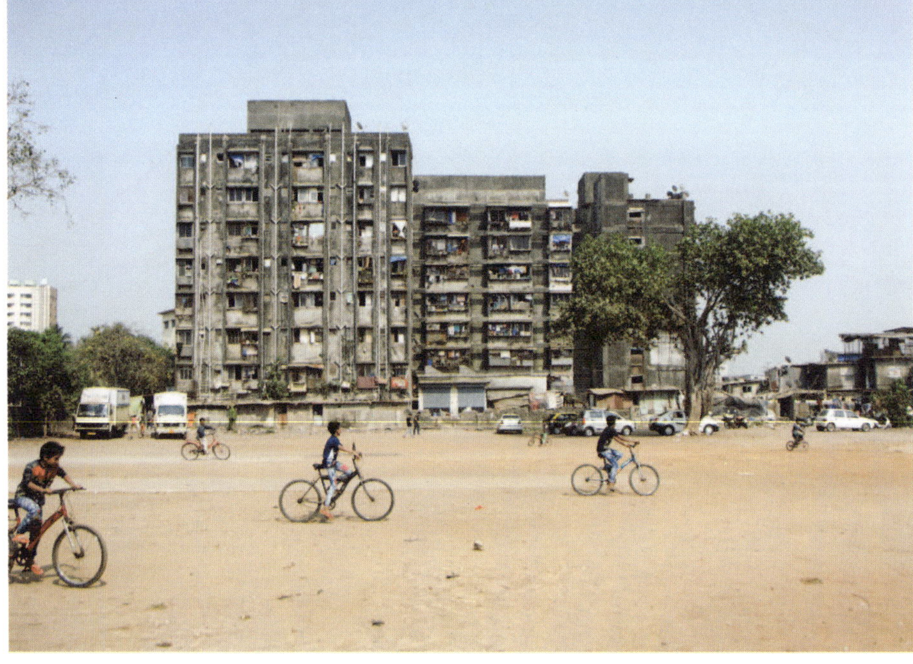

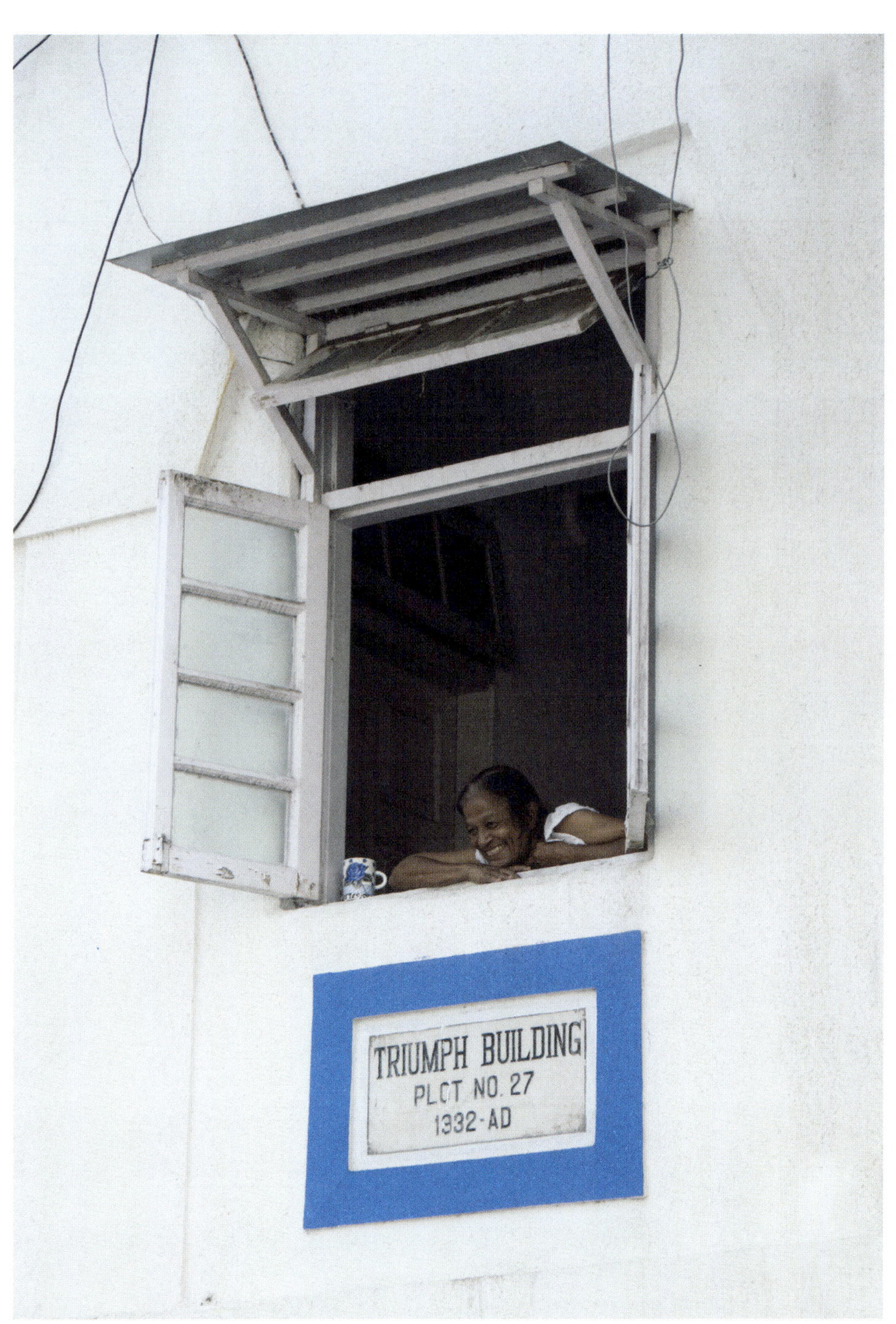
TRIUMPH BUILDING
PLOT NO. 27
1332-AD

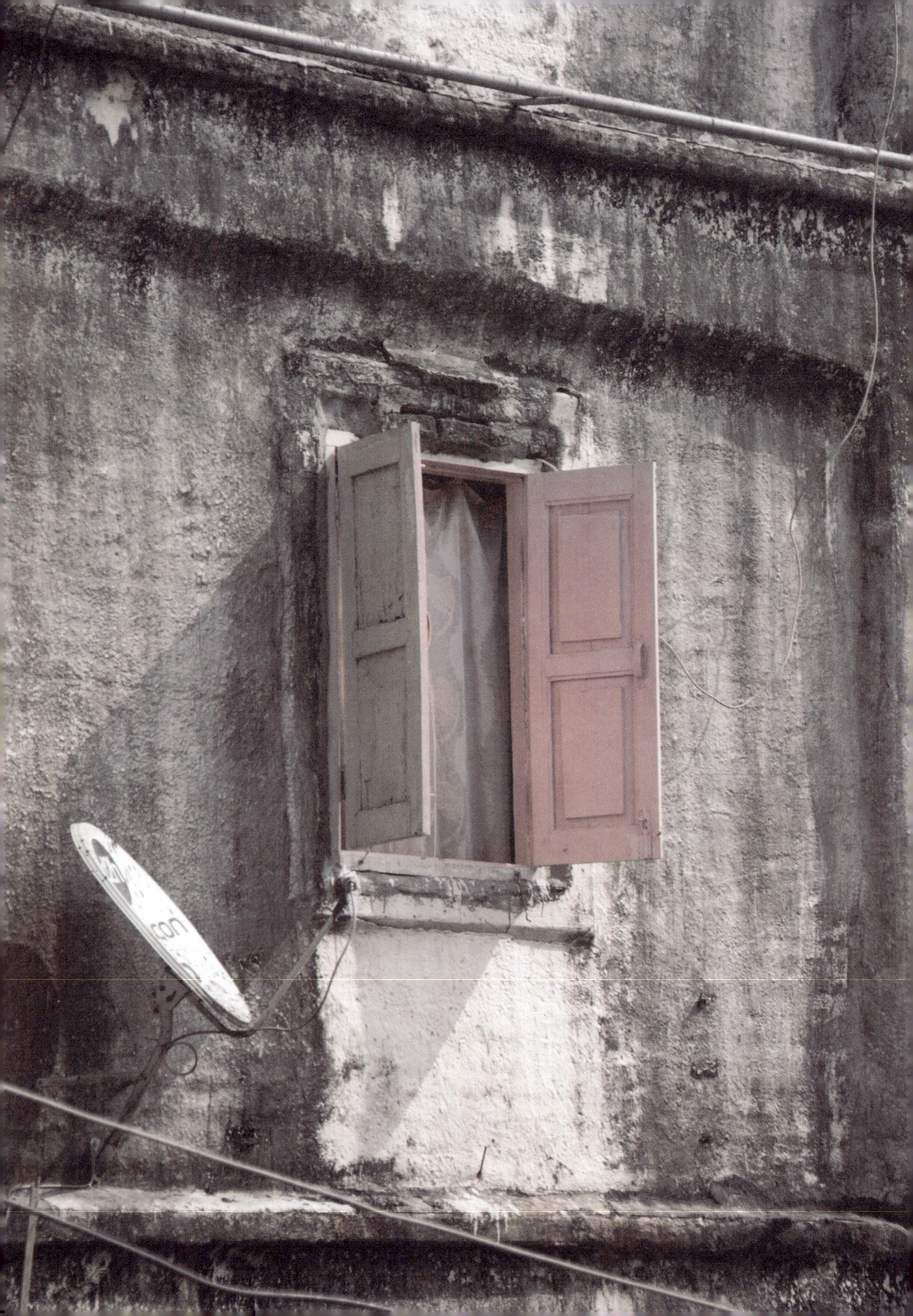

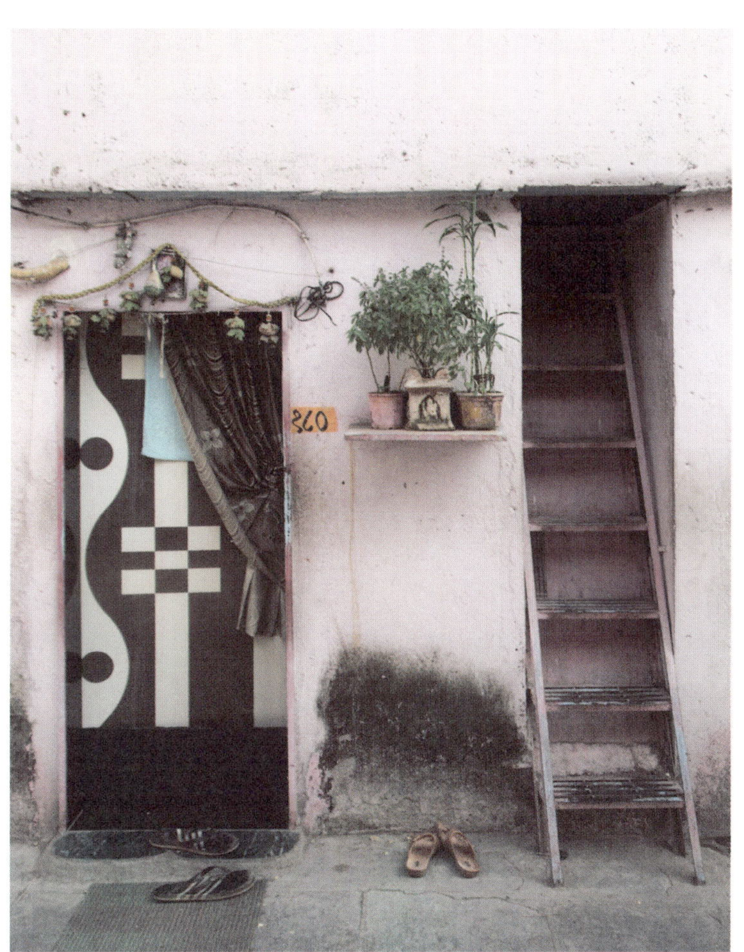

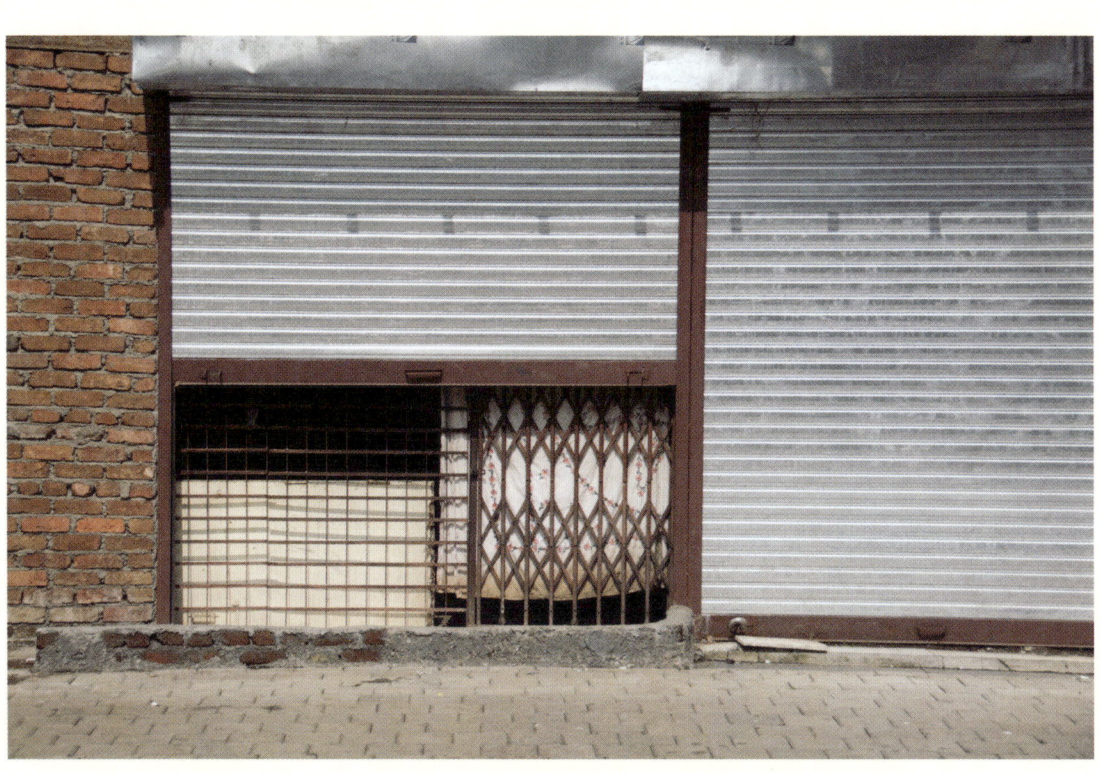

Mahim Dadar

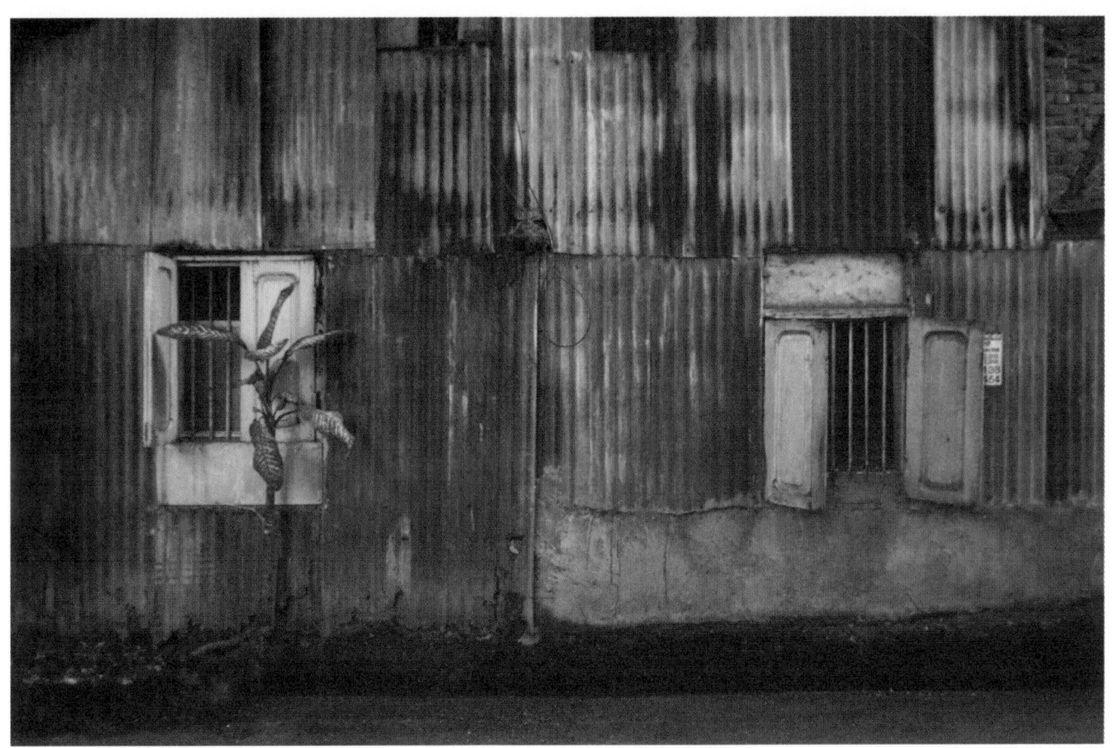

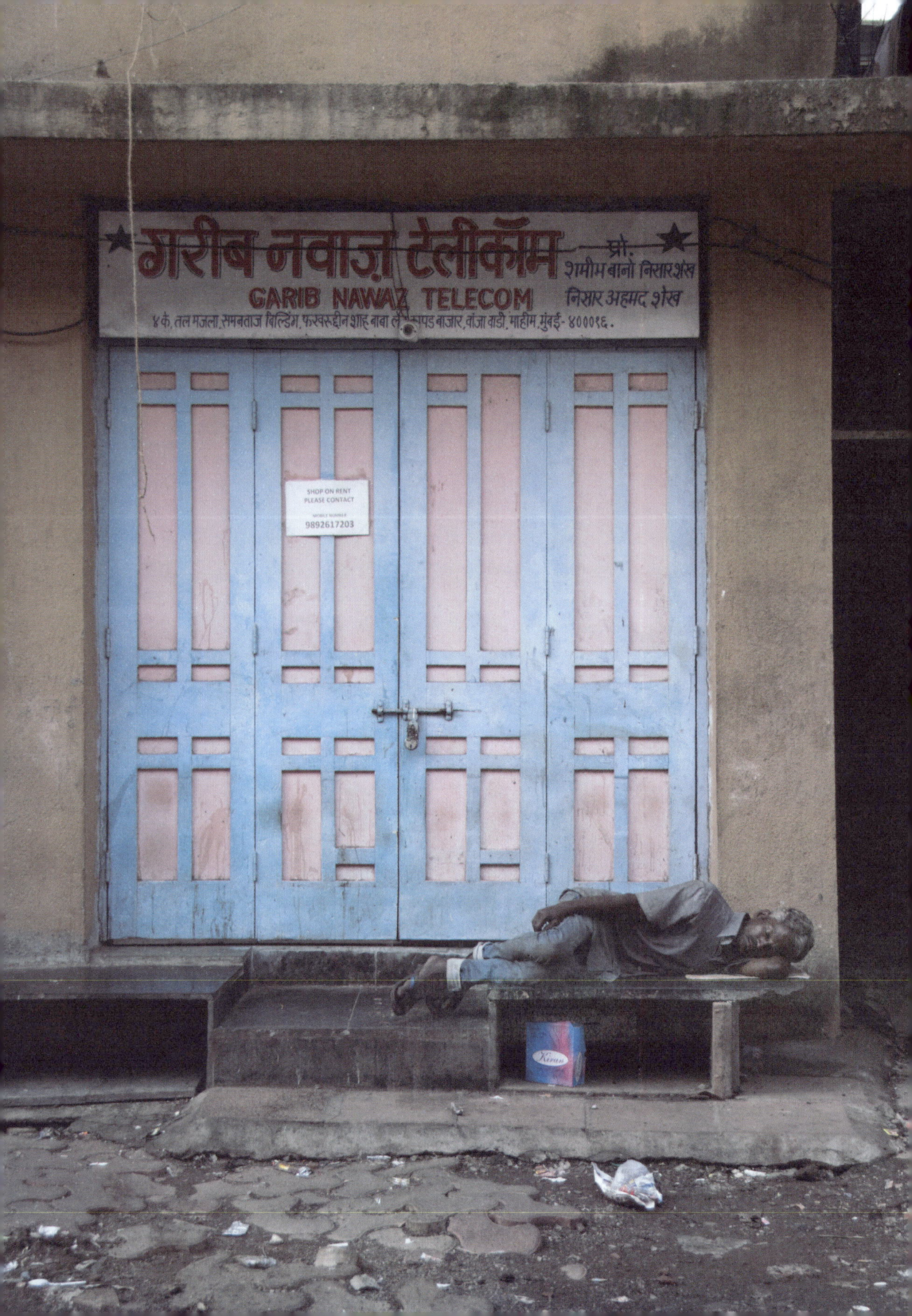
★ गरीब नवाज़ टेलीकॉम ★
प्रो.
शमीम बानो निसारअहमद
GARIB NAWAZ TELECOM
निसार अहमद शेख
४ के, तल मजला, समनताज बिल्डिंग, फखरुद्दीन शाह बाबा ले, कपड बाजार, वांजा वाडी, माहीम, मुंबई- ४०००१६.
SHOP ON RENT
PLEASE CONTACT
9892617203

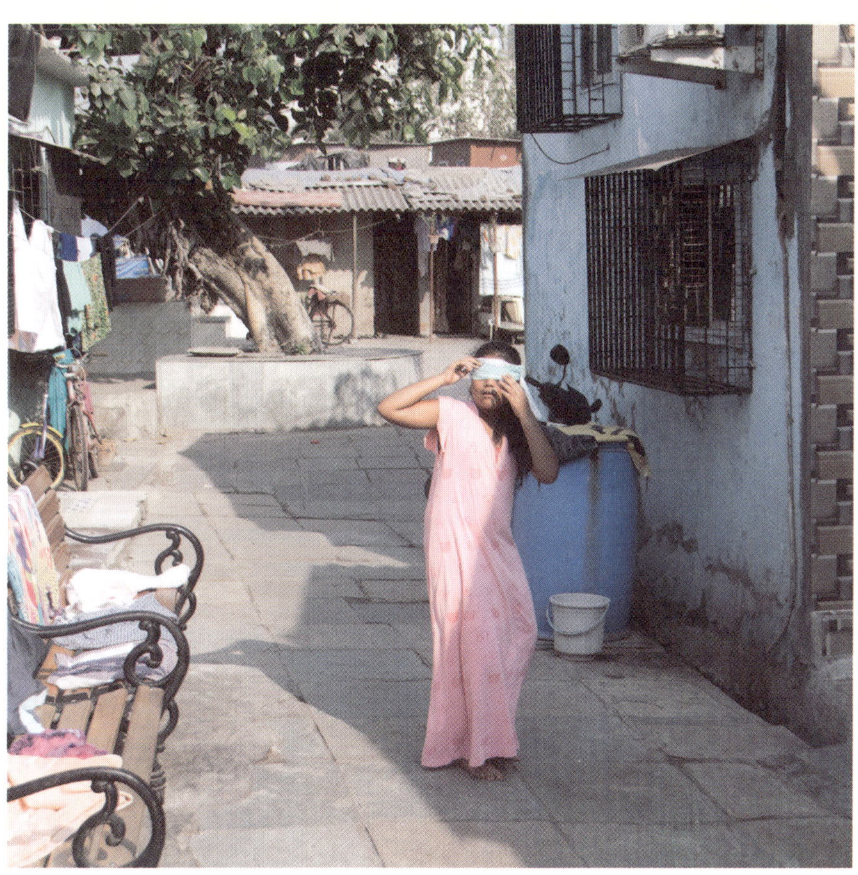

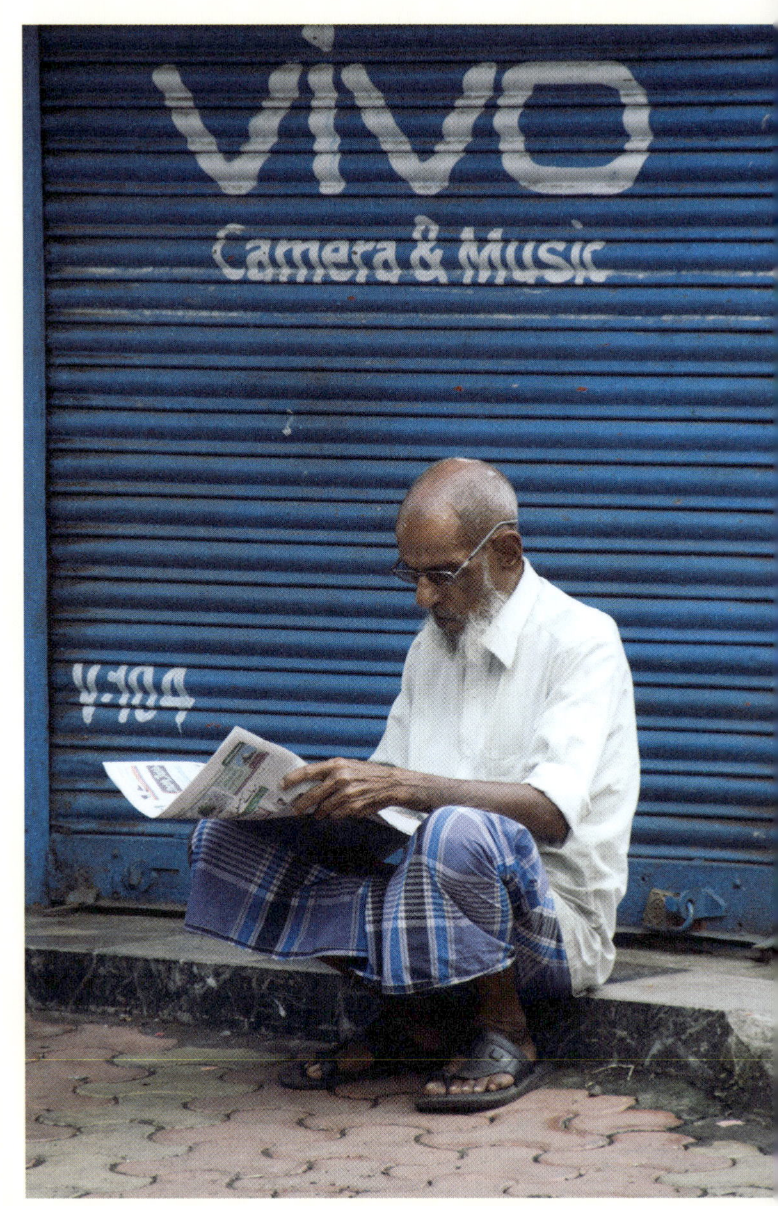

Mahim Dadar

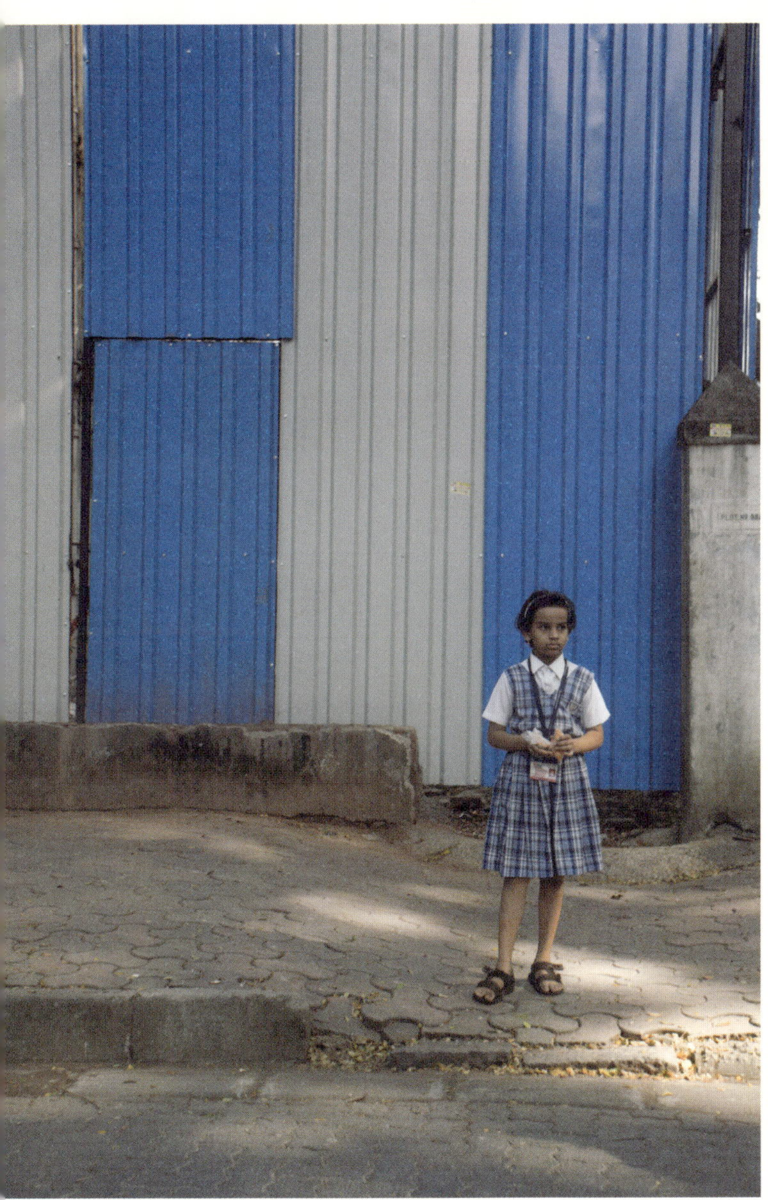

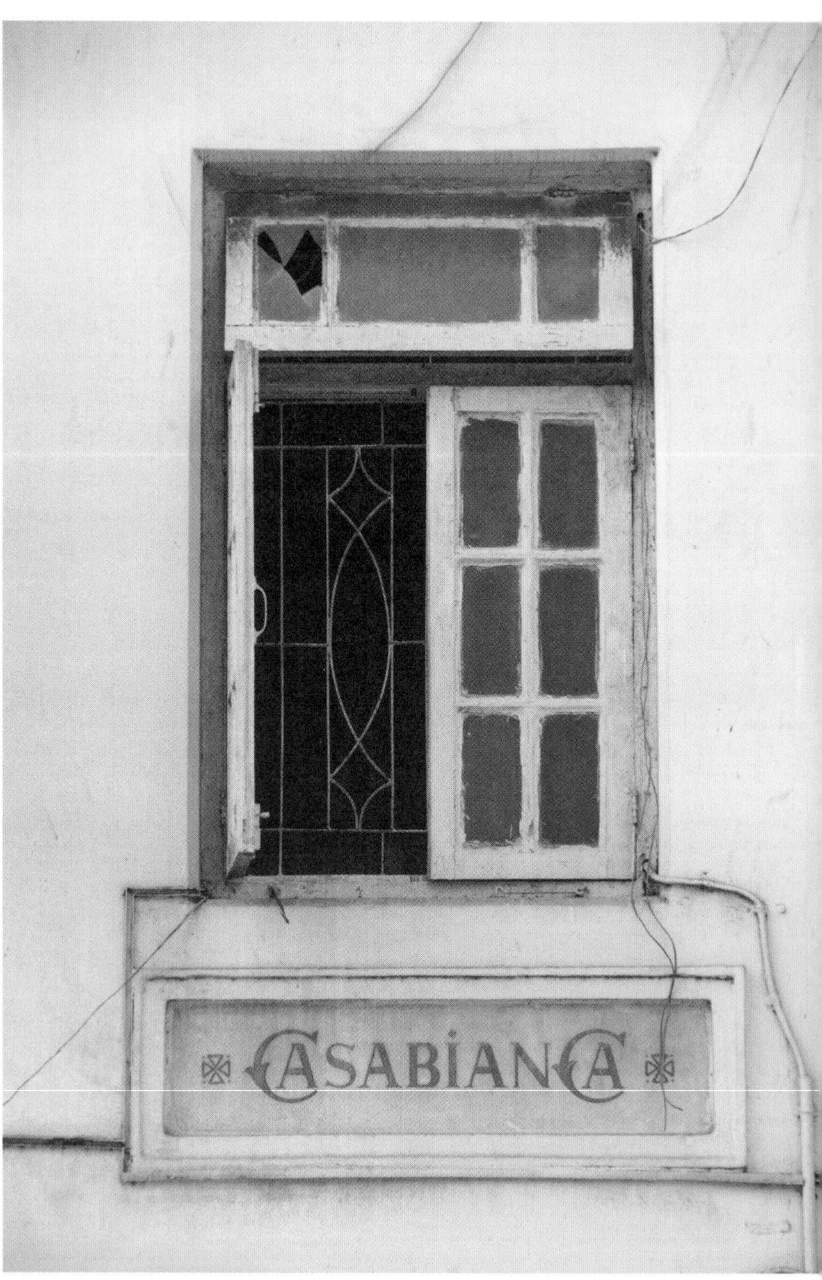

Mahim Dadar

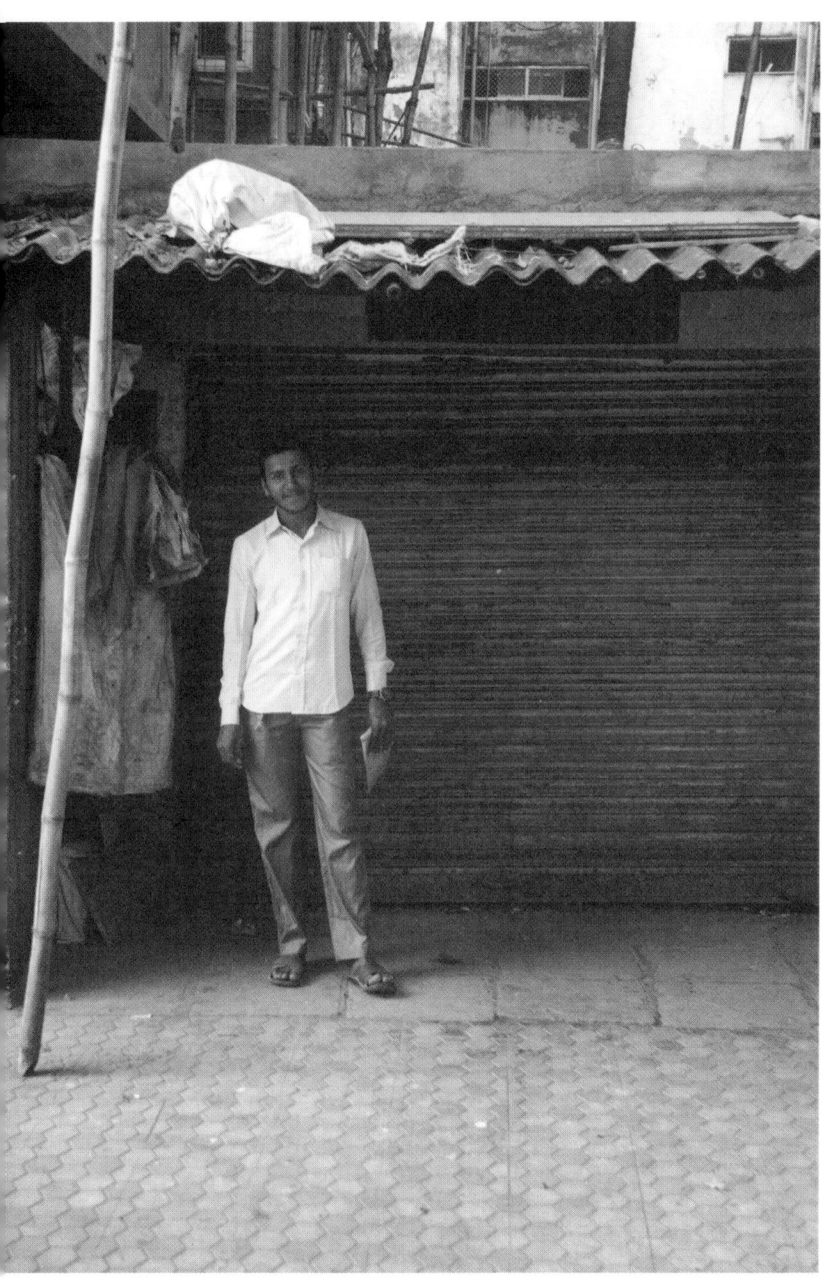

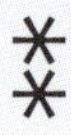

Twin Colonies

Dadar Parsi Colony and Hindu Colony in Matunga were created in the late 1800s and early 1900s to decongest the south of Mumbai. The two were the first planned neighbourhoods of the city, and remain so to this day. Of the two, Parsi Colony is better maintained as it is better regulated, but by the same token it is not as diverse, for the neighbourhood has been retained only for the Parsi community.

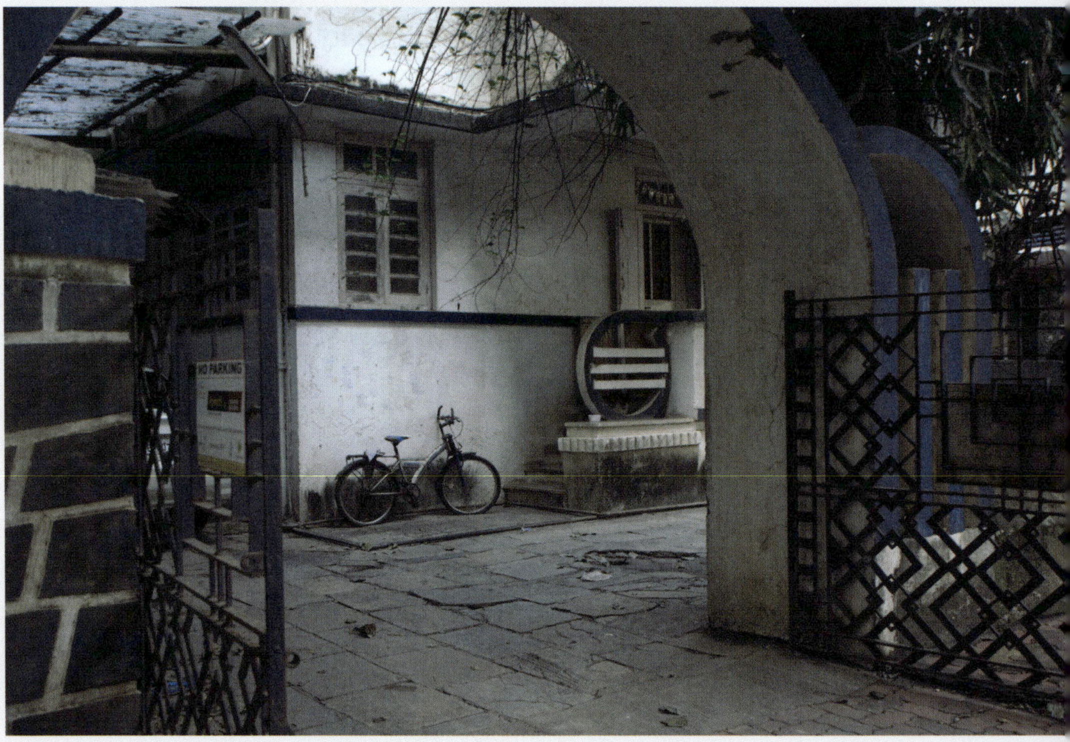

To its west are the buildings of Hindu colony. These are not as well maintained, but the area has more energy since it is more multi-ethnic. There are beautiful Deco and Indo-Saracenic buildings here, wide roads and several green parks. Controls put into the master plans of these colonies, like set building heights and defined road setbacks have made for a unified look that is yet not monotonous.

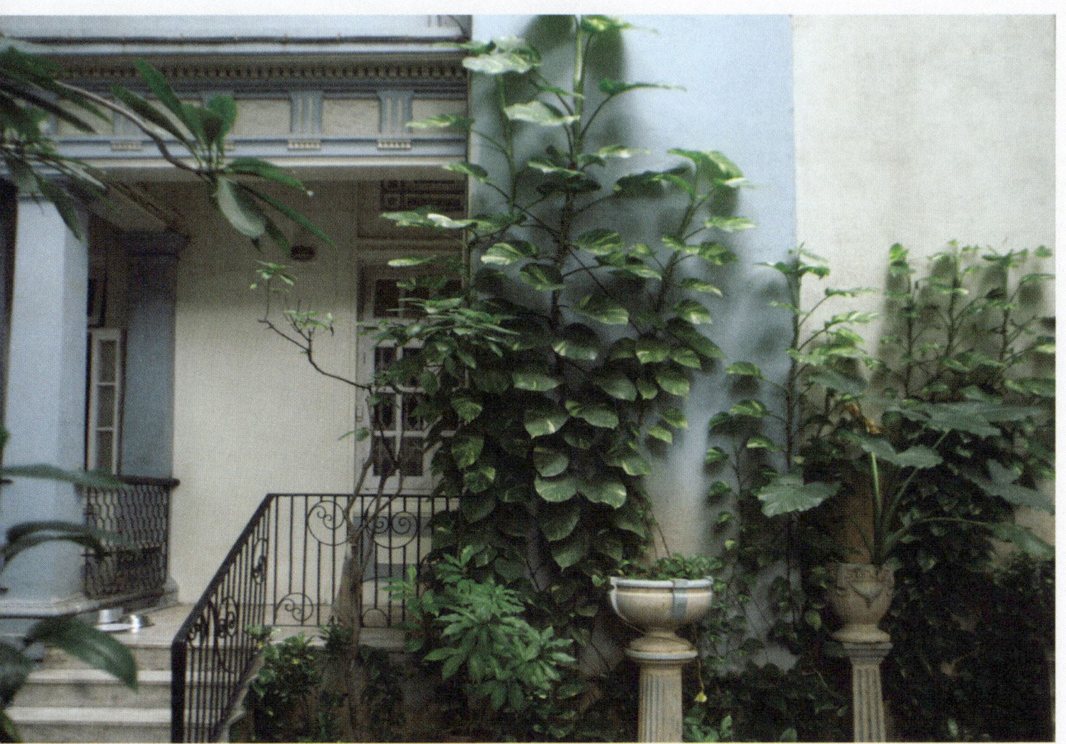

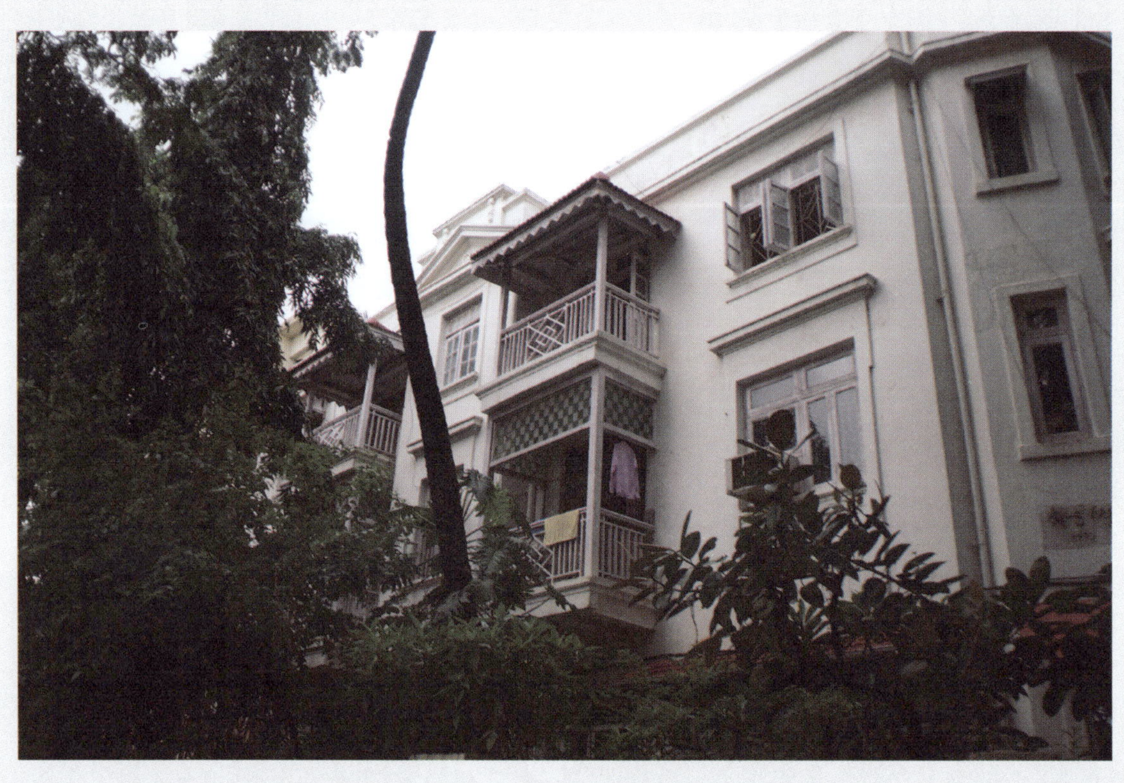

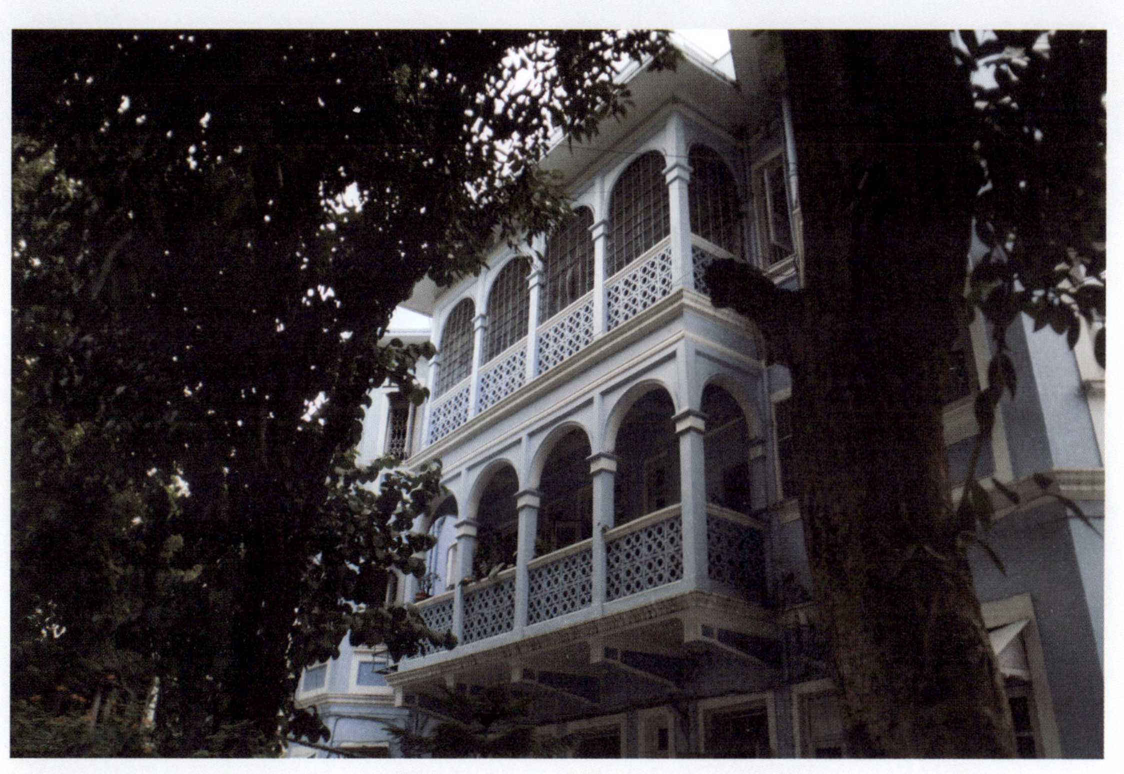

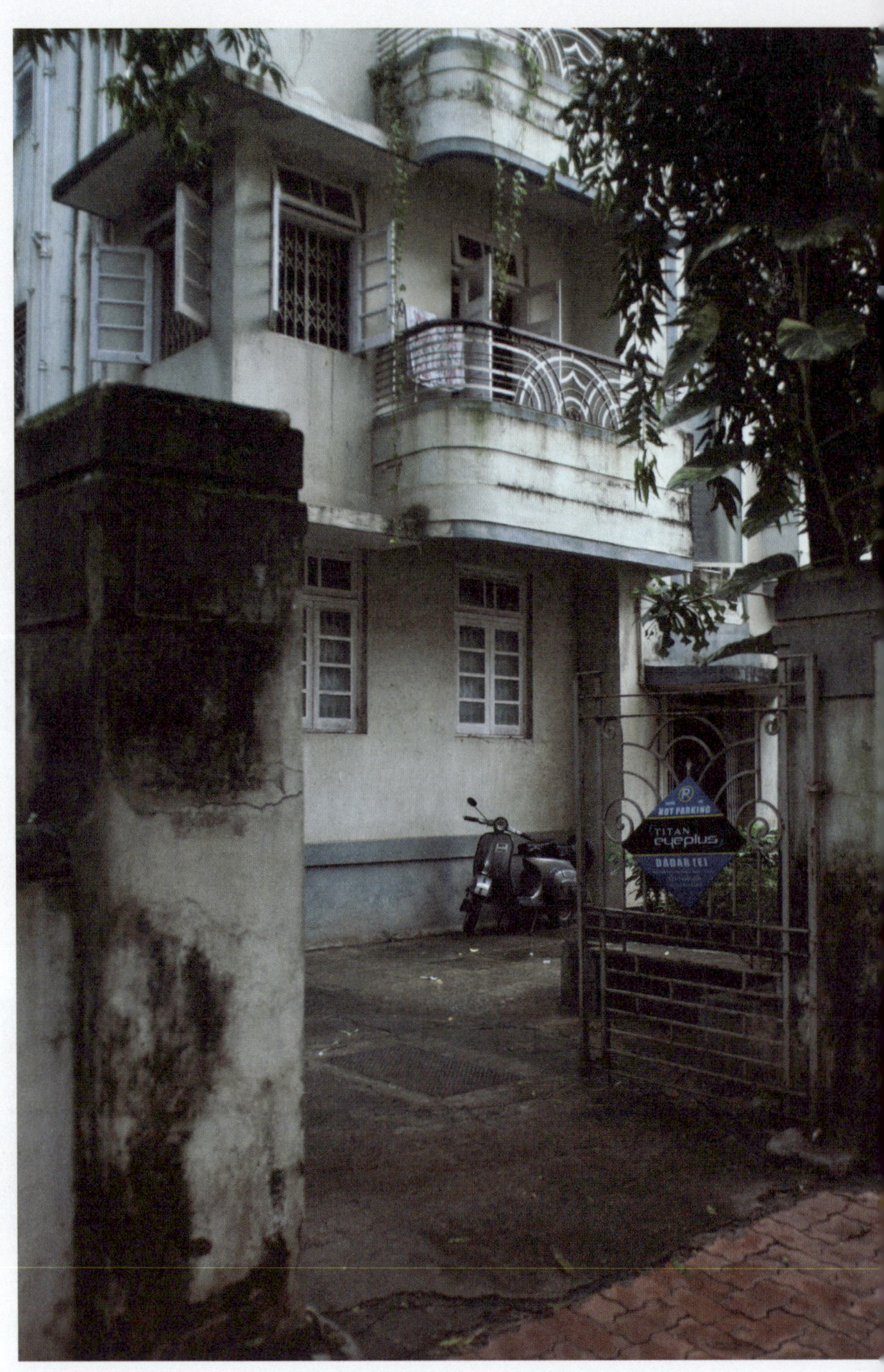

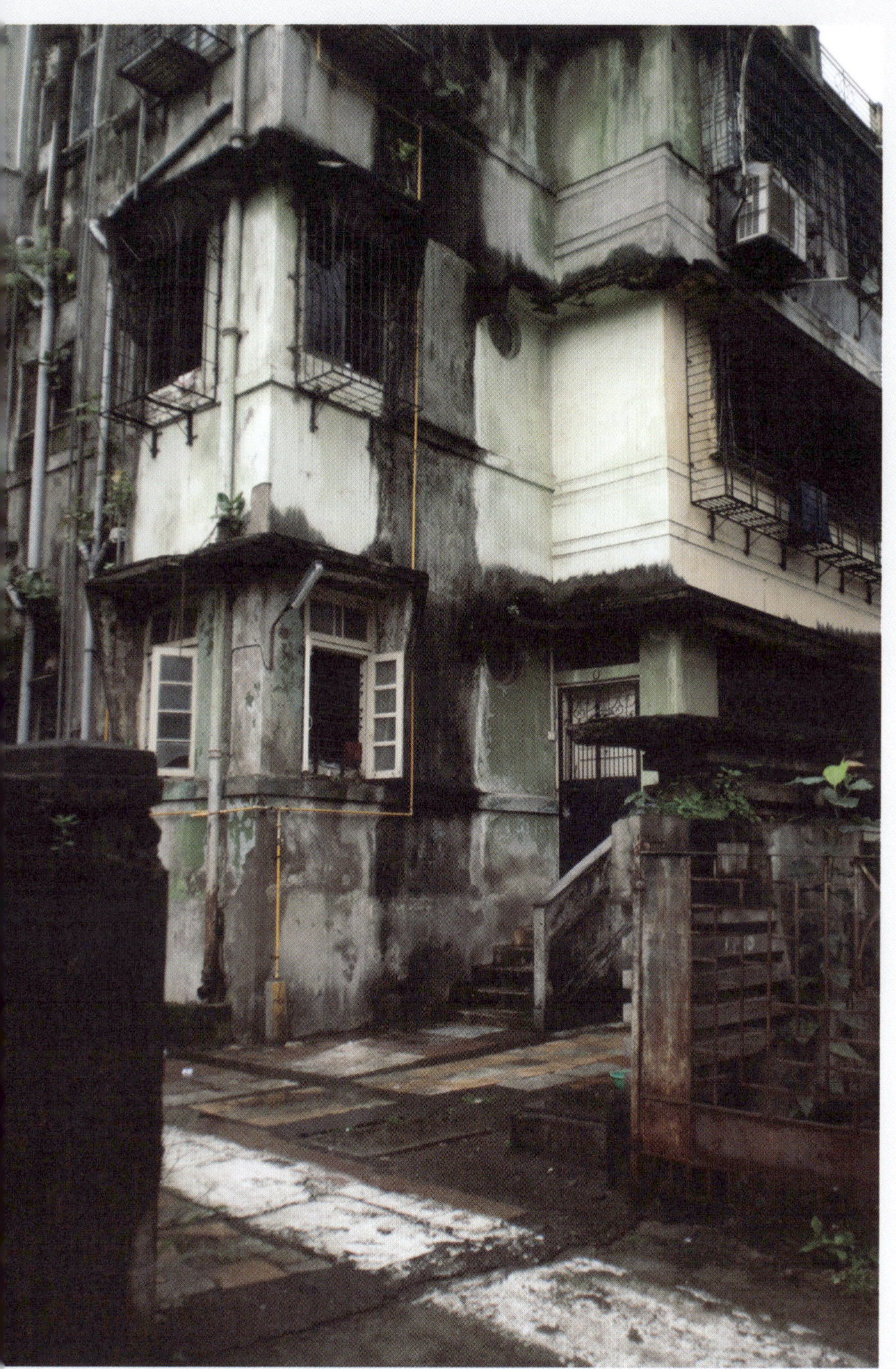

GROWING INTO THE CITY

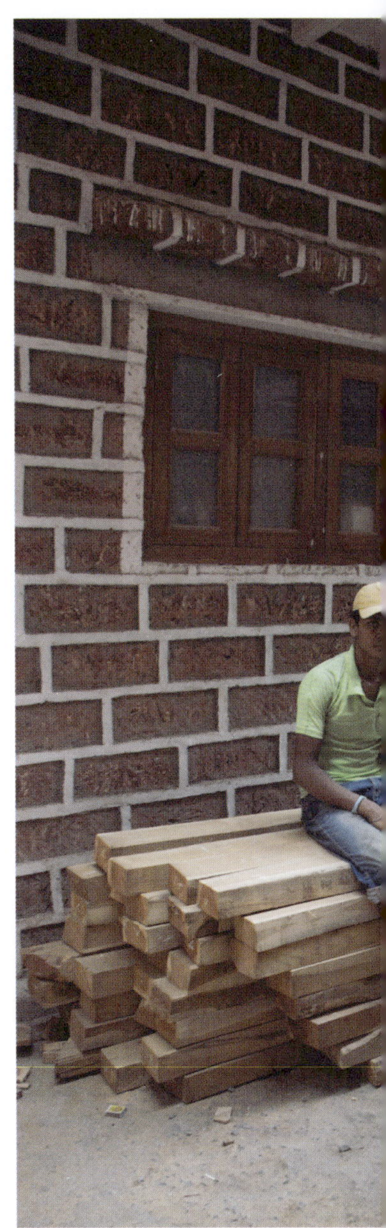

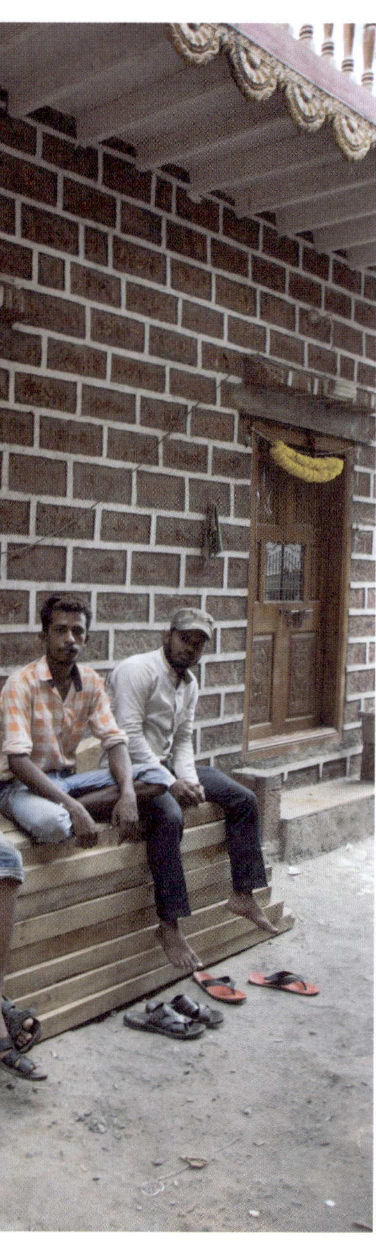

The more I walked, the more serendipity became the spirit of the project.

On any given day, only the starting point was pre-decided. It was like I was on an adventure, a treasure hunt. Thus, most things were left to chance, from the day's walk, to what pictures I got from that walk.

A Koli fishing village along the Worli Fort was one of these adventures. The village's topography is quite unique as it is located on a hilly sliver of land that juts outwards from mainland Worli towards the sea. On this strip the houses and shanties are tightly stacked on top of each other, giving the whole area a favela-like feel. Though the Koli houses overrun the Fort, some small remnants of the Fort remain.

Deep inside, it feels like any other working class neighbourhood or basti (poor people's tenements) in Mumbai, till you suddenly turn a corner to find a grand stone wall fencing in the small shanties. In the past, soldiers probably stood watch here, but today you get to see lines of freshly caught fish being hung out to dry. Many of my walks felt like this, as if I were unlocking the city's secrets.

Bandra's Mount Mary Church, a Mumbai landmark, is perched on the end of one of its hills. On one side of the hill is the Reclamation Area (that is, land reclaimed from the sea), on the other, is the picturesque seafront neighbourhood of Bandstand and on its western tip is the Bandra Fort. The Church is famous for fulfilling every wish made at its altar. No matter what your religion, caste or creed, all you have to do is offer a candle at The Mount. The candles here are not ordinary candles but come in the shape of your wish. Want to ace an exam, offer a wax book. Want to upgrade from a two-wheeler to a four-wheeler, offer a wax car. Whatever your aspiration, the vendors outside have a wax version.

Though I was familiar with this area, during my walks, I discovered that there is not one, but six ways to access The Mount and the hill that it sits on. All six are pedestrian-only paths, three from the Reclamation side, two from Bandstand, and finally, the most hidden of these is one that runs through a basti that borders the Bandra Fort.

Another gem of a landmark I explored also happens to be a fort. It sits along Mumbai's eastern bank and is called Sewri Fort. Bombay used to be seven separate islands. The British connected these islands by reclaiming the land between them from the sea. During colonial times each of these islands – Worli, Mahim, Bandra, Sion, for example – had forts. The Fort area in South Bombay is called this because in colonial times it had several fort-like structures within it.

Of all the forts I walked through, I found that Sewri Fort was the best maintained, maybe because it is along Mumbai's eastern edge, which isn't very populated. Beyond the fortress lie the Sewri mudflats, and come winter, it is on these mudflats that you see migrating flamingos. The place makes for a surreal landscape: an old stone fort, exotic migratory birds and beyond the mudflats, across the water body, industrial chimneys of a chemical factory.

On the day I visited the fort, some school kids were chilling there. They were from Mahim and had bunked school to hitchhike across town and sneak a smoke. The way the kids were navigating the fort, slipping into one chamber and then suddenly popping up at the far end on top of its dome, meant that they did this quite often. Sewri Fort's remoteness makes it a perfect playground for kids that decide to bunk school.

Sewri is along the eastern edge of the city and for my walks along these areas, beyond the harbour train line, which connects the commercial docks of Mumbai to fast-growing suburbs of New Bombay, I asked Amar, an associate from work, to accompany me. He was familiar with this area, having lived in Lalbaug all his life. This part of Mumbai is Port Trust land and taken up mostly by large warehouses. As these areas are not very populated, I didn't feel completely confident I could manage them alone.

Still, I found myself traversing through them faster than Amar, though I stopped from time to time to take pictures. He was more familiar with the area than I was, but it seemed to me that I navigated the streets with more confidence! Clearly, I'd built up this intuitive sense of finding my way through the city's bylanes. If boxed-in or at a dead end, I would look out for groups of people and follow them out, assuming they would be heading to the main road. If there weren't any people to follow, I'd rely on the sequencing of the passage widths: the wider they got the closer I was to the main road.

My three years of walking the streets passed without incident. The people of Mumbai were too busy with their own lives to bother with me taking pictures. If they did come up to me to ask what I was doing, they were cutely curious, and when they found out, I wasn't with a newspaper or with the municipal corporation, they were happy for me to create my art. The only incidents I did have were with local street dogs, and I had to be wary of them.

I saw a lot of things on my walks and had a lot of experiences, and though I continue to be a shy person, I do feel I'm more comfortable with myself and appear to have higher self-esteem. I think my quietness now doesn't come from a sense of fear but more from an awareness that there is so much more out there than my problems or my limited worldview.

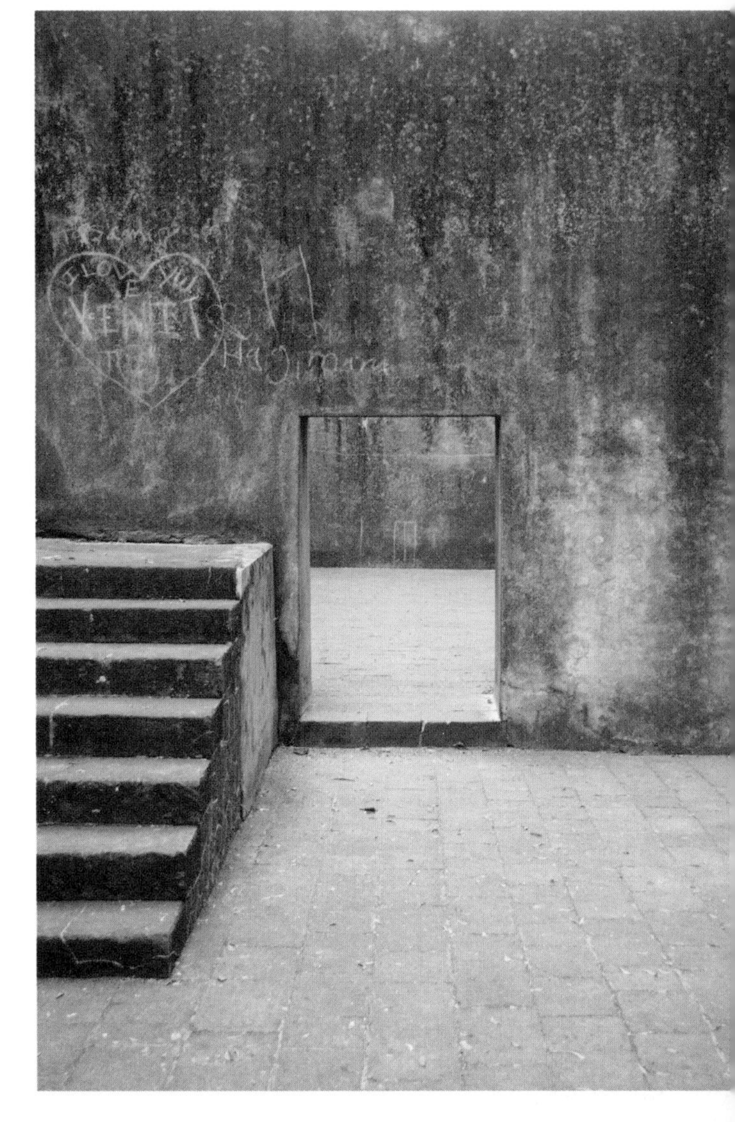

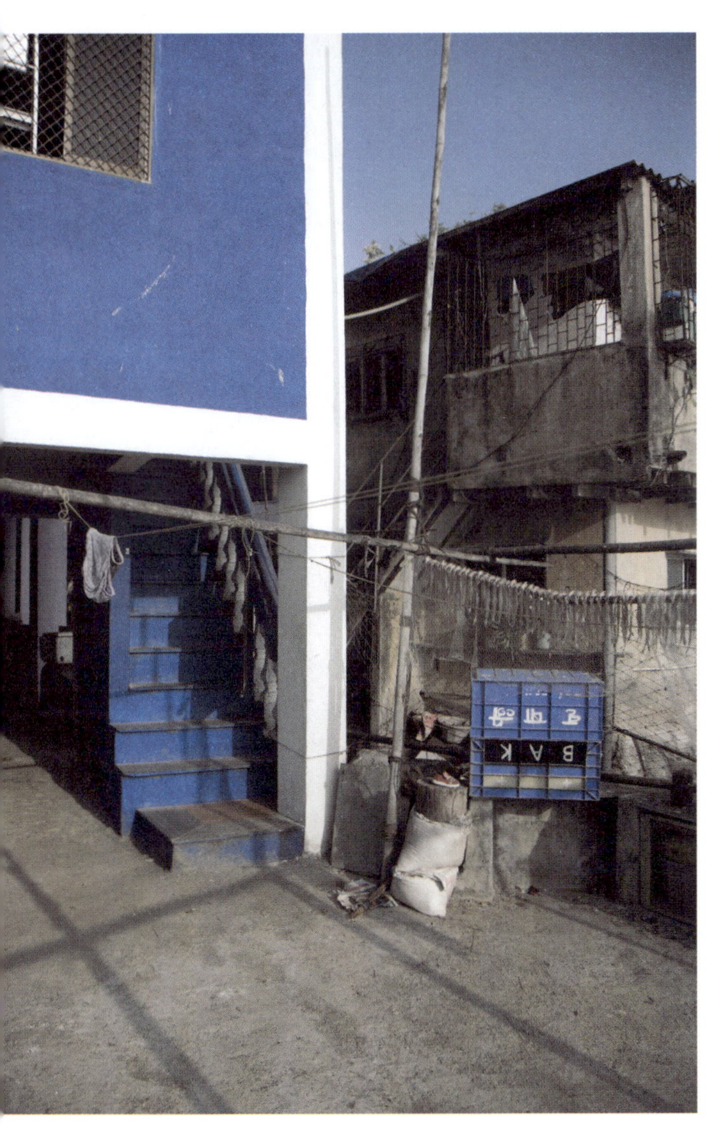

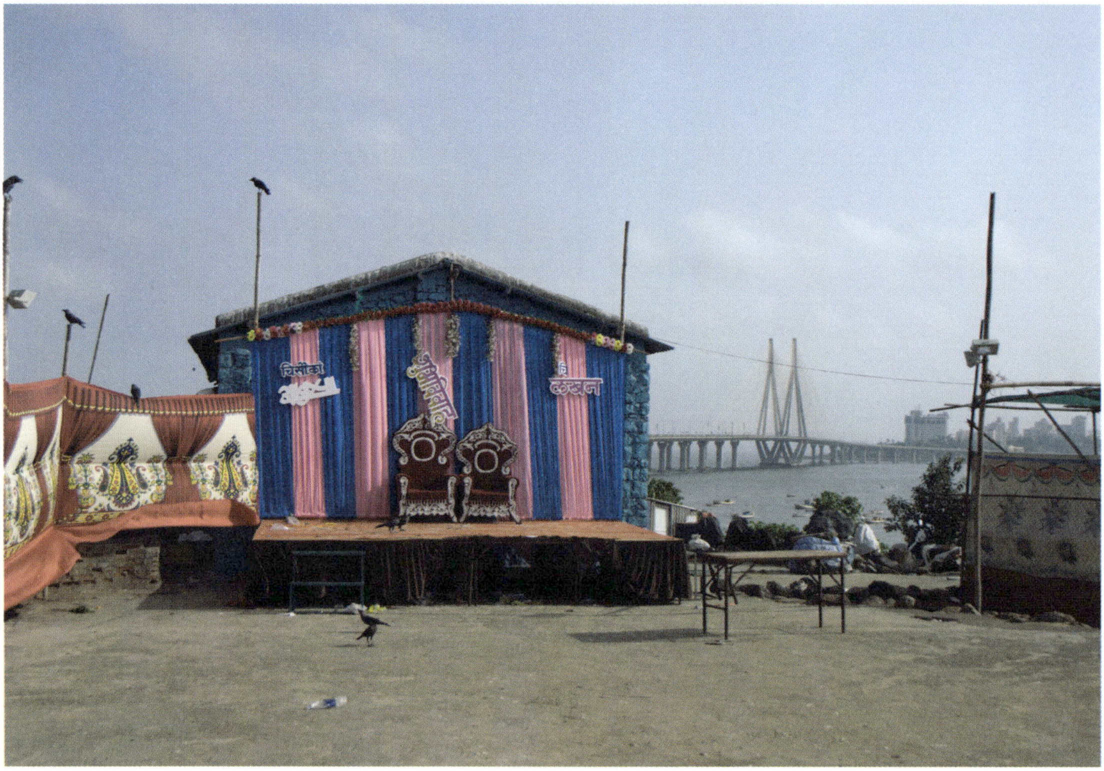

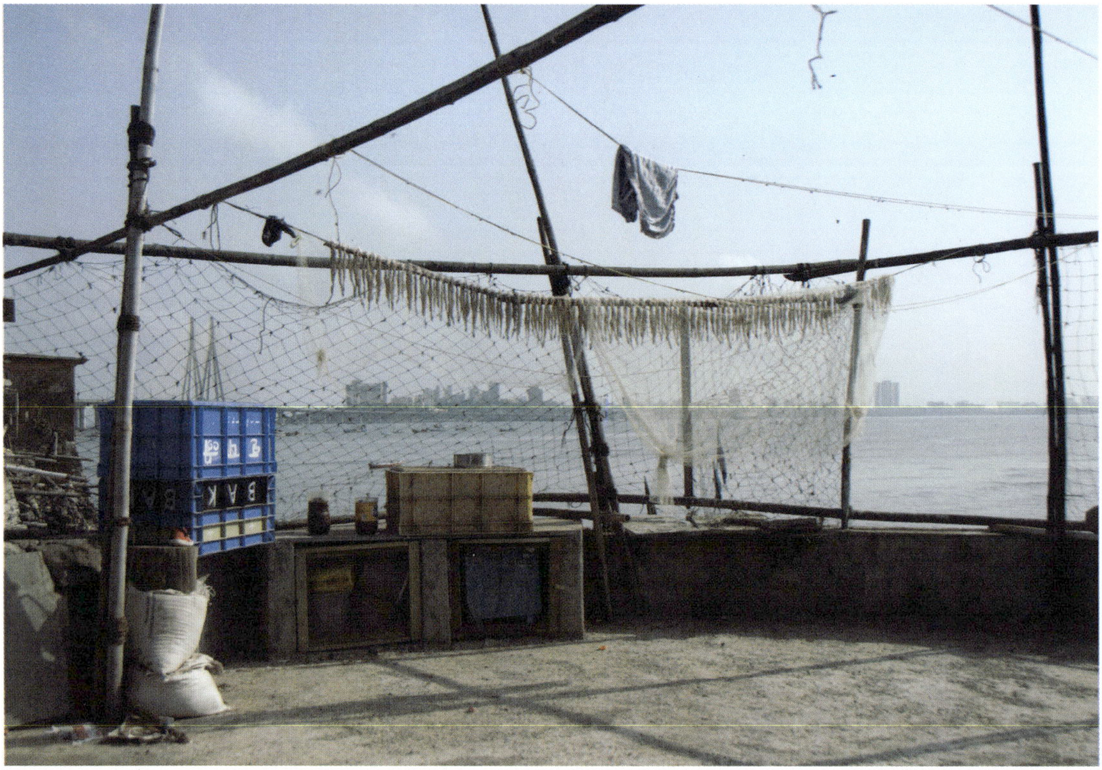

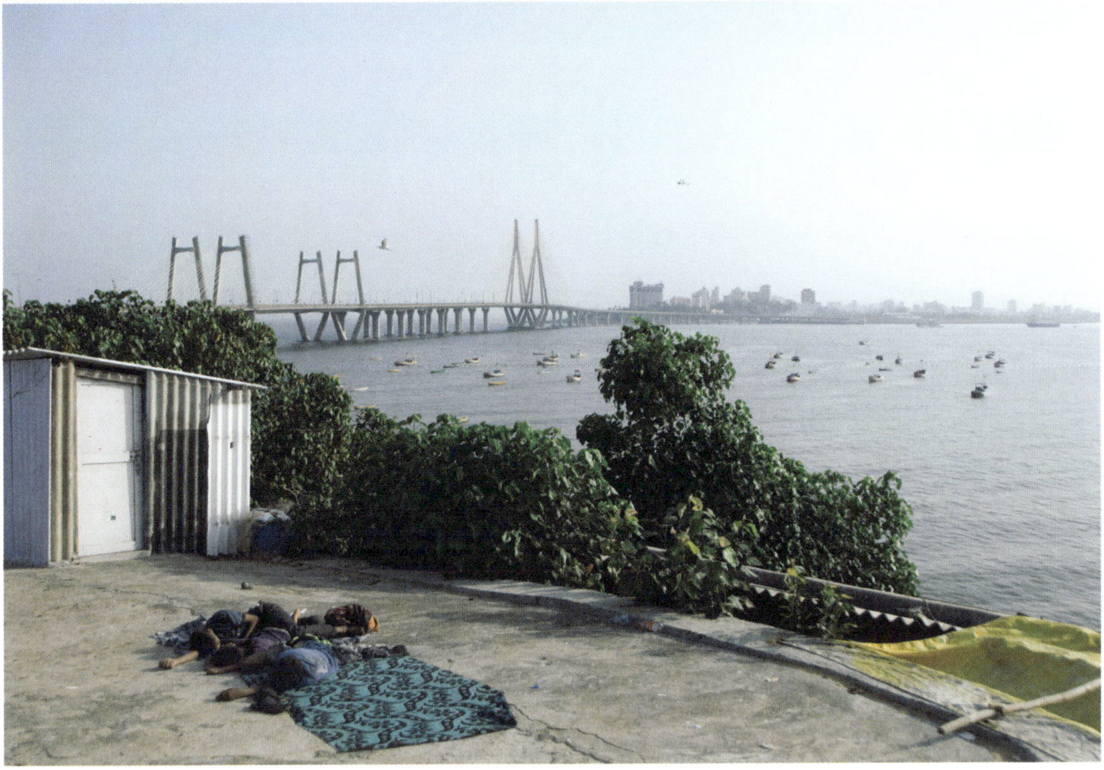

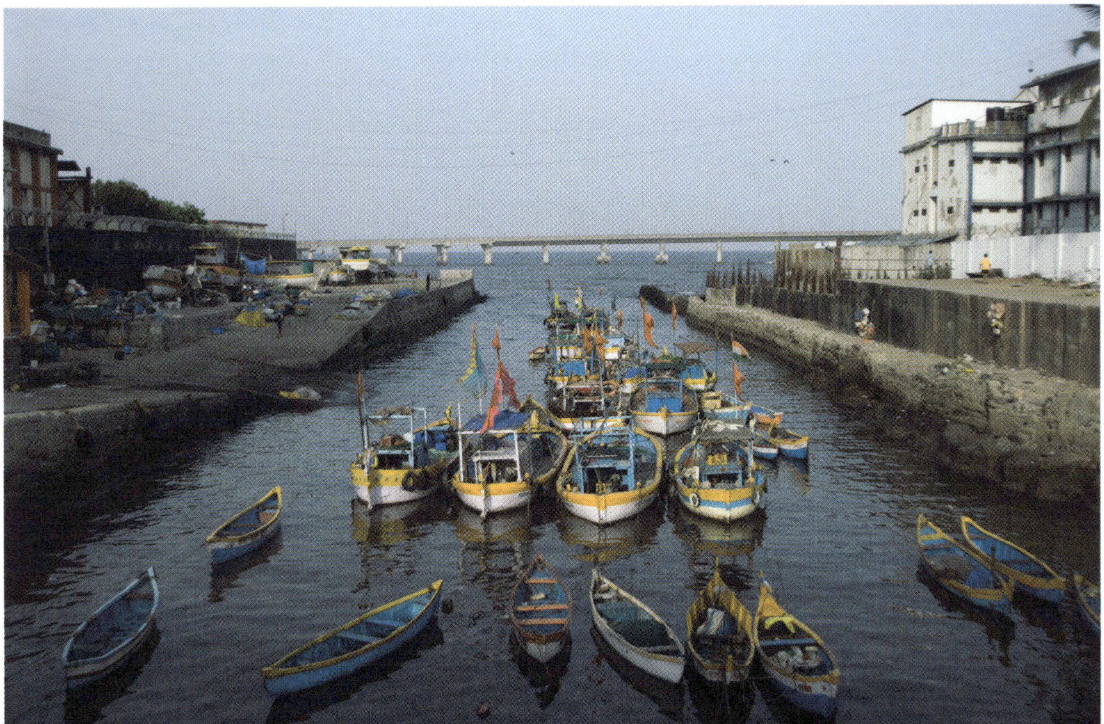

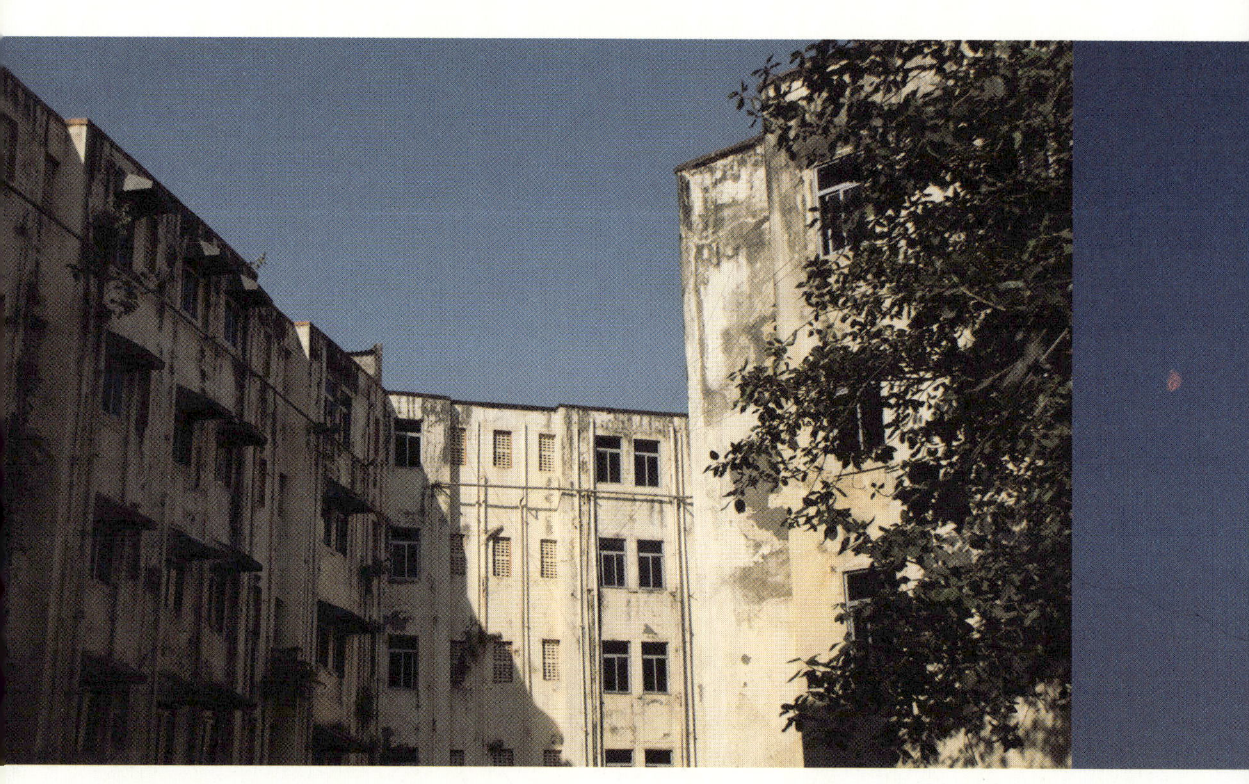

Worli

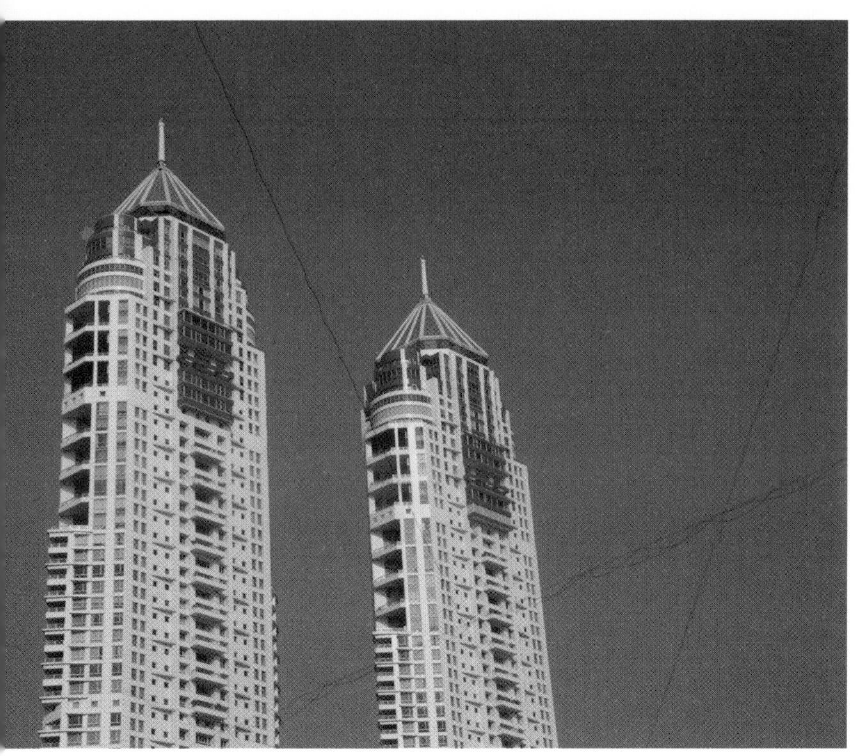

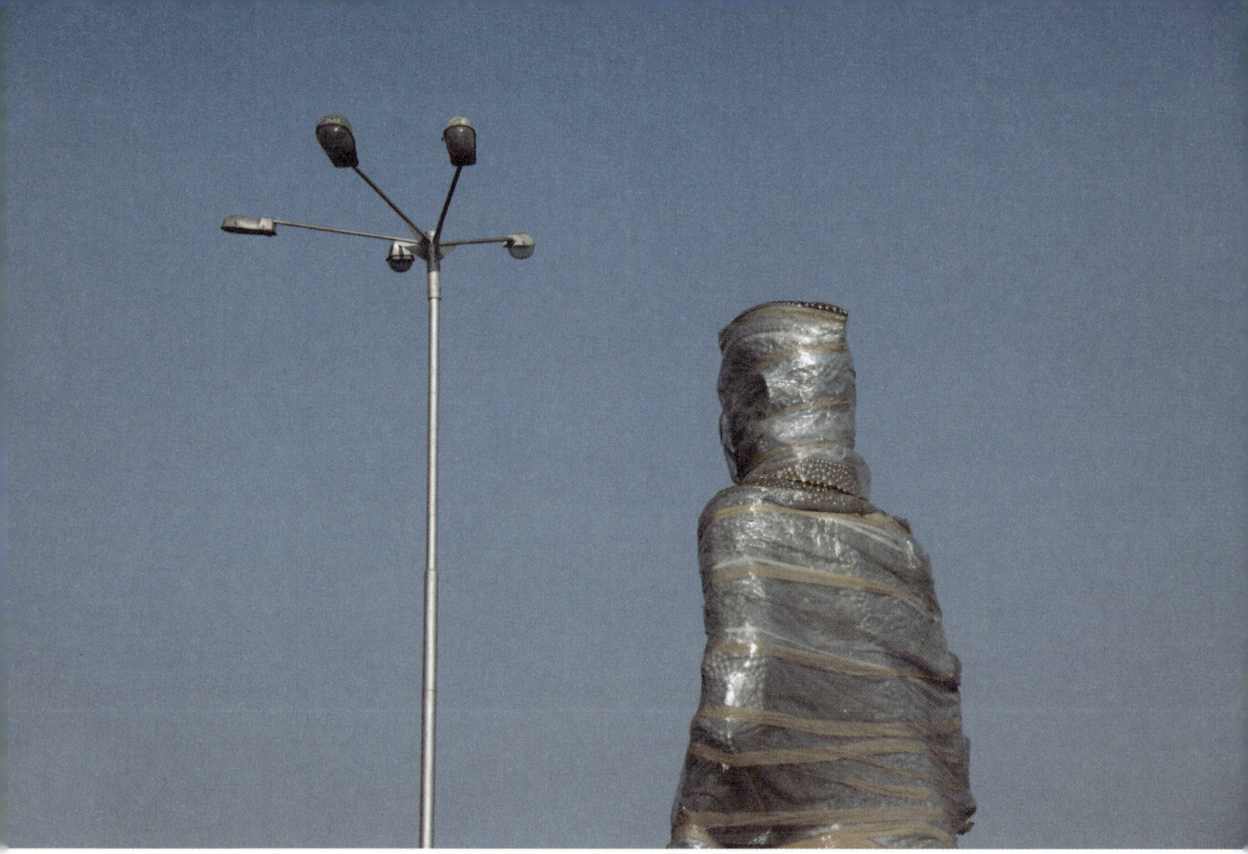

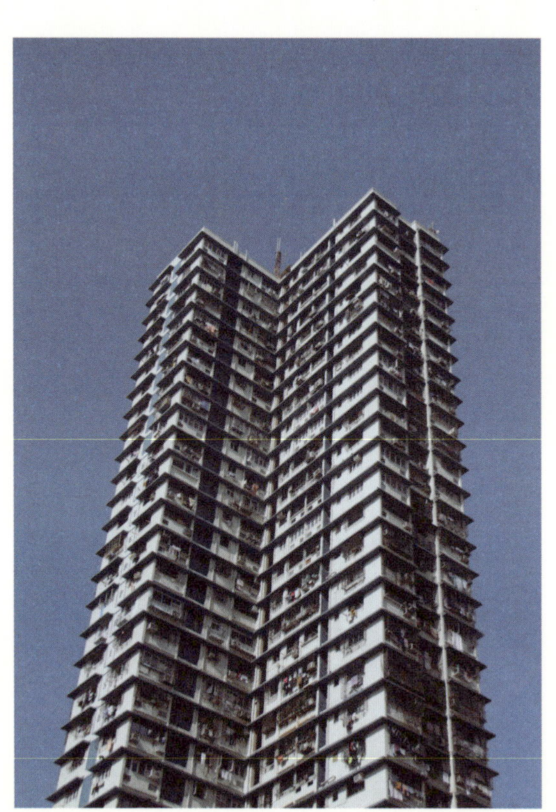

Worli

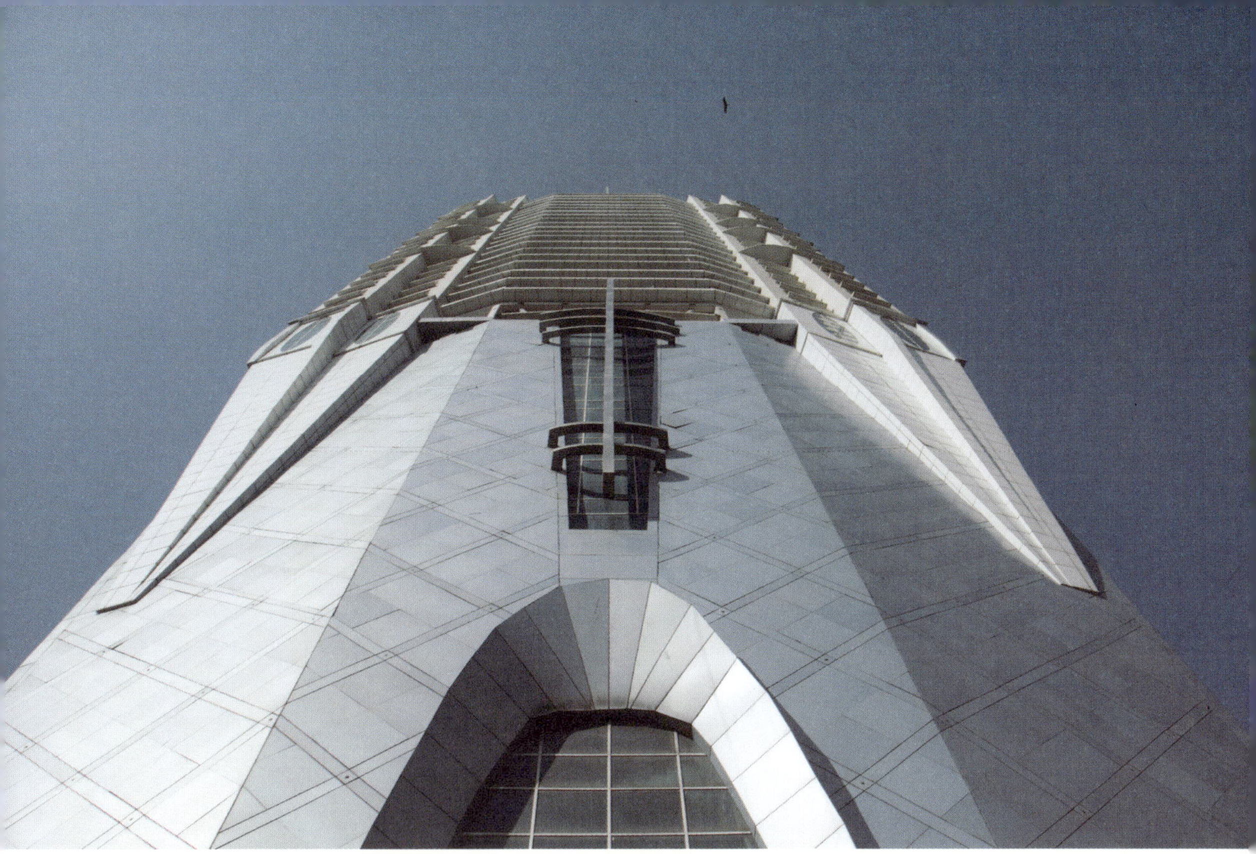

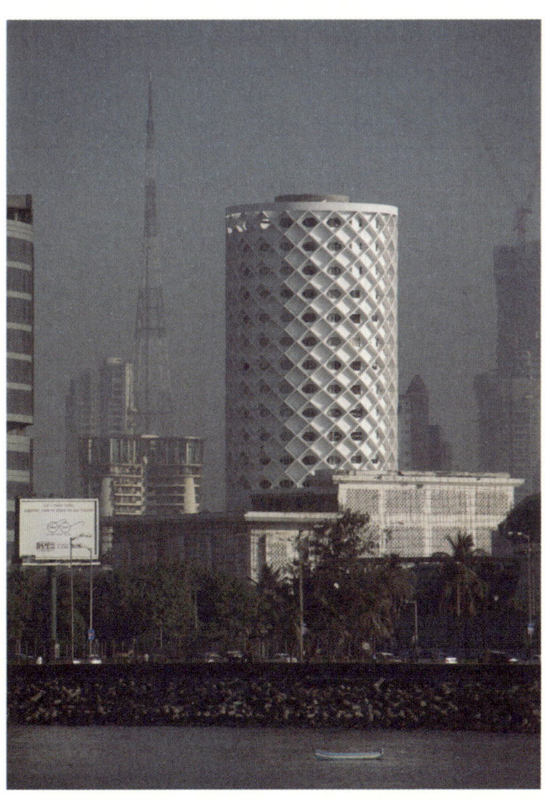

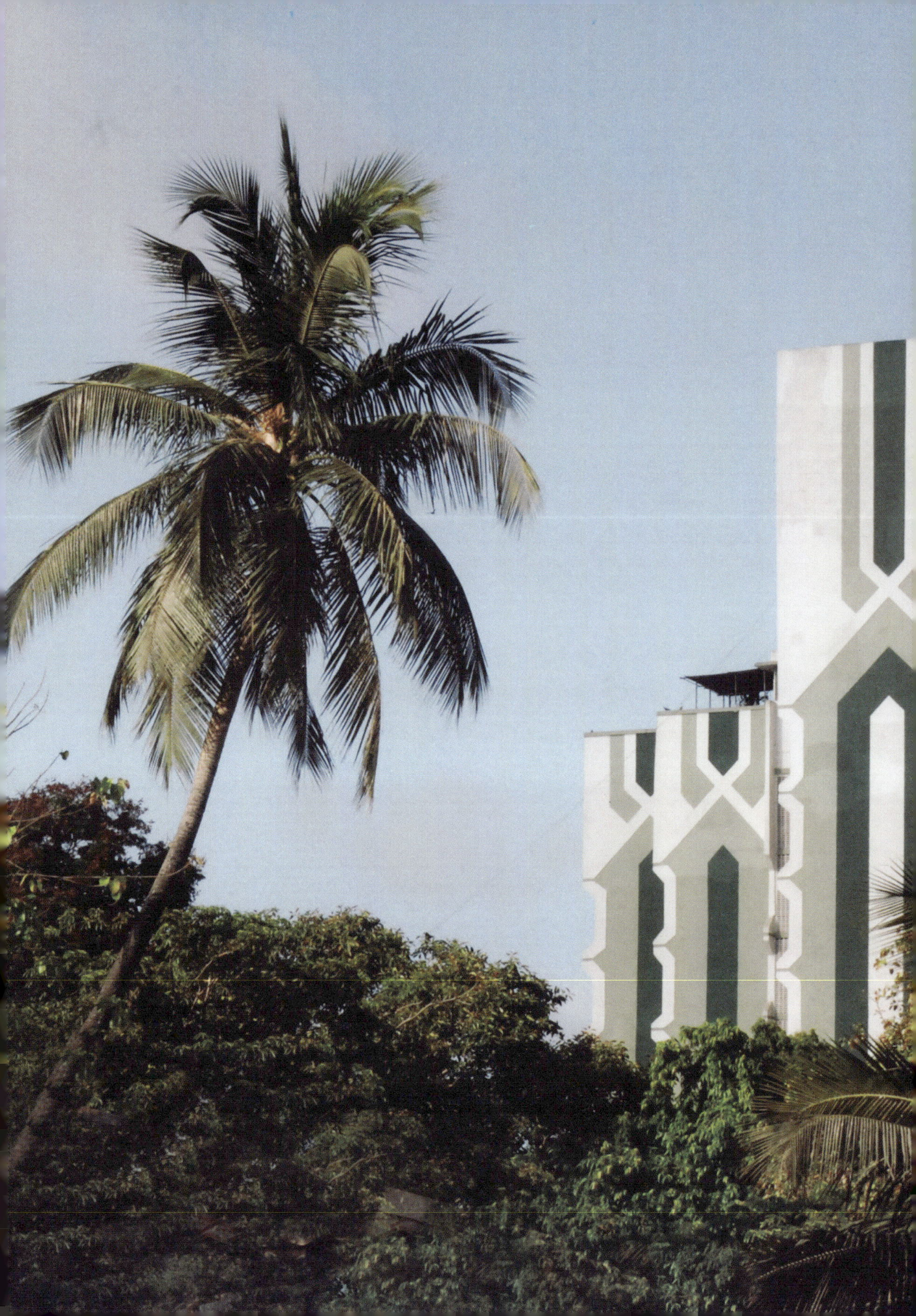

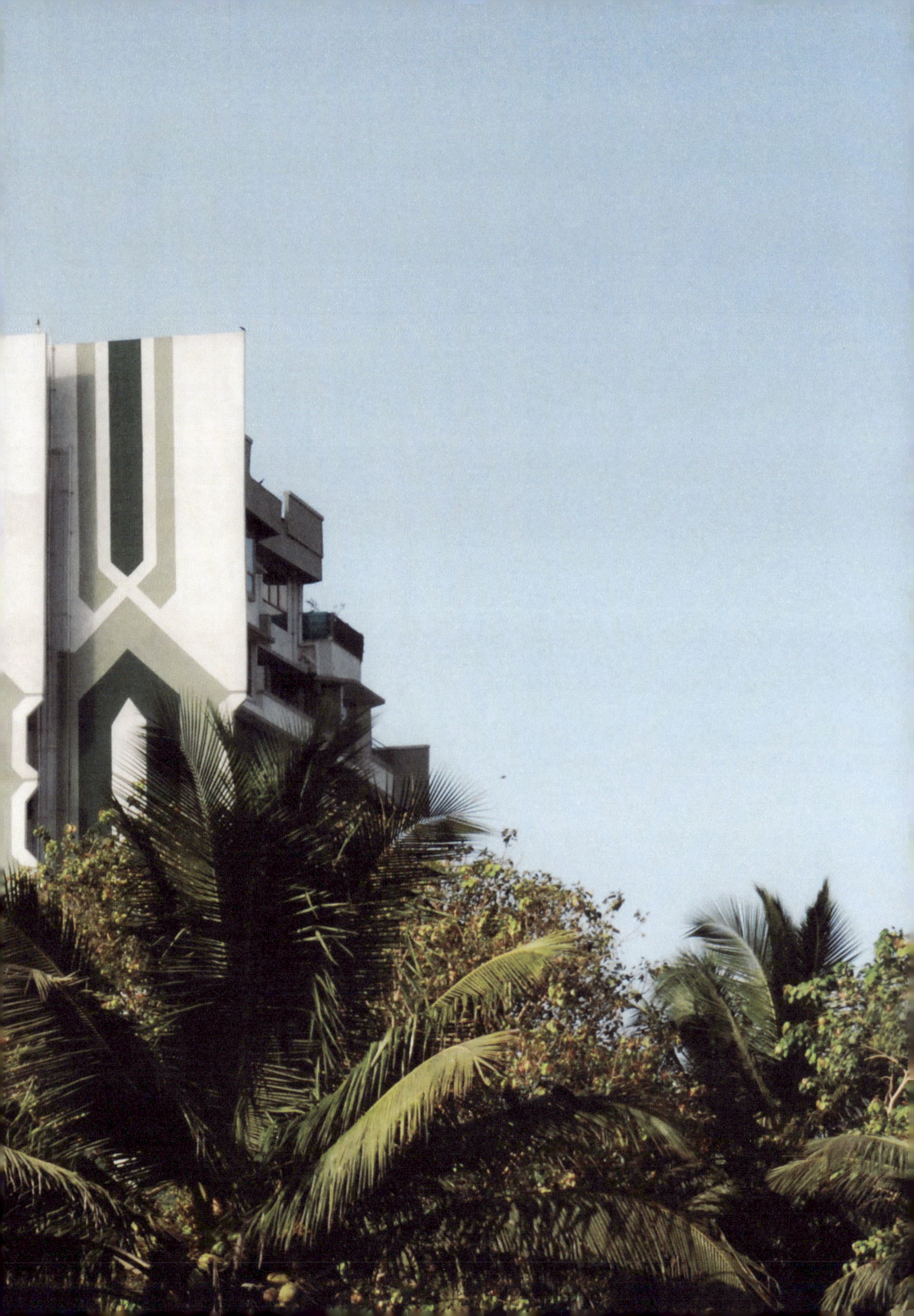

§

Time Travel

Most of my walks were early in the morning.
At this time, one can see the city take a pause,
take a deep breath before the day's chaos
begins. I could feel the city fill its lungs, give
itself a pep talk. Walking and observing the
city from the street, forced me to slow down,
and enabled me to reflect on what I was
photographing: so that I could try and see the
city past its daily cycles and plot its graph on a
longer time frame. Thus, I was able to capture
where time had been kind to the city and
where it had taken a toll.

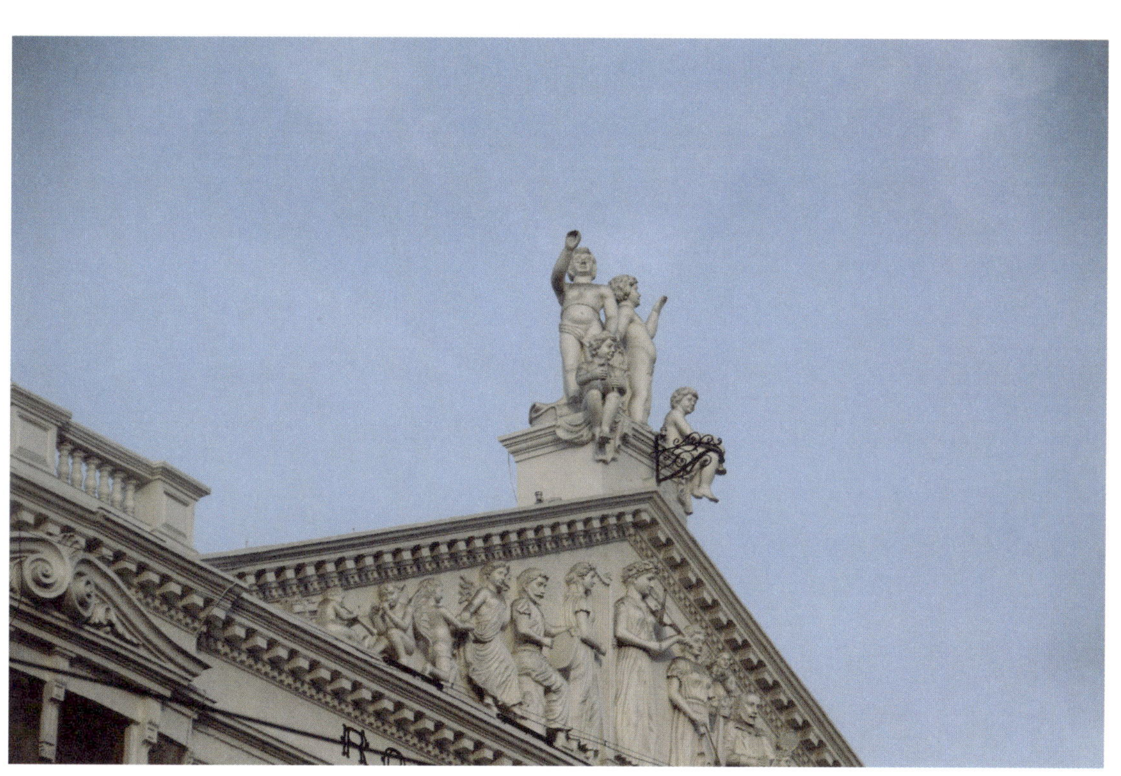

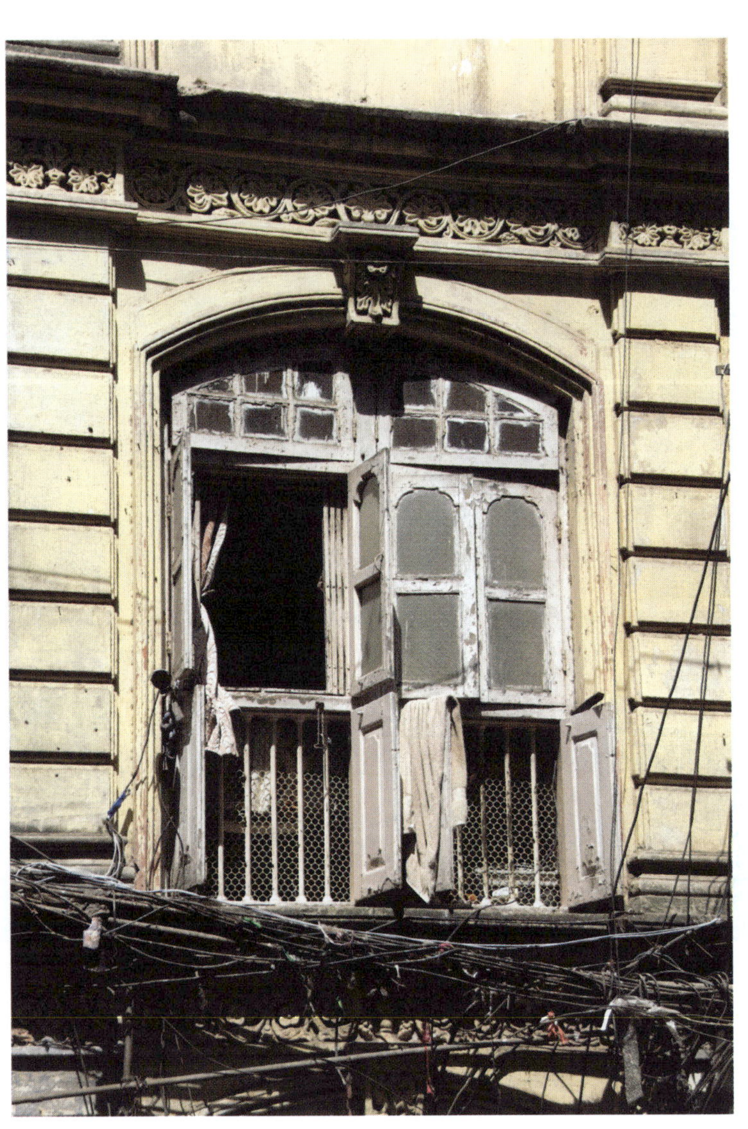

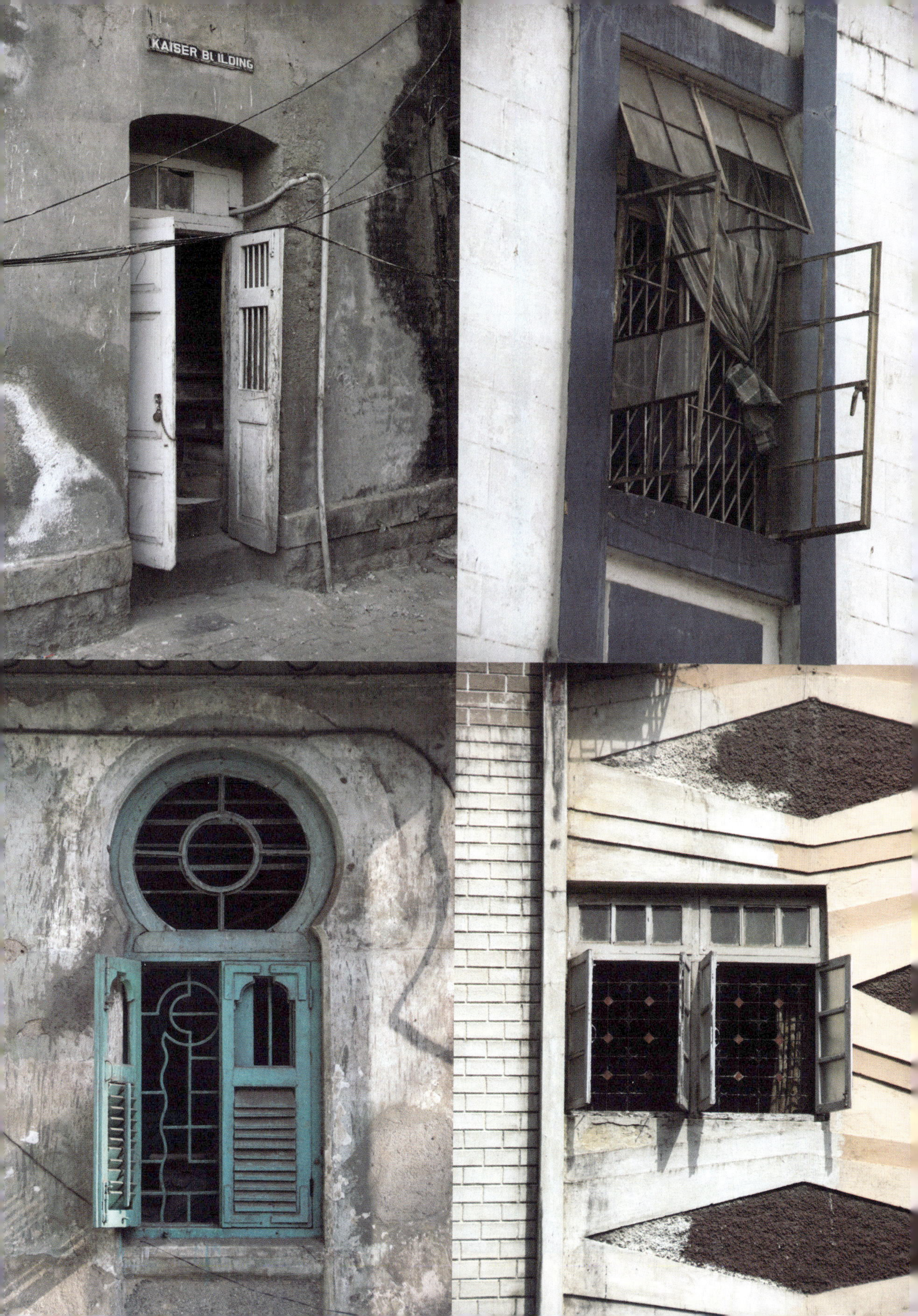

KAISER BUILDING

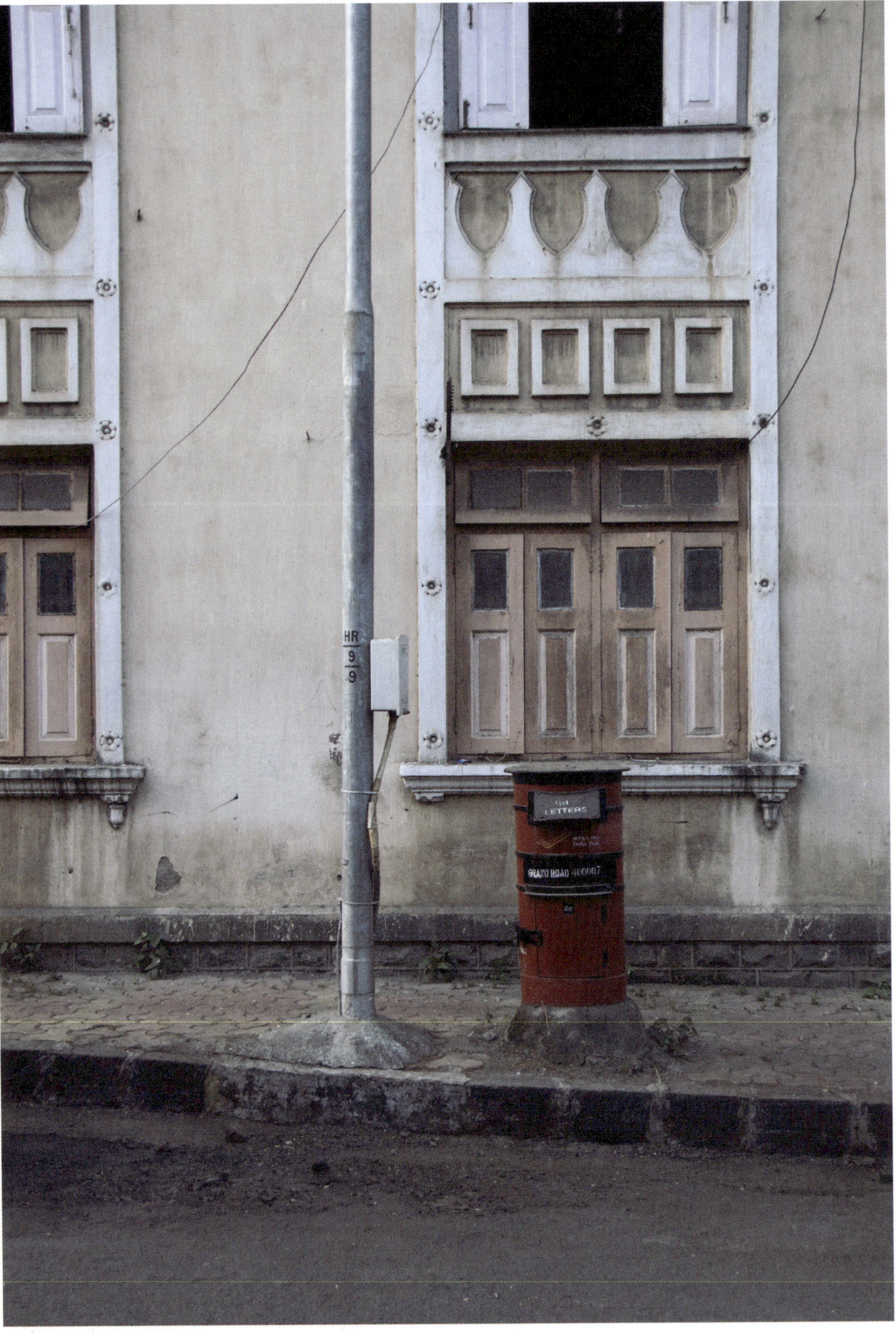
LETTERS
GRAND ROAD 400007

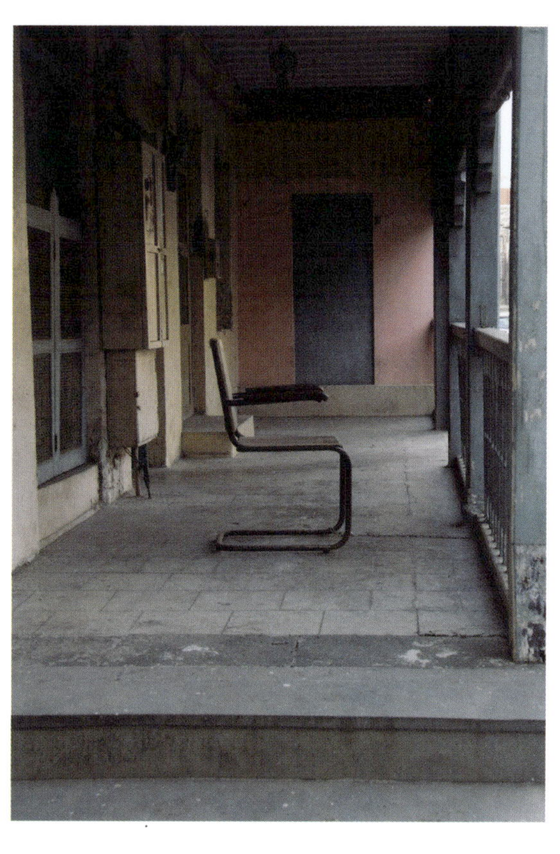

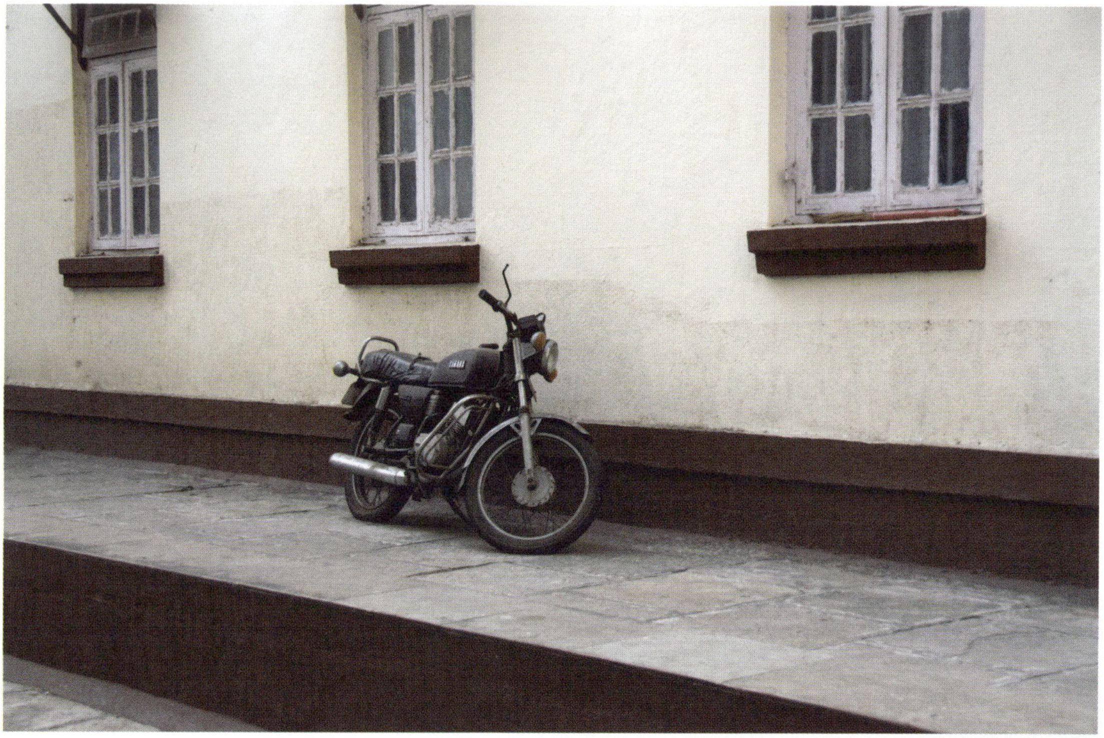

WHY THE LONG SHADOW?

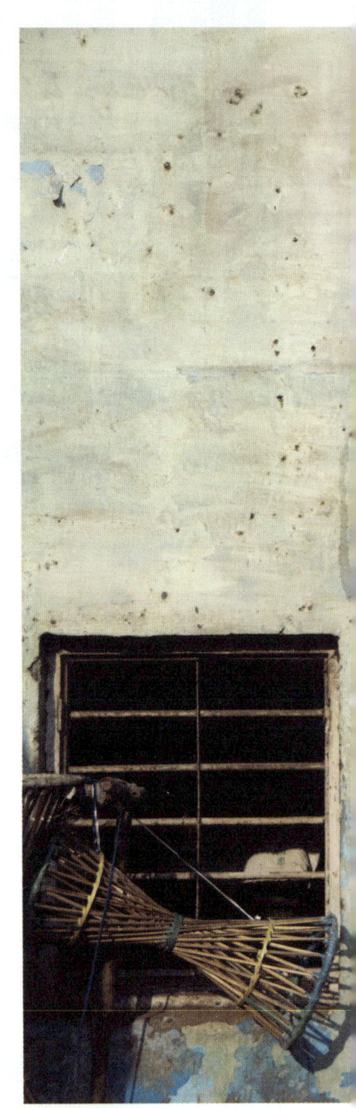

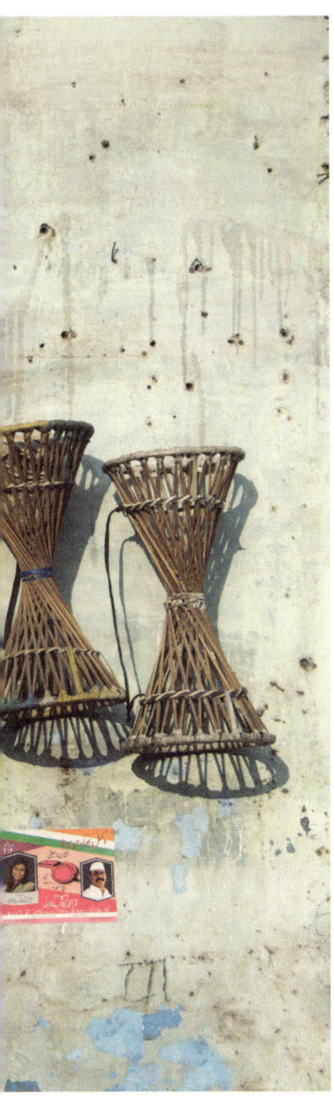

My wife and I have two young kids, and since
we've had them, we've become early risers.

The kids get on the school bus by 7.00 am and I get into work by 10. So when I chanced upon this project, mornings, between 7.00 am, and 10.00 am, was the time I could dedicate to it.

Walking the streets early in the morning enabled a whole different experience of the city. I shared the road with sleepy school children, municipality cleaners, barefoot devotees returning from their morning temple visit, morning walkers with their funny walking styles, joggers, paowallahs (bread-sellers) on their Atlas cycles and lots of people catching up with the morning newspaper.

Being relatively peaceful made the city much more navigable: fewer people, lesser cars, lesser noise and lower levels of pollution. Perfect for someone trying to capture the beauty of the city. But Mumbai is not immediately beautiful, at least not aesthetically. It has a vibrant culture, great diversity, high energy, but to look at, it is rough. All pictures of the city that you see in museums or hotels are framed pictures of pre-independence Bombay. In such a beautifully located city, this shouldn't be the case, but sadly Mumbai has been hard done by pretty much everyone involved.

In the morning with fewer distractions, I was able to extract its beauty. It helped that in the morning the light is softer, right for the kind of story I wanted to tell. The sun in Mumbai is unforgiving, and once it is out in full force, everything becomes high contrast, chiaroscuro: harsh light to expose the harsh realities of the city. That's not exactly what I was going for. I was documenting, to be sure, but I wanted my commentary to be subtle and I was looking to be optimistic, even flattering.

Therefore, when I did get dramatic light, I went for a softer poetic version. It would leak through the densely packed buildings and fall gently on my subject, either a person or building. It would act as a spotlight extracting my subject from its background, highlighting its best features. I was getting a quality of light that one gets when setting up lights to take a studio portrait.

Since the sun was at a steep angle, I would often get these exaggerated long shadows. For photos of architectural details, this worked well. All the windows of Mumbai apartments have grills on and around them. These wrought iron cages give a false sense of security to the homeowners and are ubiquitous throughout the city. They are an eyesore on the cityscape, but for me, they made beautiful pictures as these floral or graphic patterned grills threw patterned shadows onto the otherwise unimaginative building façades.

The city has been through many cycles of change. It is in a state of constant flux, driven as it is by a progressive restlessness and healthy competitiveness. Some of these changes have proved successful, some less so. Bandra, for example, has maintained its relevance, by being open to new ideas. But there are parts of the city which look like they were glorious once but are past their prime now.

My first job in Mumbai was at MTV India and their office was in Parel. To get to and from the office, I commuted through parts of Central Mumbai. I'd look at the once-glorious grand structures along this route and wonder why they had fallen by the wayside. Now after walking through these areas, some of them frozen in time, I felt that they were stubbornly holding onto their past, exhibiting almost an aversion to change.

On some of my walks through Central Mumbai, I could feel unwelcoming eyes peering at me and I sensed a clear sense of entitlement. It was out of these parts that local leaders launched their regional movements to reclaim the city for what they considered its original community. They used the latter's resentment and mobilised their members against the more successful minority communities that had migrated to Bombay. Turning the clock back to past glories to propagate the growth of indigenous movements, in place of imported cultures, did make the area proud. But at the same time it gave it a sense of entitlement which has led to stasis. I'm all for celebrating one's culture, but people change, they need growth, they need movement, or else they get claustrophobic. The slower pace of walking through city streets enabled me to reflect on these and other related thoughts about Mumbai.

The quieter shots I got made it easier to focus on one idea at a time. I got many wide shots with no one in them or with one person walking across the cityscape. If my frame was busy, I could zoom in and isolate out a quiet moment, or I could wait for a few minutes for the rush to move out of the frame. On Worli Sea Face, one of the busiest spots in the city I got a shot of all the benches without a soul on them. When I showed these pictures to my peers, their universal comment was that they didn't recognise the city.

Perhaps there is an element of sleight-of-hand in these pictures, and they certainly don't capture the experience of day to day life in the city. On the other hand, that is what I was trying to explore and communicate, remind people of the potential of the city, interrupt their apathy towards the familiar, by highlighting Mumbai's small graces. Could I nudge them beyond their immediate personal concerns? In the hope that their appreciation of what was and is, would move them to show more care for what could be?

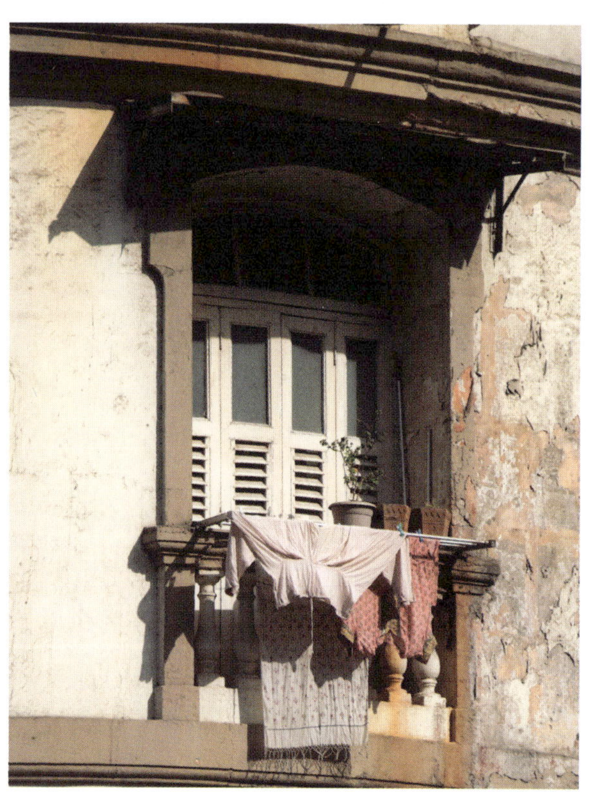

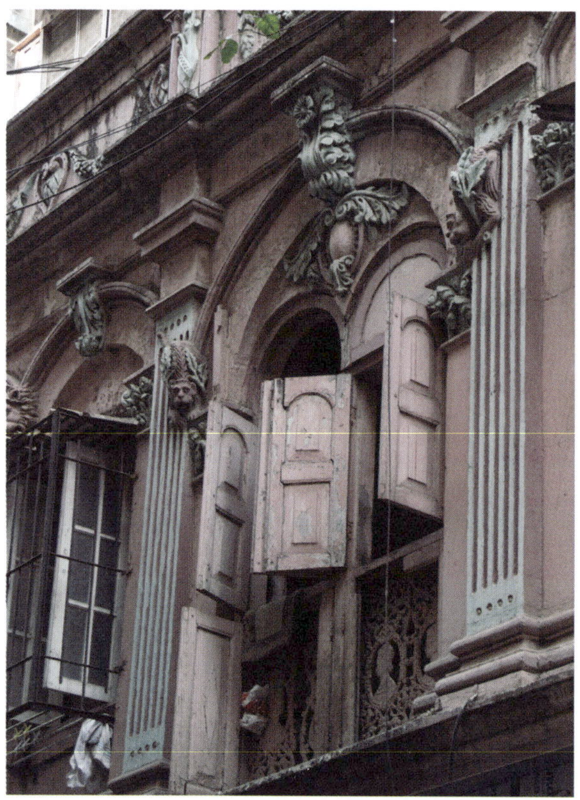

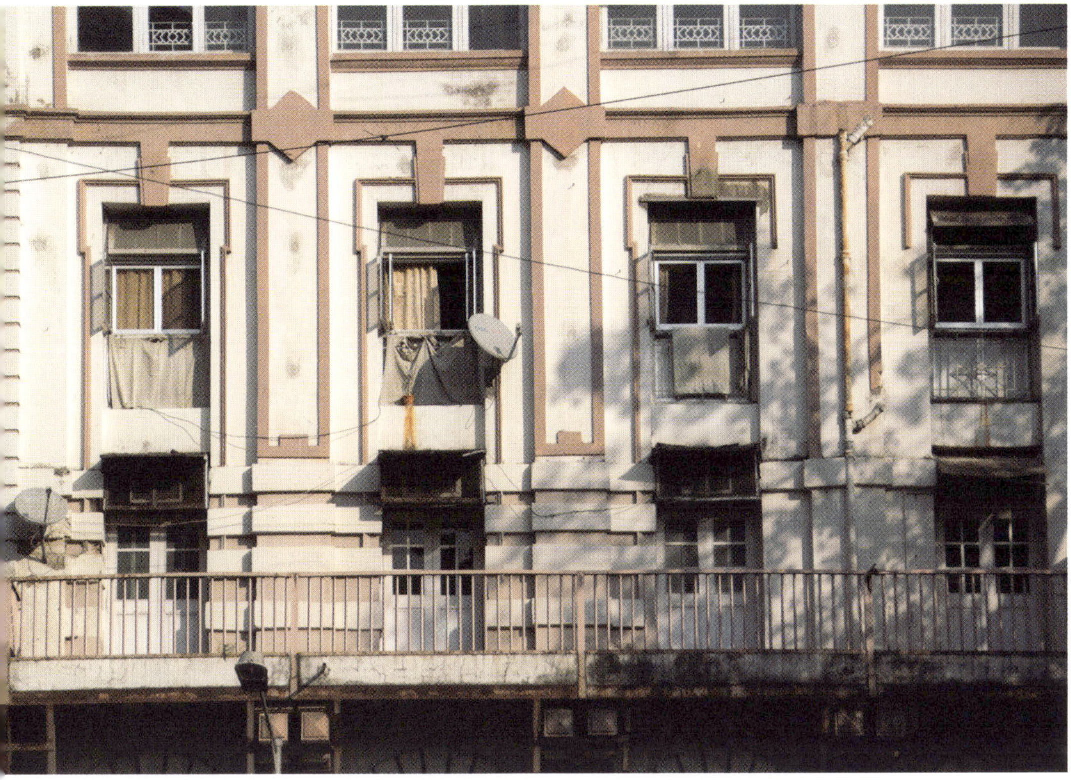

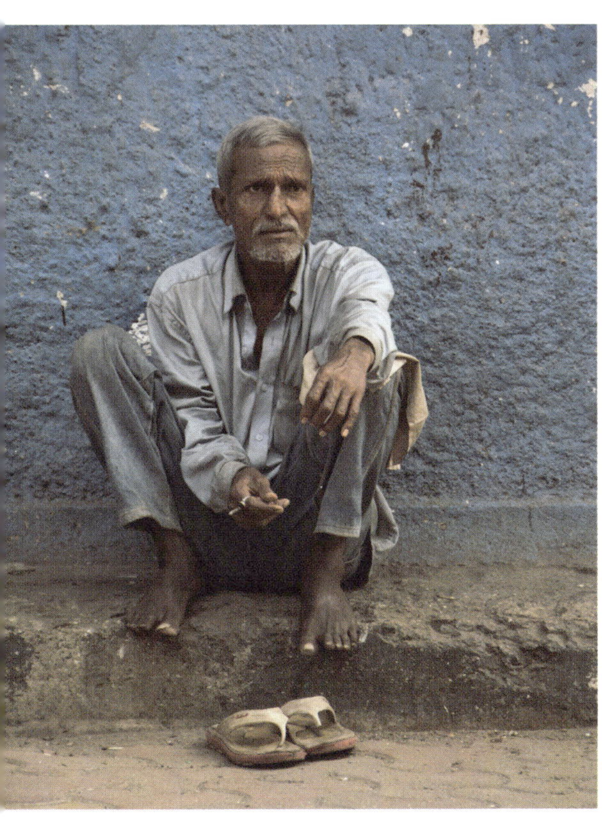

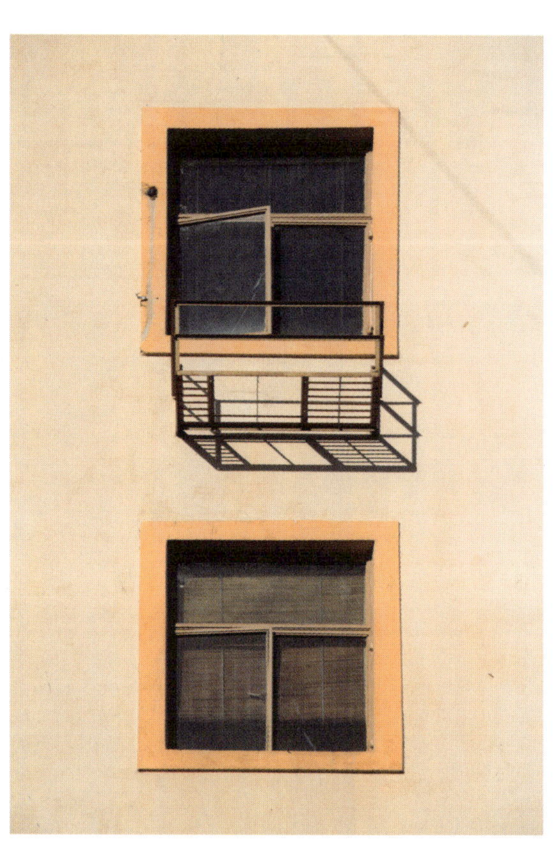

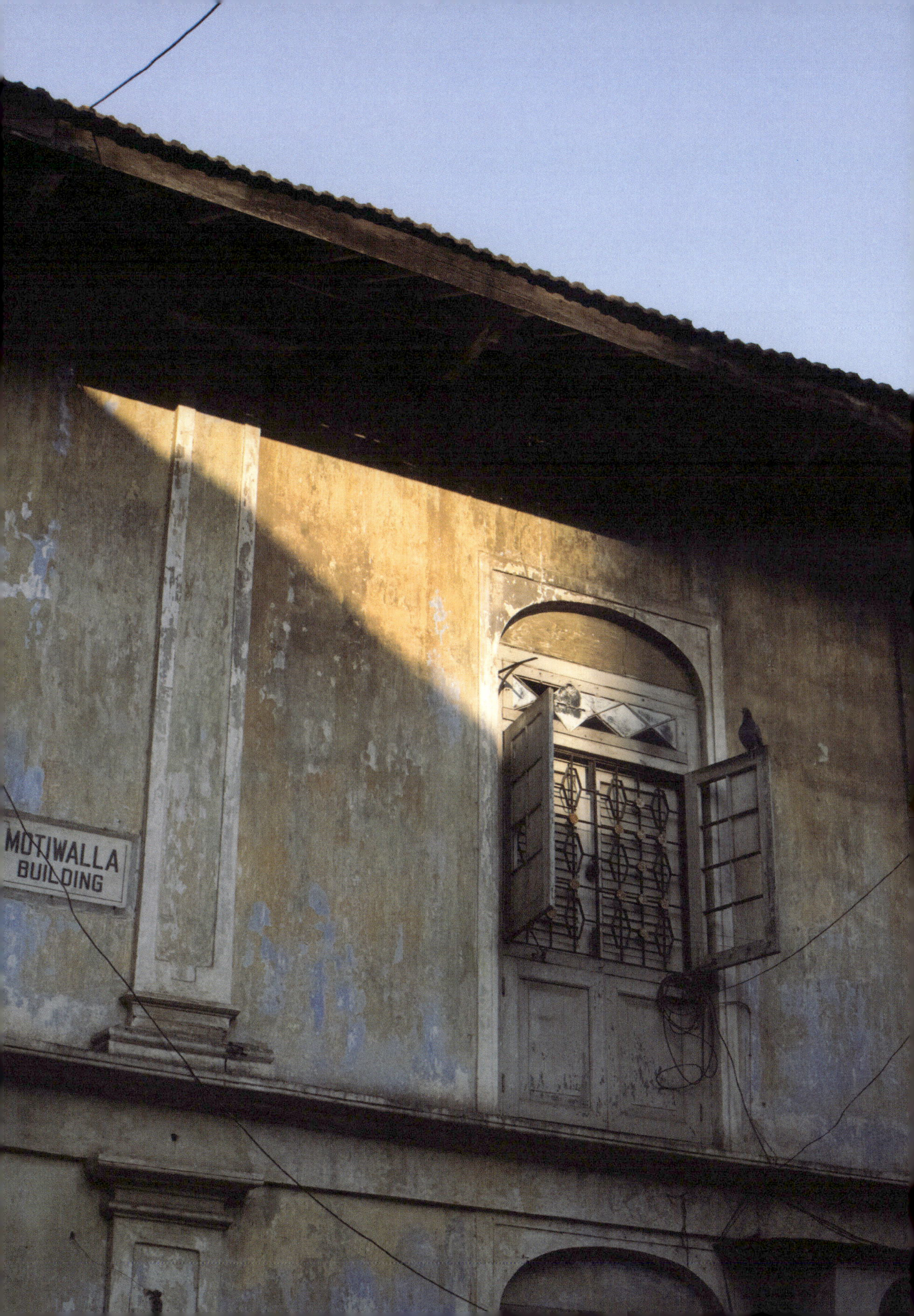

MOTIWALLA
BUILDING

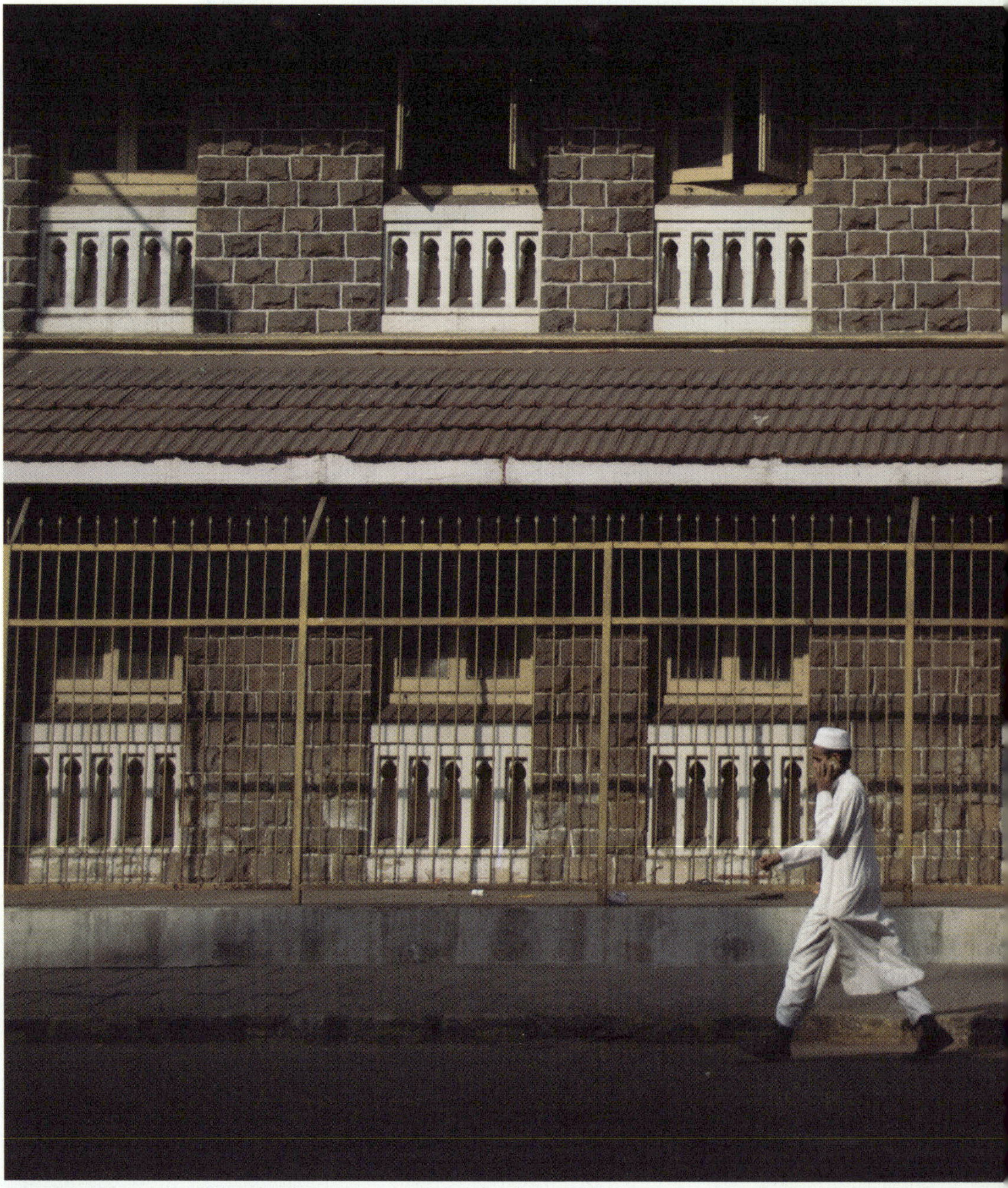

Mumbai–Central Opera

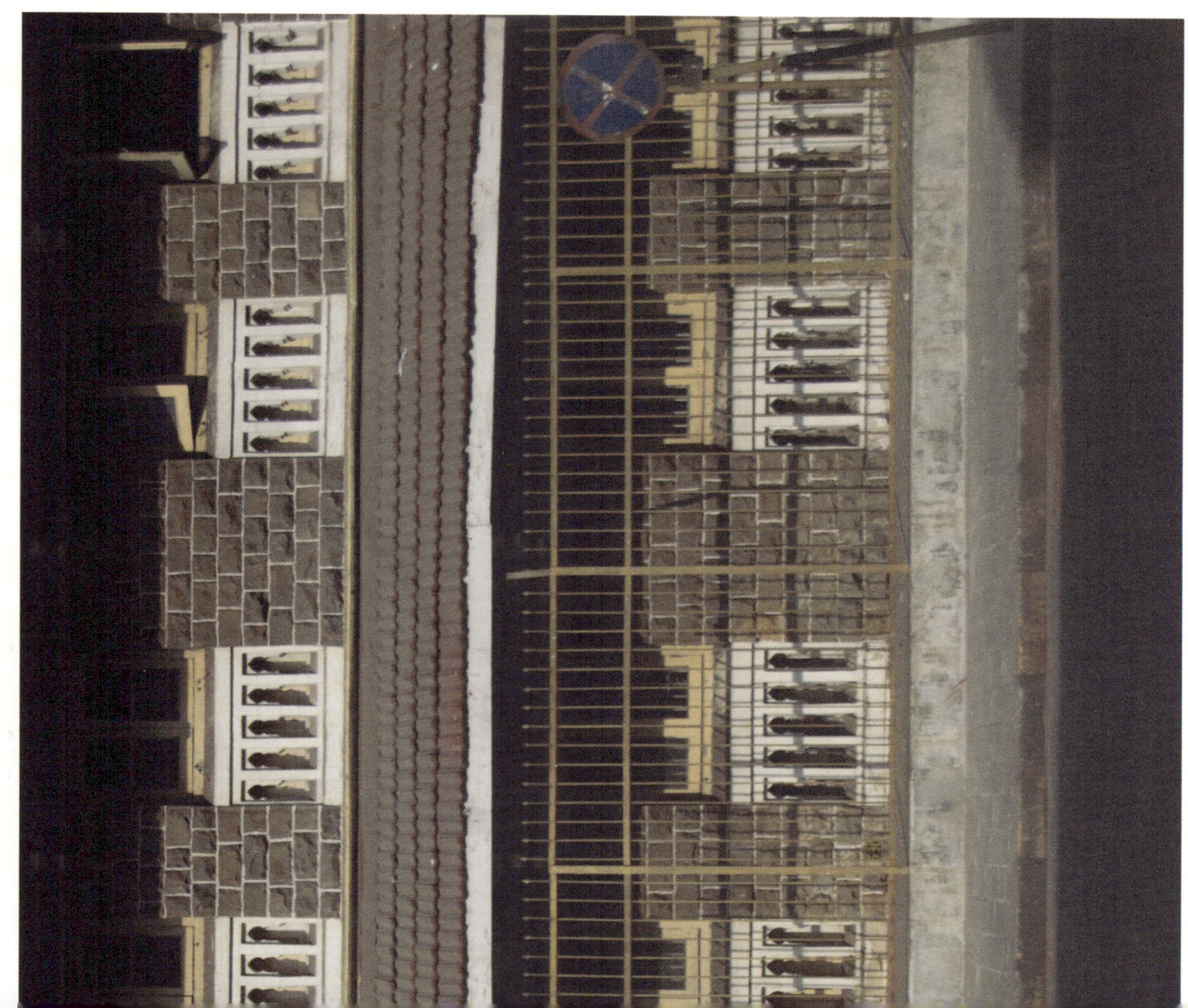

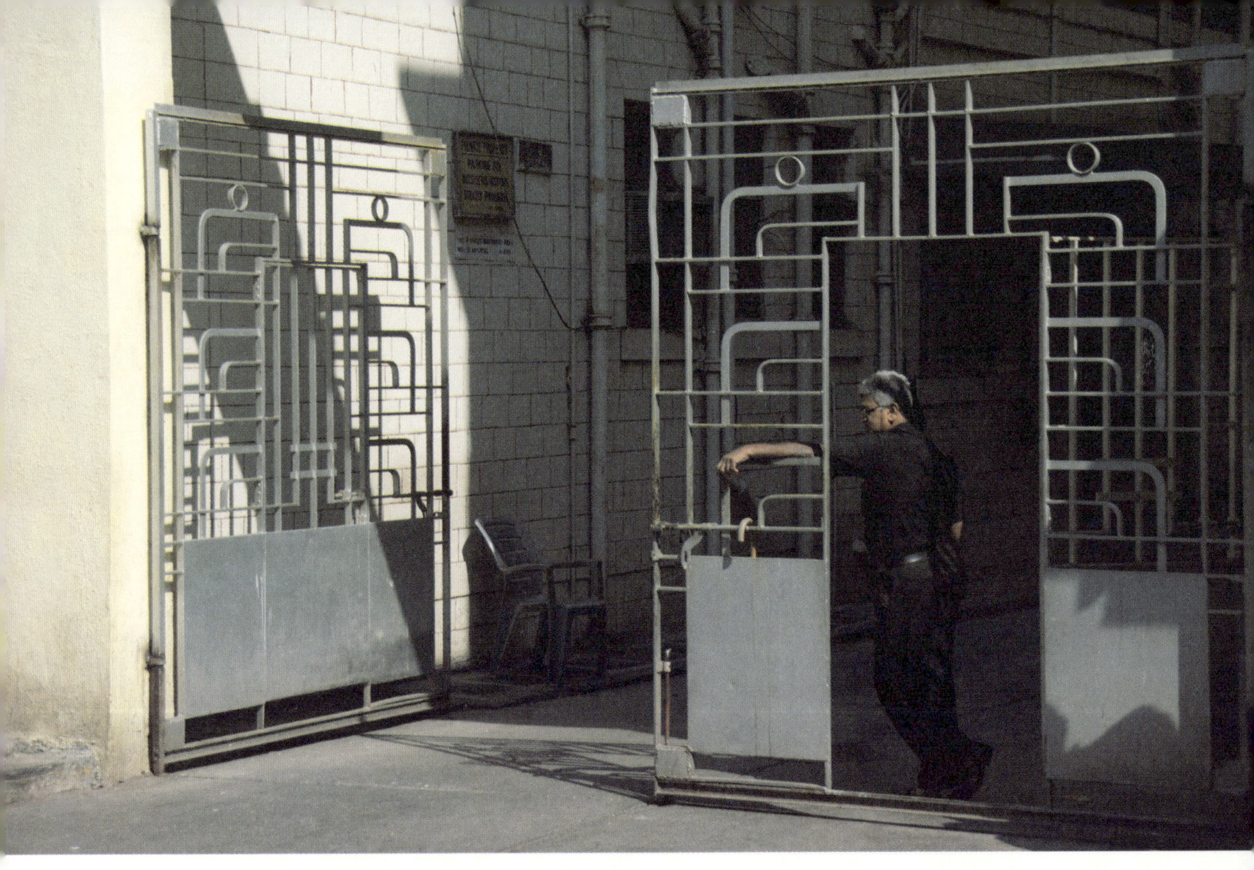

Mumbai–Central Opera

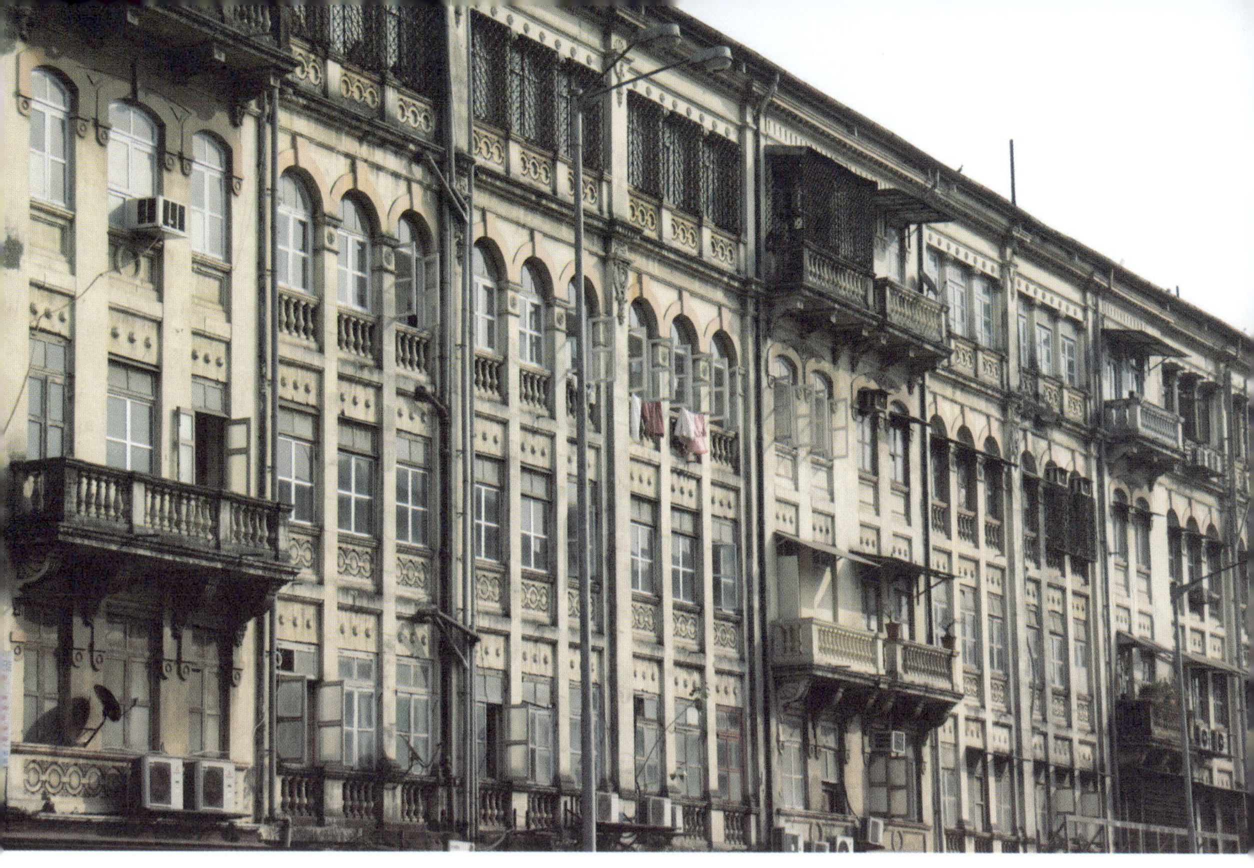

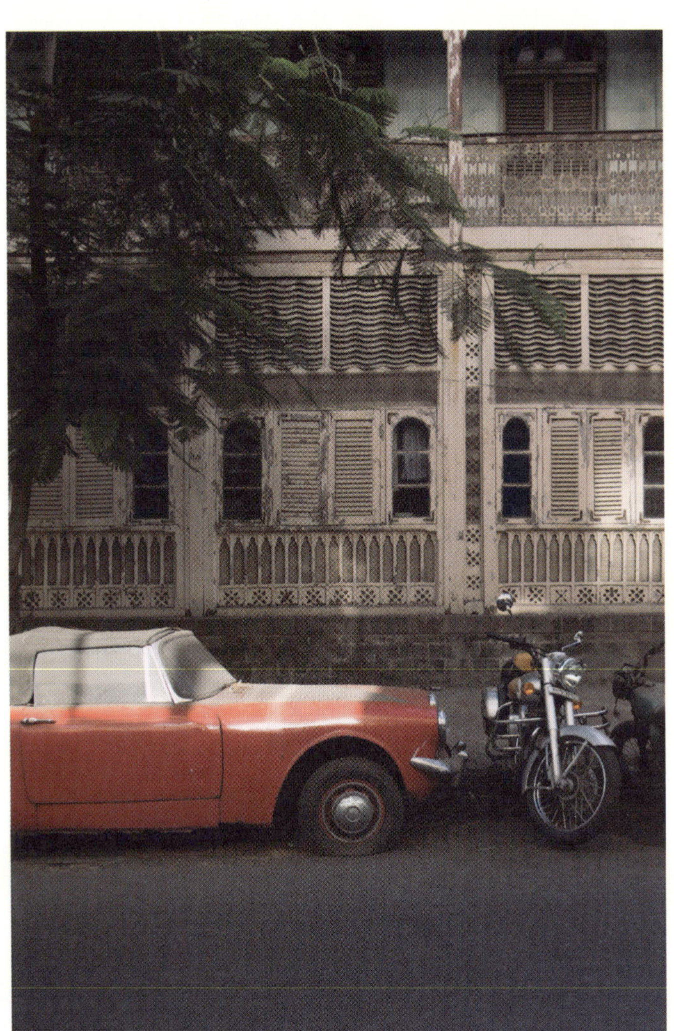

Mumbai–Central Opera.

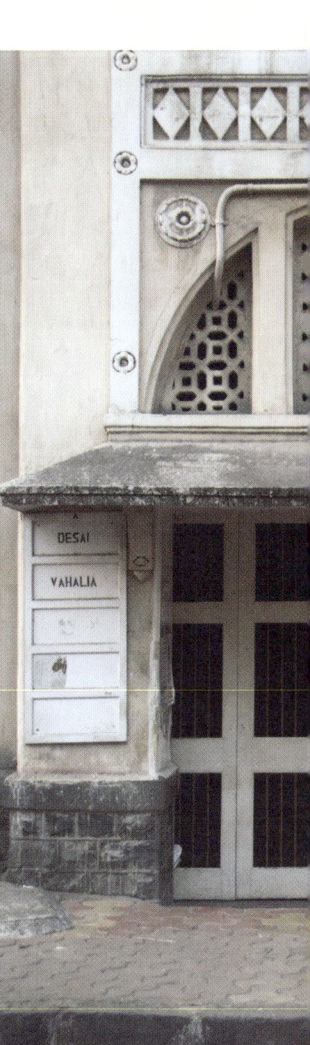

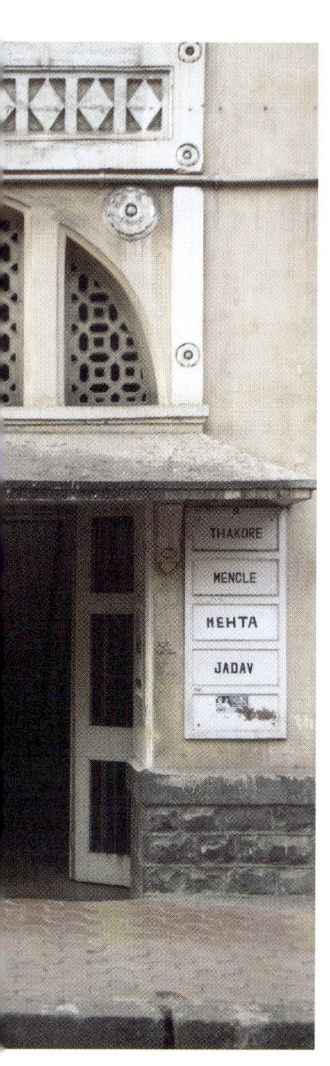

THAKORE
MENCLE
MEHTA
JADAV

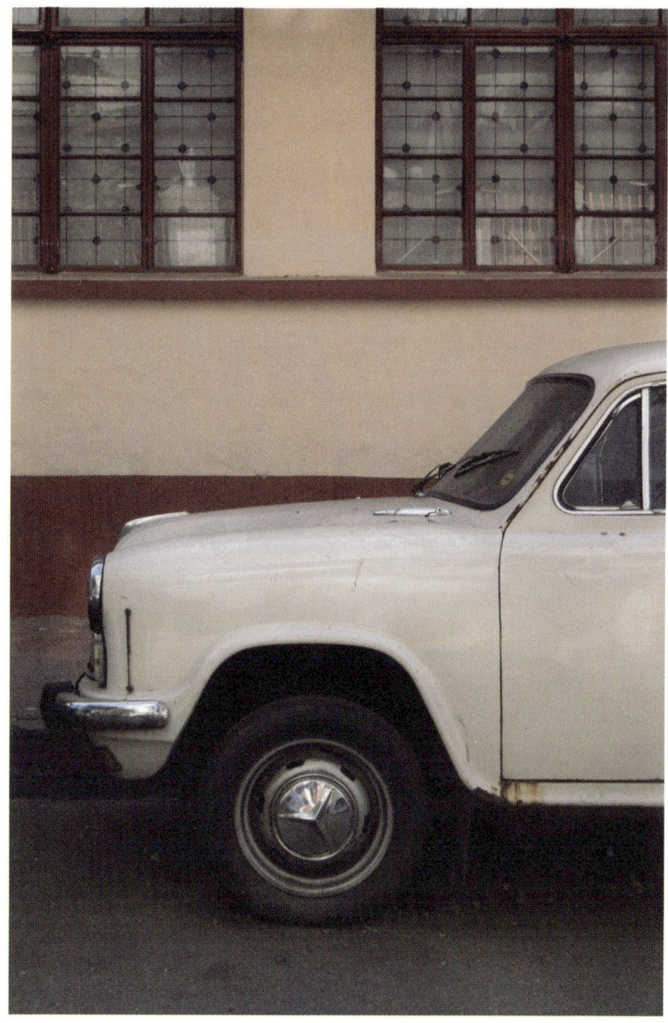

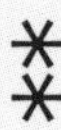

Banganga

Banganga is one of the places in Mumbai I'd heard of but never
visited. It is on the outermost tip of Walkeshwar, and its centrepiece
is a large rectangular sweet-water well. When I was at MTV, it was
a favourite shooting location because it doesn't feel like Mumbai.
It is surrounded by temples and the legend is that Laxman, Ram's
brother, created it for Ram as they made their way to Lanka. Thirsty
and exhausted, Ram needed water. Laxman shot an arrow into the
earth and exposed a tributary of Ganga, miles away from that river's
natural path from the Himalaya to the Bay of Bengal. That's the
origin of the name: Ban (arrow) plus Ganga.

What interested me more than the myth was that like many
places in Mumbai it was a little snapshot from another part of
India: Banganga was a mini version of the ghats in Benares. Taken
together these places added to the sense that Mumbai indeed was
the 'gateway' to India.

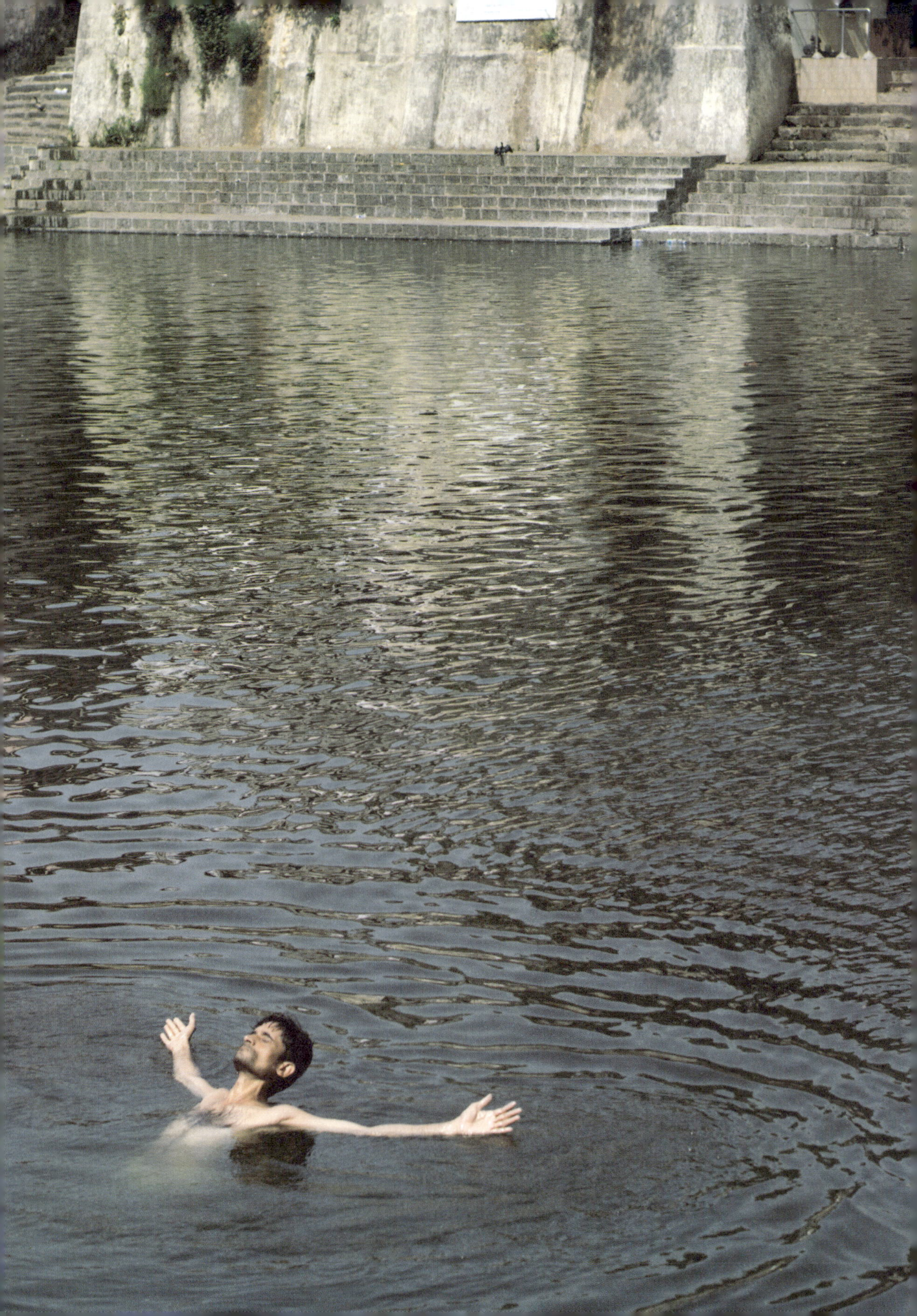

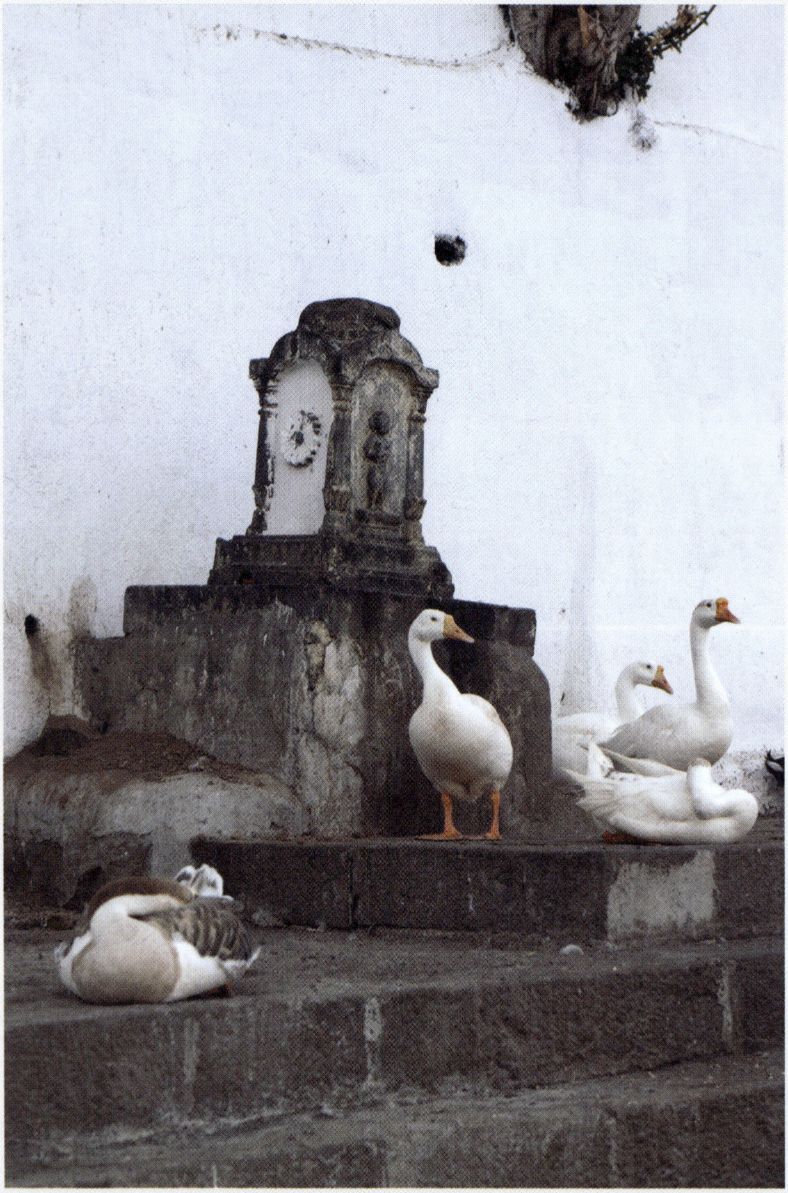

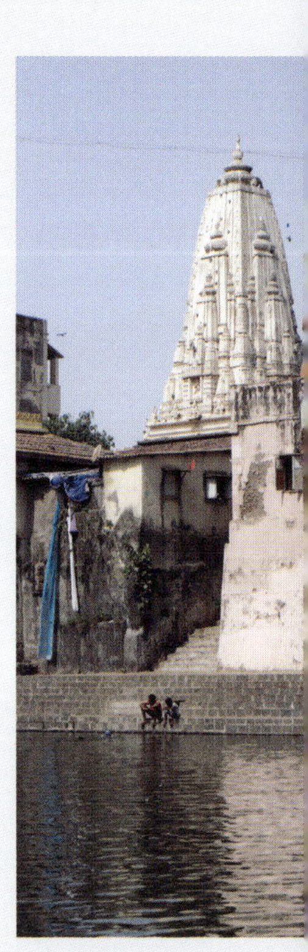

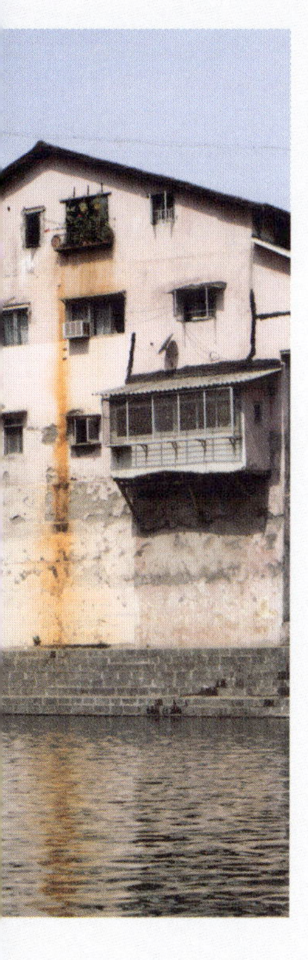

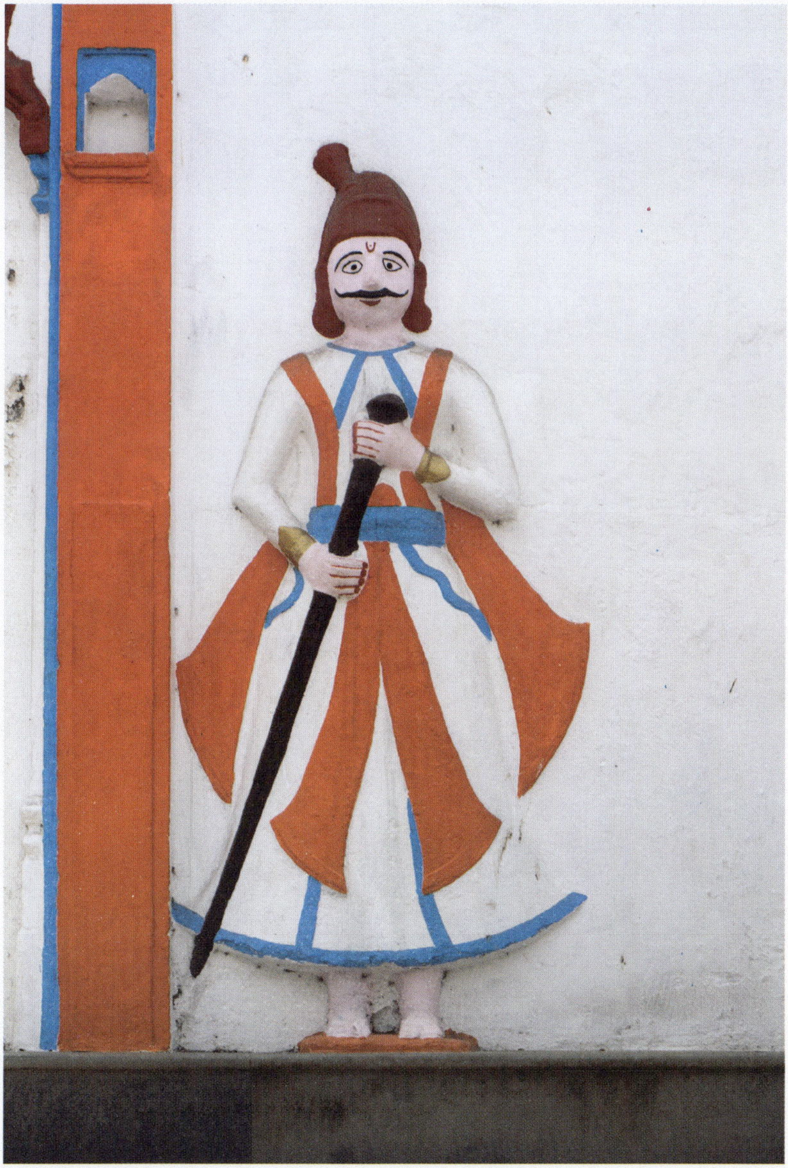

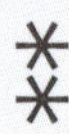

Kamatipura

Kamatipura is Mumbai's largest red light district. In sequence, it is the last walk I did. Two reasons for this: one, I had heard of a photographer losing his money and camera in here. Second, I didn't quite know how to approach it. I was looking to make a document but also capture a sense of hope. As it is, that was a hard task in Mumbai and to do that in Kamatipura without being inauthentic was likely to be difficult.

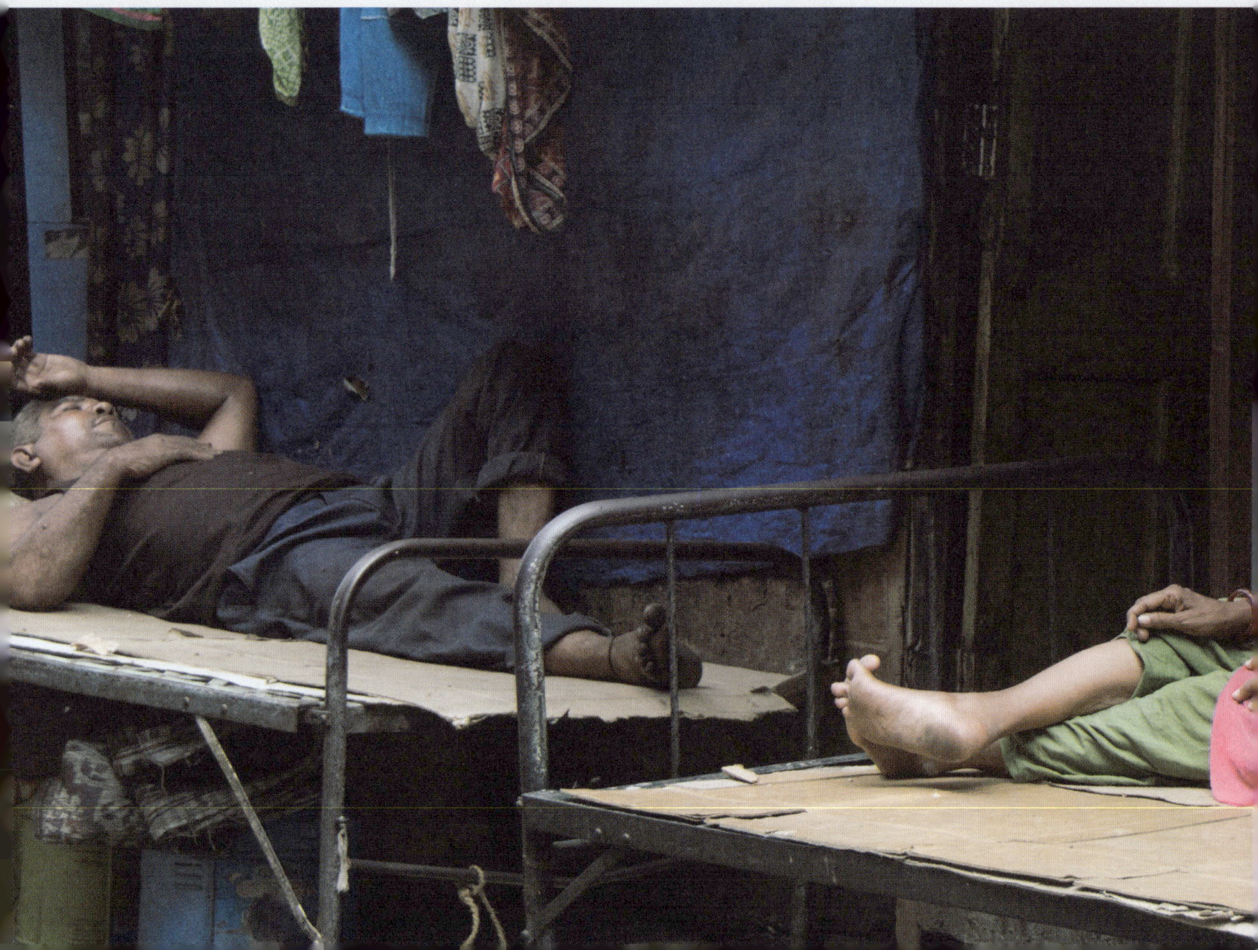

I'd been through this area before. If you go shopping at Chor Bazaar near Crawford market, then it is very likely you cross this area. During this project, when I first encountered Kamatipura, it snuck up on me. It was early in the morning, and I was walking east from Lamington road. I saw a hoard of men standing on one side of the street. I found that odd, especially at this time in the morning. I looked around, and

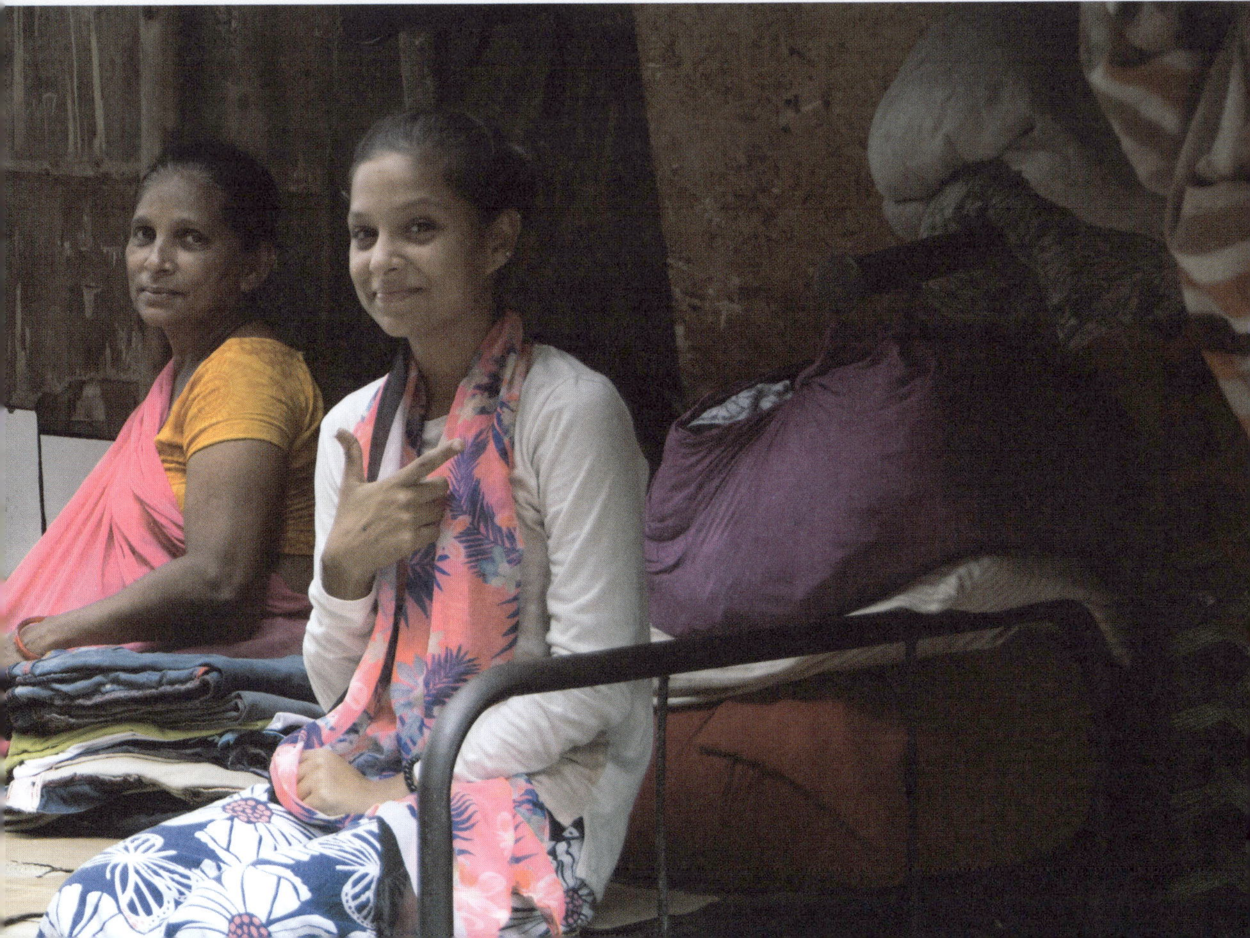

suddenly realised where I was. I walked through
some of the skinny bylanes but wasn't prepared to
photograph yet.

When I finally walked through Kamatipura
and took pictures, I was surprised to see how
it is much more than its cliché. Beyond the
bright colours, heavy make-up and flirtatious
personalities of the women, which mask an
inherent sadness, the neighbourhood also
has all the other shades of everyday Mumbai.
There are many small industries here, like
tailoring, recycling, metalworking… You see
schools, families and places of worship. It has
a big market and many different communities
inhabit its bylanes. Kamatipura, I realised, was
a Mumbai neighbourhood like any other, and as
deserving of empathy.

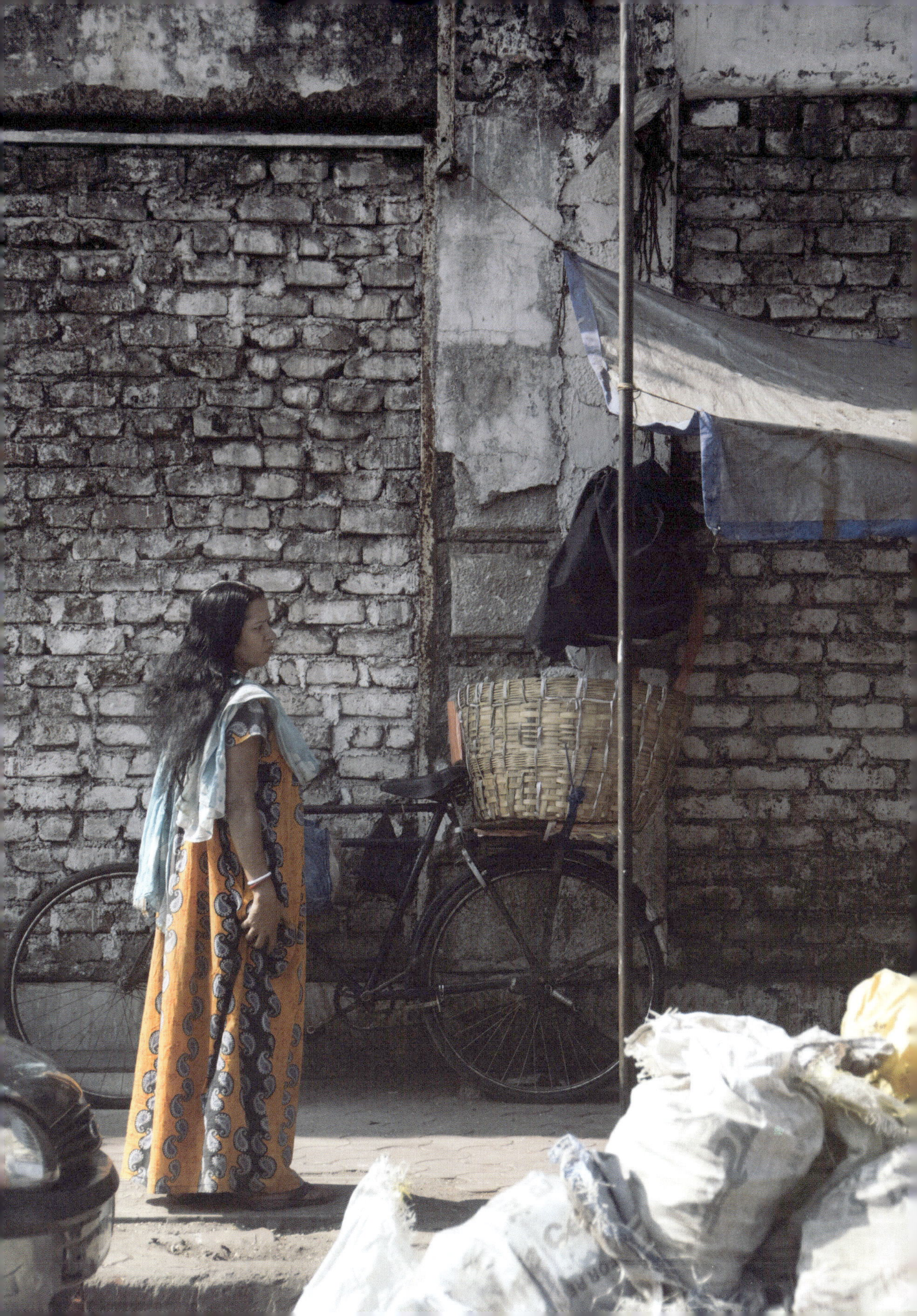

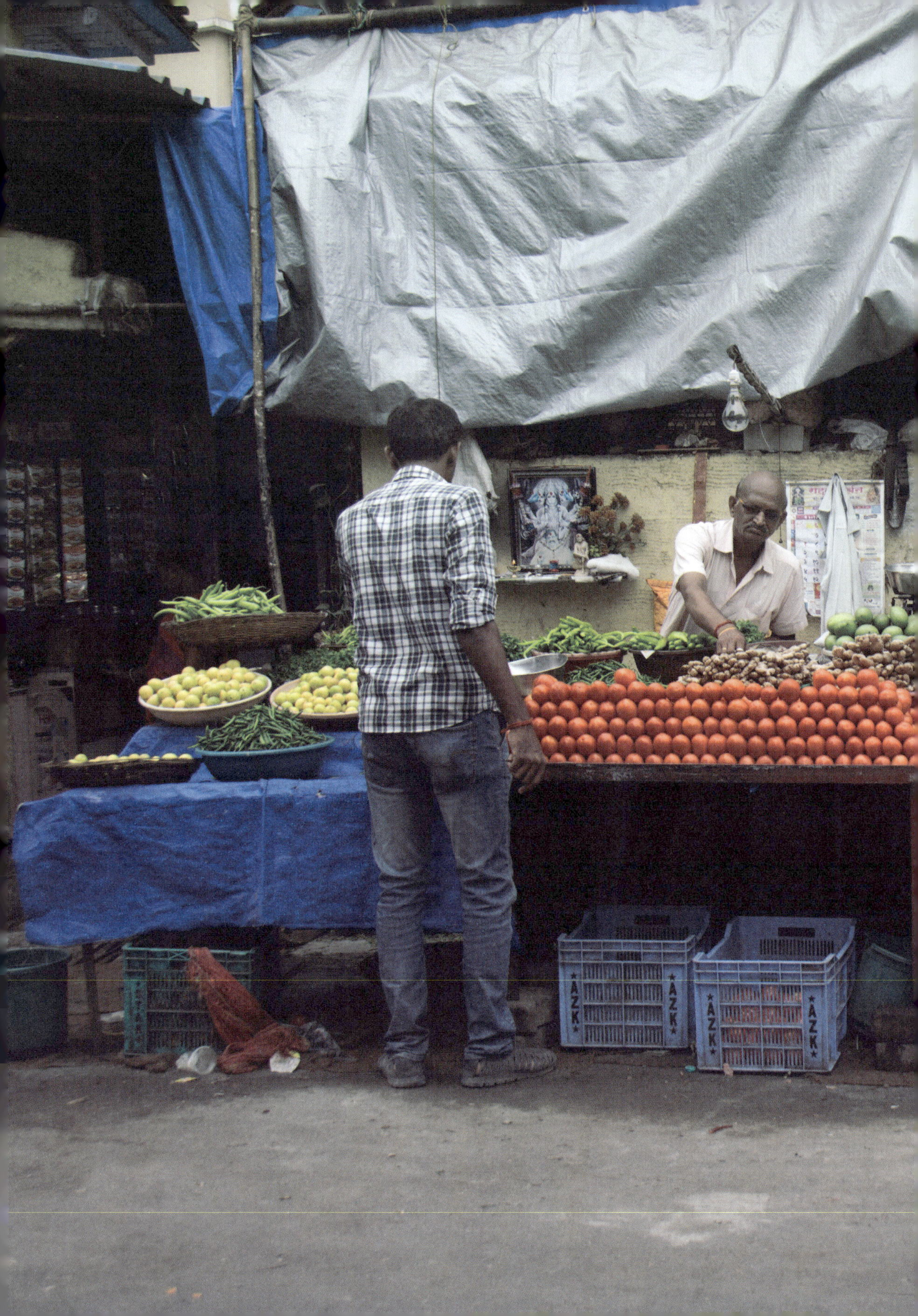

AZK
AZK
AZK
AZK

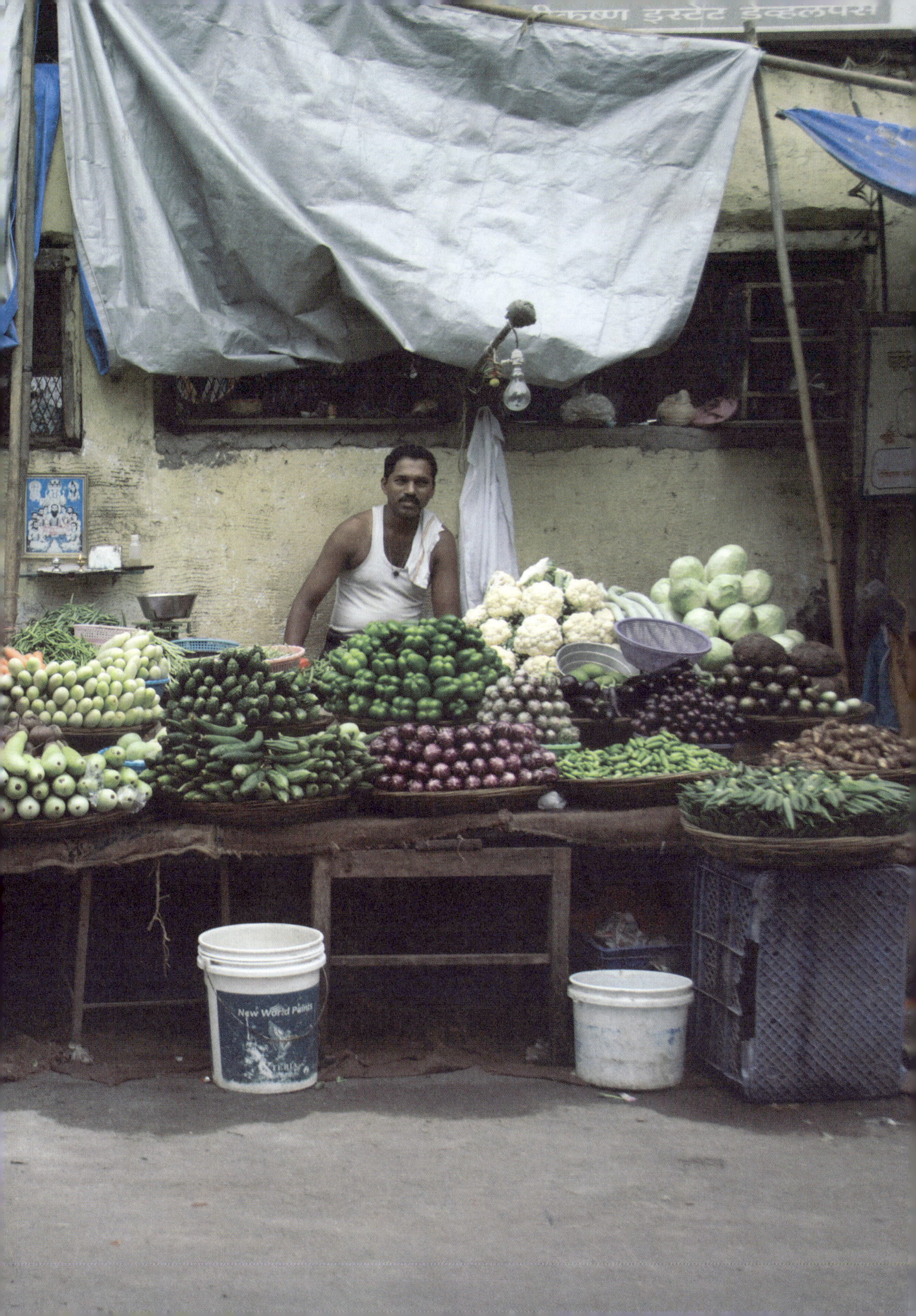
कृष्ण इस्टेट डेव्हलपर्स

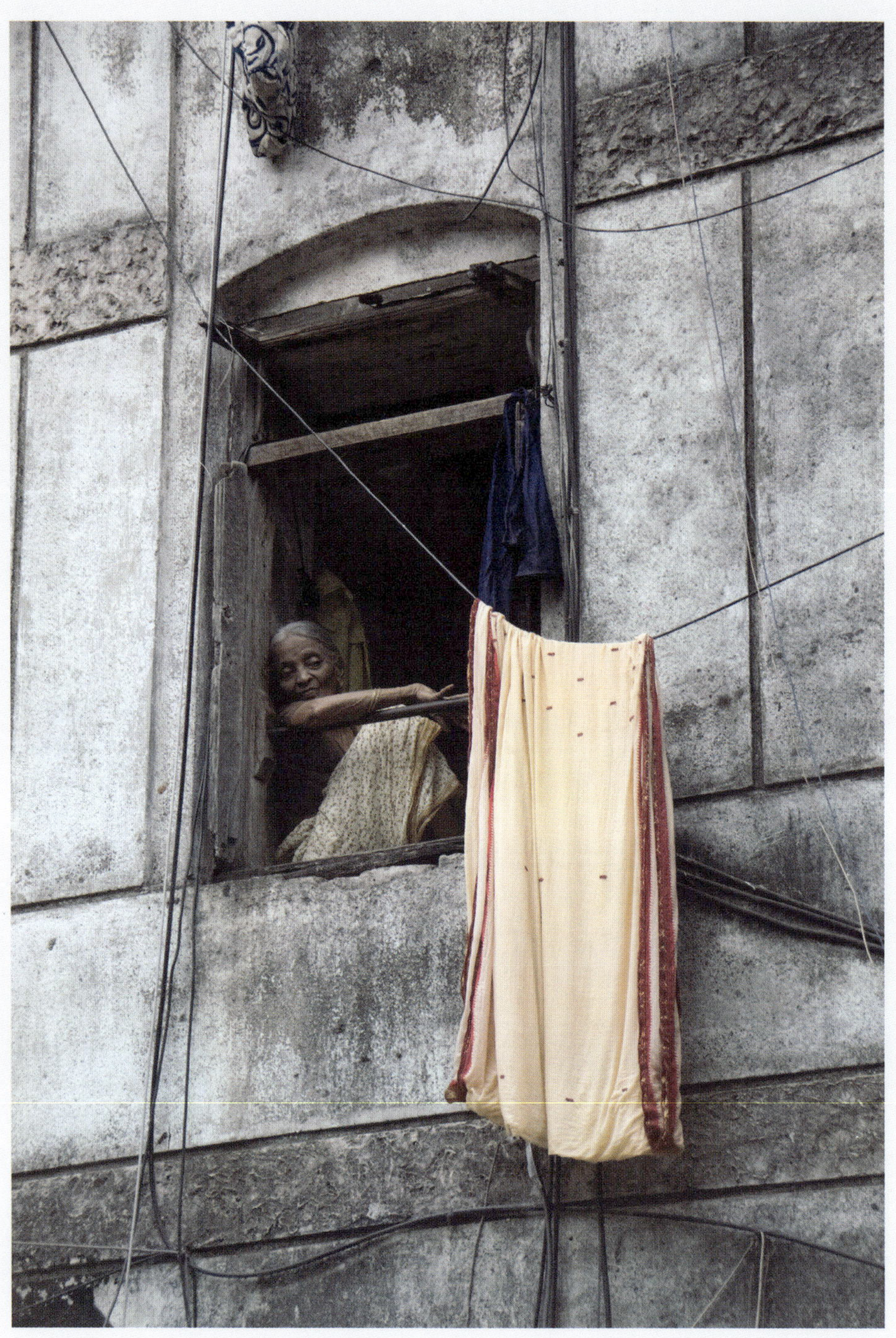

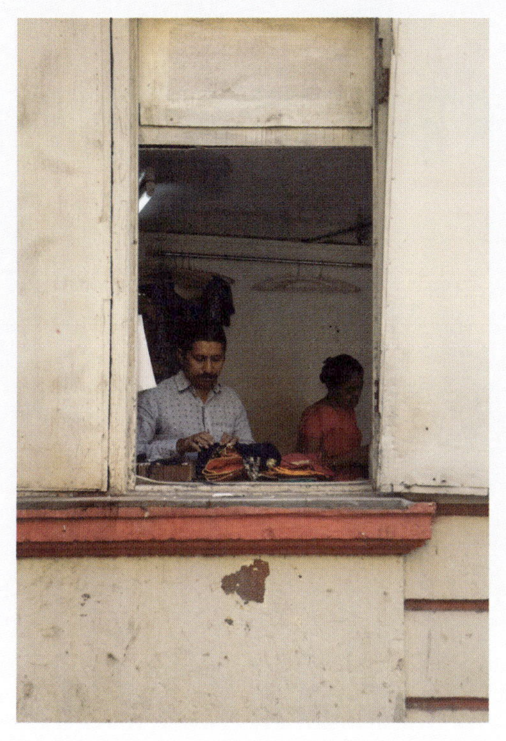

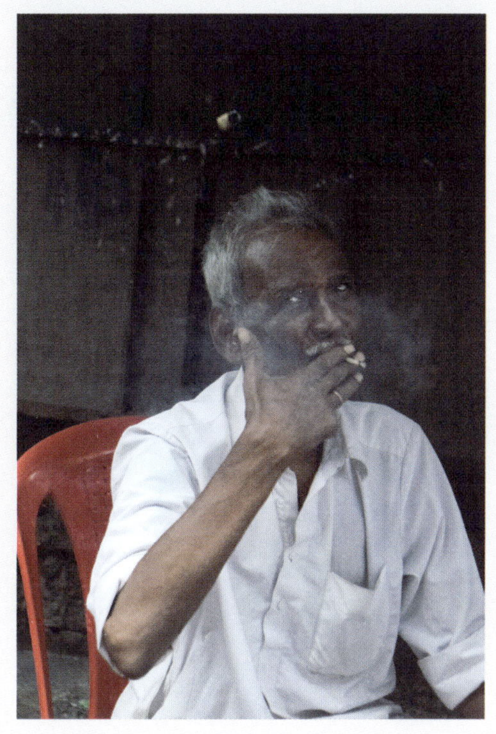

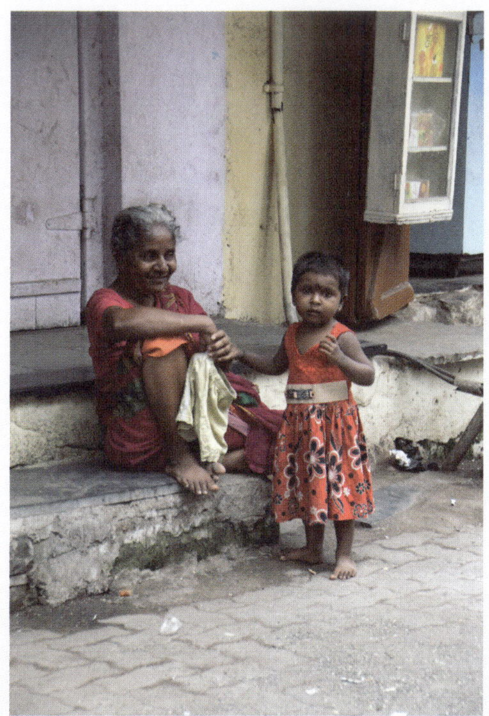

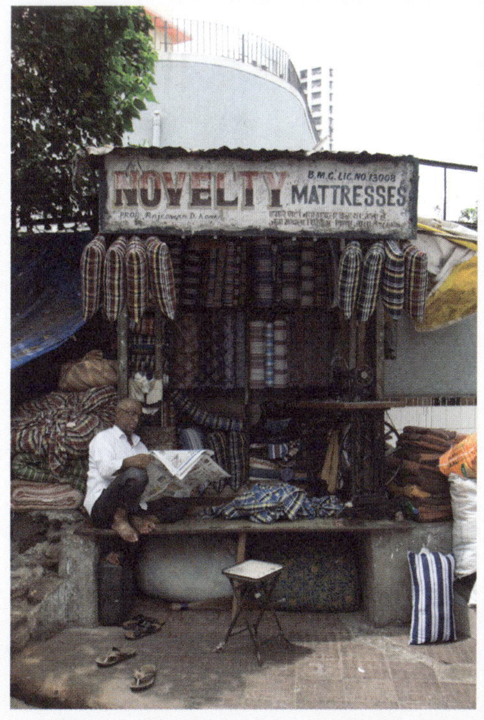
NOVELTY
B.M.C. LIC. NO. 13008
MATTRESSES

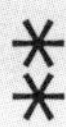

Deco District

Mumbai is only second to Miami in the total number of Art Deco inspired buildings that are here. These buildings have remained a significant factor in Mumbai's aesthetic appeal and add to the sense of Mumbai as a global city.

Most of the best-maintained ones are on a couple of streets in the south of the city. There is a string of them along the picturesque Marine Drive and another set opposite Oval Maidan. The collection along Oval Maidan has been accredited UNESCO heritage status, which would ensure that the buildings are maintained and protected. You can see Art Deco influences in buildings all over the island city. The areas of Wadala, Dadar and Matunga also have some beautifully detailed Deco buildings.

Bombay fell in love with Art Deco and vice versa for several reasons. In the early 20th century, when it was booming and aspiring to be a global metropolis, Art Deco was on-trend. Unlike Delhi, Jaipur or Mysore, it didn't have a significant local architectural identity. So because of timing, and the Indian love of ornamentation, Bombayites were attracted to the decorative but cost-effective modernity of Art Deco.

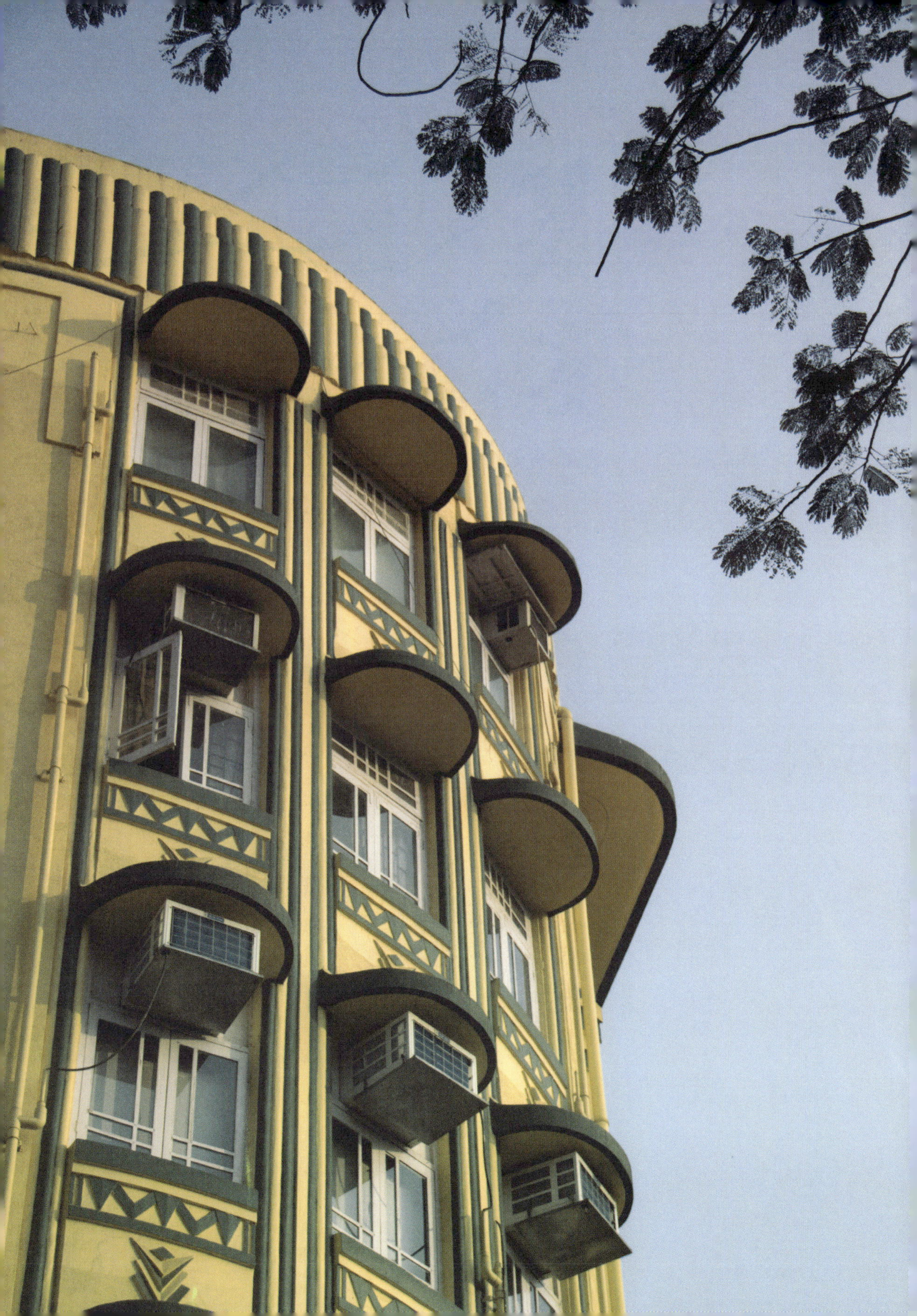

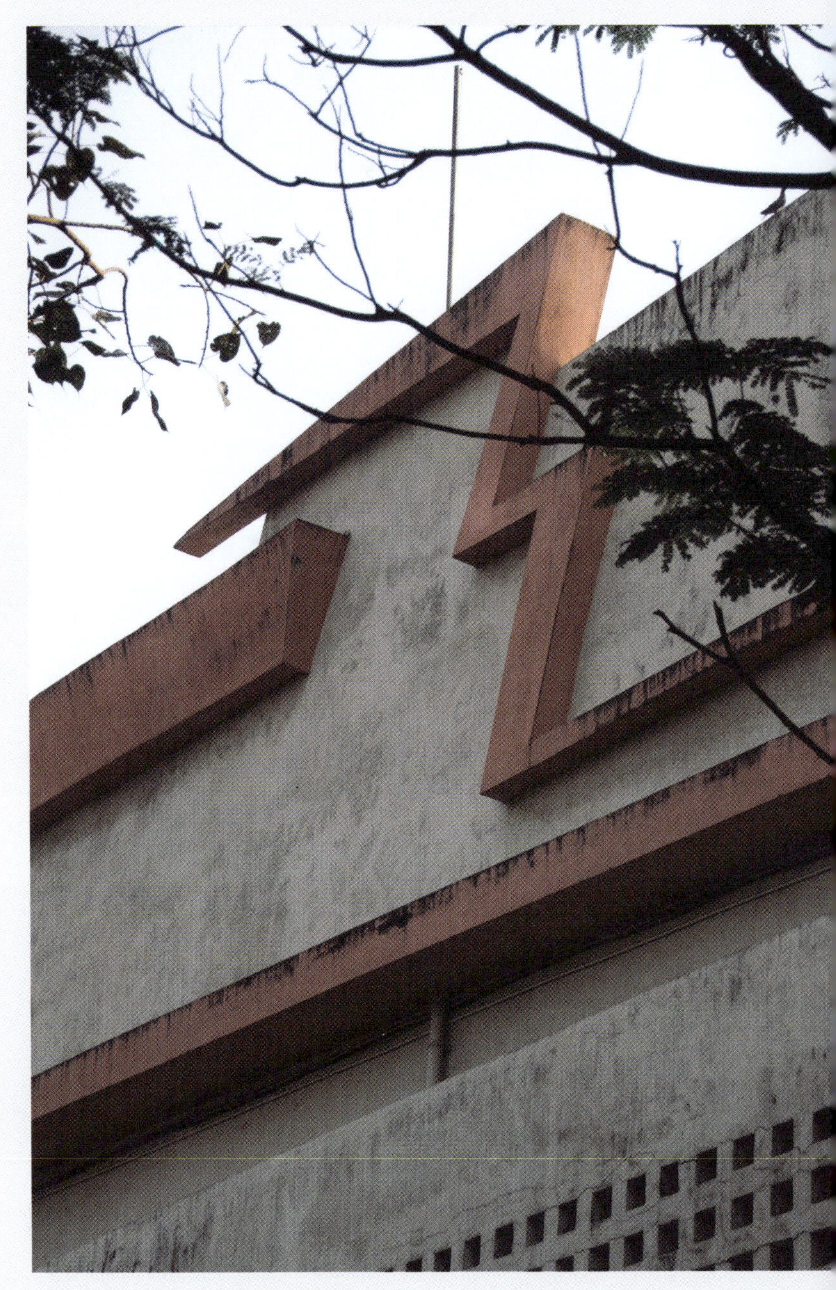

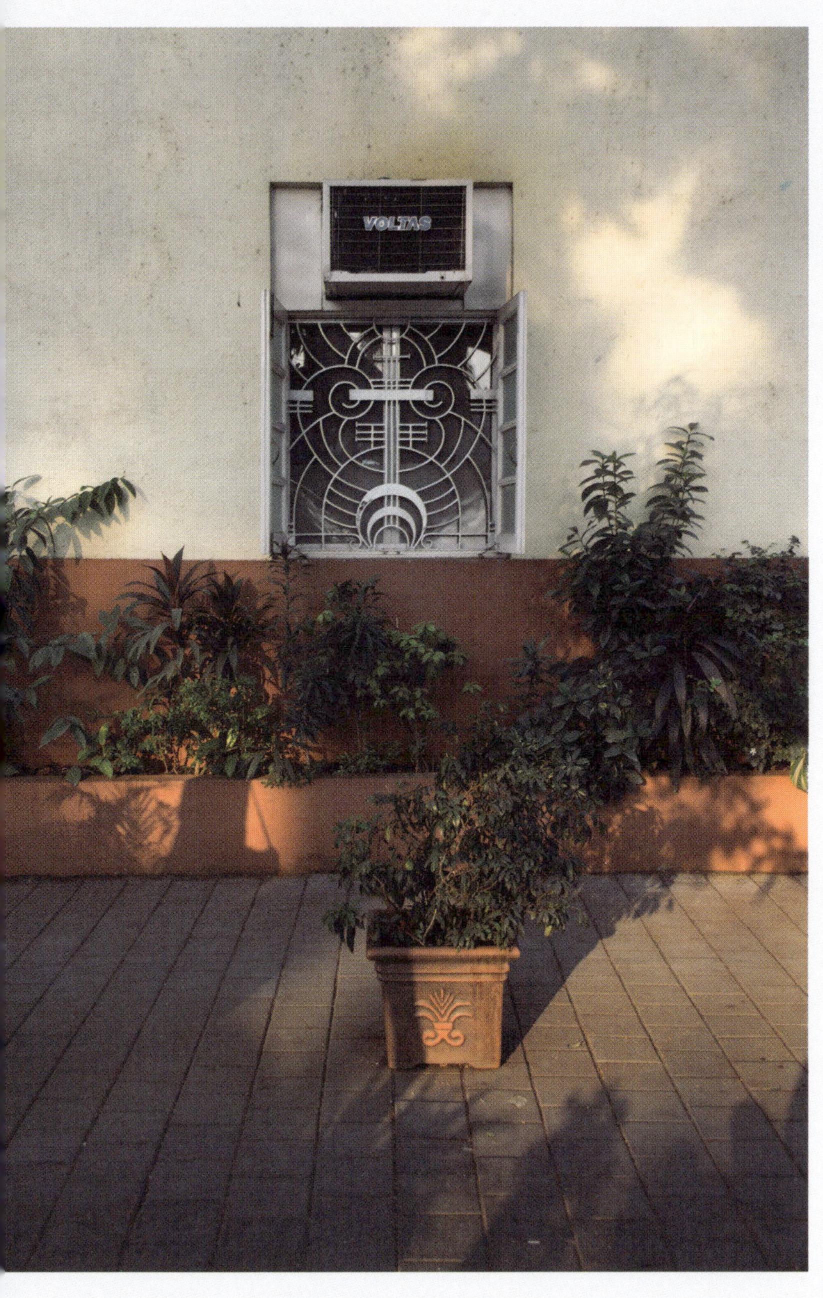
VOLTAS

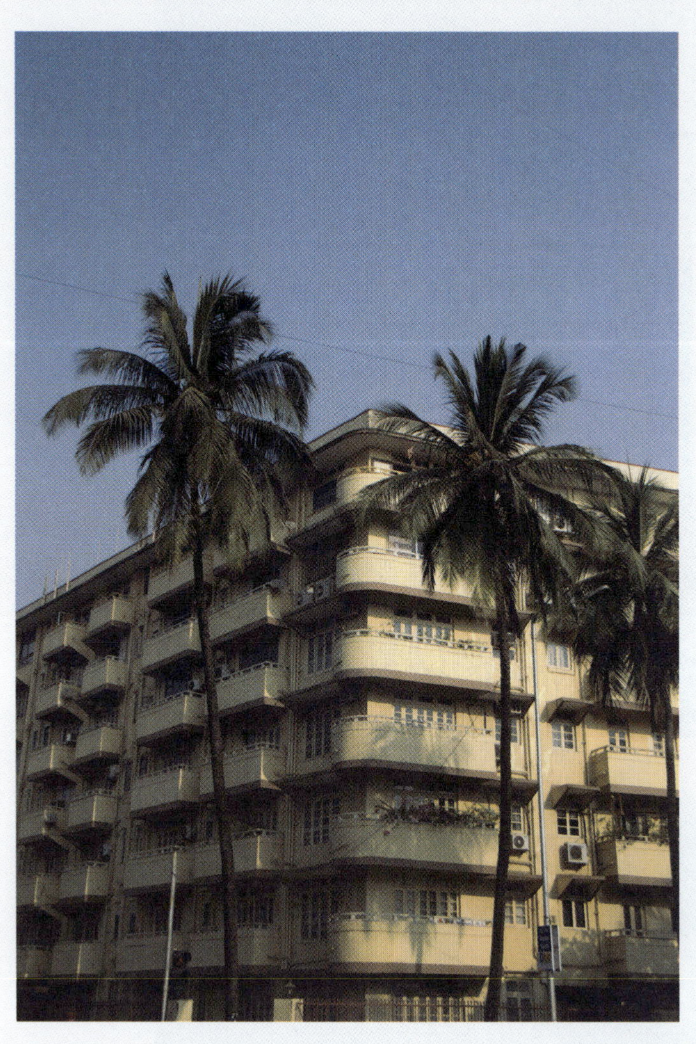

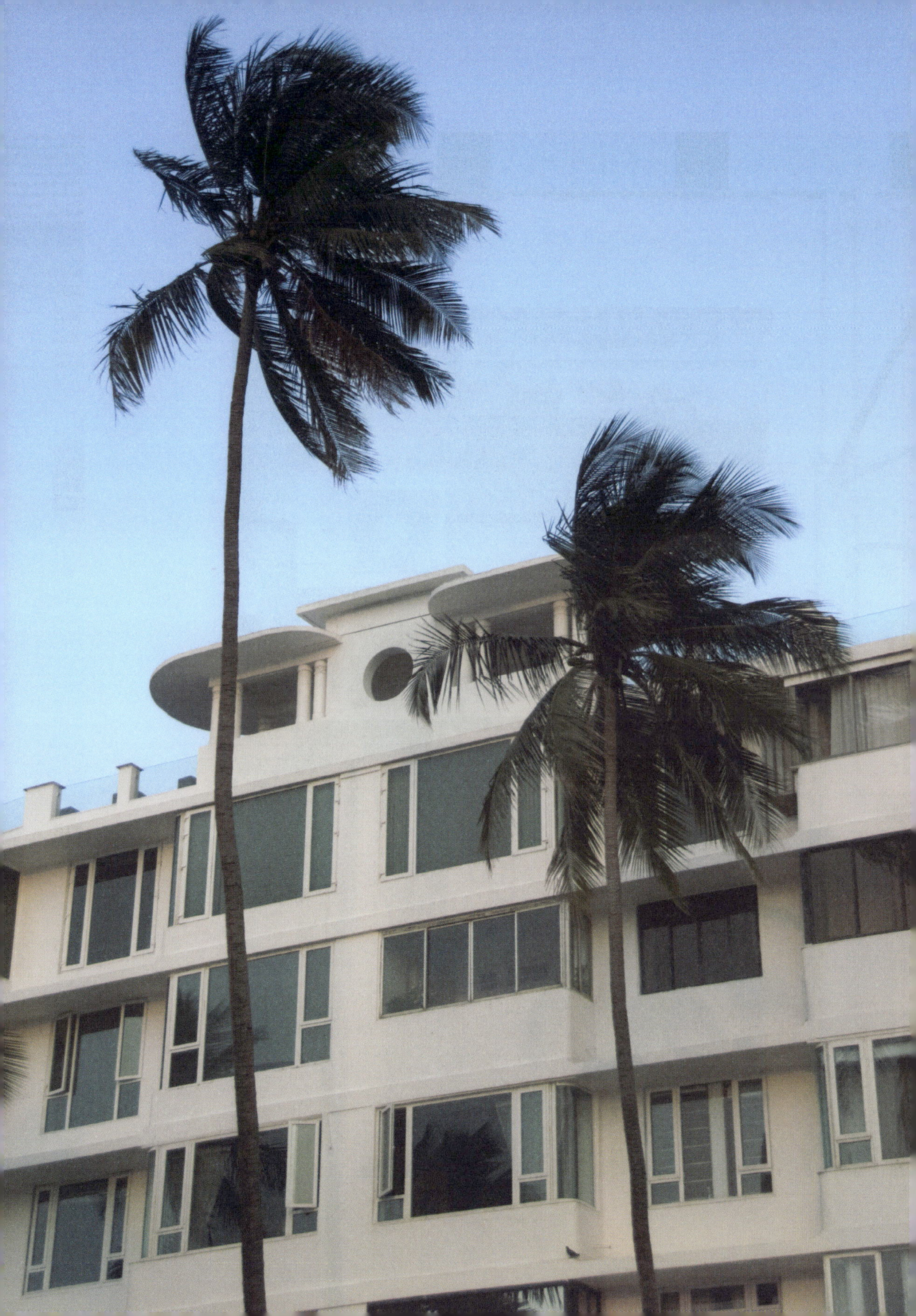

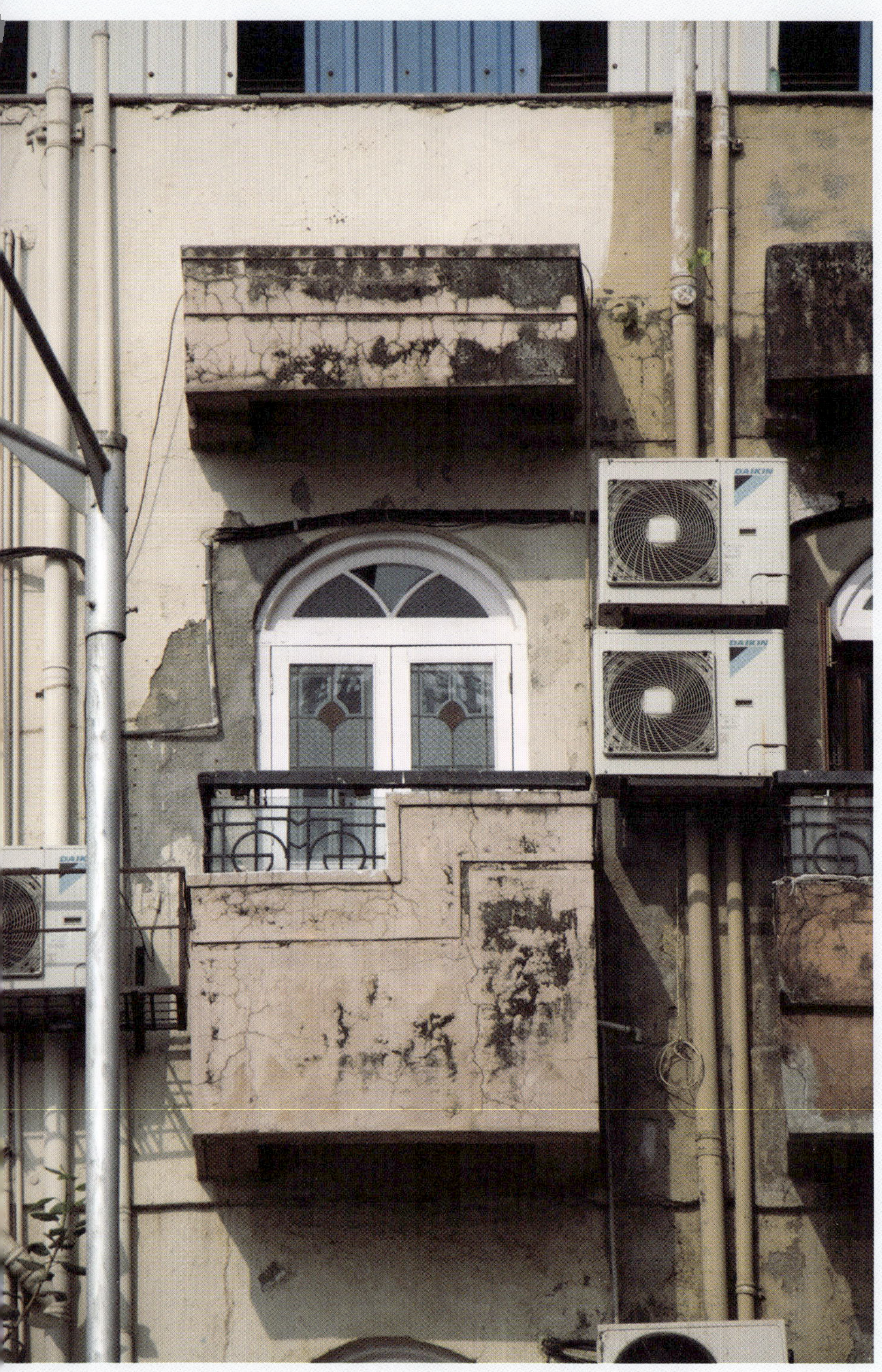

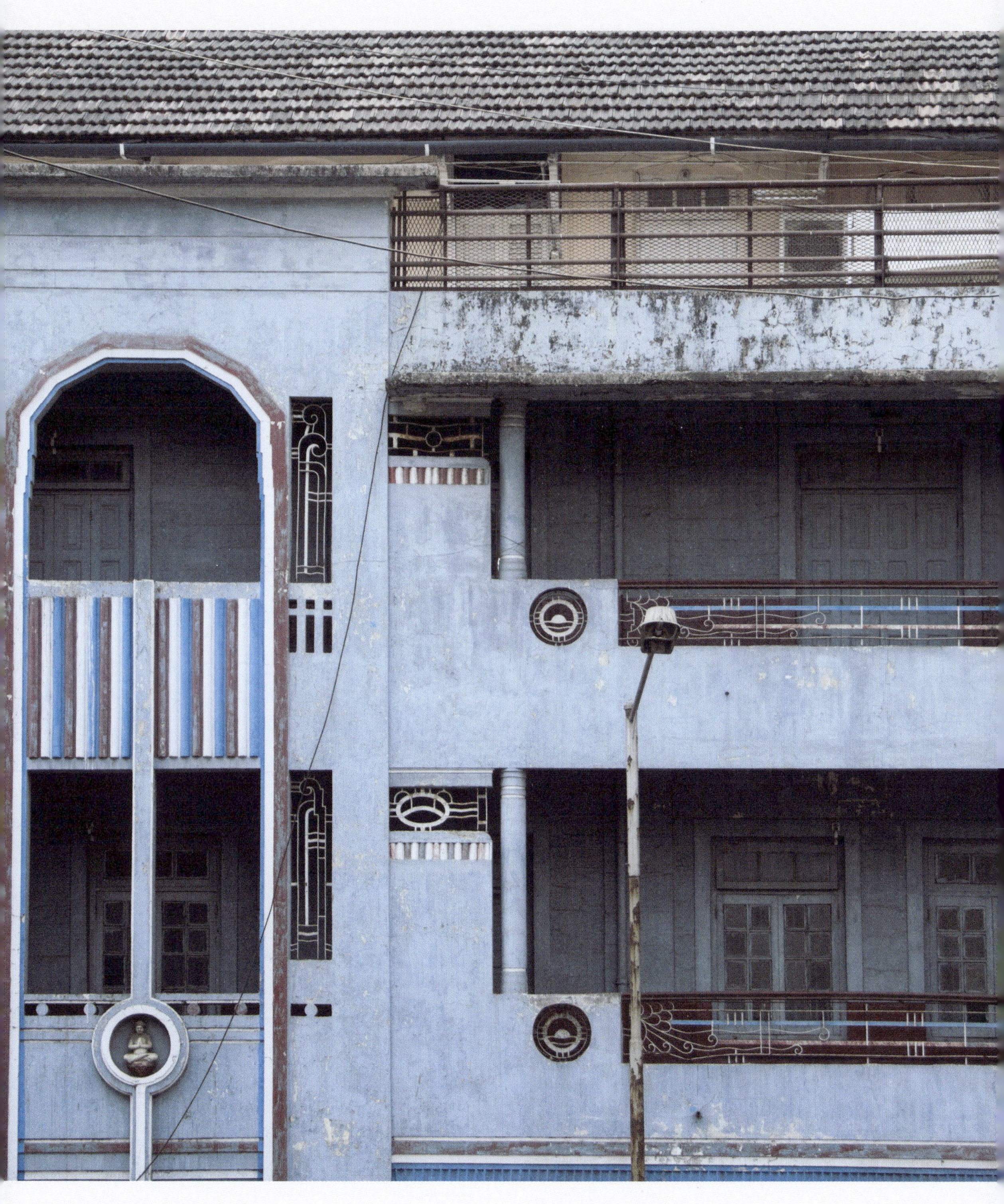

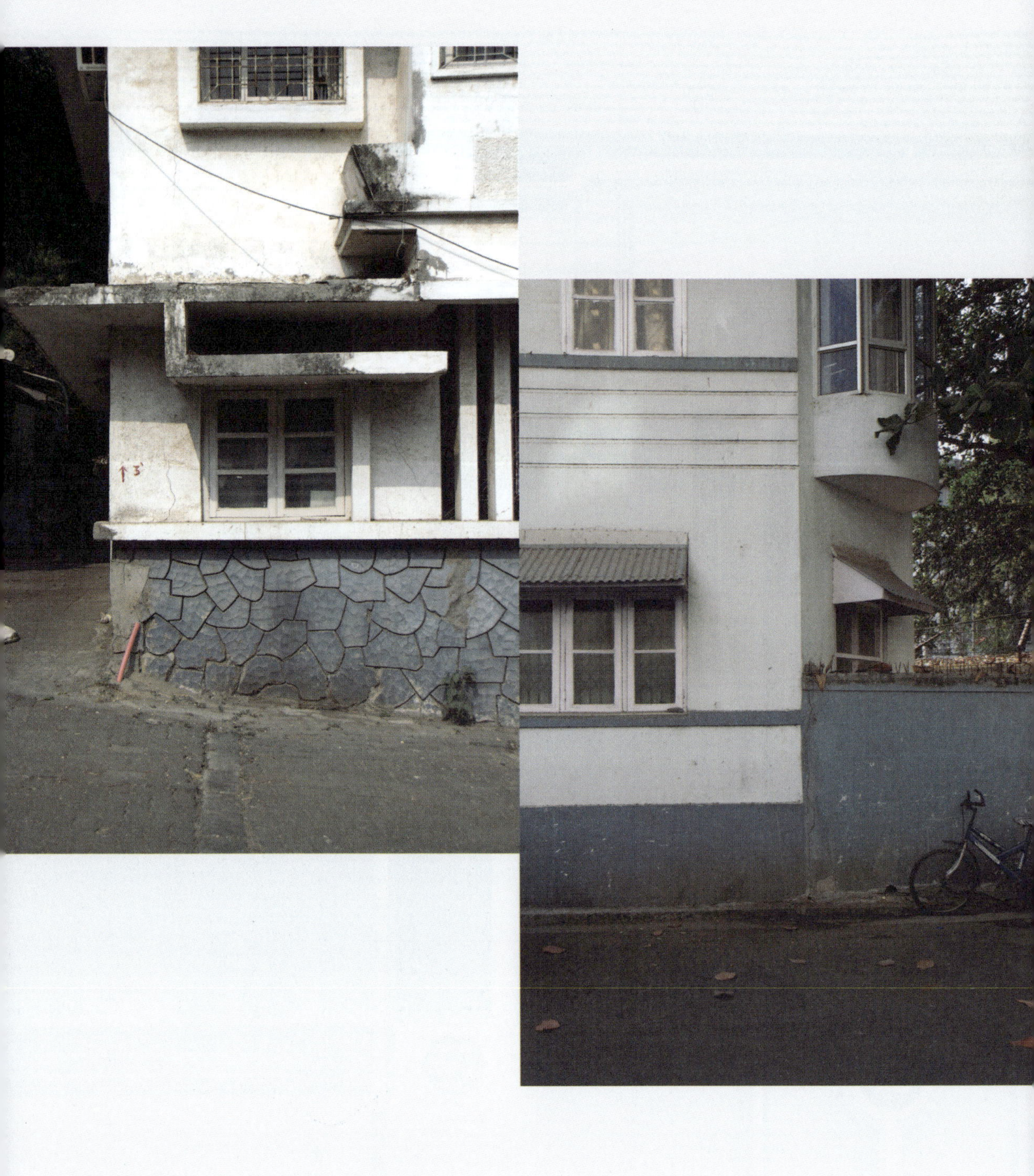

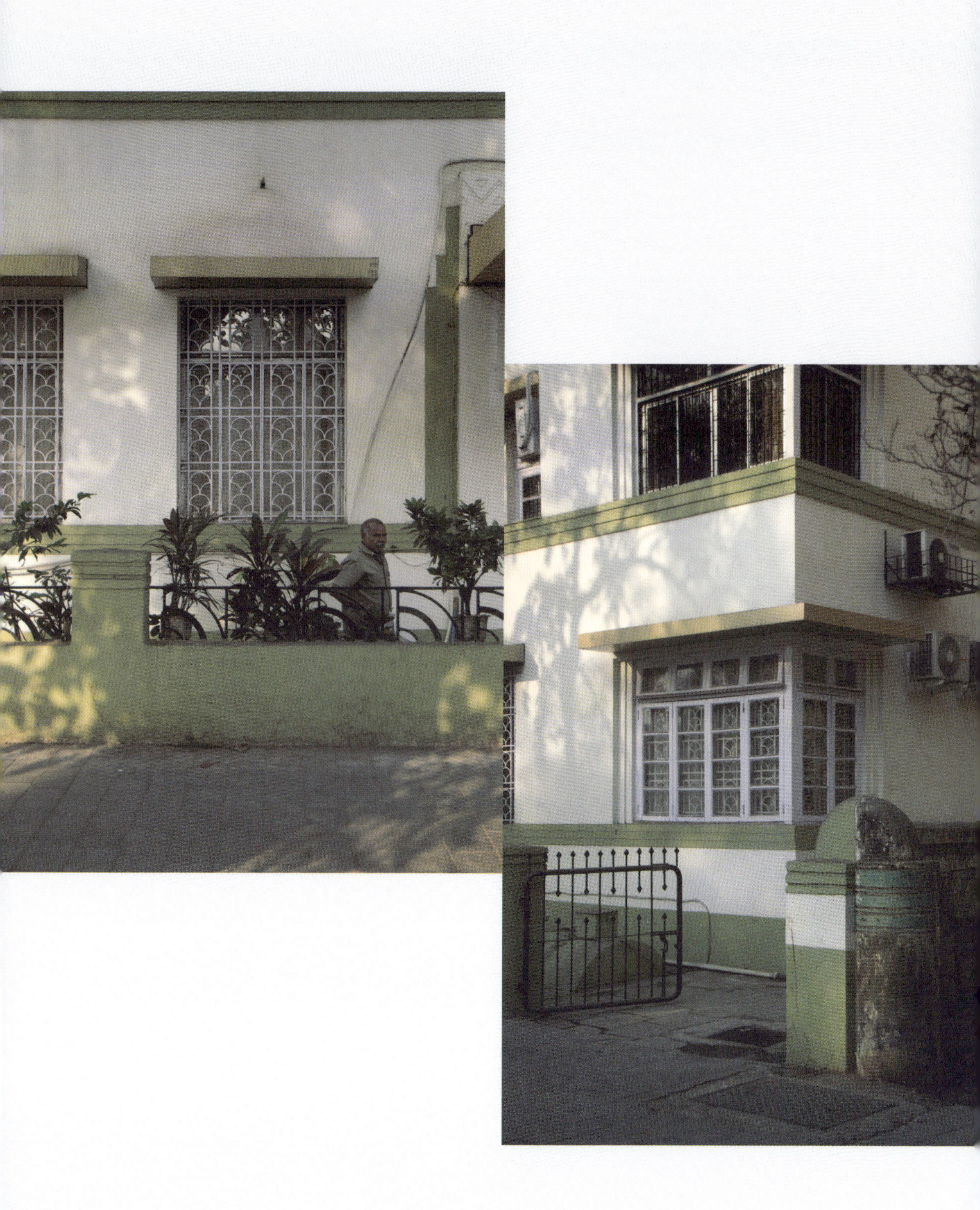

✳
✳

SoBo: From Shangrila to Antilia

SoBo (a shortened name for South Bombay) is Mumbai's Champs-Élysées, Grosvenor Square, Park Avenue… it has some of the most expensive real estate in the city. If Mumbai were the city of dreams, then living here would be the ultimate realisation of that dream. It has some wonderful pieces of architecture, including Deco buildings and my favourite building in Mumbai, 'Kanchenjunga'. Designed by Charles Correa, Kanchenjunga is a perfect example of form following function. It takes into consideration Mumbai's climatic conditions and while being practical is beautiful.

    My least favourite building is also in this area. 'Antilia' is the single family home built by the Ambani family (associated with Reliance Industries). It is the world's costliest private residence. When it came up, like many other people in the city, I found it offensive. It physically upset me: how could something like this exist in a developing country, I wondered. Over time I've realised that it is not fair to judge it in such a black and white manner. Antilia after all doesn't exist in isolation, and in that sense, it is an extreme instance of inequality. And it not being there would not mean that we've begun to address inequality.

    I also wonder why we continue to build these Antilias, or, for that matter, Shangrilas or Camelots. Names of many buildings that exist in the SoBo area today are from mythology. Do we somehow start believing that in our case, these myths will become a reality? That we've managed to build paradise, where we could live forever?

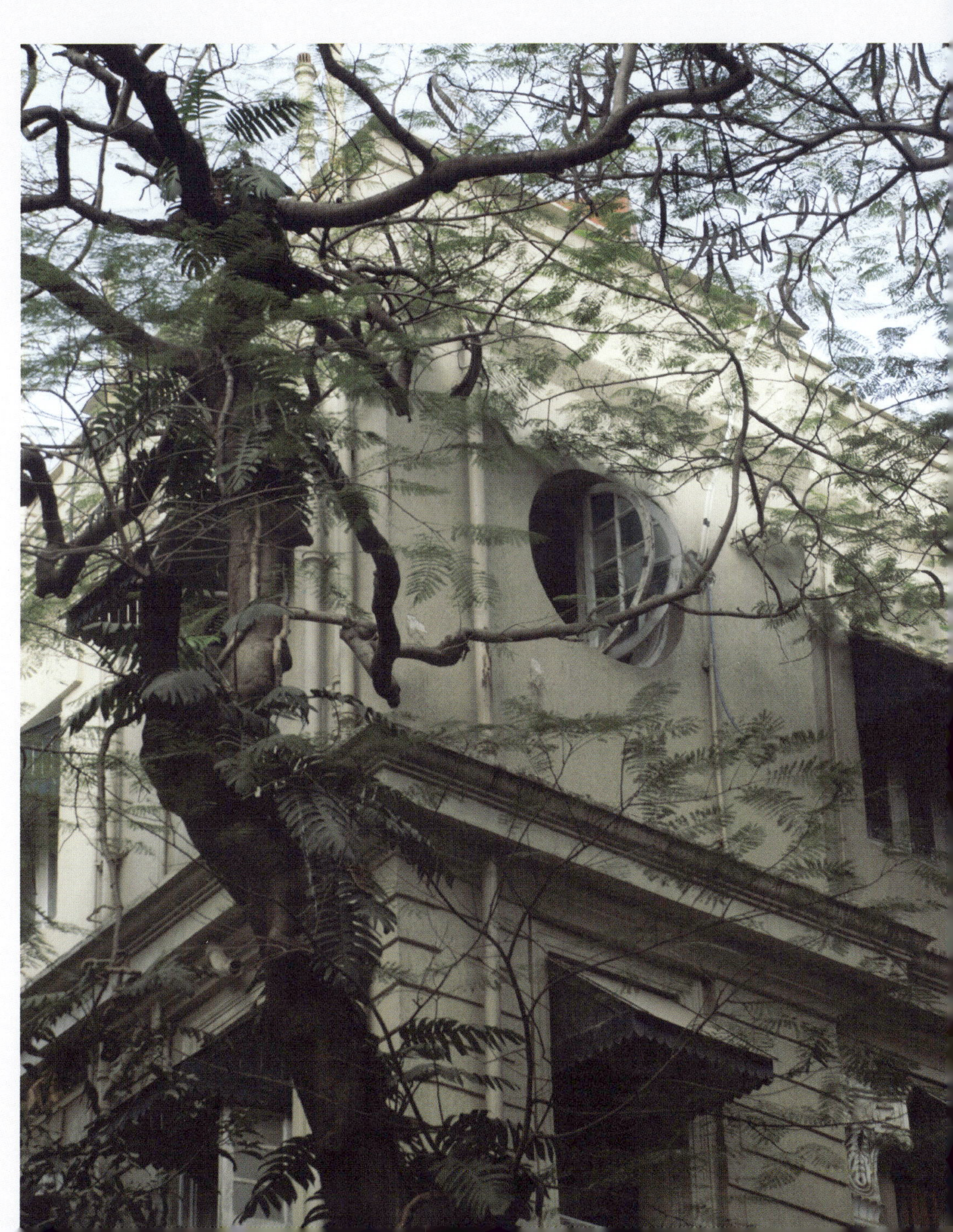

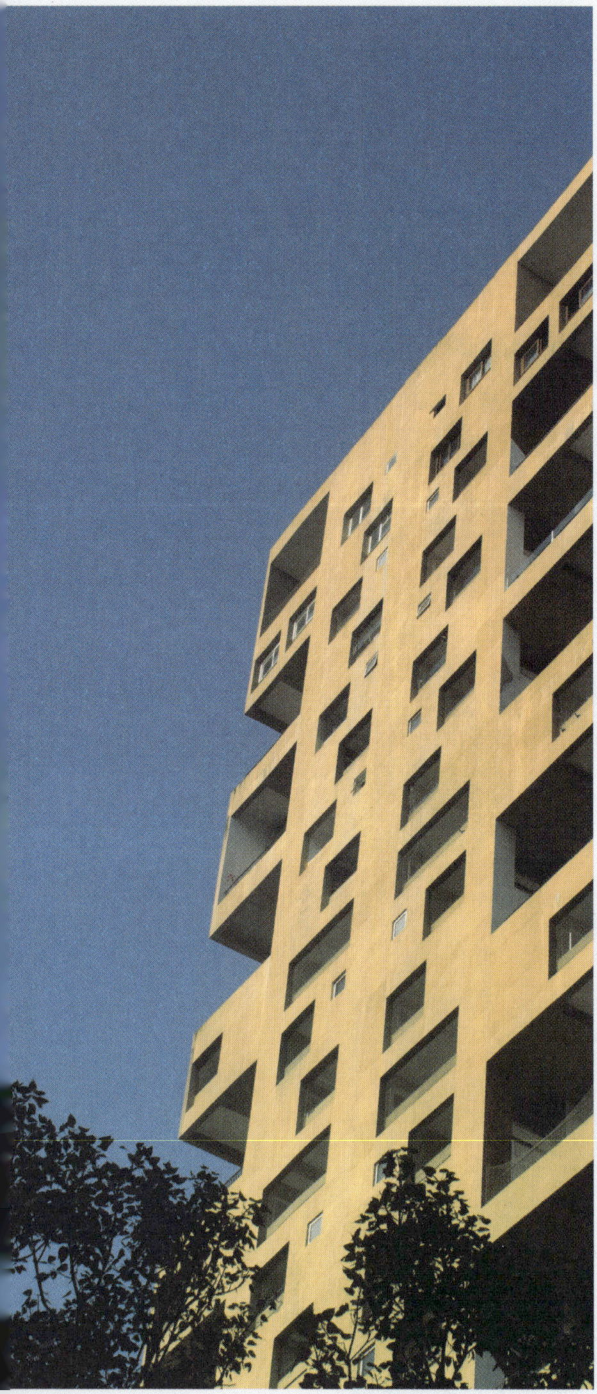

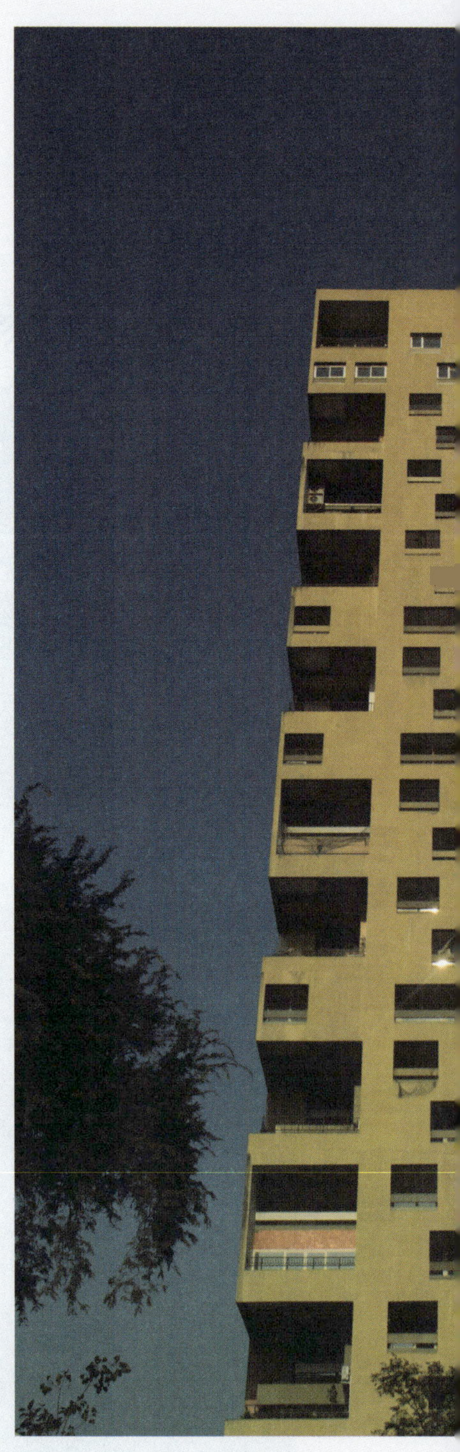

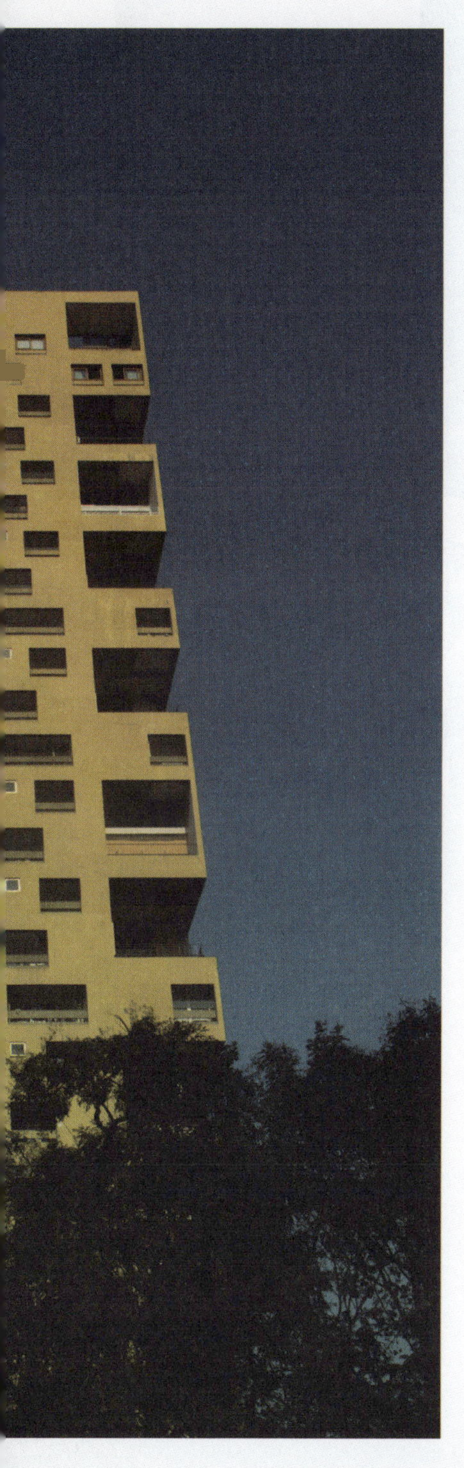

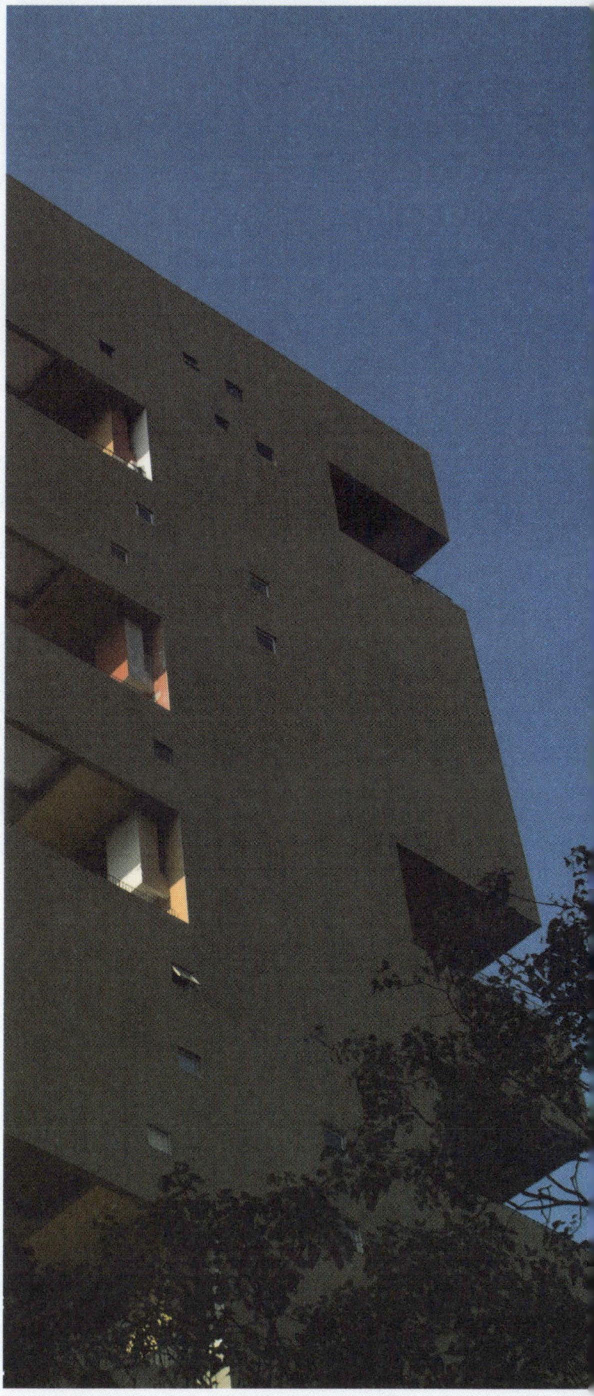

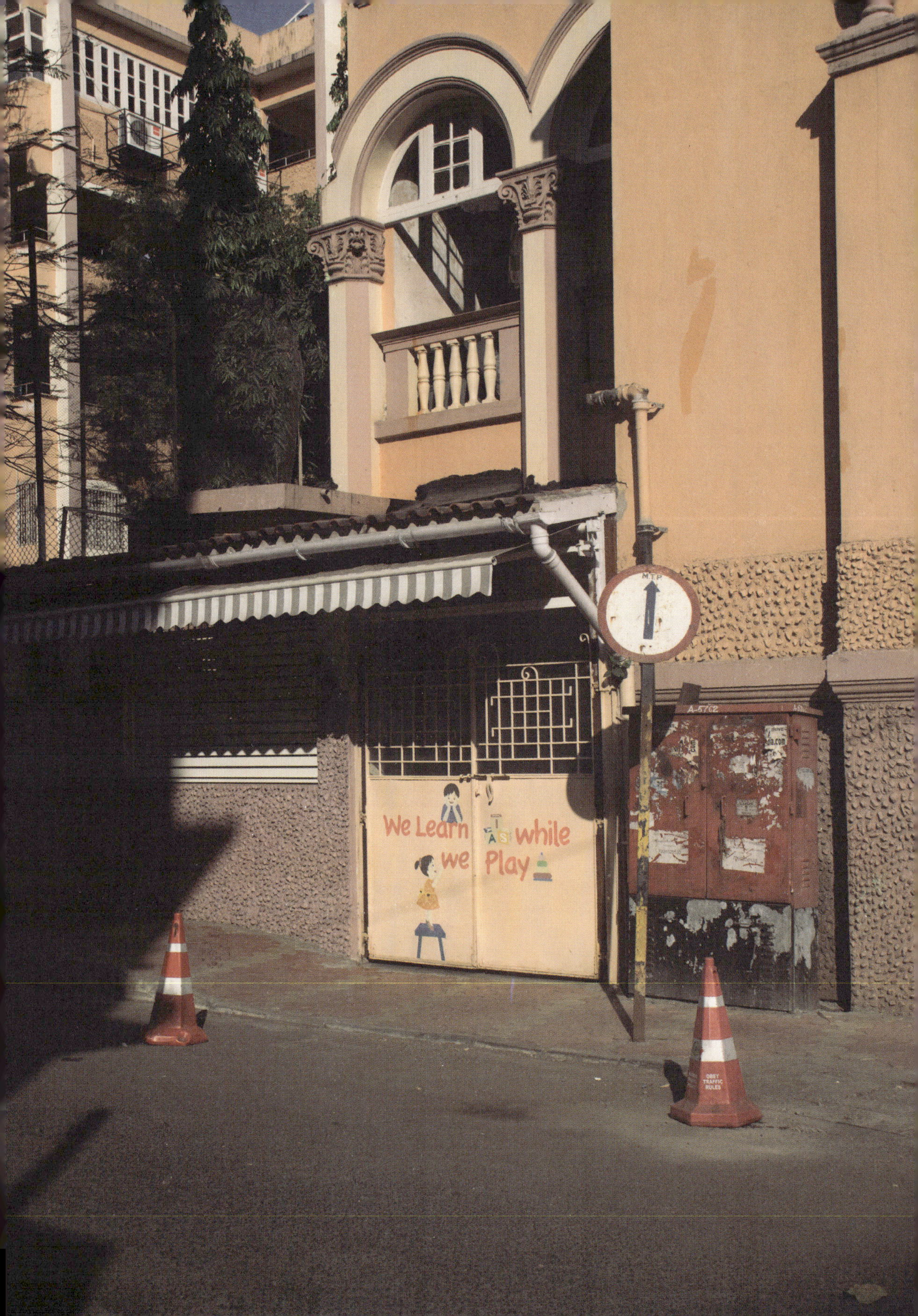
We Learn while
we Play
A-5/62
OBEY
TRAFFIC
RULES

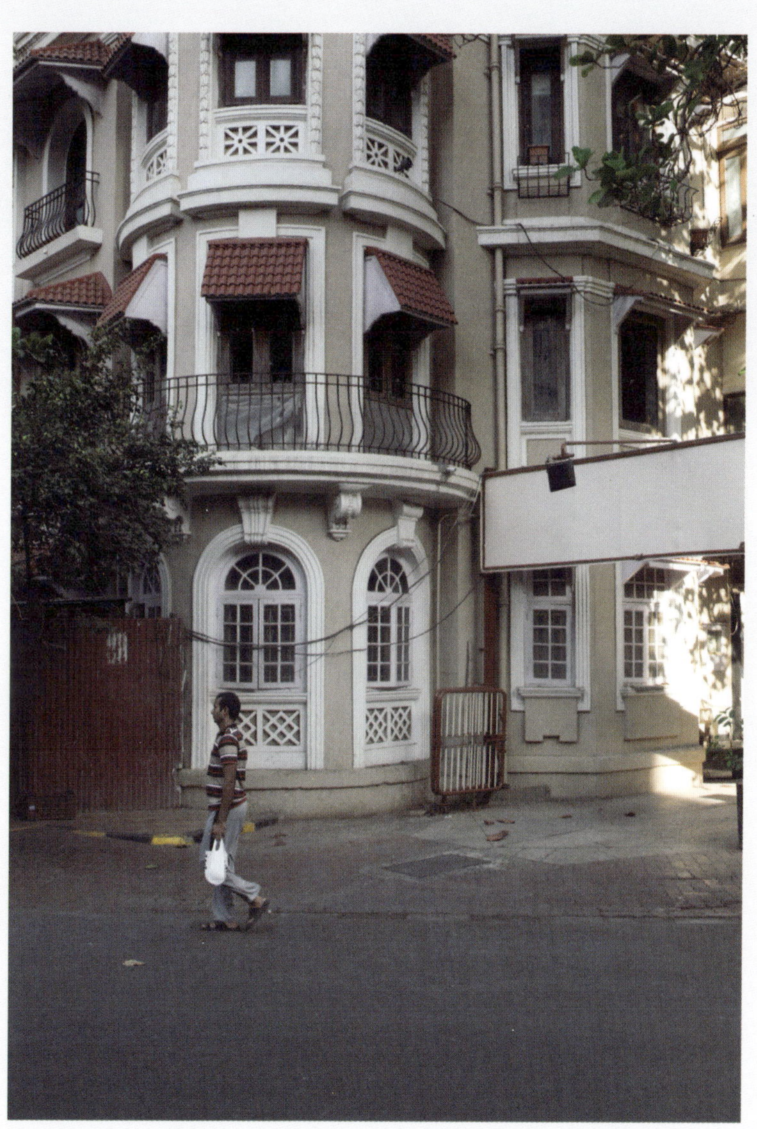

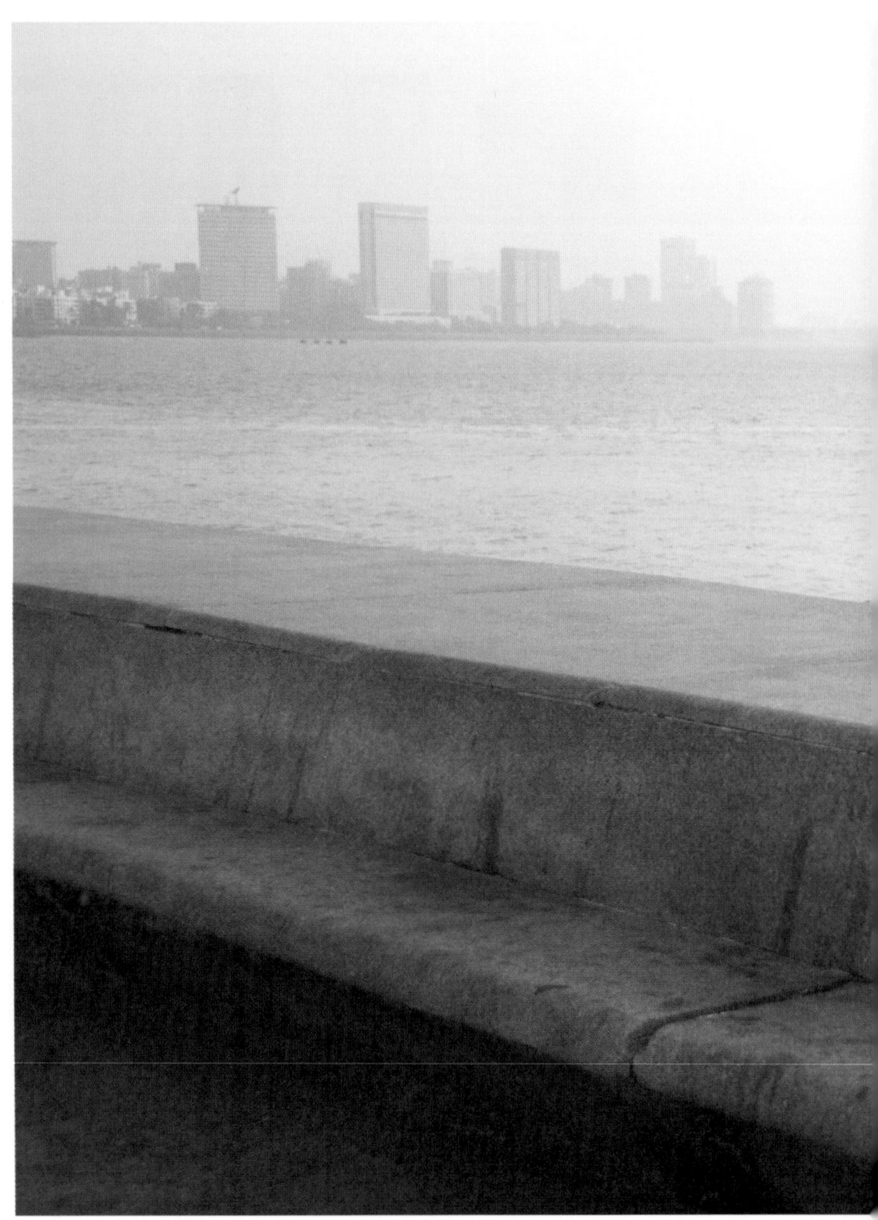

Chowpatty

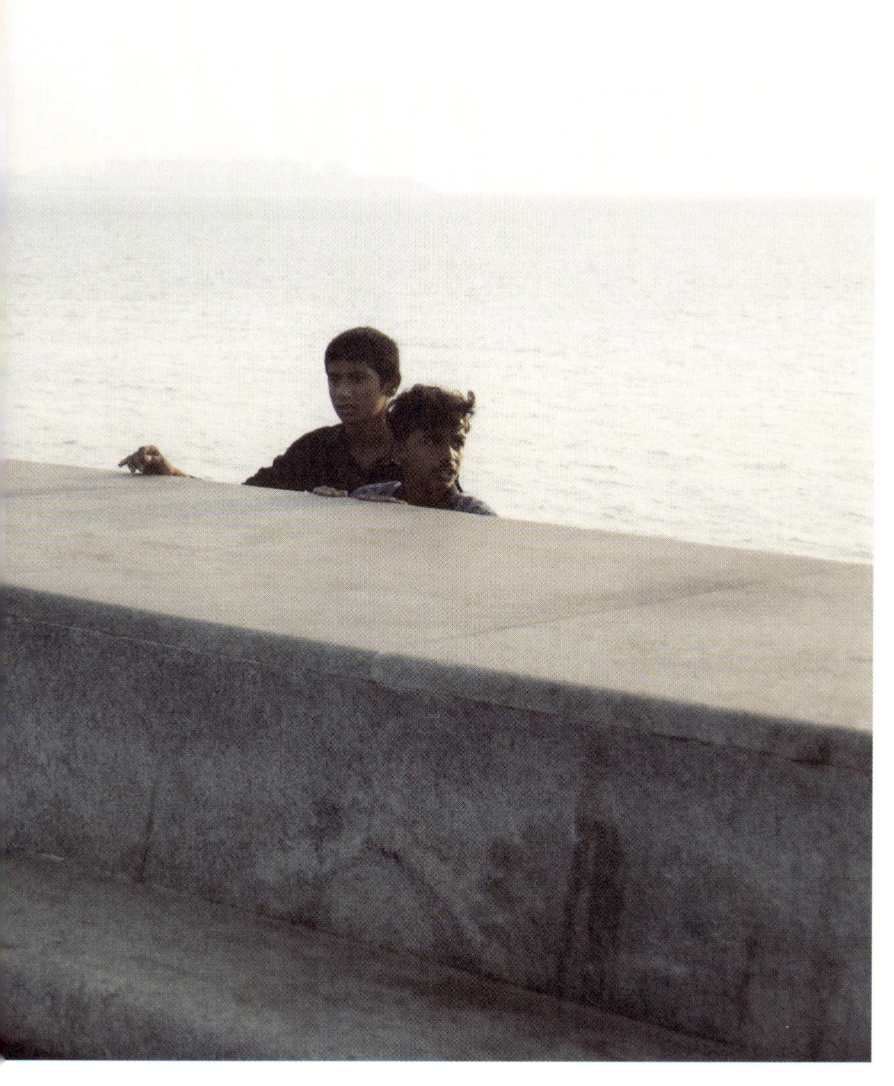

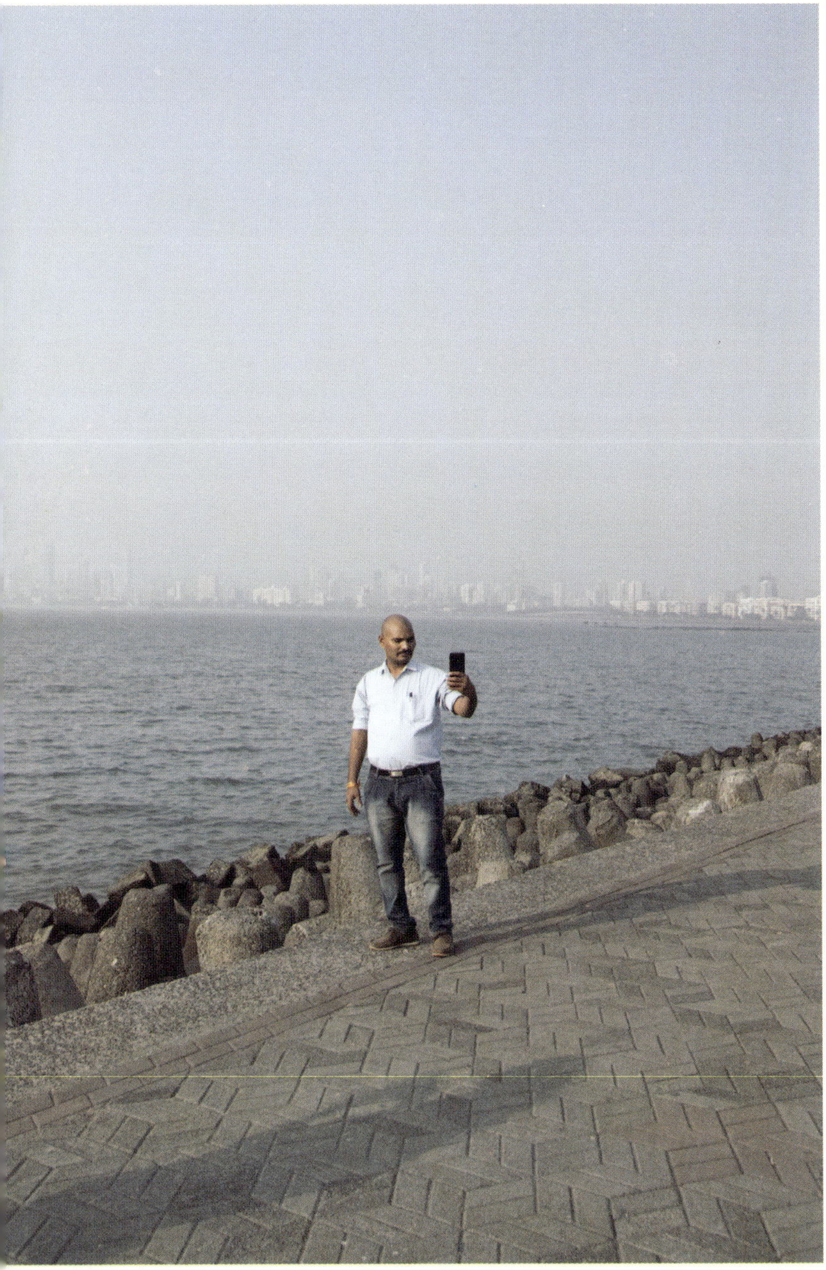

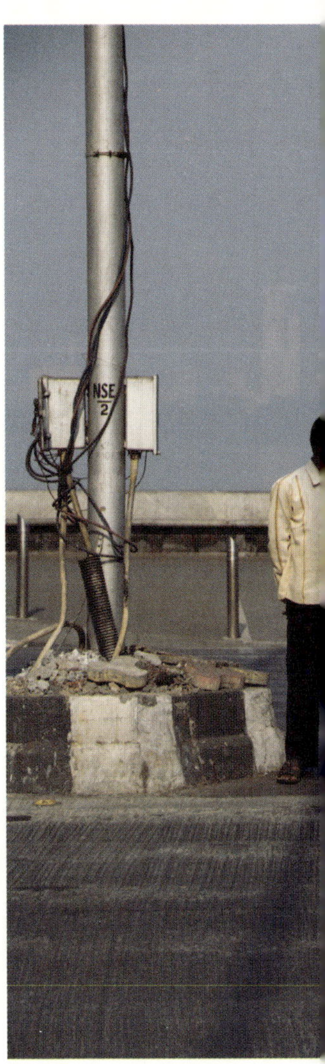

Chowpatty

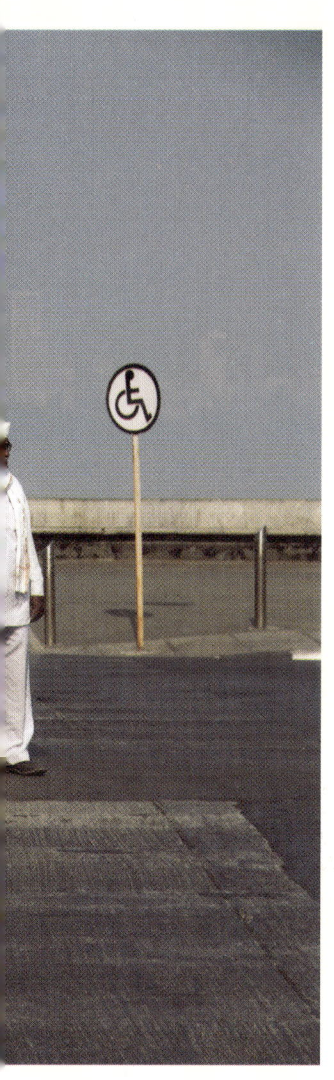

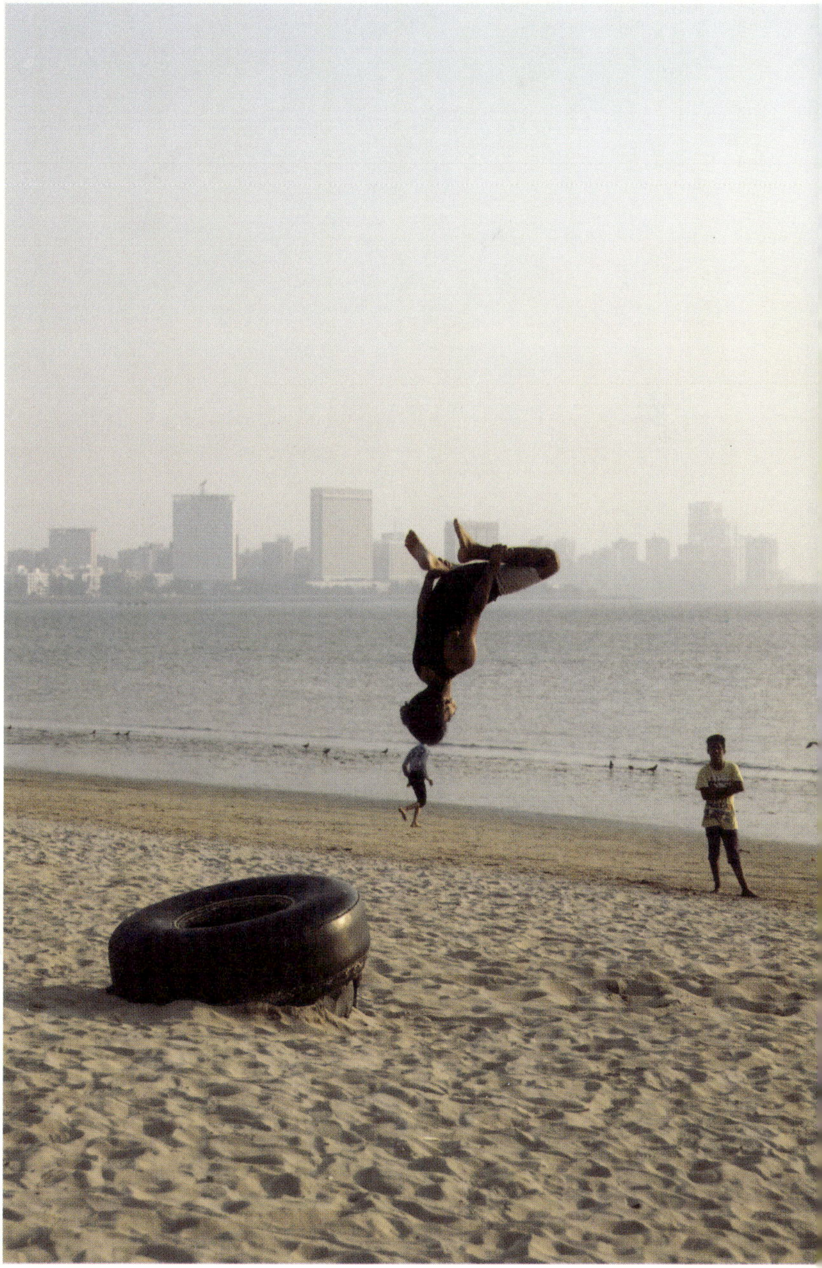

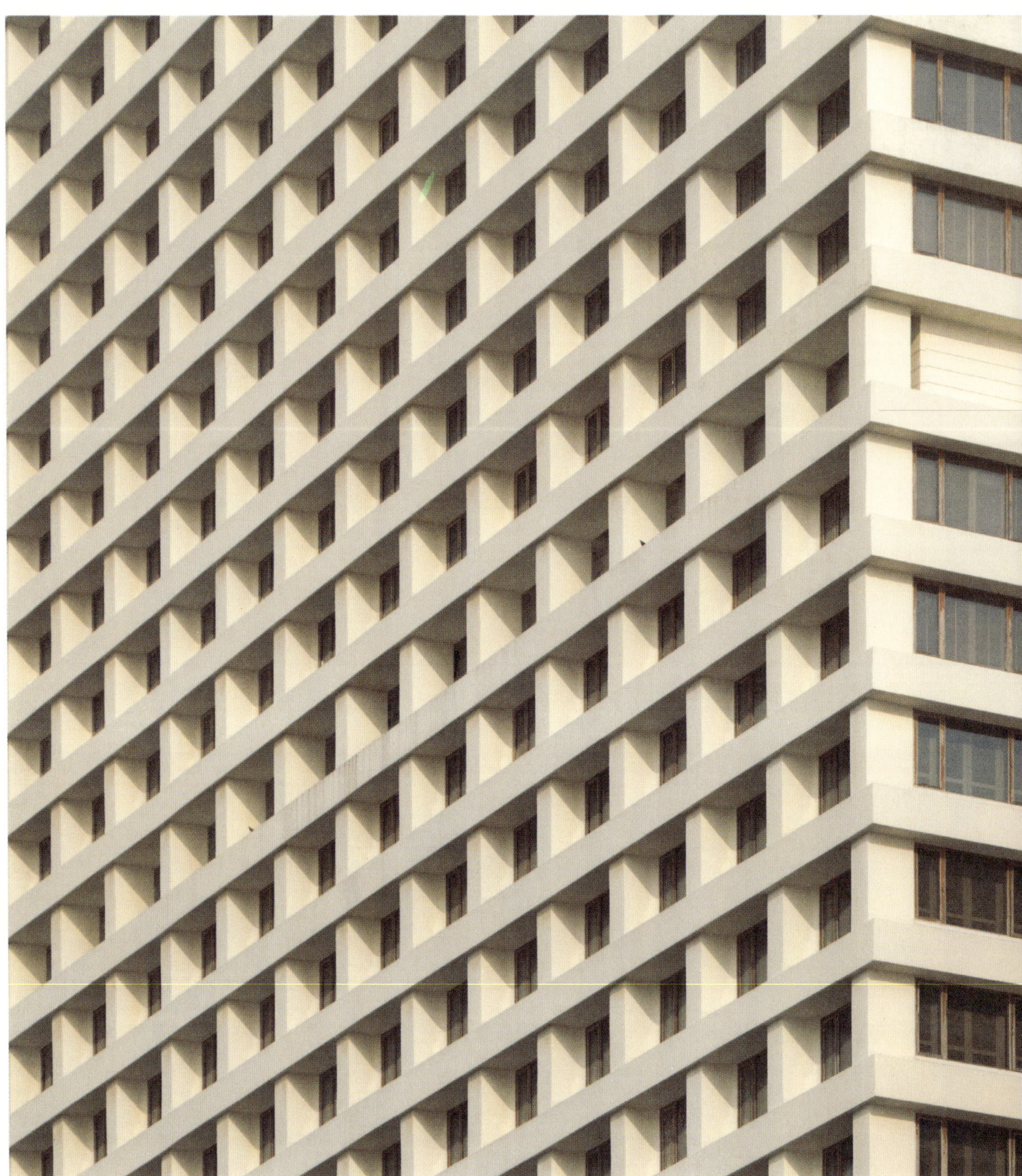

Nariman Point

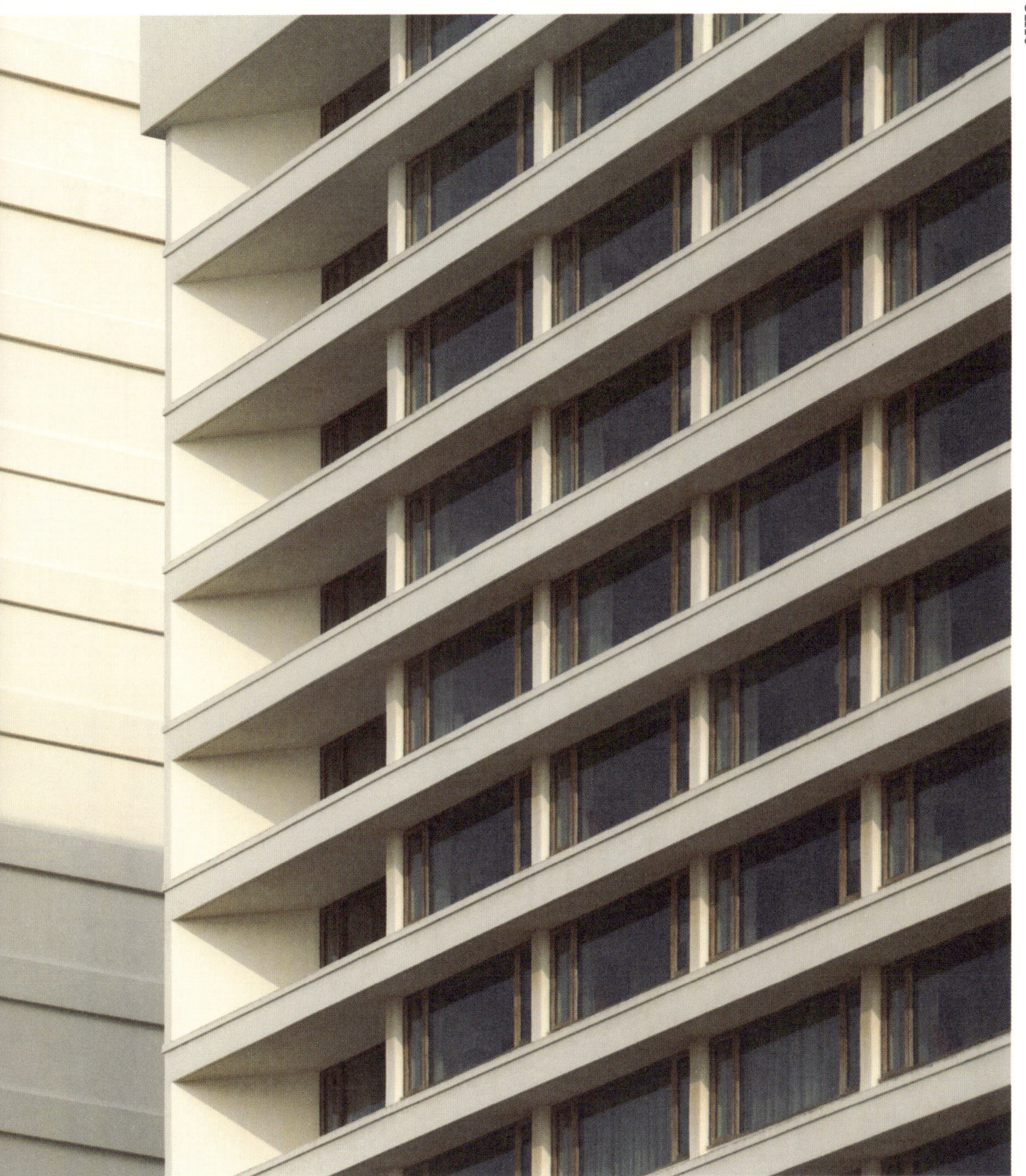

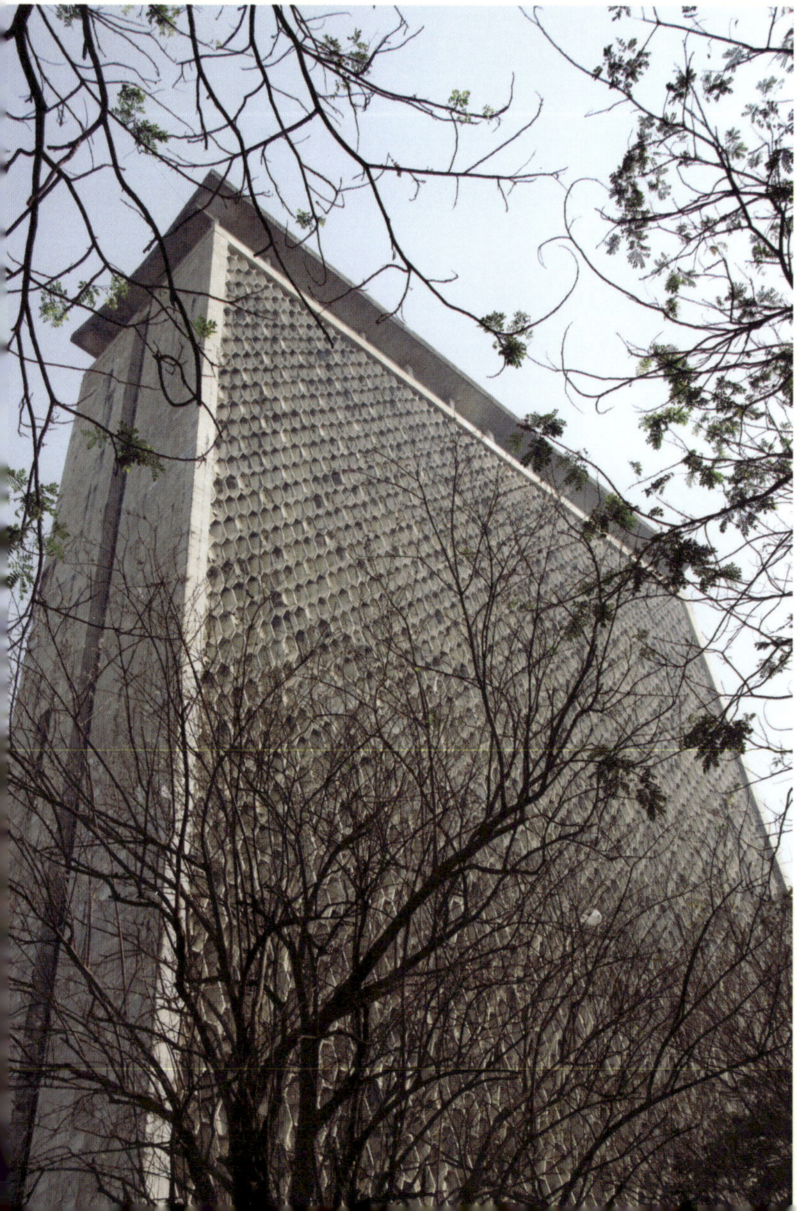

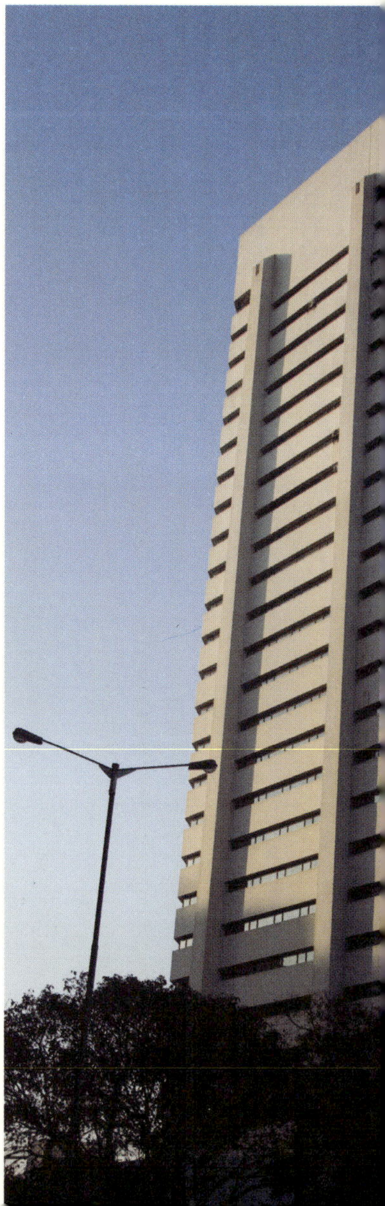

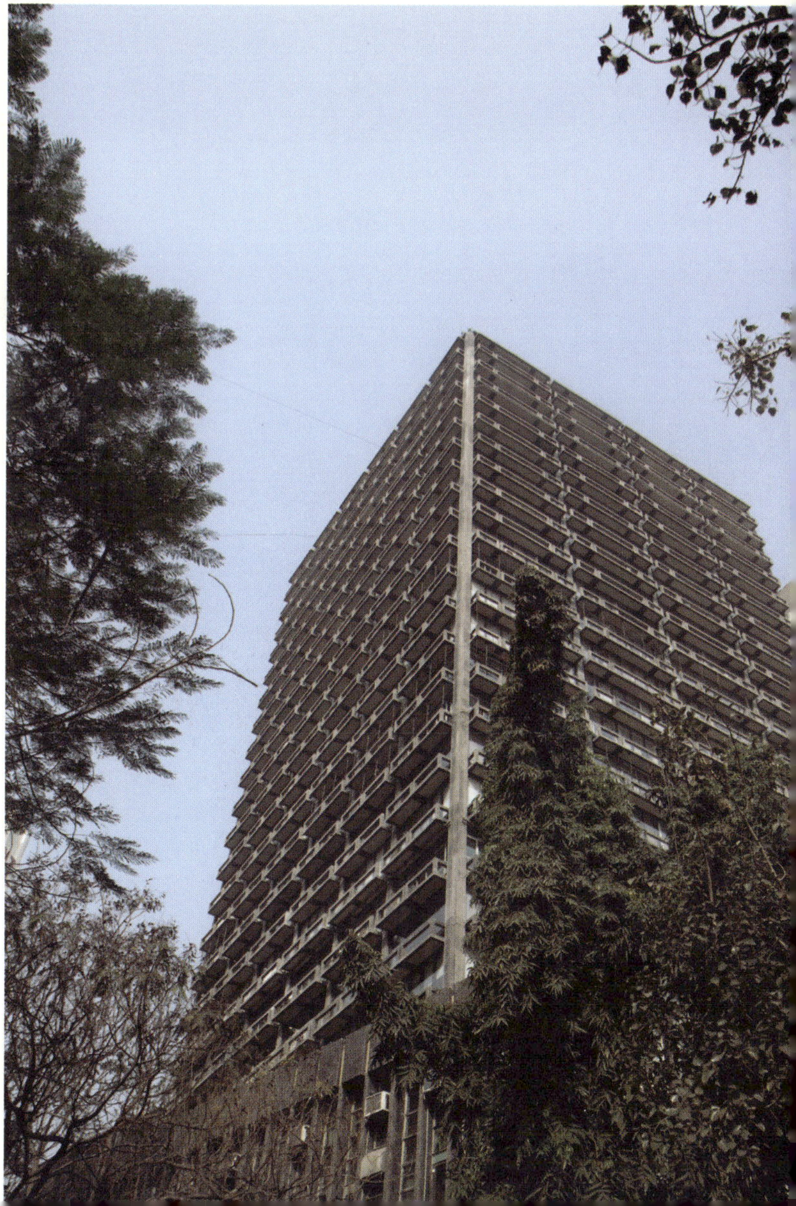

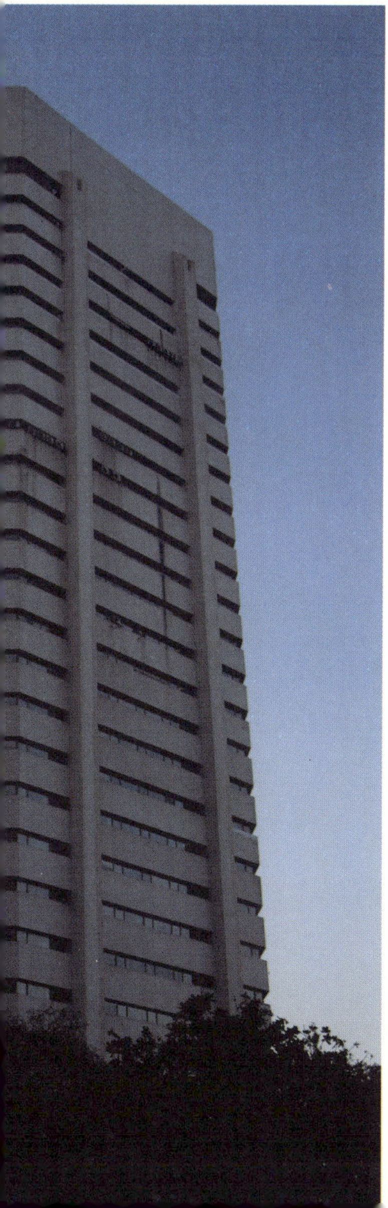

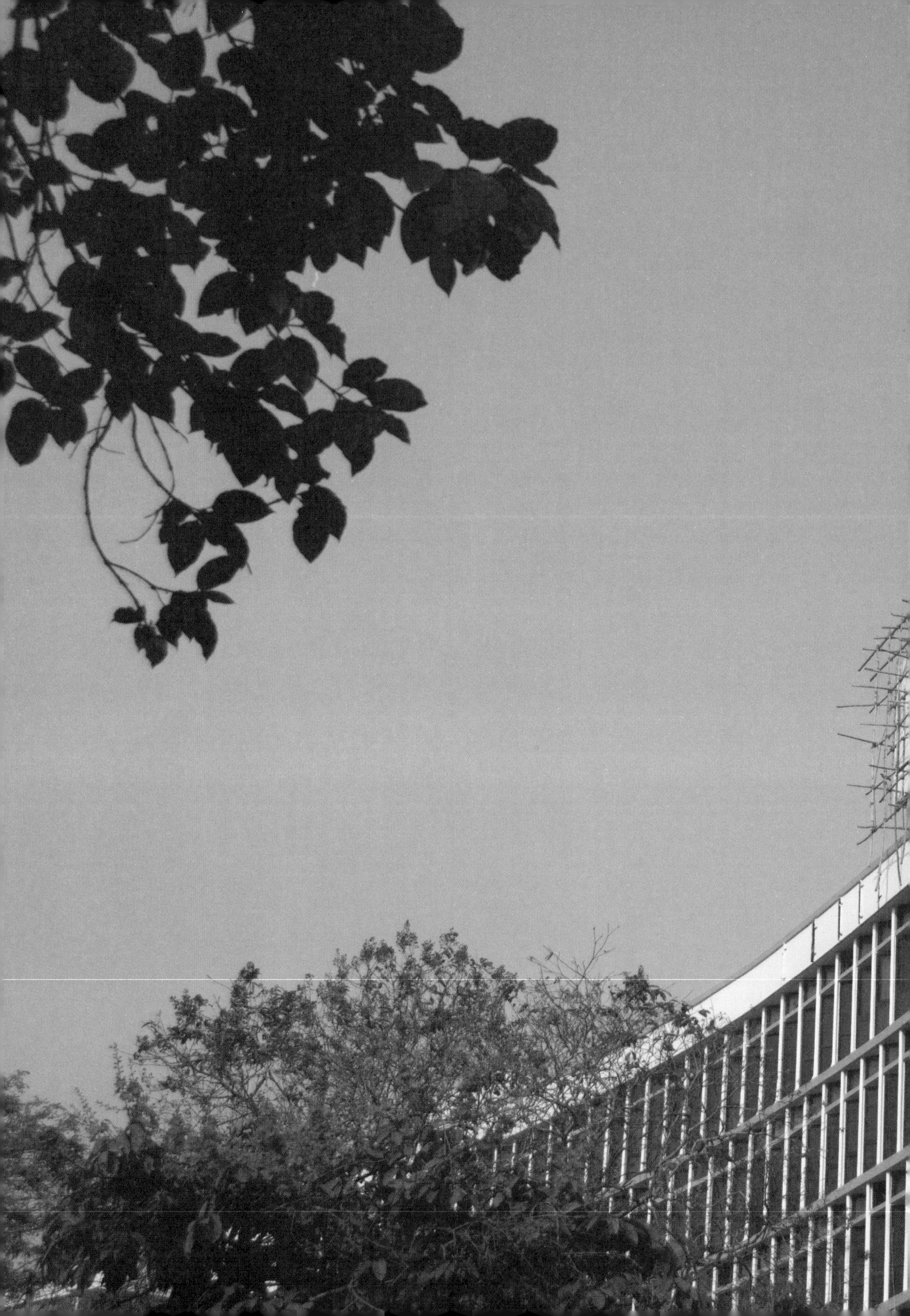

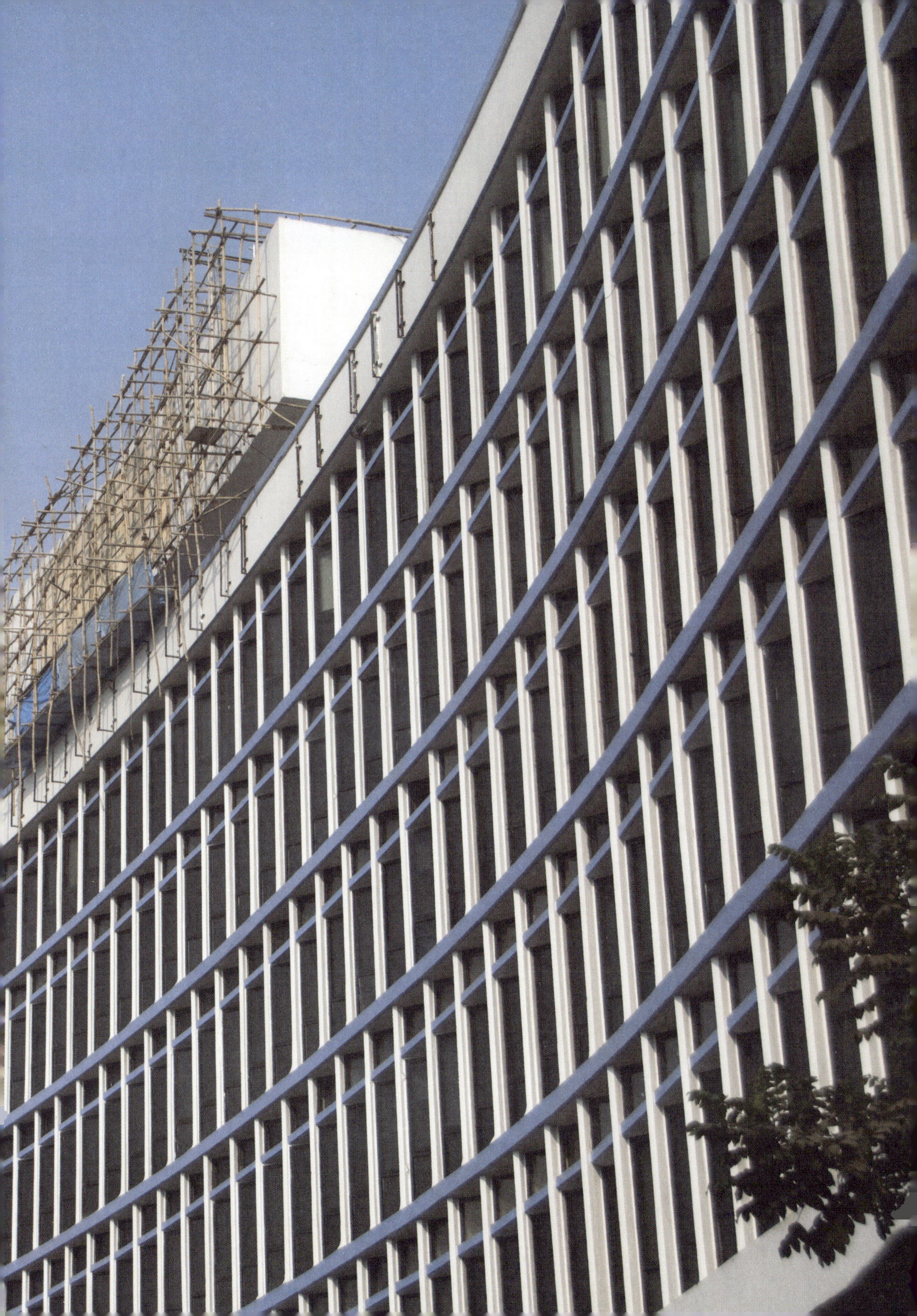

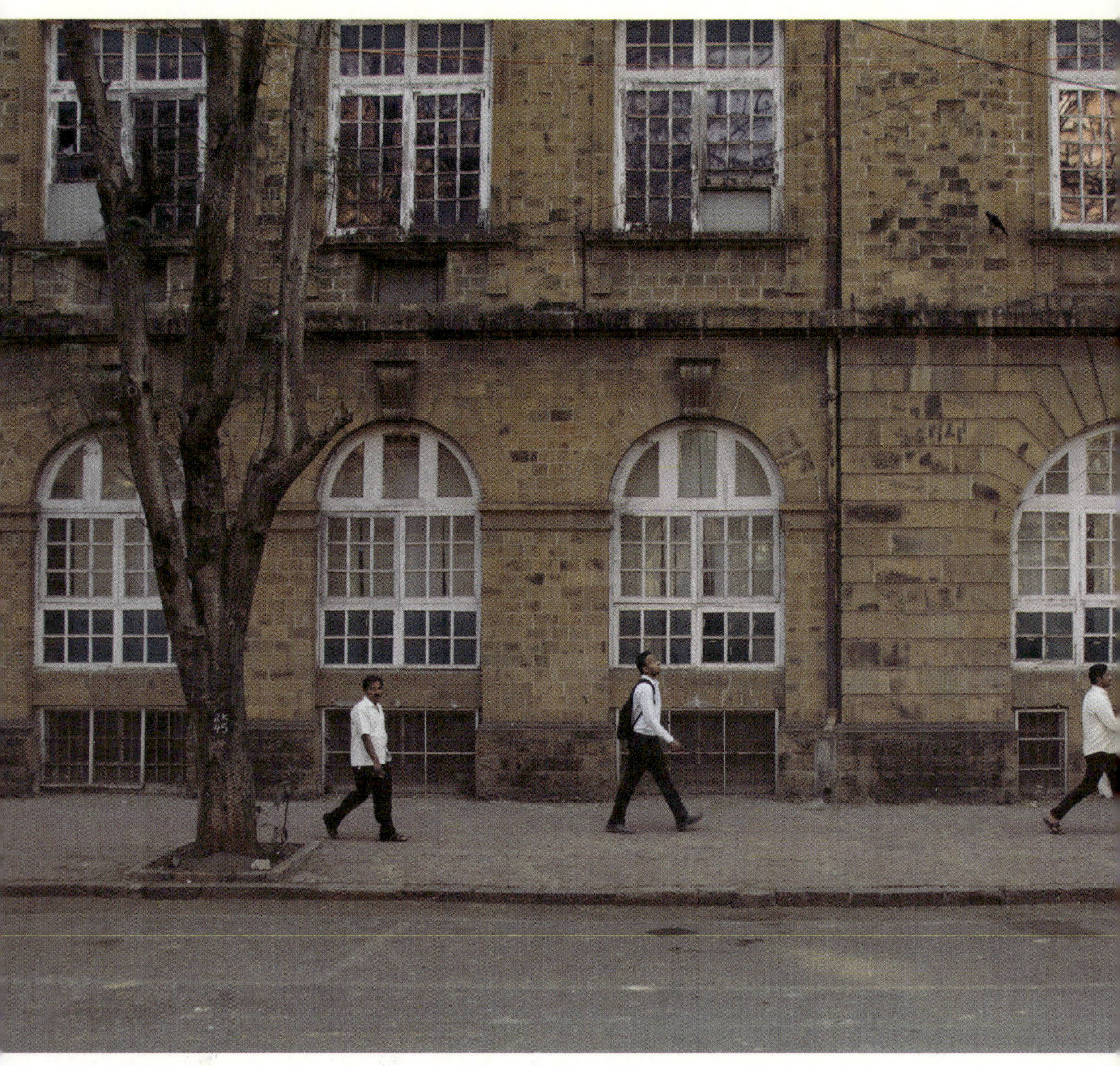

Fort

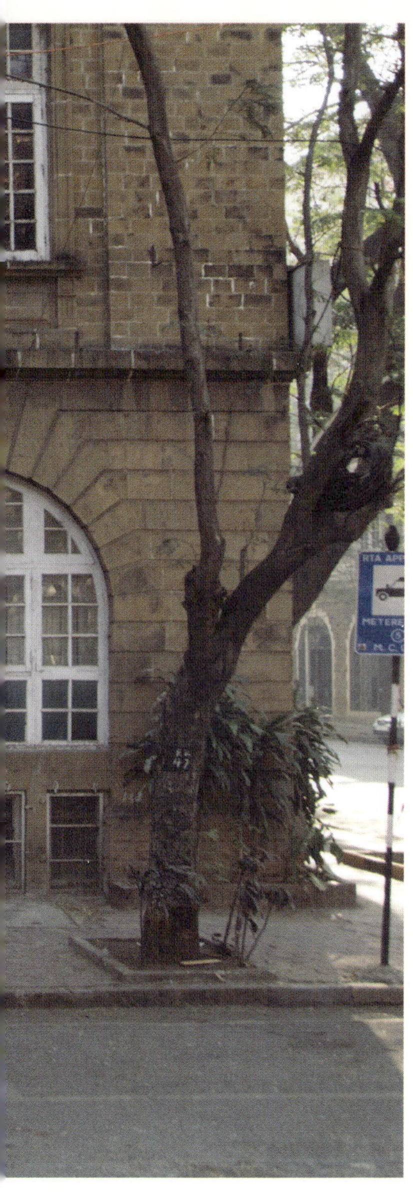

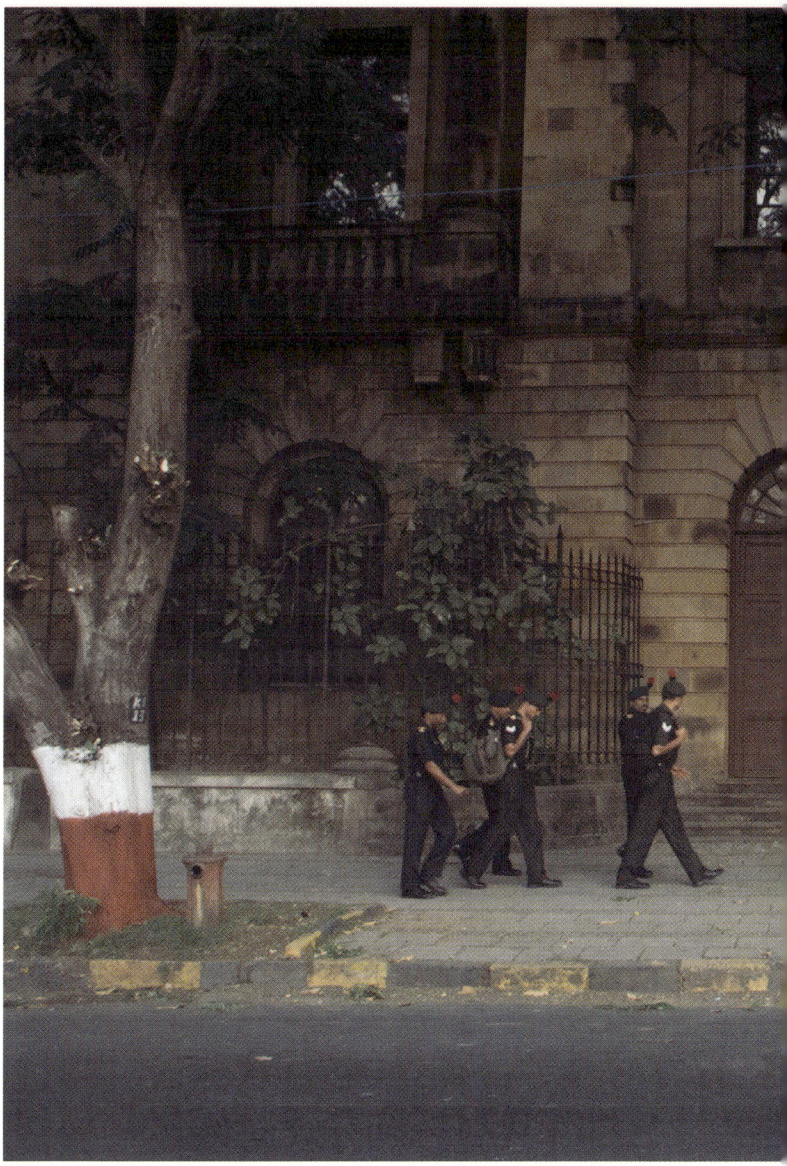

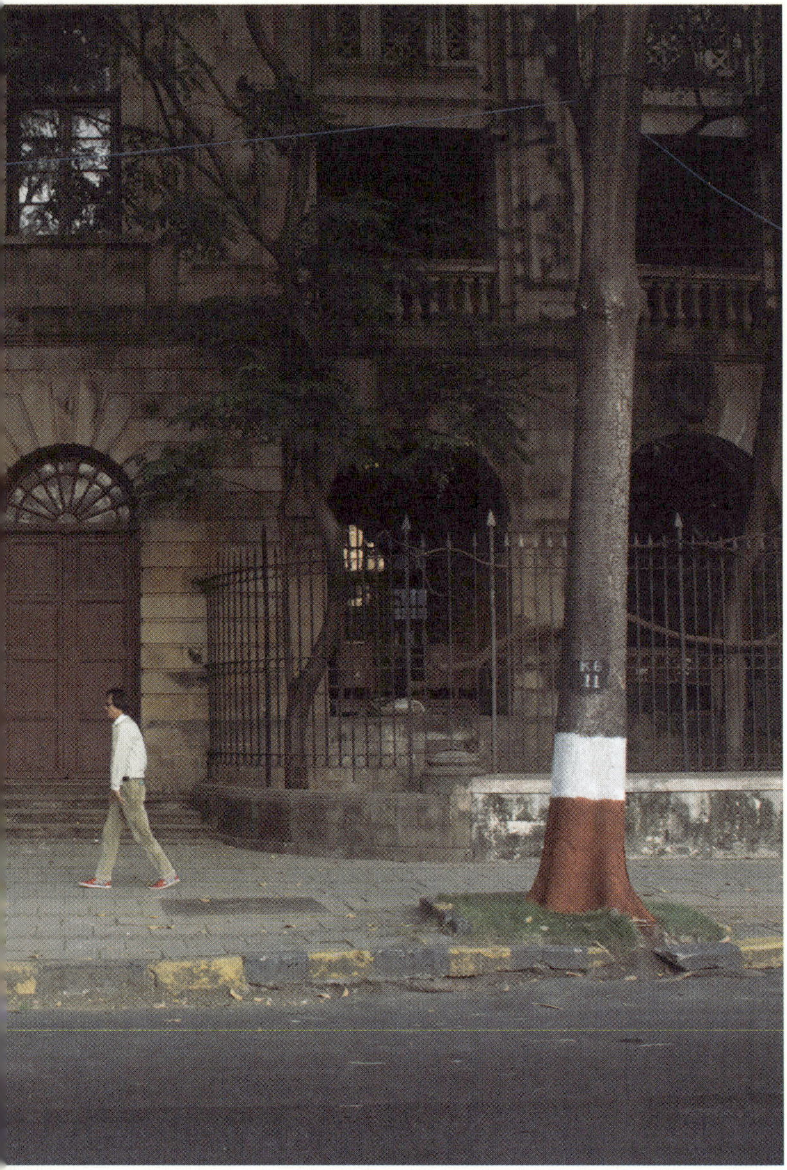

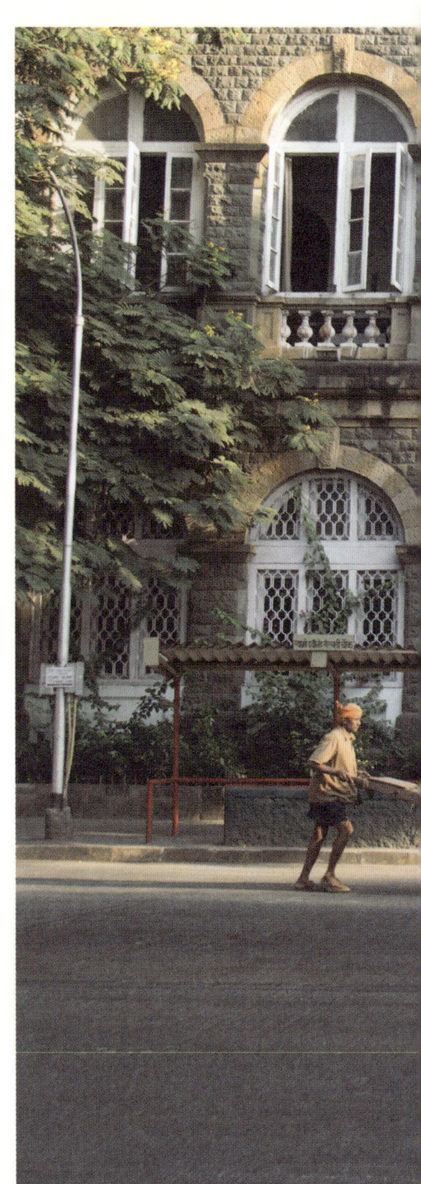

Fort

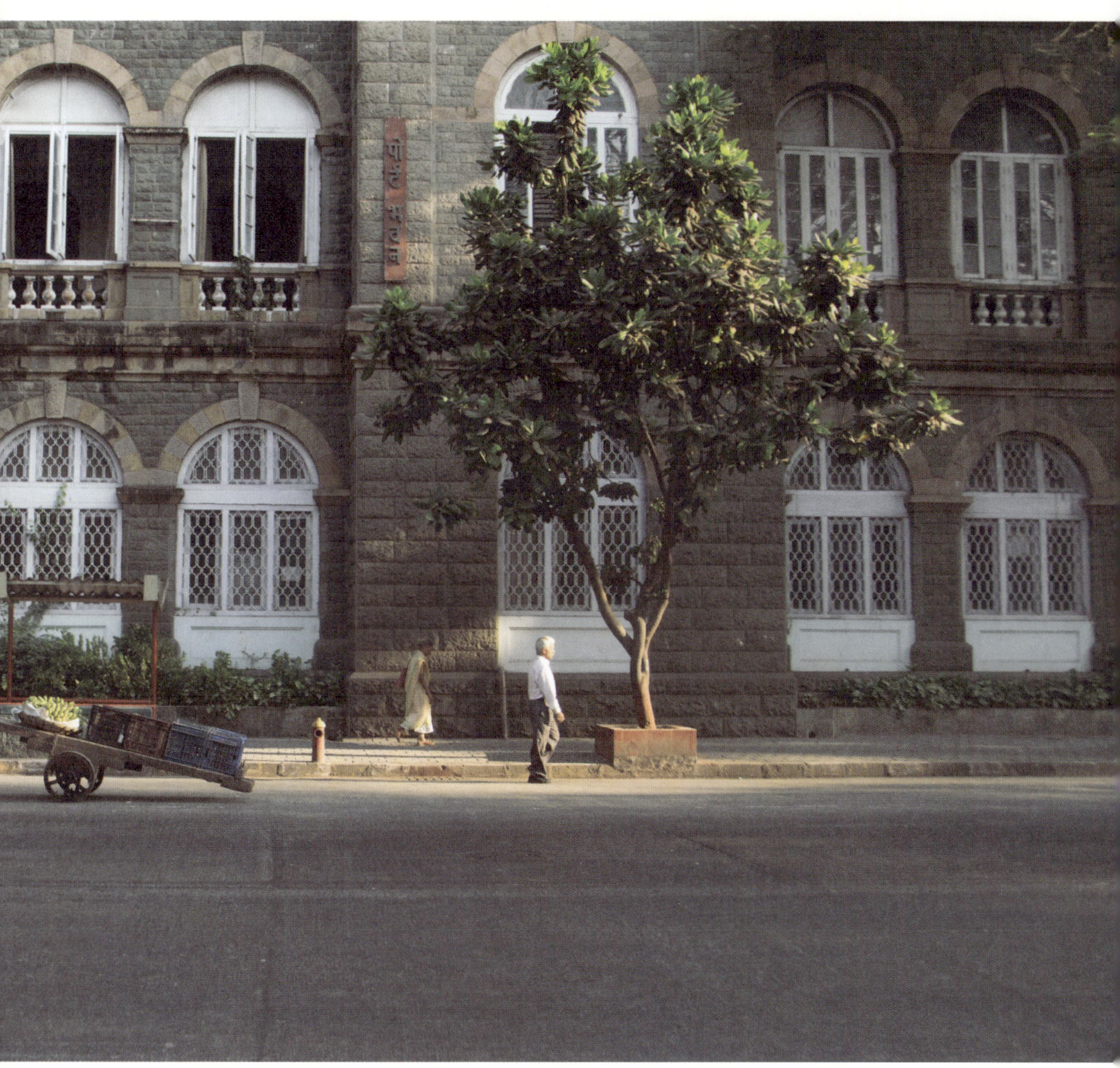

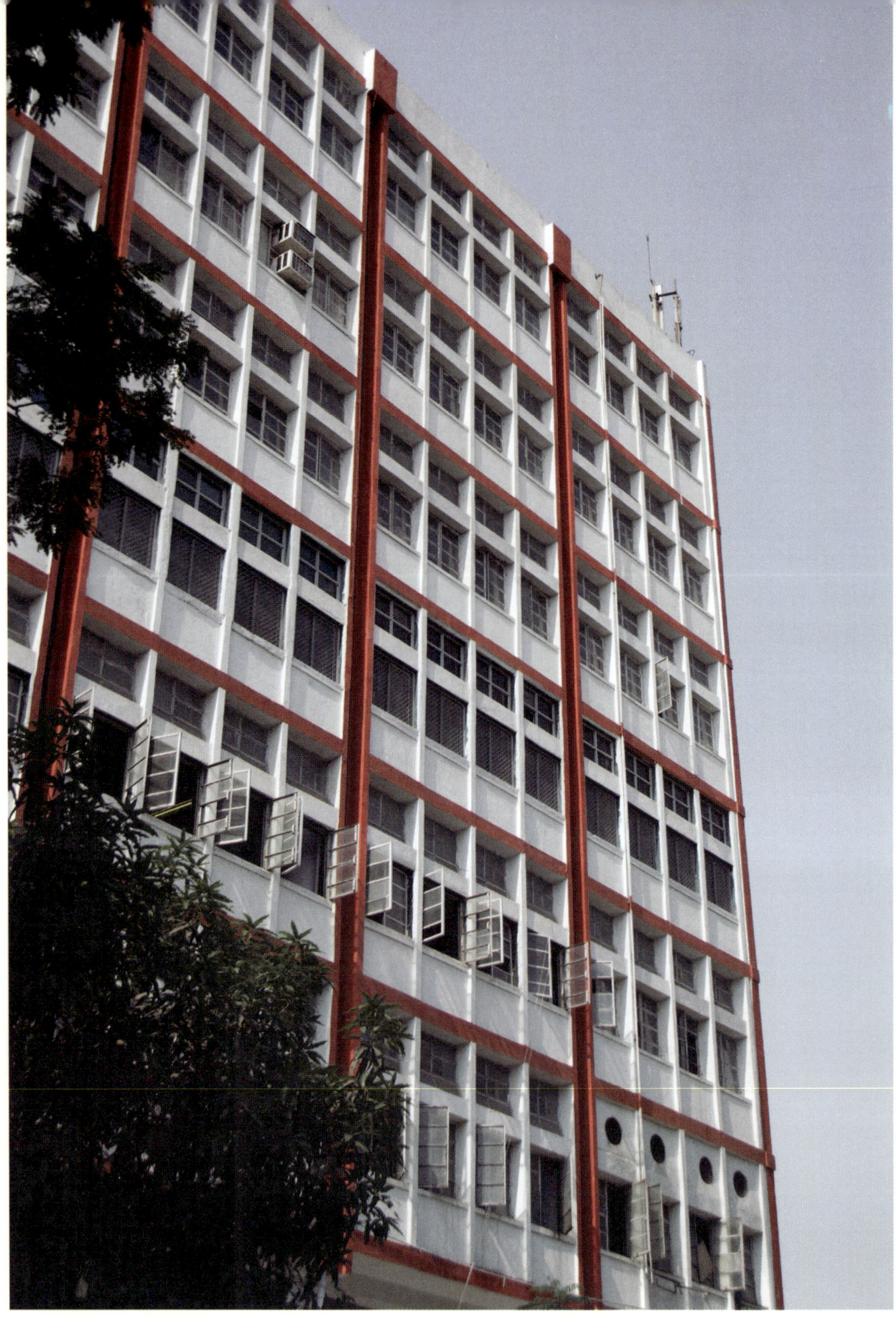

Fort

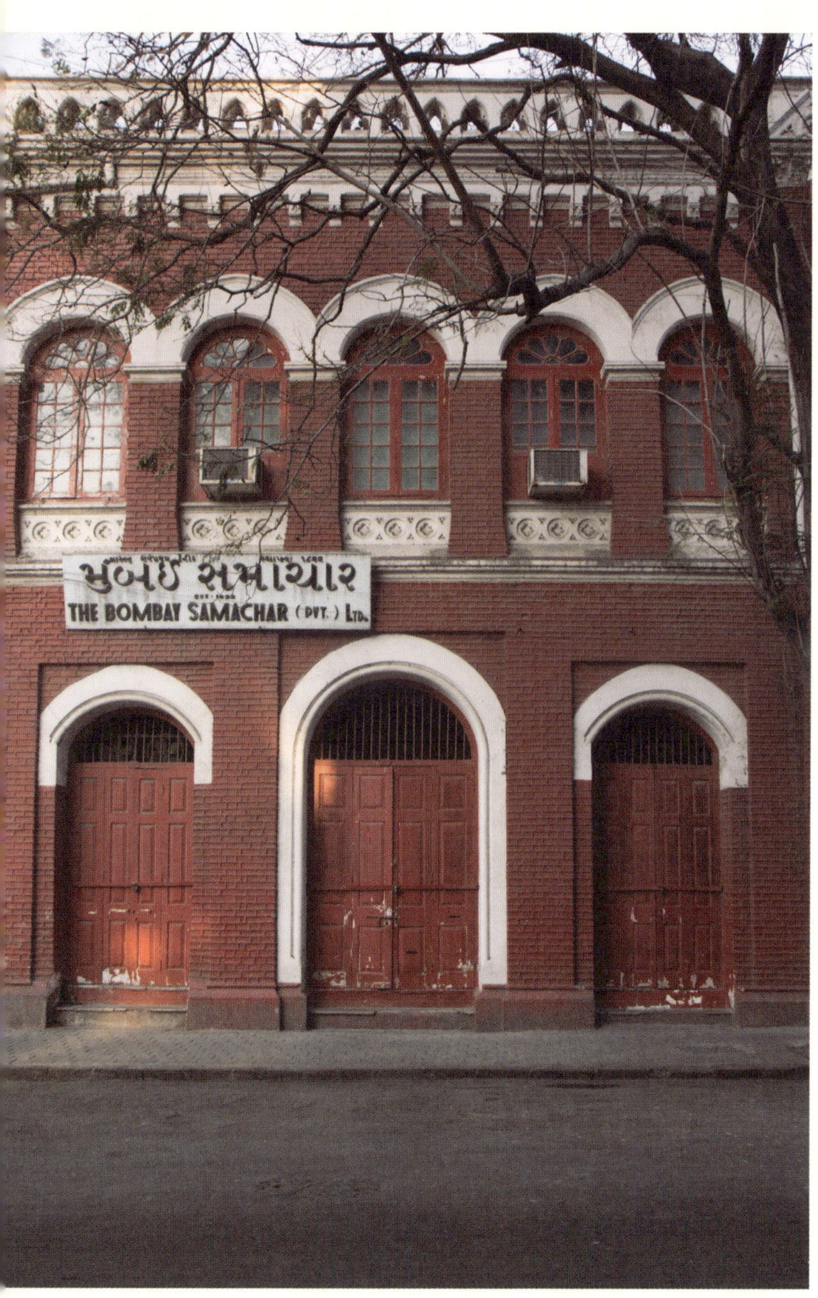
મુંબઇ સમાચાર
THE BOMBAY SAMACHAR (PVT.) LTD.

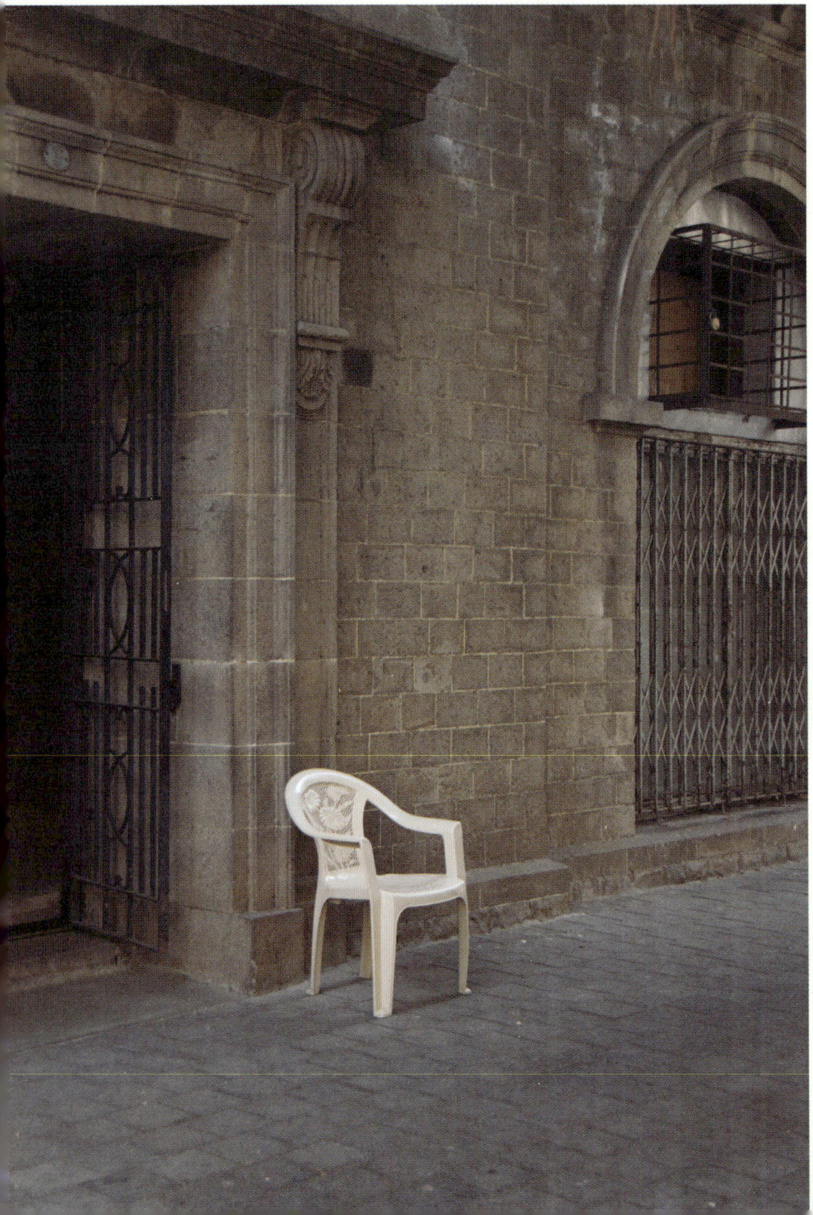

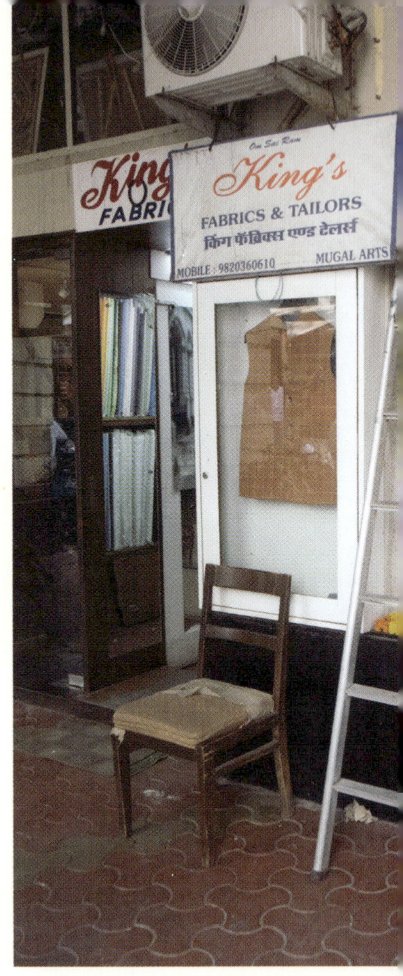
Om Sai Ram
King's
FABRICS & TAILORS
किंग फॅब्रिक्स एण्ड टेलर्स
MOBILE : 9820360610
MUGAL ARTS
King's
FABRIC

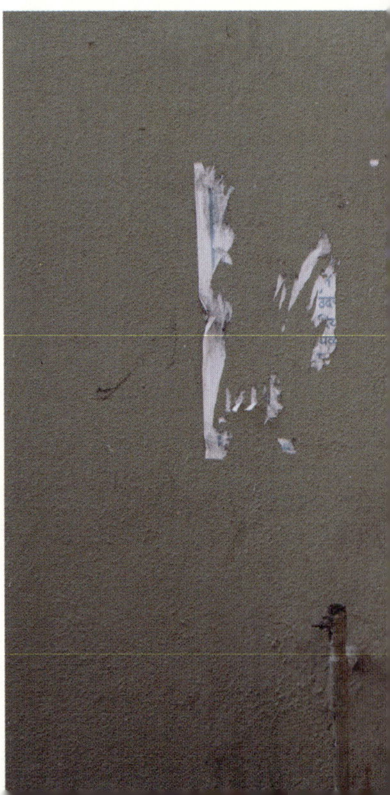

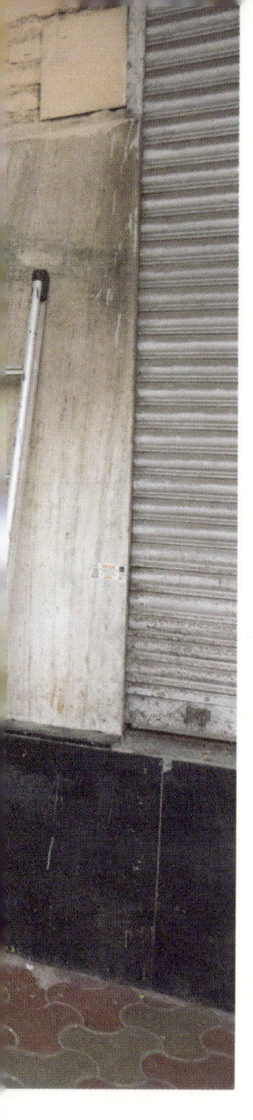

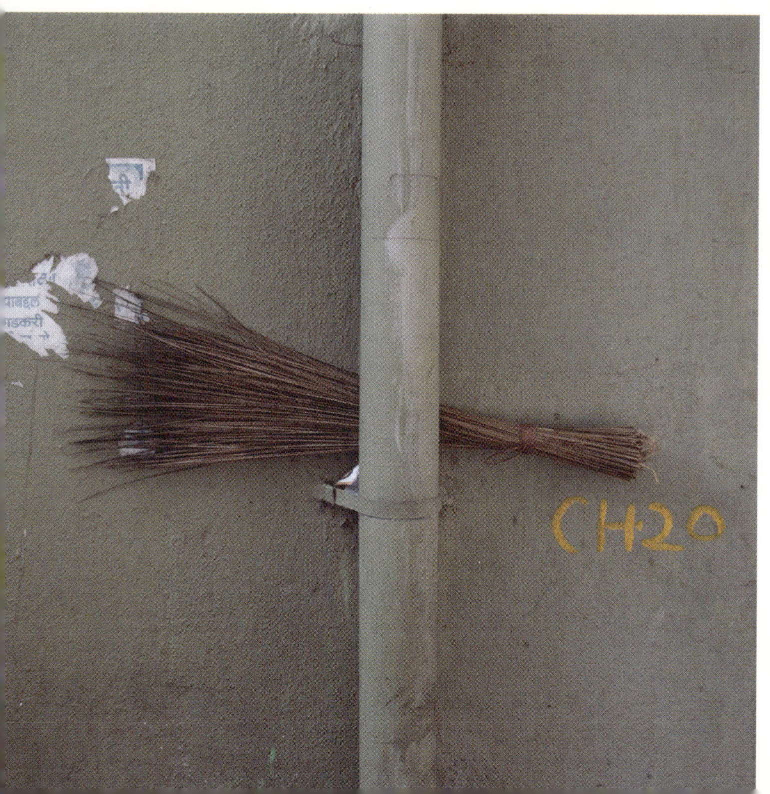

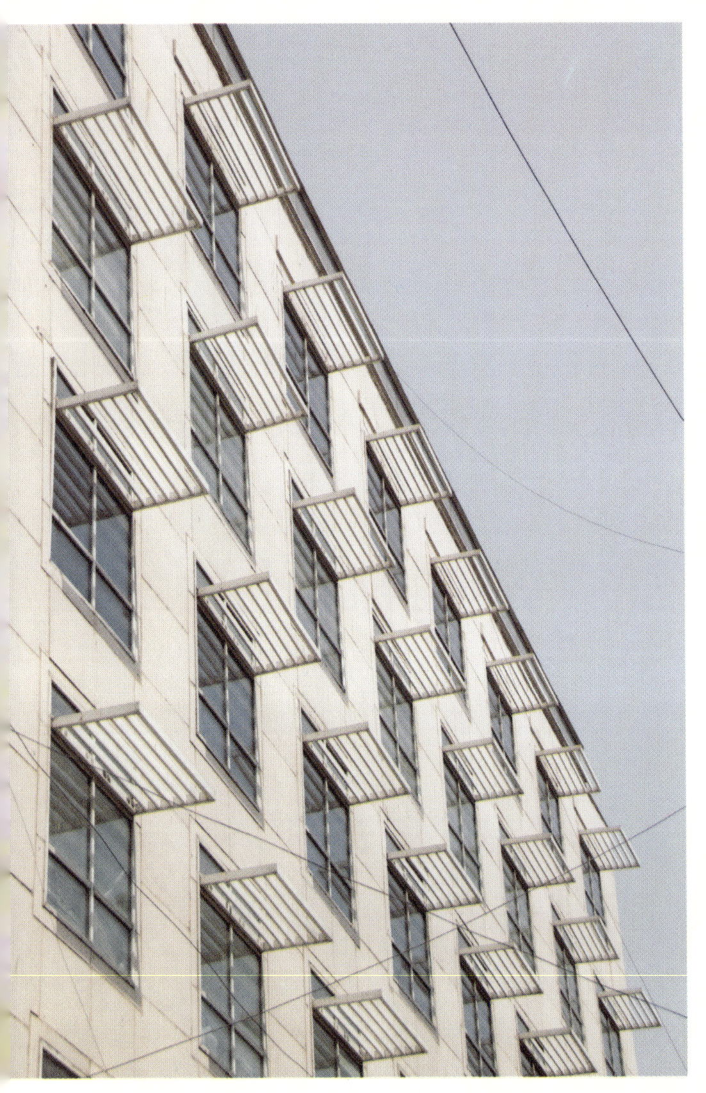

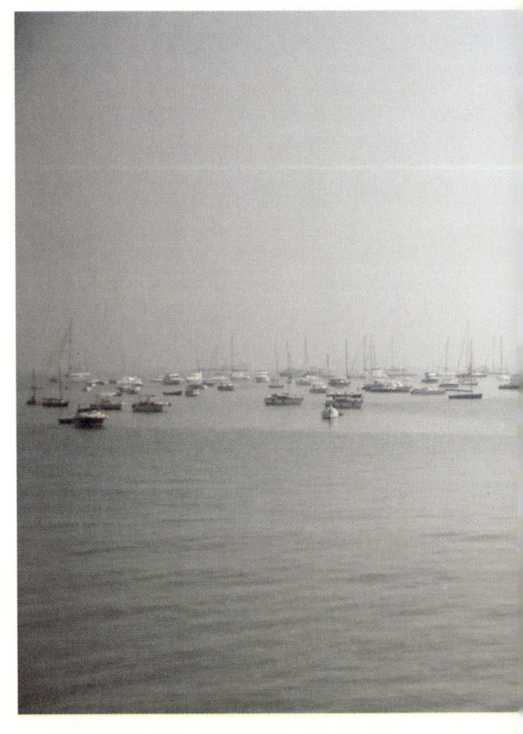

Colaba.

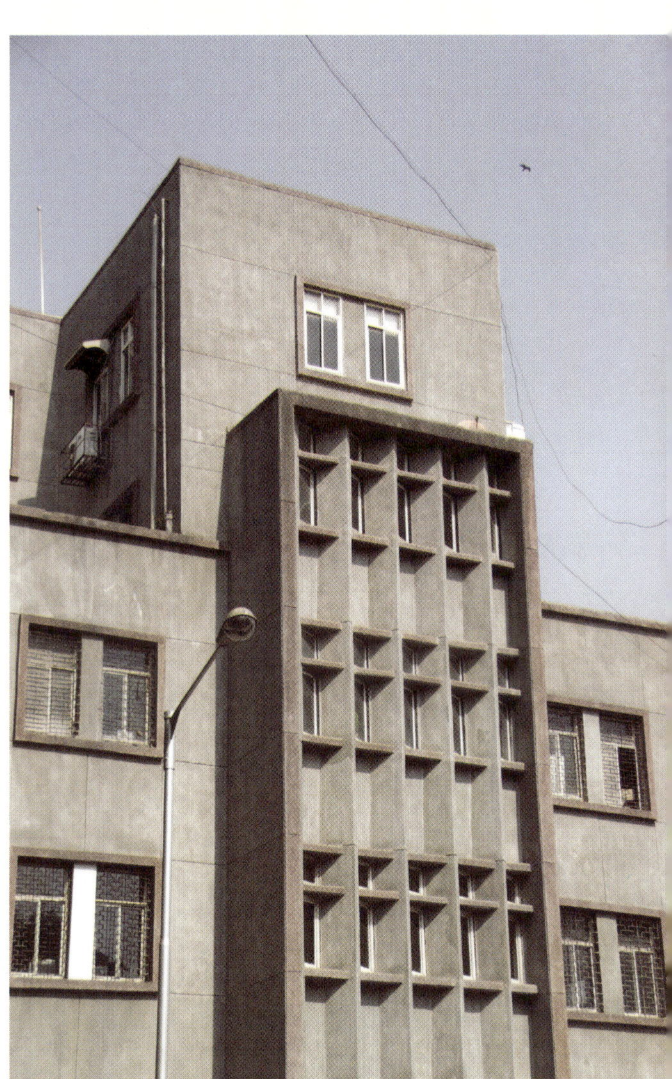

FANTASY

Though my walks were unplanned, a lot of
them felt staged.

It was like the city was putting on a show for me. Firstly it was the setting. While walking some streets, I thought I was on a film back lot, and that a set had been put up for my benefit. For example, I'd find all the things you find spread across a city block: a bakery, a tailor's shop, a copy shop, places of worship, all miniaturised and lined up next to each other, a series of facades along a single street. Then there were the actors, fisherwomen with attitude, kindergarten kids in picture-perfect school uniforms, men from all castes and religions reading newspapers in various regional languages to catch up with the day's events, as if the streets were selling the idea of a vibrant heterogeneous society to me.

Sometimes it seemed that what I saw was a compressed version of Bollywood, whose art directors created city streets in their studios, often lining up various city sights into one space.

But, equally, there were dystopian scenes, apocalyptic landscapes of abandoned or dilapidated public housing units whose open spaces, free of security guards, had become playgrounds for kids to run amuck. And as happens while reading or watching a good thriller, you never know what you would see next. You turn a lazy corner and bam! Something unexpected hits you. The switch between dream and nightmare happens so fast that you begin to wonder what megacities like Mumbai are: some sort of a lucid dream or a big scam, sold on ideals of a better life, of diversity, variety... What is the nature of the gap between the 'dreamland' you buy into and reality?

I've worked in the media for most of my career, in television and then directing advertisements, so I understand the need for aspiration, for hope. But I wonder whether the gap between dreamland and reality is getting more and more drawn out. When I worked at MTV in the early 2000s, I remember a lot of people acquiring pugs, inspired by the then Vodafone TV ads. The cell phone company had this friendly four-legged mascot tell their customers that they were always happy to help. Up until then, the go-to dog for Indian families was the Pom, short for Pomeranian, a handsome dog with a luxurious, pure white coat, but with an unpredictable and sometimes colourful personality. To me, a Pomeranian felt more Indian, feisty, shrill and in your face, versus the benign pug.

It is the same with cars, I thought we as a people were more Maruti 800s, Ambassadors, Innovas…. And seeing Ferraris and Lambos zipping between speed breakers in Mumbai felt weird and out of place. Those are beautiful machines but can you stretch a Ferrari on the roads of Mumbai?

I guess megacities are really about projections, stating that we will become Shanghai by building more super built-up Grecian villas in the sky. But at what point does the bubble burst? In 1983, for the first time in mainstream media, Kundan Shah's cult film 'Jaane Bhi Do Yaaron' lifted the veil on the builder-politician-bureaucrat nexus, and one that essentially controls the Mumbai real estate market.

During my walks, I saw many disputed properties: at least 30% of Mumbai has signboards stating the High Court had seized a particular property because of a dispute between X and Y. It made me wonder if these conflicts were resolved sooner, we could actually solve Mumbai's housing crisis. For, these pieces of land tied up in law suits seemed like wasted resources.

The next significant land parcel in Mumbai slated for redevelopment – as of 2019 – is along the eastern coast. Owned by the Port Trust, these vast swathes of land house unused warehouses. If properly planned, these new developments could solve a lot of Mumbai's congestion and quality of life issues. But I've realised that it is more than likely that the status quo will hold. The perceived value of everything in Mumbai is so high, always in bubble territory that everyone fights for that square inch that much more. A fight for something that, in reality, might not be that valuable, that scarce.

Maybe Mumbai, New York, London, Tokyo aren't meant to be grounded in reality. Their role is to be in a constant dance with the limits of the possible, higher, bigger and faster. They are meant to fuel our instincts and push us to not be rational. They function as dreamlands, enticing you in with the idea that out here anything is possible: super built-up dreams, not very different from the buildings that go by that name.

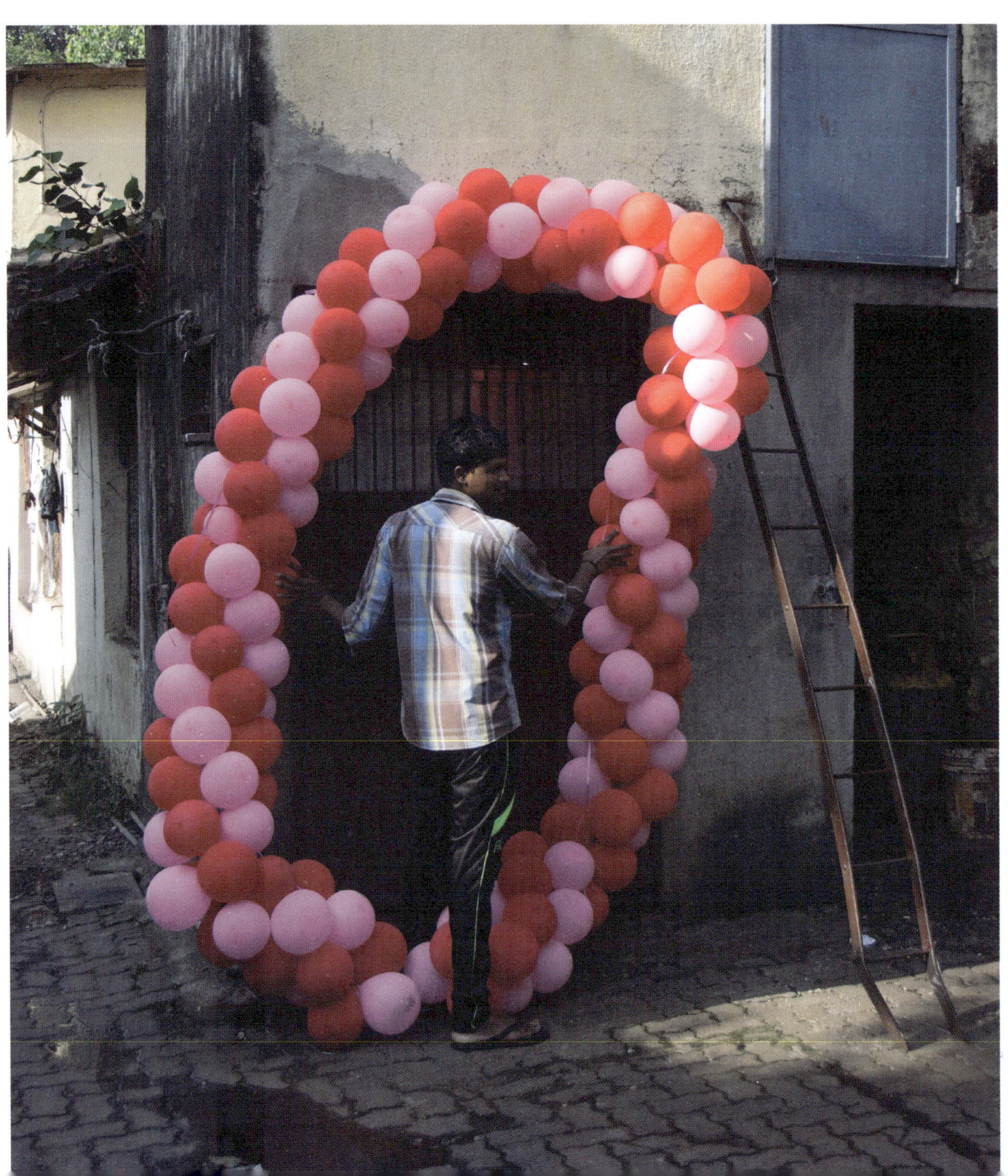

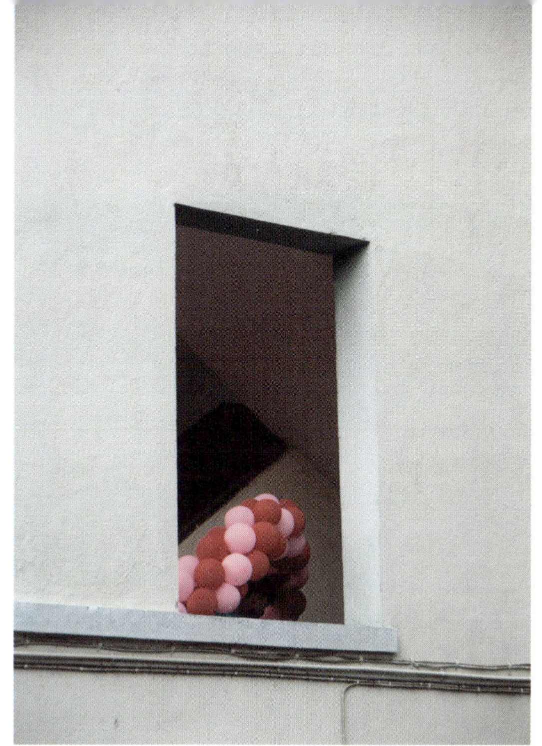

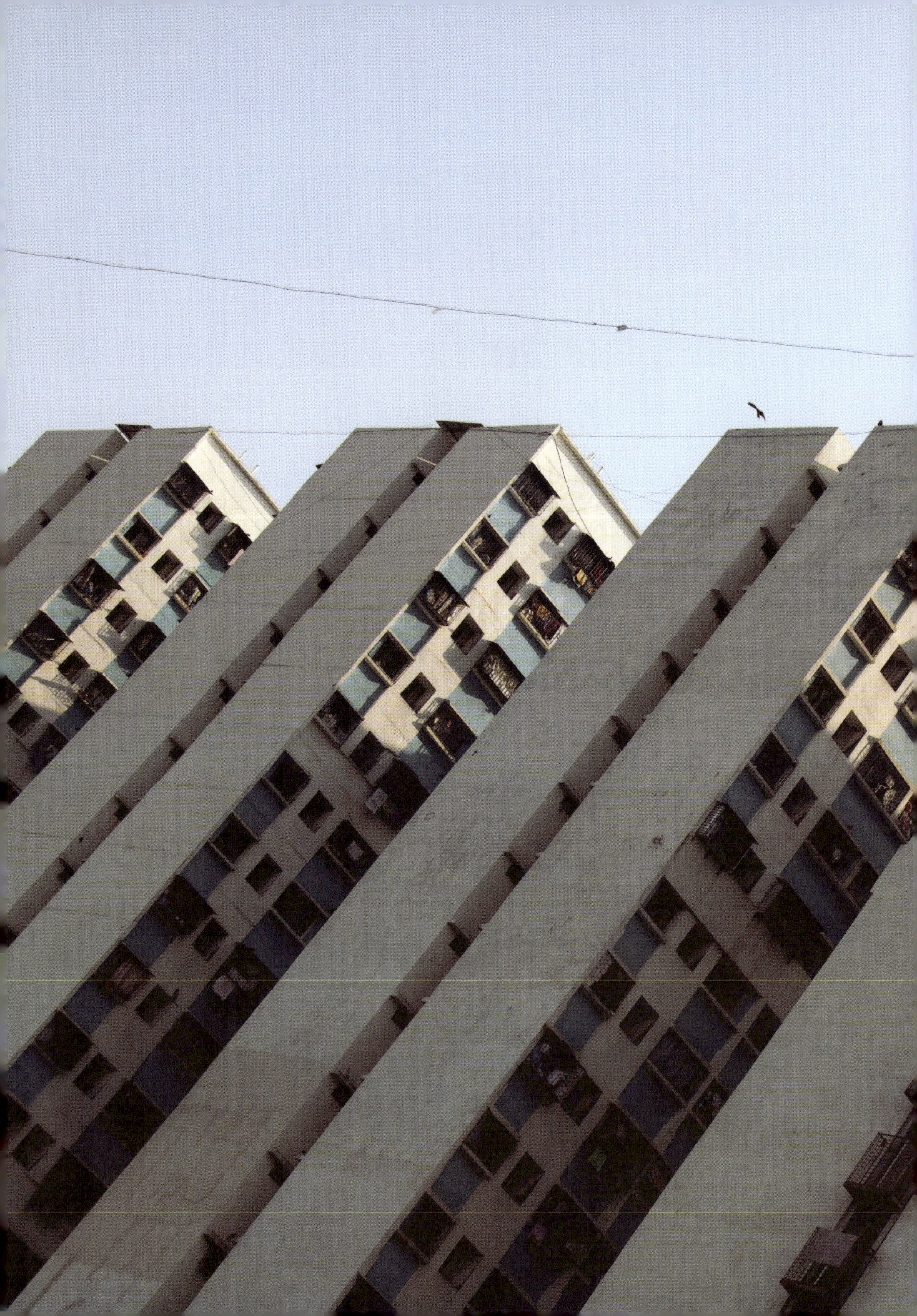

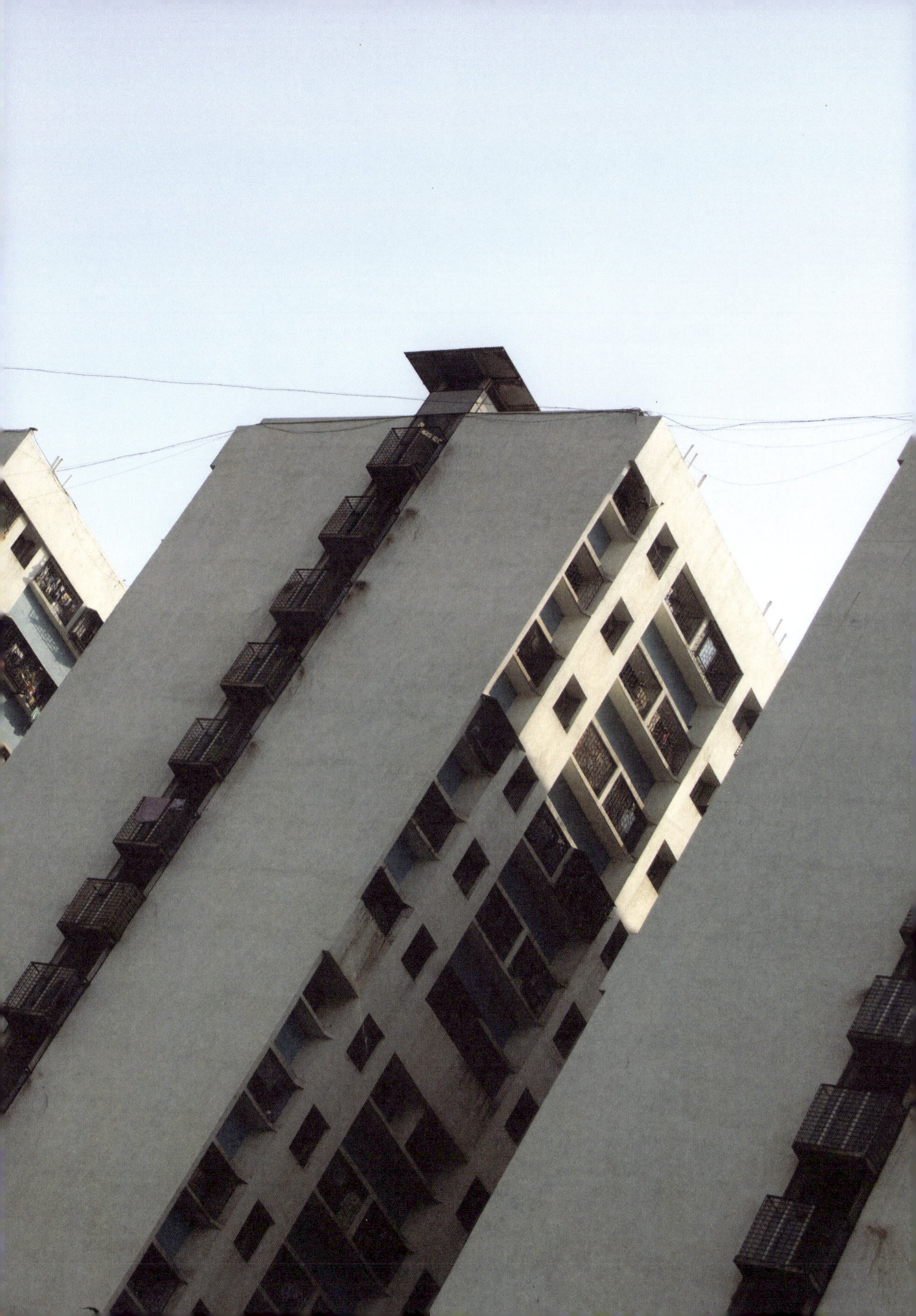

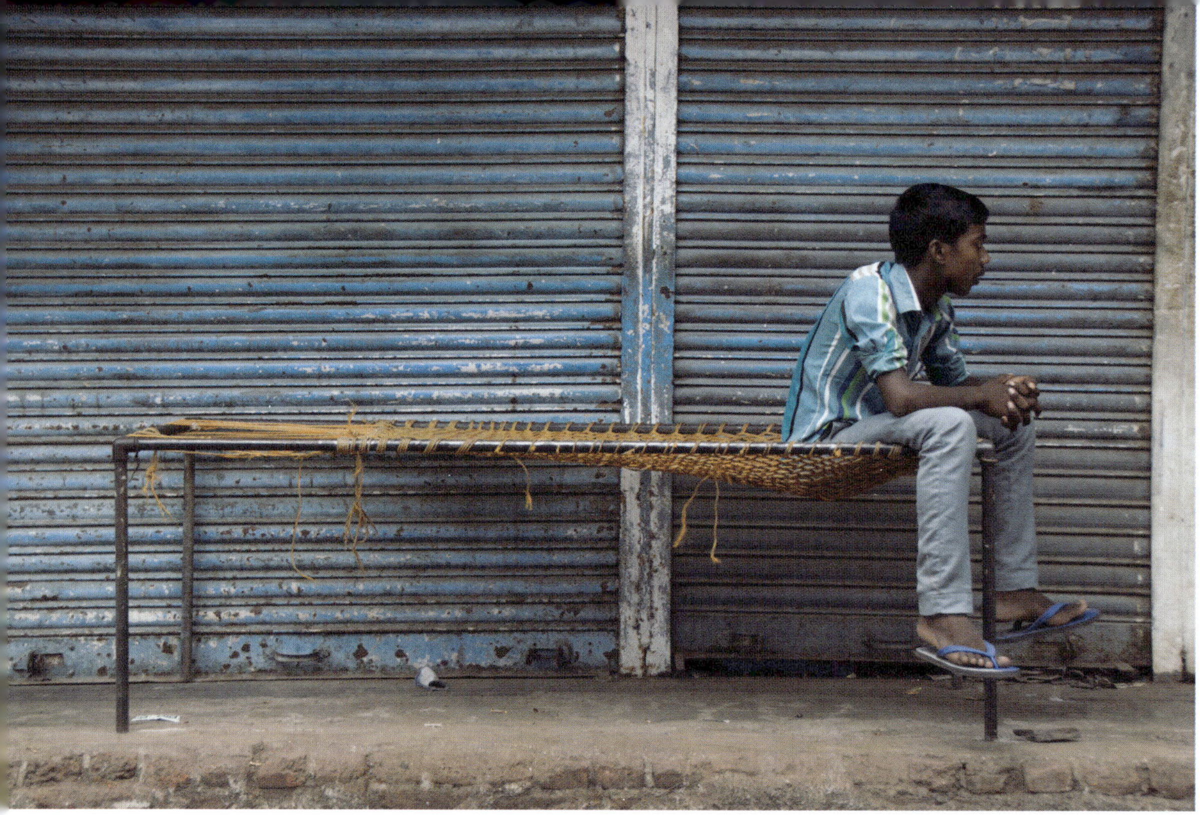

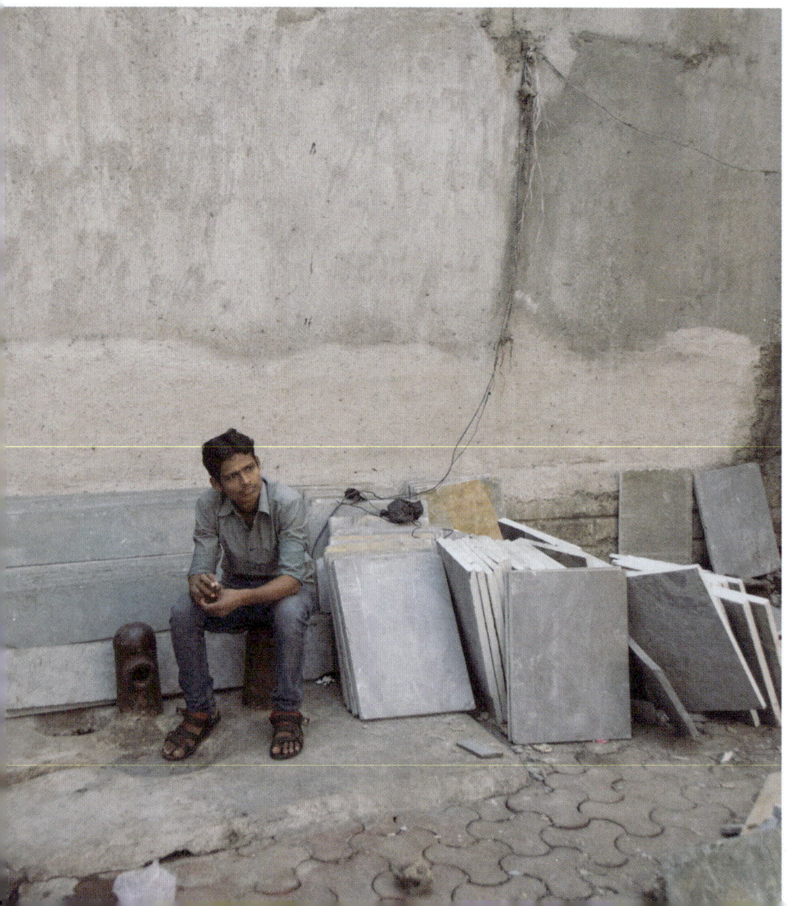

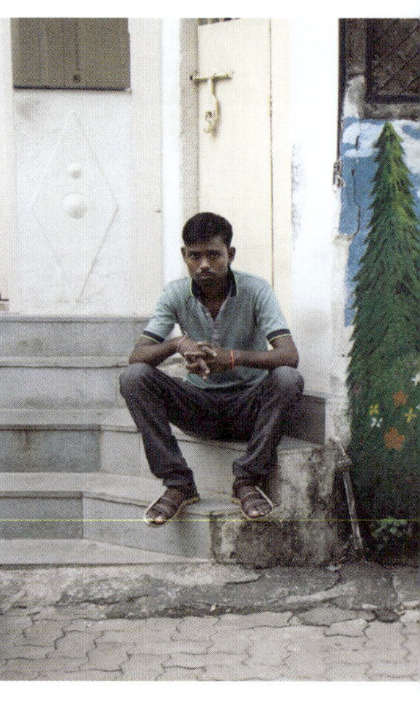

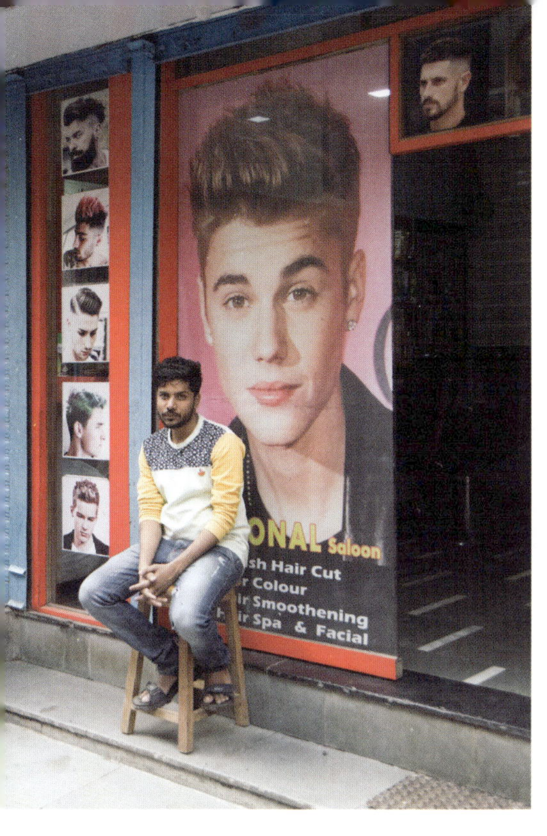
ONAL Saloon
sh Hair Cut
r Colour
ir Smoothening
ir Spa & Facial

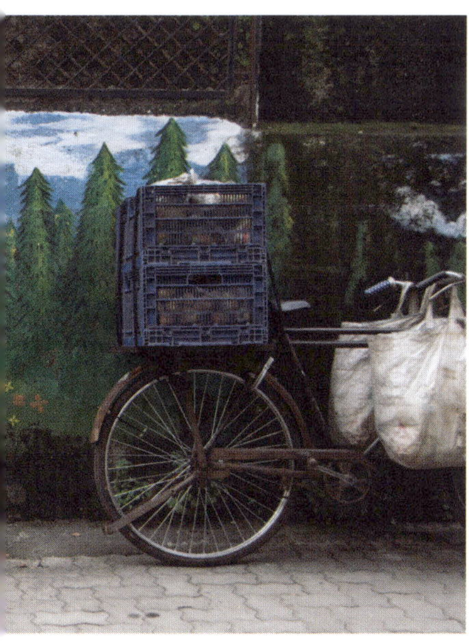

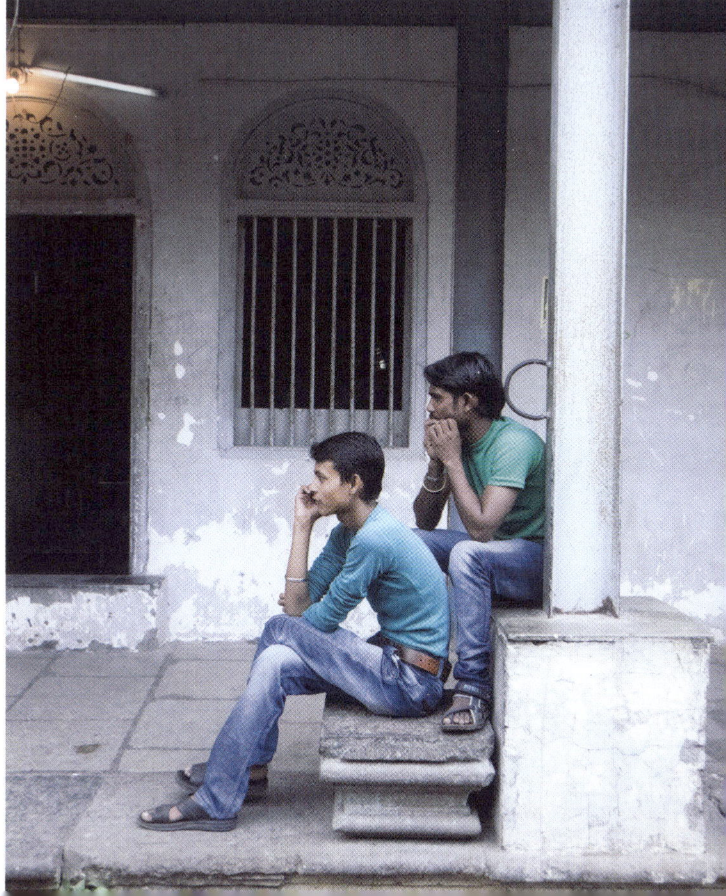

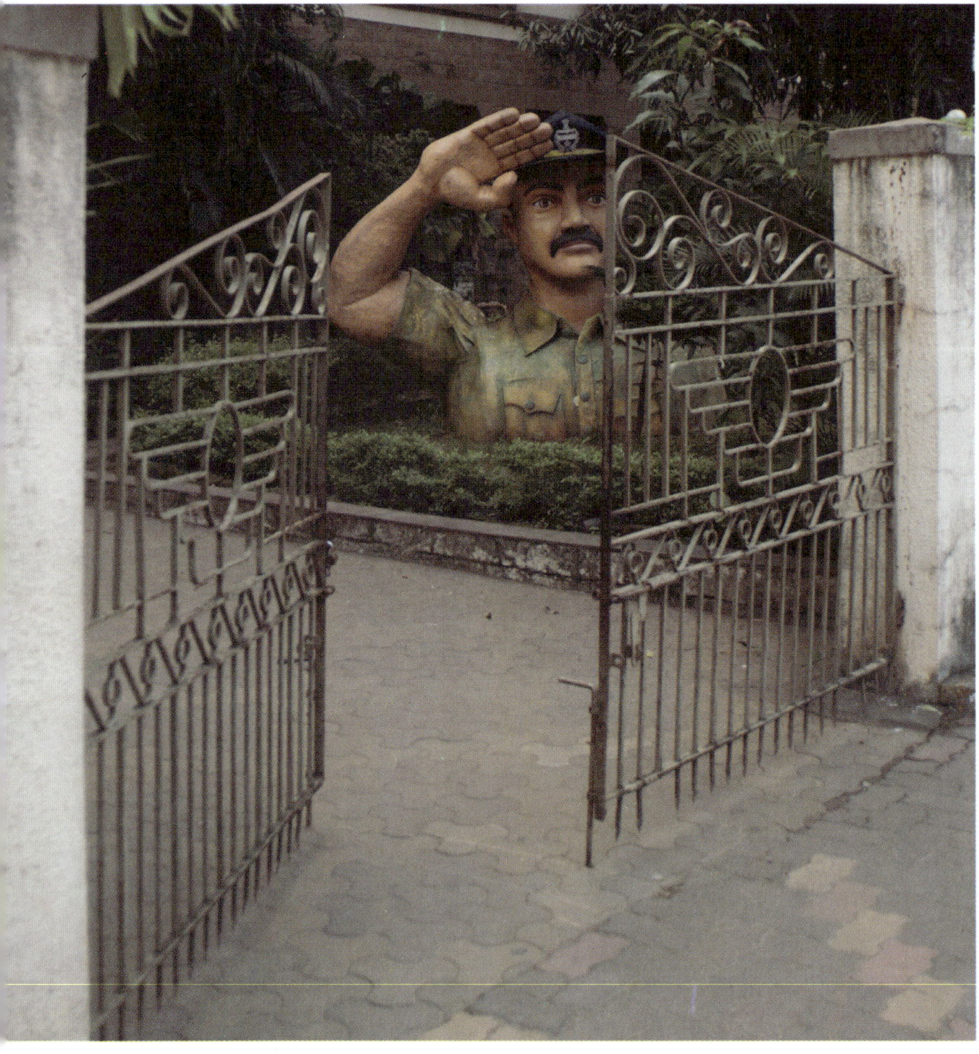

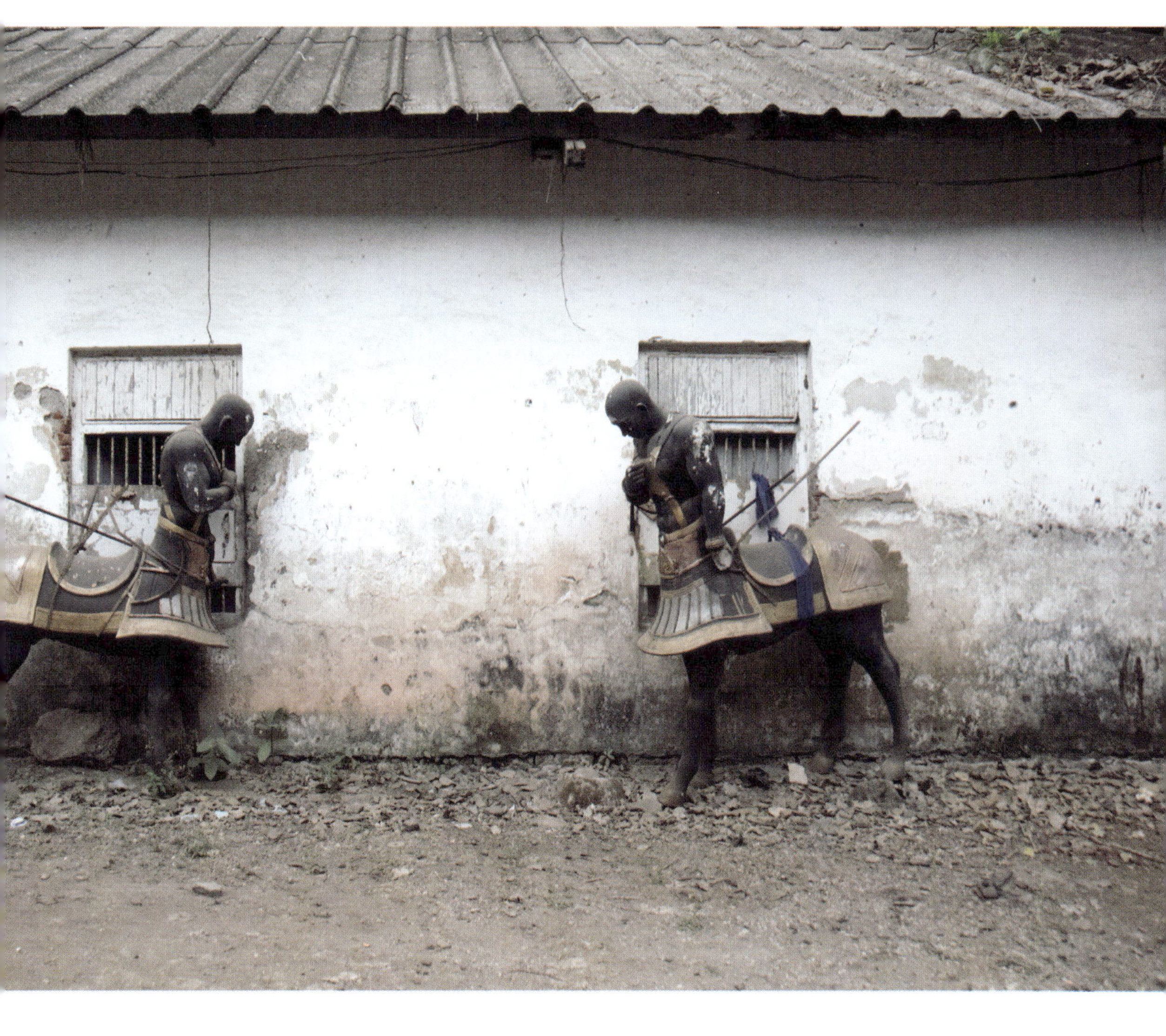

DREAMLAND

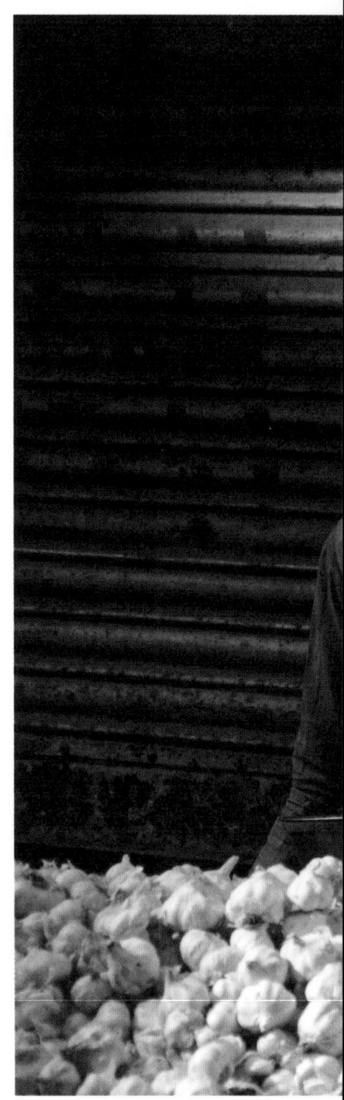

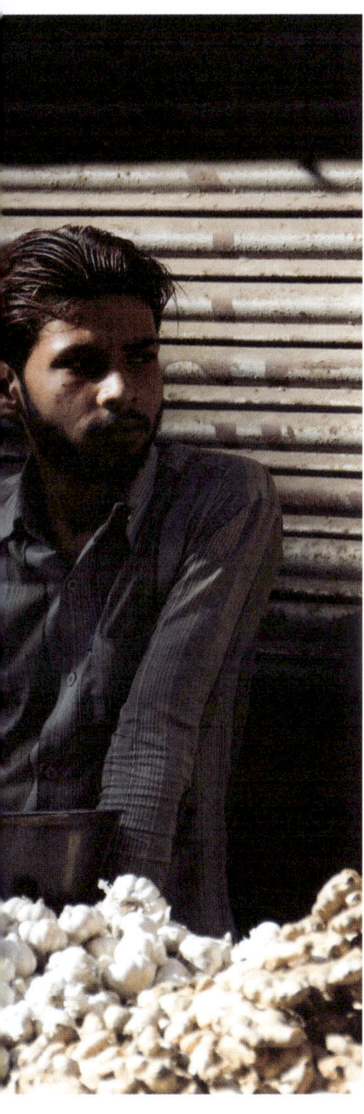

When I first started photographing the streets
of Mumbai, I had a different concept in mind.

I had noticed a change in the building names in the suburb where
I lived. When I was a kid, the buildings were named 'Little Flower',
'Shantivan' and since Mumbai is by the sea, 'Sea Breeze', 'Sagar
Darshan'. Even if they appeared exotically named, they felt grounded.
Take the name of my building 'Casa Maria': Maria was probably the
name of the previous landowner, an East Indian, and the building
bordered Bandra's East Indian-dominated Salcette Society.

Today's new buildings have faux luxury names like 'Pallazzo
Opulence', 'Dheraaj Grandeur', 'Gorwani Excellenzia' and besides,
today's posh neighbourhoods are those that have appropriated
adjacent localities and renamed them. Thus DN Nagar has been
upgraded to Upper Juhu, while the old mill area along Senapati Bapat
Marg in Lower Parel became Upper Worli. In Wadala bordering RCF
Chemical factory emerged a new development area, the New Cuffe
Parade.

Once a cabbie told me that five thousand people come to
Mumbai every week. Most of these people stay. No matter how harsh
their living conditions, they prefer these to the places from where
they came. Like in the acclaimed director and actor Raj Kapoor's
films. These films were family favourites. My parents loved the
songs that featured in them and we listened to them daily. We made
sure we caught them when they were shown on national television.
When my dad bought a videocassette recorder, these were the first
movies he recorded. A lot of them had Nargis starring in them and
she reminded me of my mum. But basically I loved Raj Kapoor.
I liked especially that a young idealist Raj would come into the big
city with big dreams and would find love, success, prevail over his
moral dilemmas but always at a loss of his innocence.

Incidentally, our movies, especially those from Raj Kapoor's
time, have always been made for the broadest audience possible.
They've celebrated our multi-ethnicity, and the titles often appear in
English, Hindi and Urdu, at least in the past. And in the street set they
built in studios, art directors would build a temple, a mosque and a
church all next of each other.

My walk in Mumbai's Sonapur area, also called Dhobi Talao,
which lies between Princess Street and Metro Cinema, took me back
to a time where I felt I was watching a Raj Kapoor film. I felt as if
I was on a soundstage and everything there had been choreographed
for me, transported in from another time.

It started like all other walks at around 7.30 in the morning.

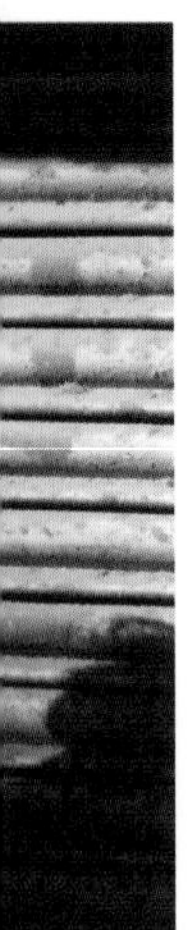

I started on the foot-overbridge on Marine Lines and proceeded to walk along Our Lady of Dolours Church. A few early office-goers were walking along with me, dressed in their neatly pressed office clothes. In front of us was a woman who stood out from the pant-shirt clerks. She had red heels on, red pants and a patterned Versace-type scarf. I consciously overtook her because I didn't want her to feel or think that I was stalking her. I was very curious about her, but when she turned into a lane, I continued to walk straight. As it turned out, this wouldn't be the last time I would see her that day.

To the left of the Church, which is more like a tiny chapel, was a mosque, and one street down, a temple. Taking a right from the temple, I turned into a small Gaothan, only two lanes long. When I got out from there, I passed a beautifully decorated single block building called 'Camy House'. It looked like a Parsi dormitory, and once I walked past it, I came back onto the main street right in front of a bakery called 'Paris Bakery'. According to my mother-in-law, Paris Bakery always had the best macaroons in town. Her aunt would take her there all the time when she was a child and lived in Cusrow Baug, Colaba.

Twenty minutes into the walk, I saw the same woman in red pants, this time she drove past me riding pillion on the back of a scooter. I continued walking, making my zigzag pattern through the inner streets of this old area of the city. I ran into some Japanese tourists taking a walking tour through the area. They also seemed like extras in this movie scene. I walked by what looked like a bar and it had a neon sign above the entrance. At the door of this bar was a hospitable-looking little person smoking a cigarette, giving me a big smile. It was as if Toulouse-Lautrec himself had popped out of Moulin Rouge to tip his hat at me, a friendly gesture, commending me for this creative endeavour I'd set out for myself.

To top it off, I saw the woman in red pants again, this time sitting in an Irani café having filter coffee. Sadly I couldn't take a picture of the lady. I couldn't find a red backdrop to match my colour story. Imagine the irony: I couldn't find a backdrop on a film stage made out of backdrops. Now you may think the woman in red pants is a ruse as I have no photographic evidence. But to me, the whole walk felt like a ruse, like the city was pulling a fast one on me, setting up this entire charade of a walk. I must say though that I did take a photo of the hospitable little person.

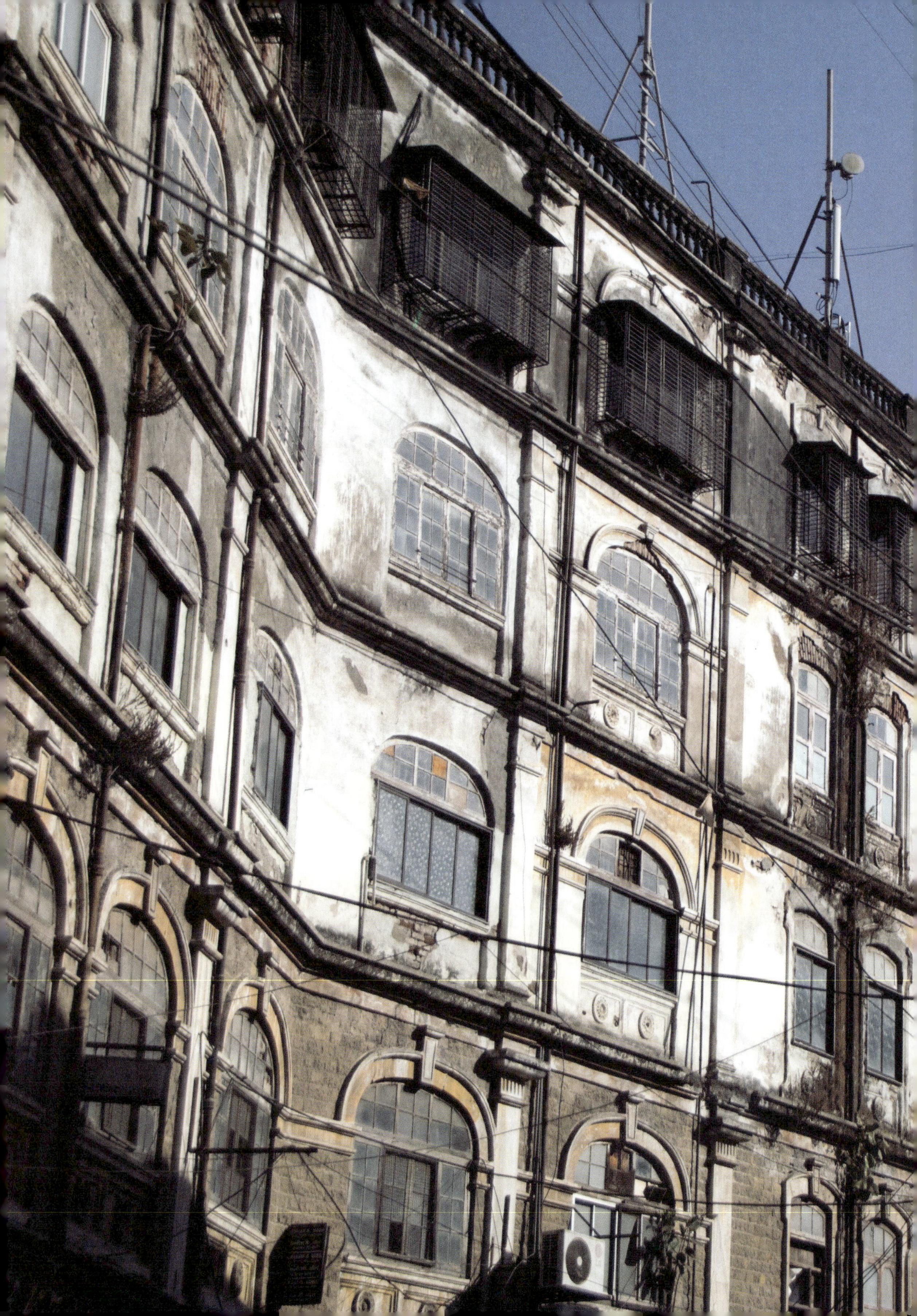

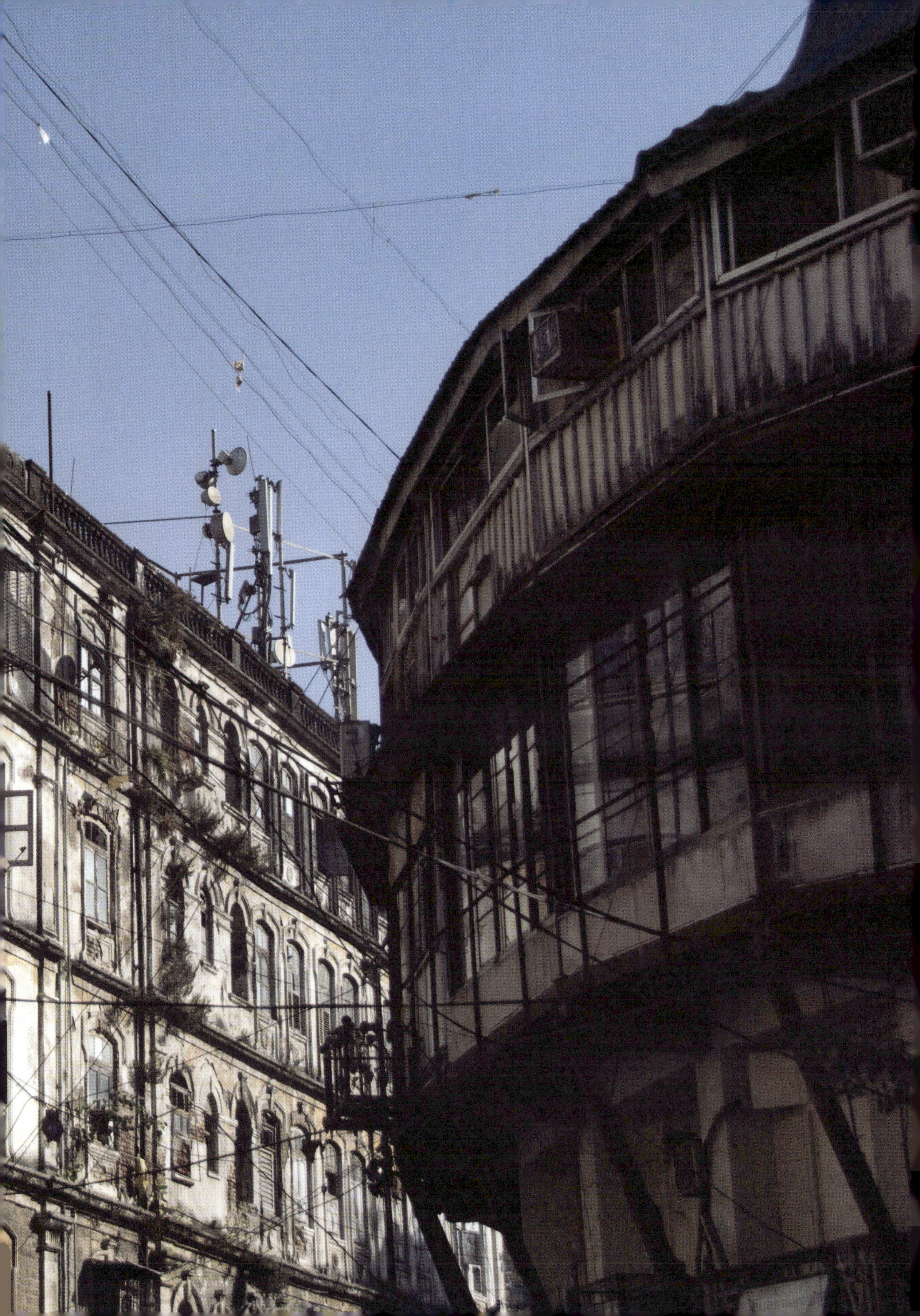

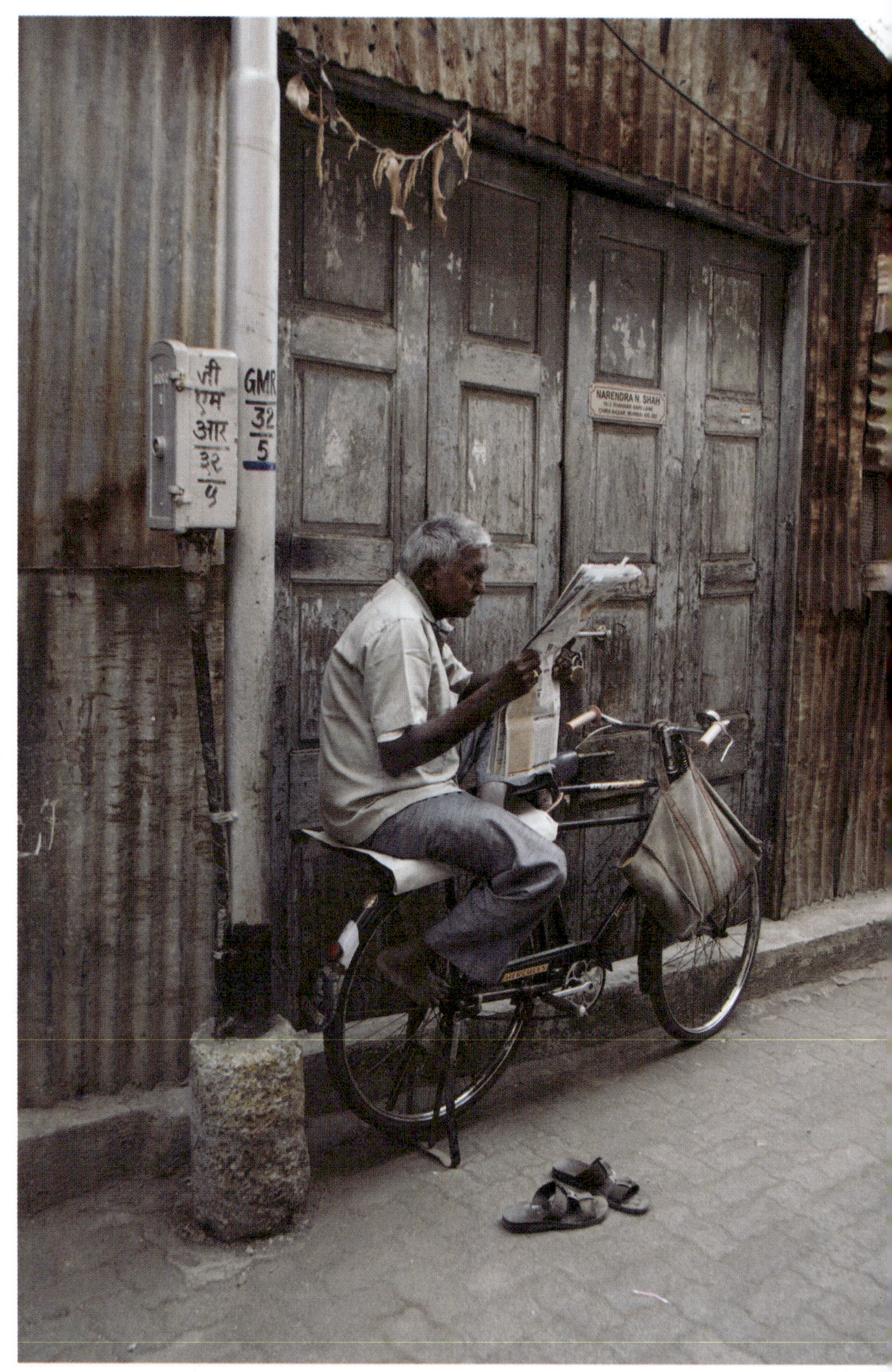
जी
एम आर
GMR
32
5
NARENDRA N. SHAH

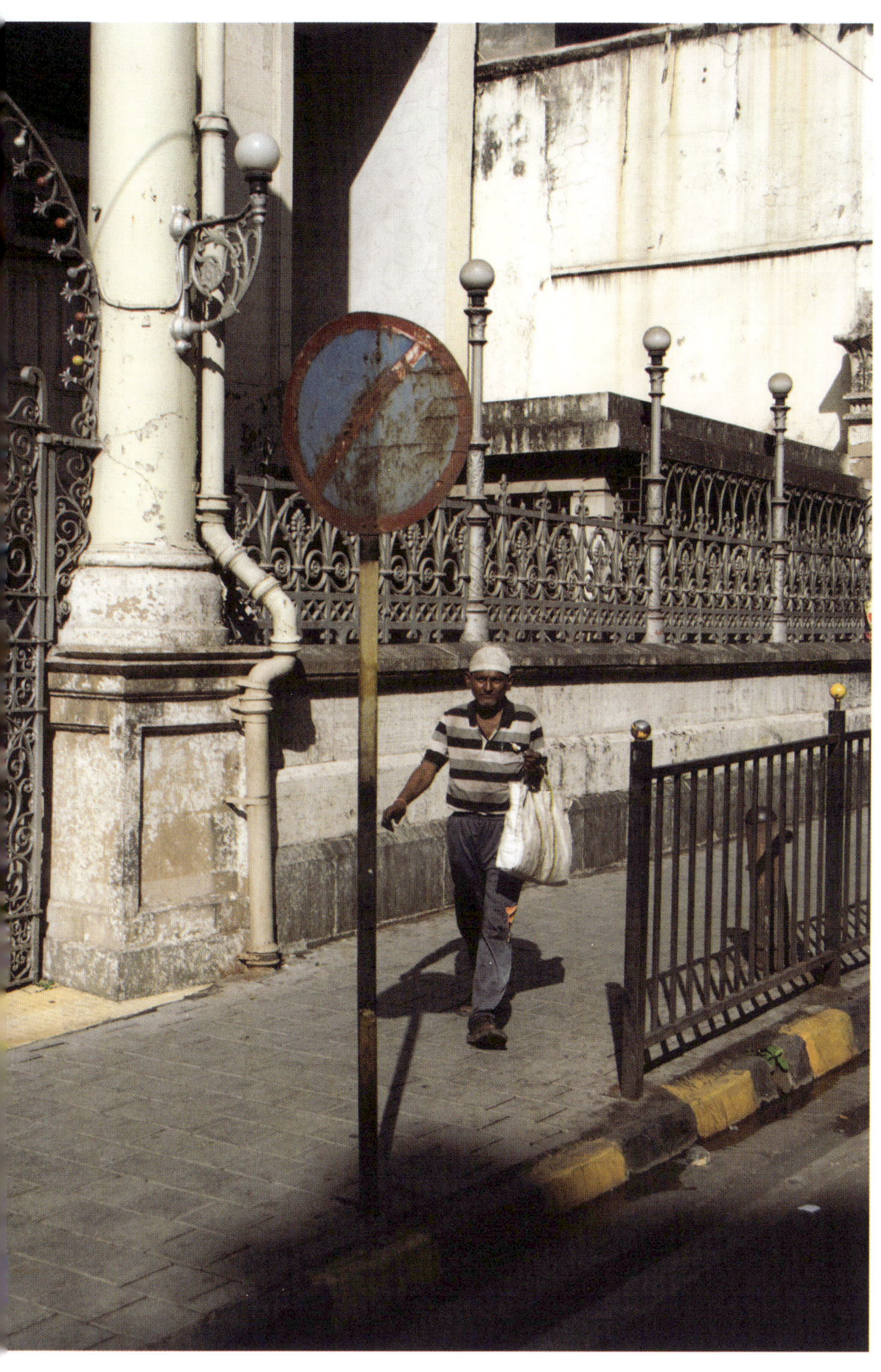

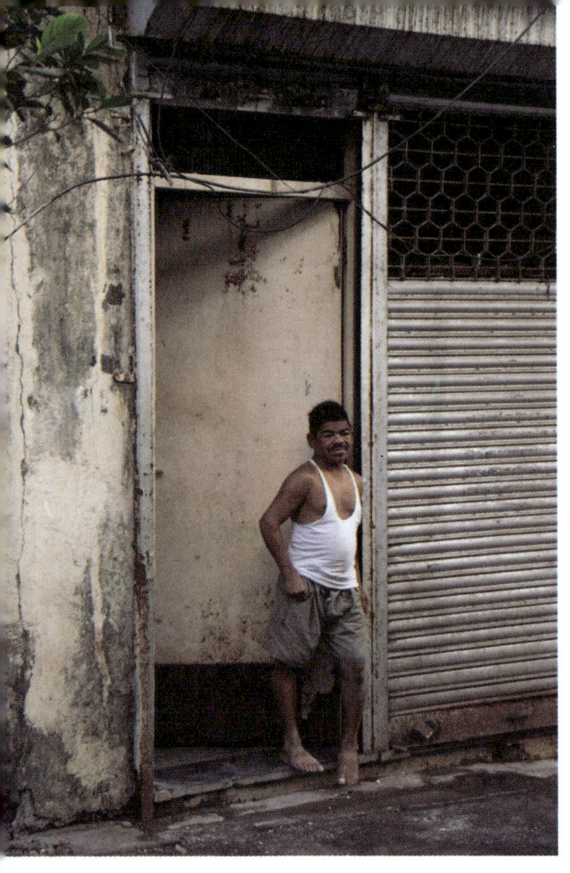

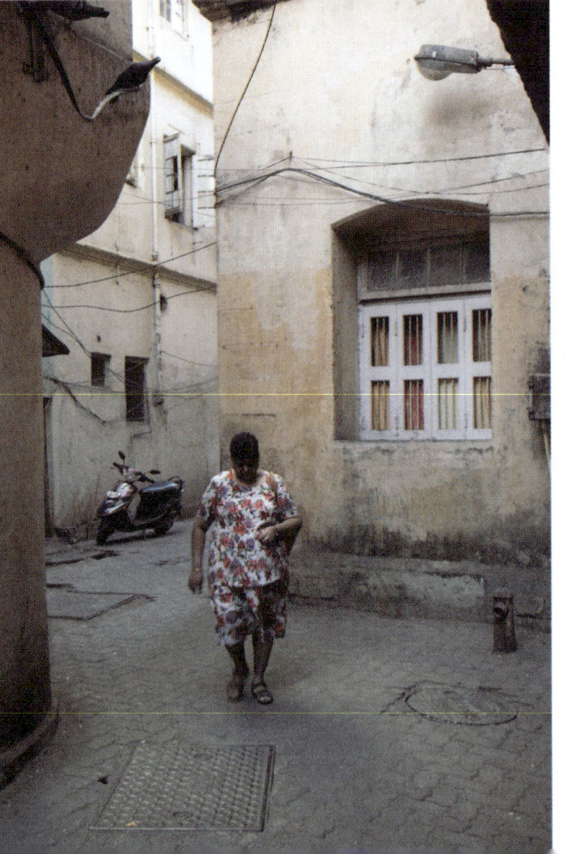

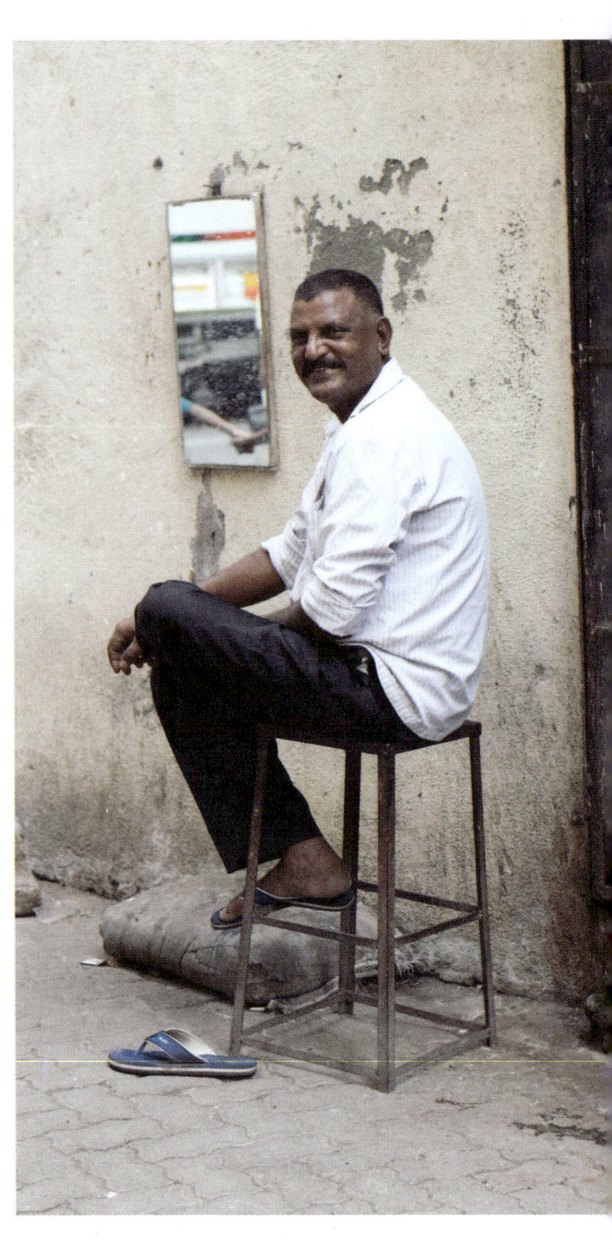

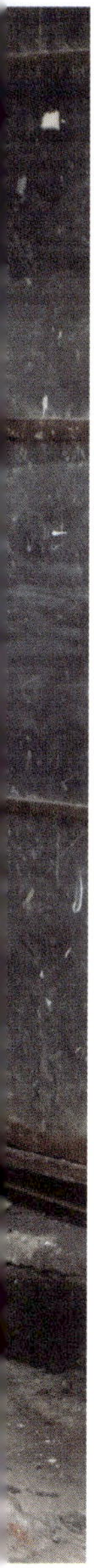

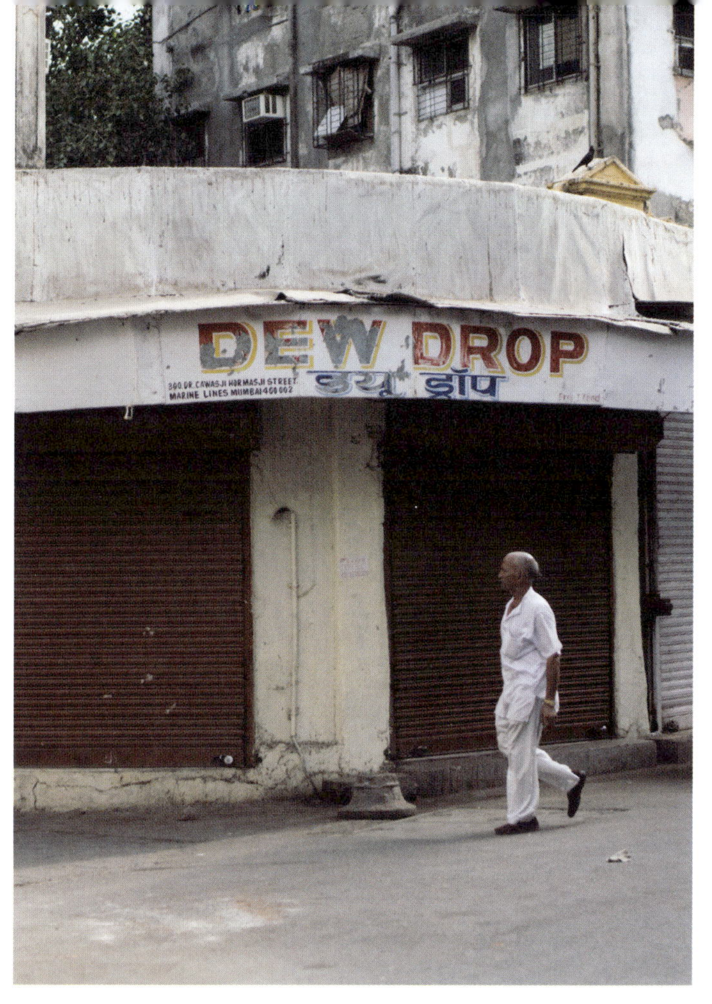

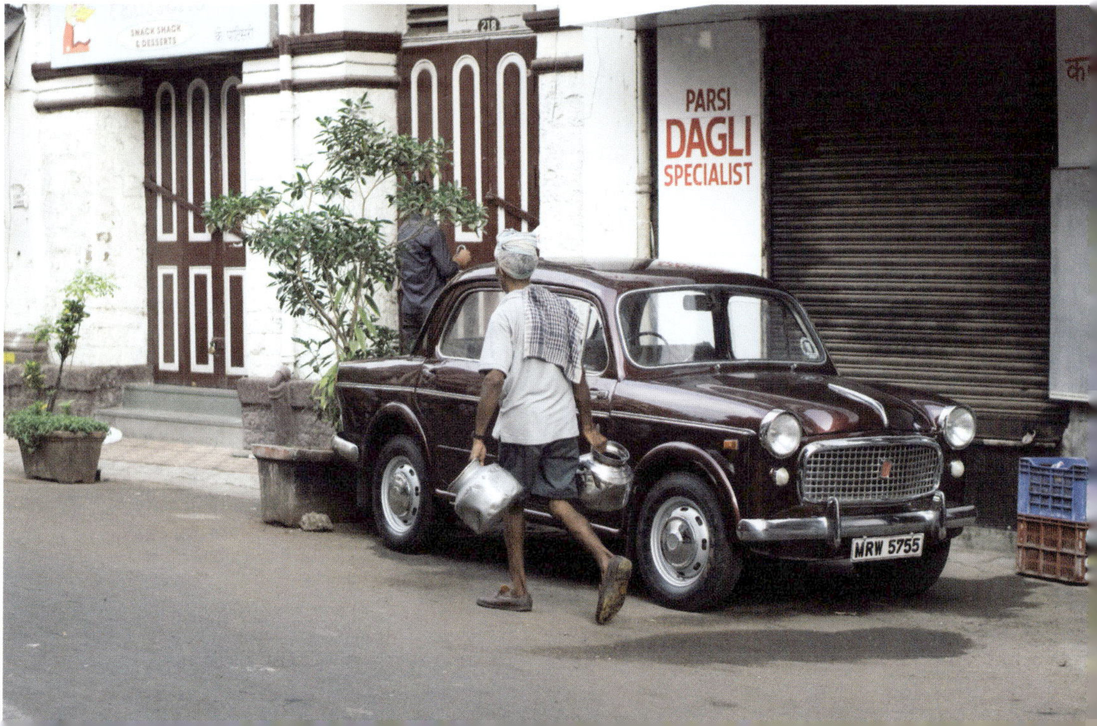

§

Audacity

Mumbai to me out of all the cities in the
world is the most human. By human,
I don't mean humane, but Mumbai as a
median for where humanity stands today.
In Mumbai, more than any other city in
the world, the human struggle to leave its
primitive self behind is visible, in its people,
in its structures. There is an organic
wildness to how the city has grown. It is
like looking at human anatomy exposed.
It is overwhelming, to see the guts, the
gore, the grime, condensed in such a tight
place, throbbing, pulsating. Looking at it
makes you want to throw up, but at the
same time, the sheer audacity of it blows
your mind, humbles you. The city shouldn't
work, but somehow it does. Every year
thousands of migrants come to the city
with the hope of making a better life. The
city has no plan for this influx, and every
time a plan is presented, it is redundant
the day it is published.

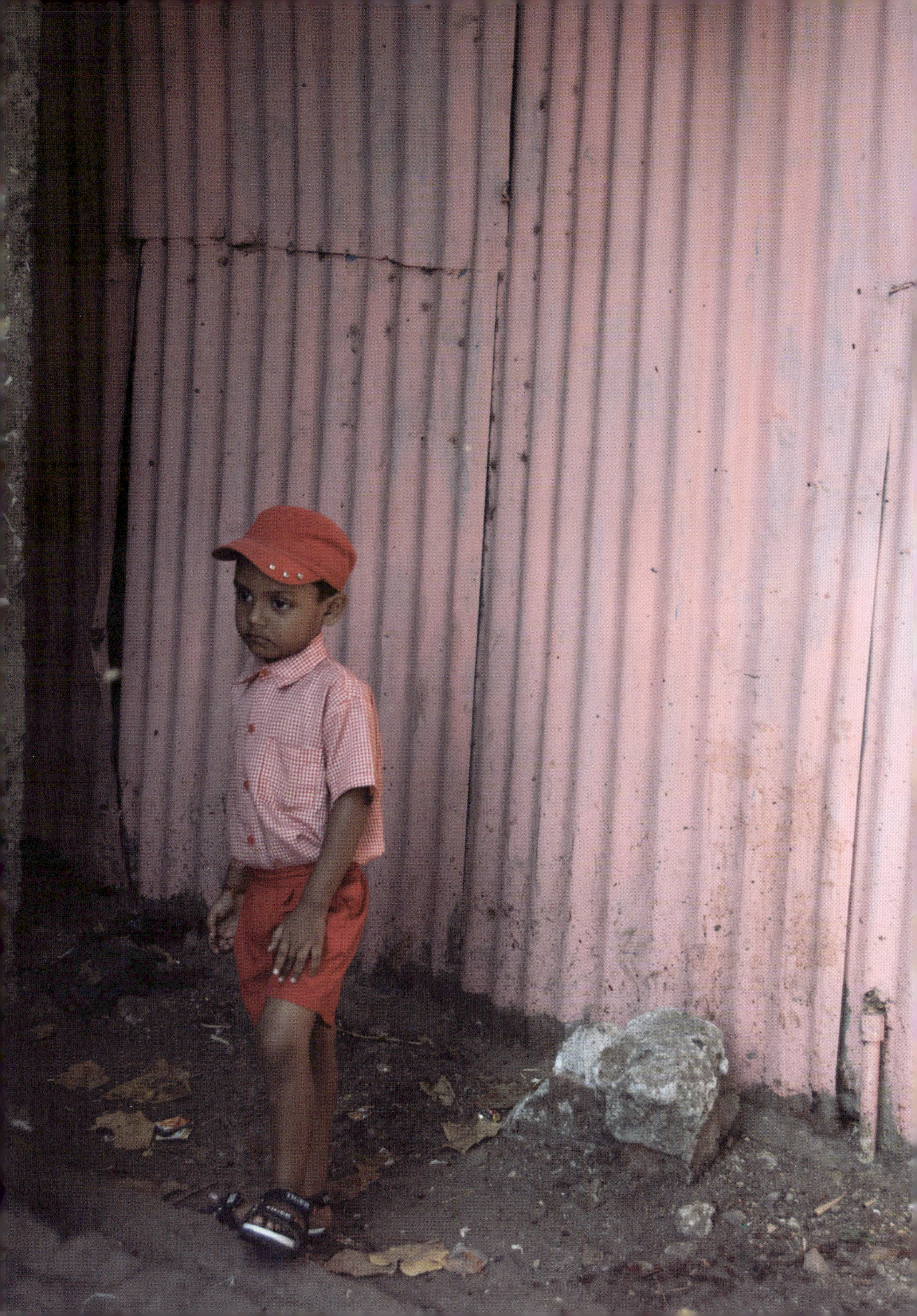

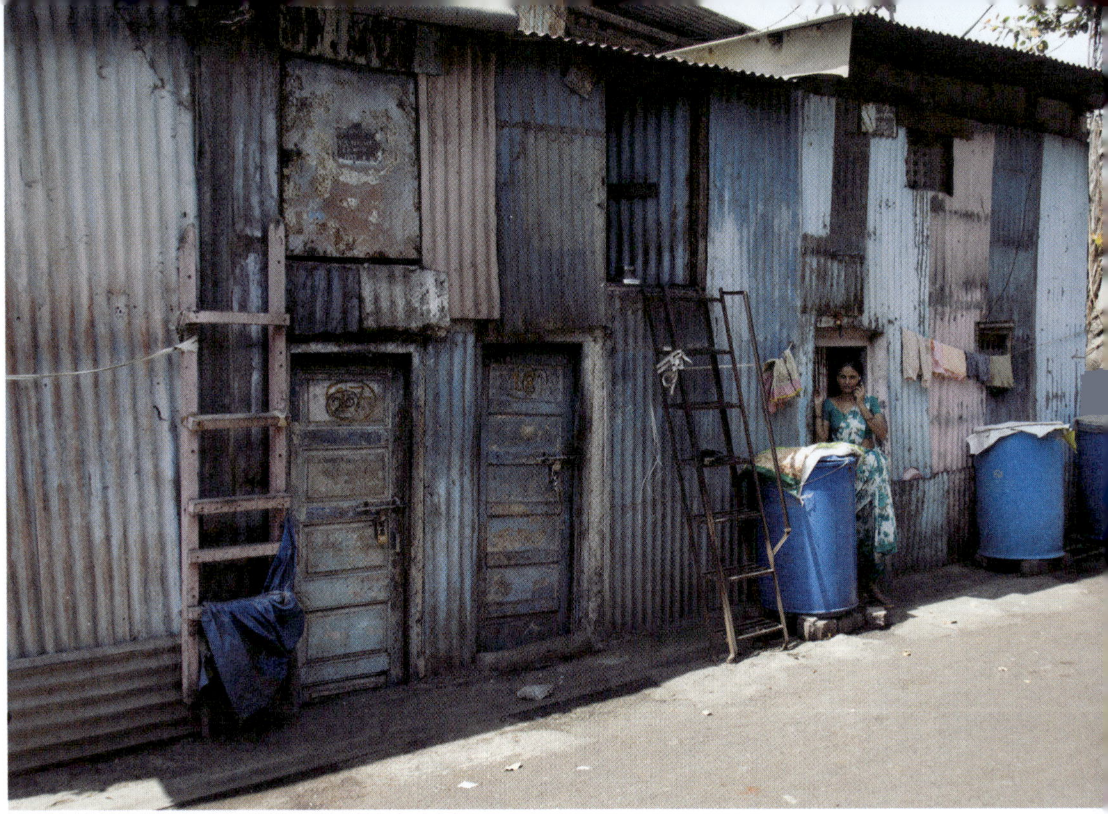

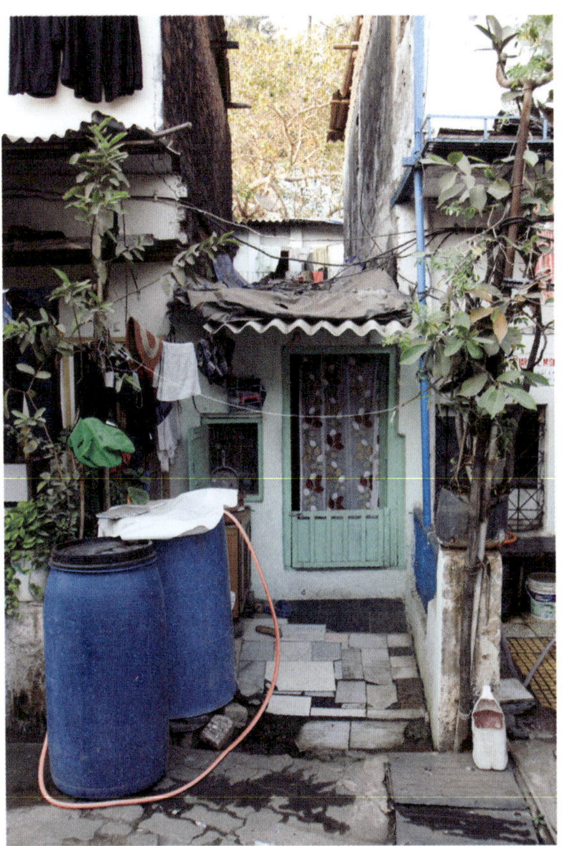
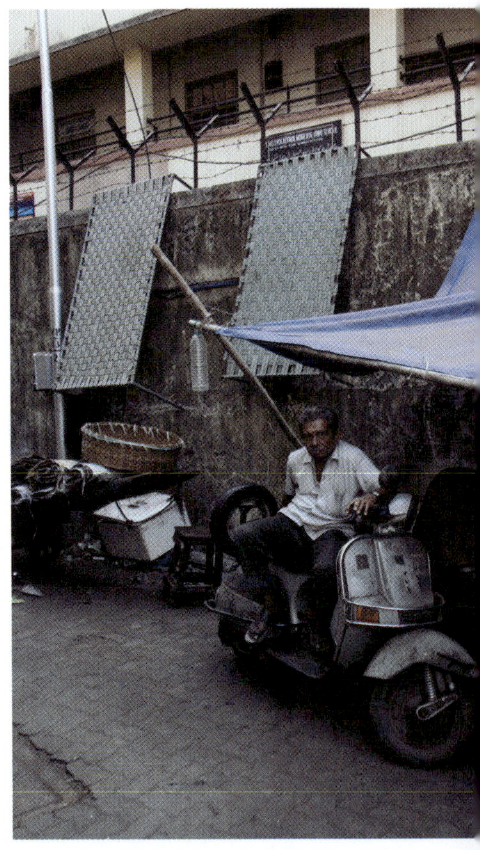

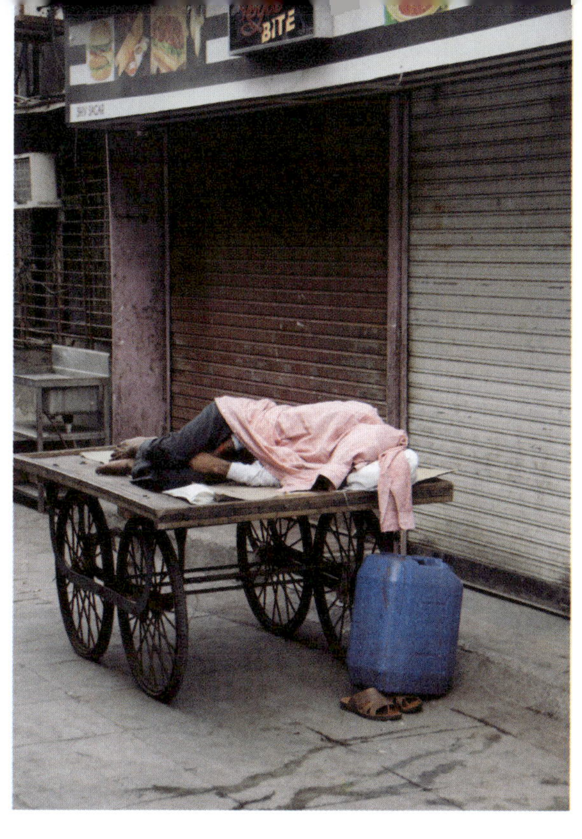

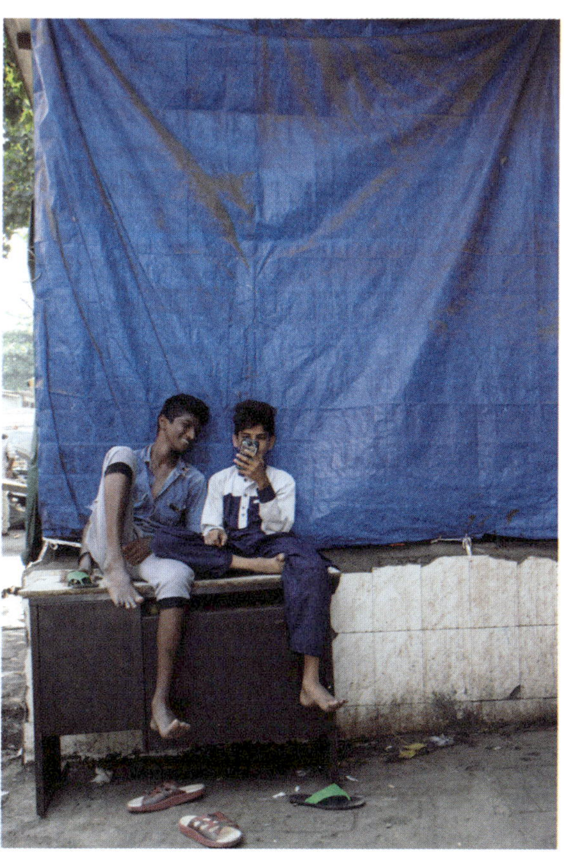

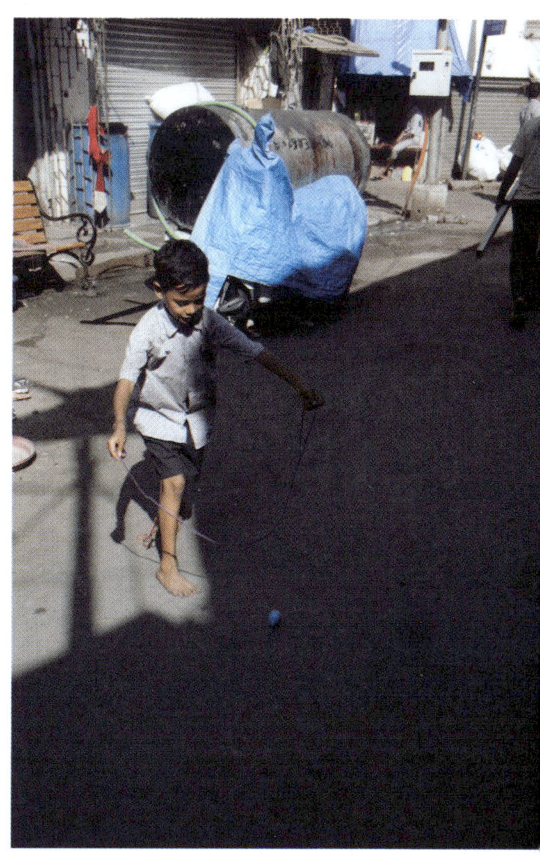

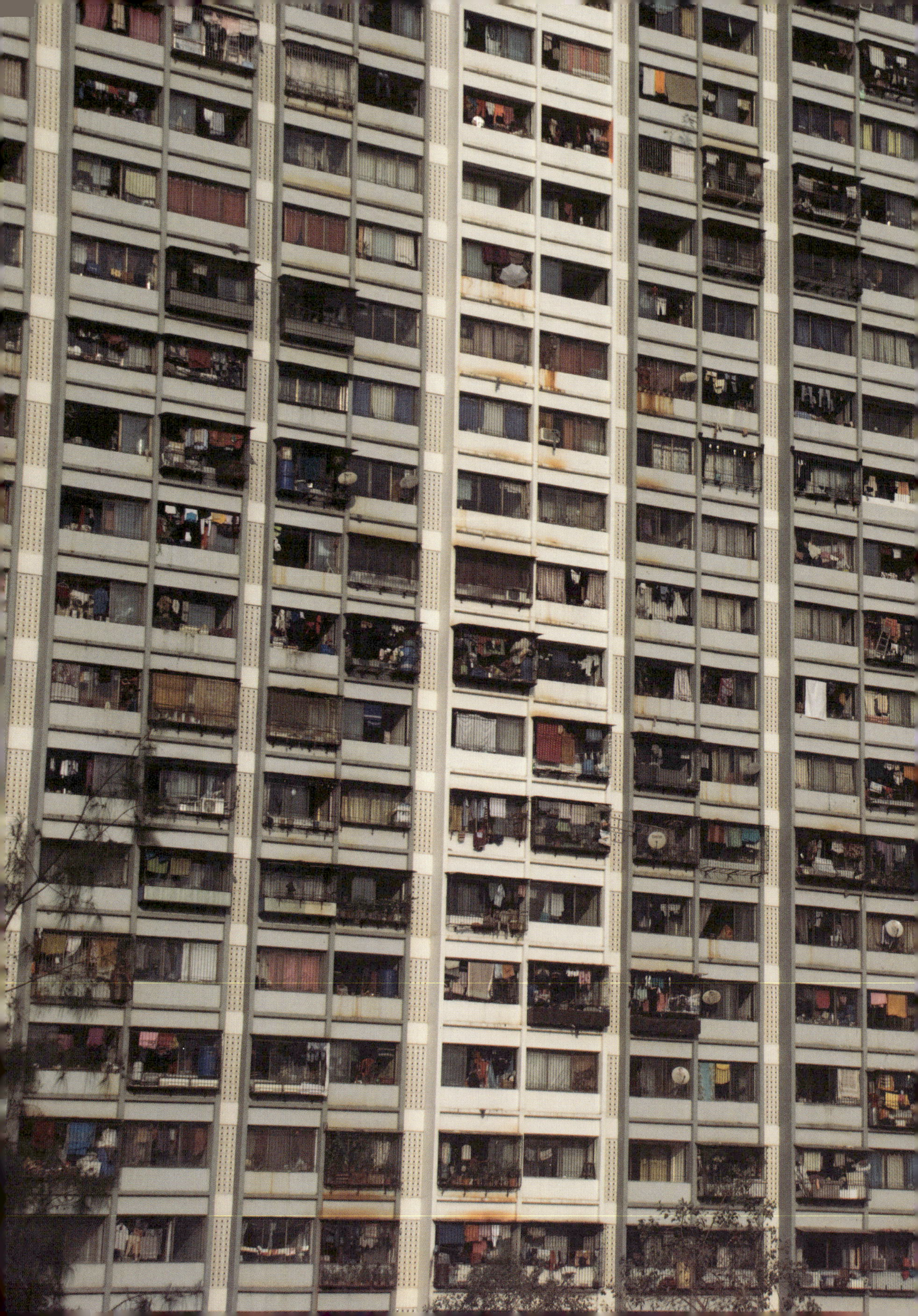

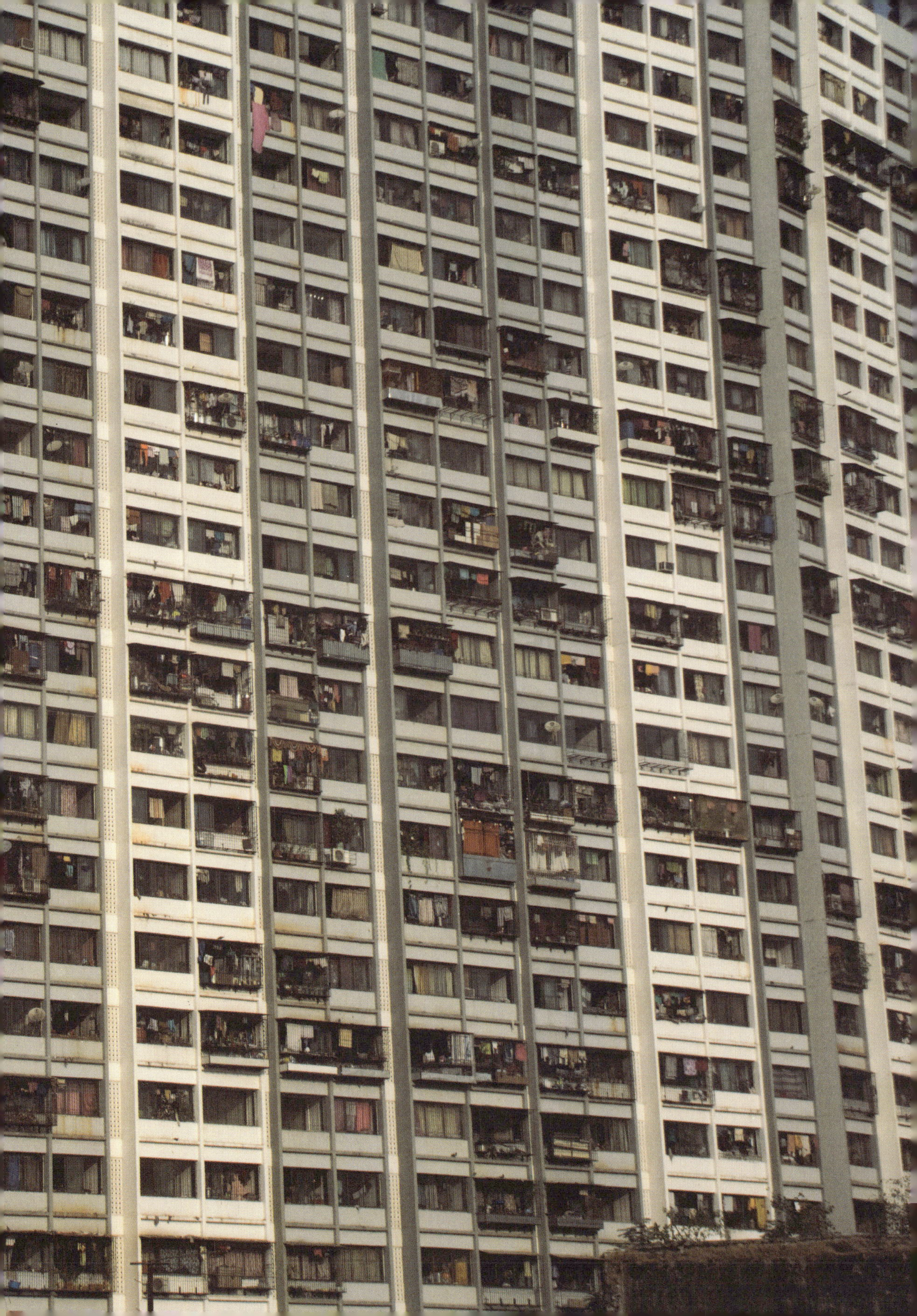

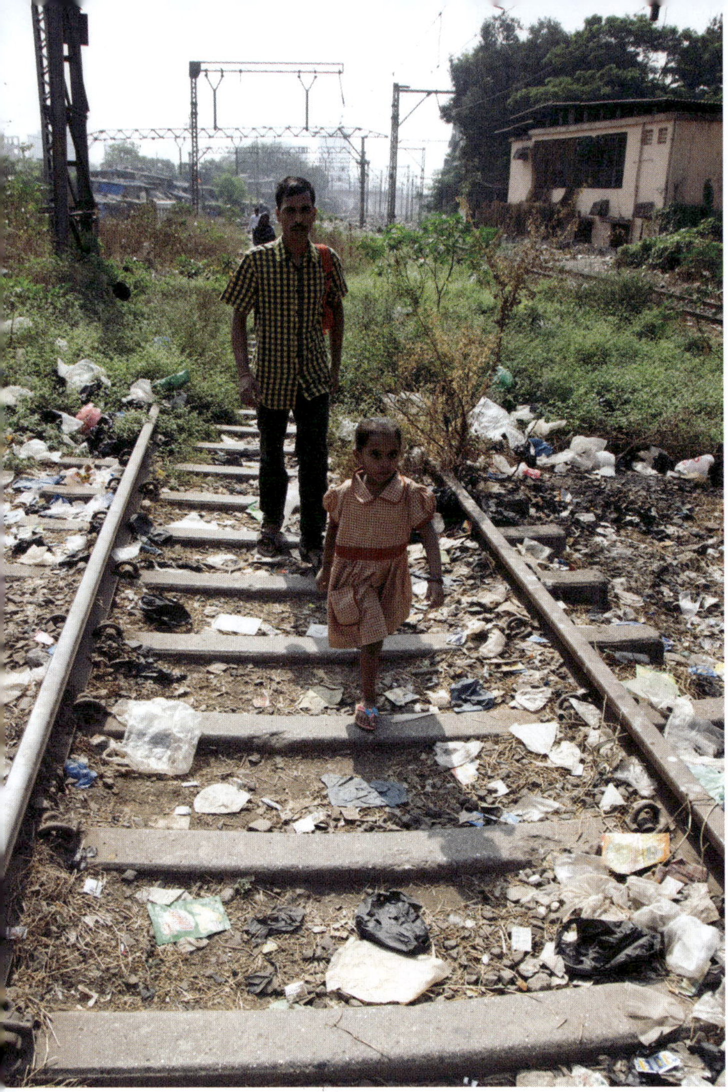

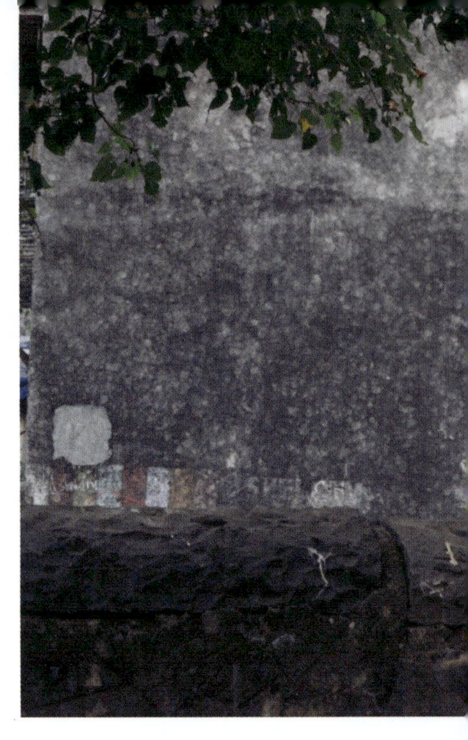

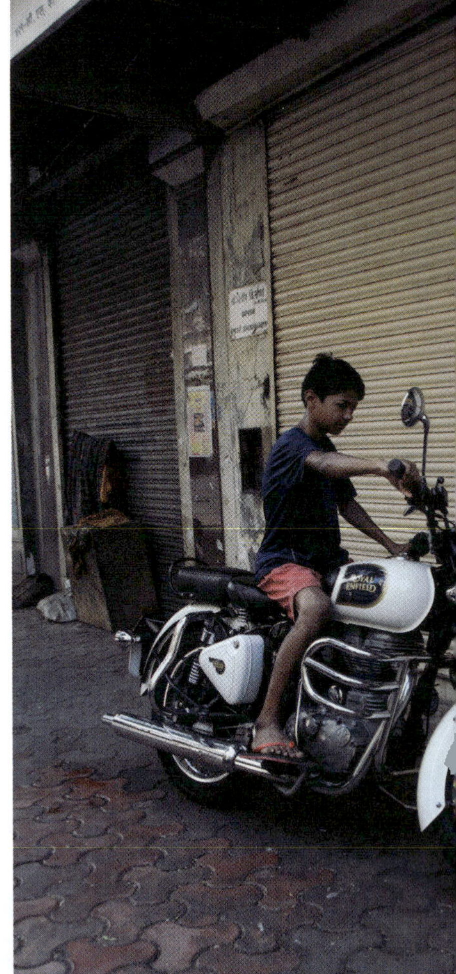

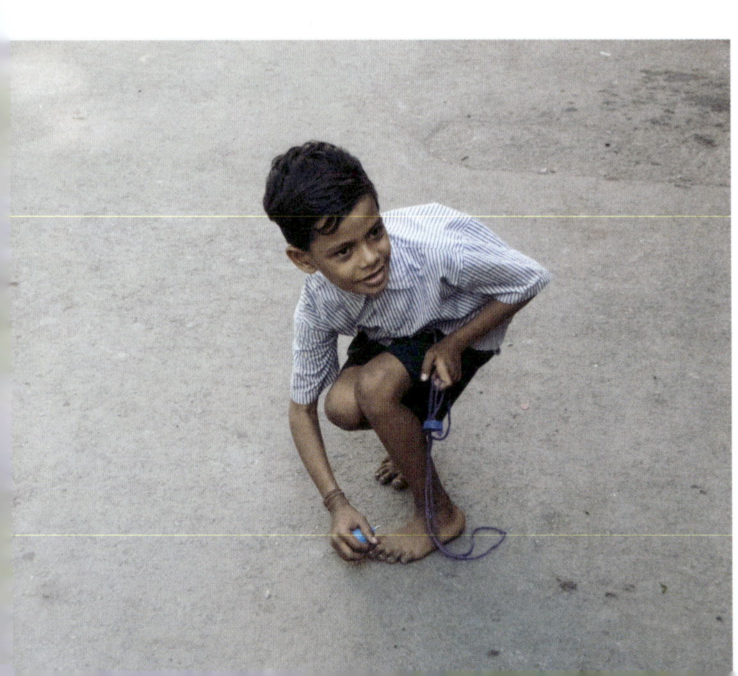

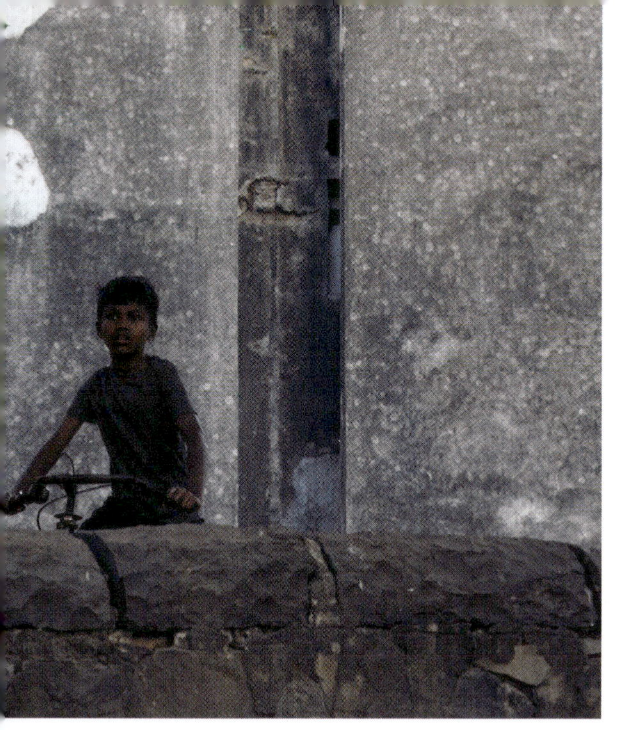

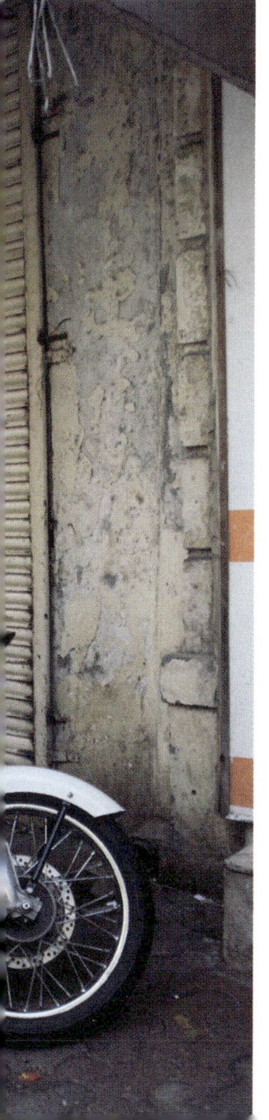
ABDUL KADAR ABDUL LATIE
SOPARIWALA EXPORTS

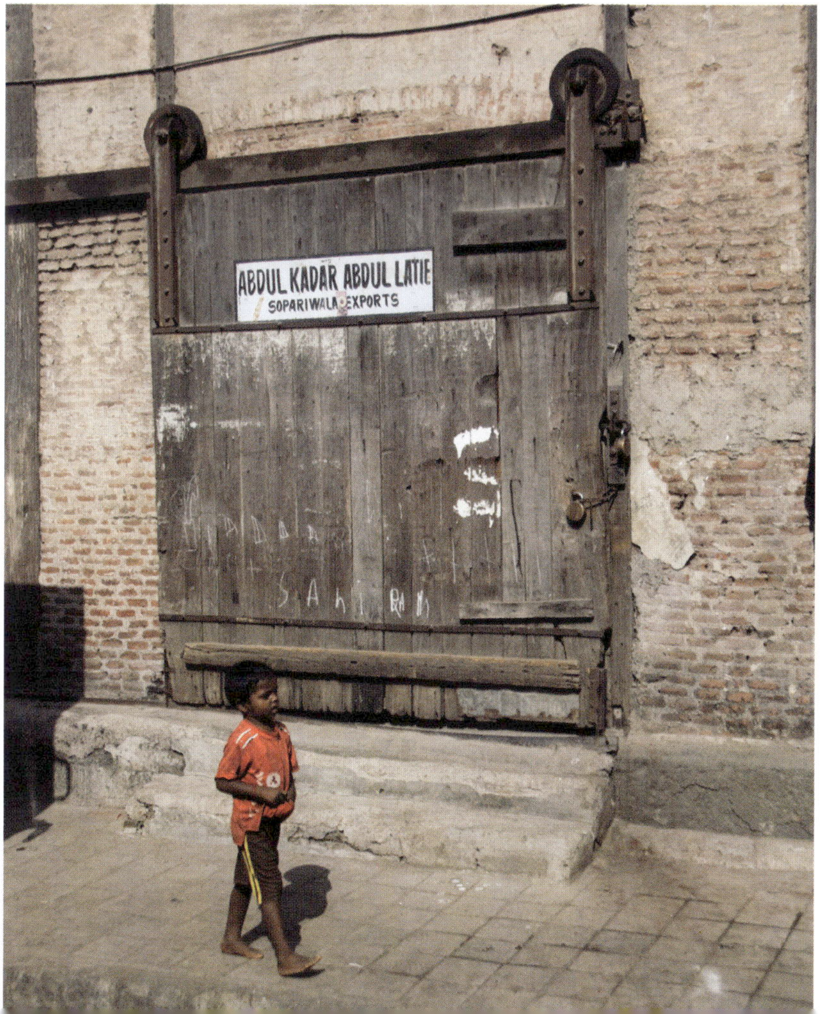

TWO CITIES

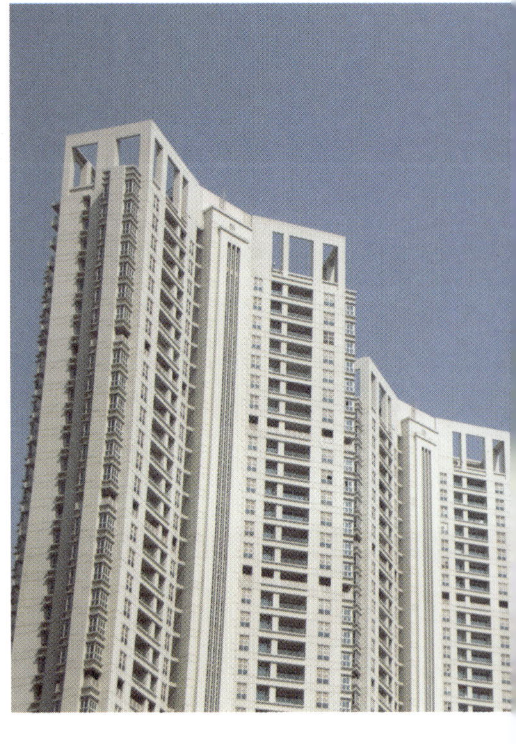

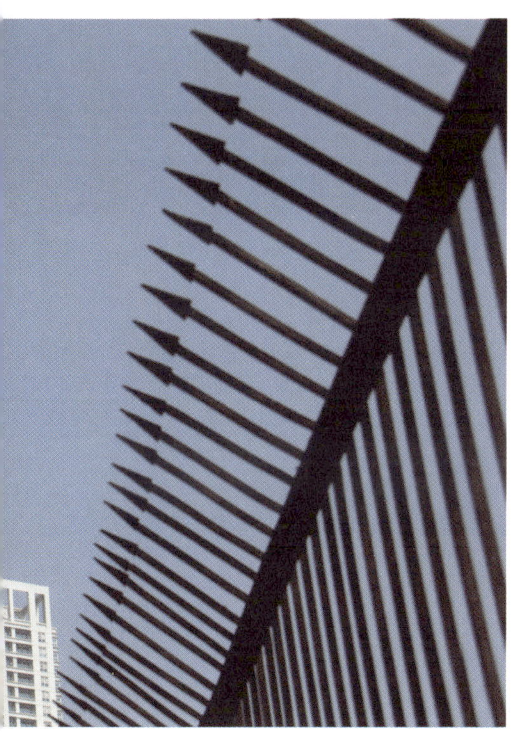

Walking the entire city, meticulously tracing every street was quite a tedious exercise.

Today's Mumbai is not walker-friendly. I remember my dad
telling me that in the 1970s he'd walk to his guitar class in
Bandra. He'd walk from the train station to Bandstand,
a distance of about four kilometres. It must have been a pleasant
walk then, but today, not many people would voluntarily walk in
Mumbai. Shops or bastis encroach the footpaths, and if not, the
footpaths are either dirty or broken. The elements are harsh –
the weather is often hot, muggy, or rainy. Finally, there is the
emotional toll, to walk through the desperate conditions that
most Mumbaikars live in can be disheartening.

Living conditions are difficult all over Mumbai, but the
ones who have it the hardest are the ones who live on the street:
migrant labourers who have to manage in makeshift shacks
along the roads and bridges they are helping to build. There are
other parts where the people haven't just arrived, forgotten
areas that were once thriving. In Central Mumbai, for every one
of the Saat (seven) Rastaas (roads) that is sprouting a gated
community, the other rastaa is falling off the development
wagon.

In Mumbai, the two worlds, polar opposites, have always
existed. In Bandra, next to our apartment building was a large

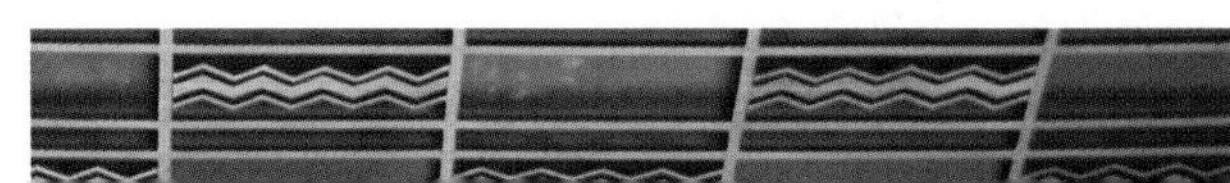

basti. But some of the parts that I just saw during my walks were worse than anything I had ever seen before. New apartments in the city are now ten times higher. Earlier, all the building gates were see-through, the compound walls open. They were private property, but they felt transparent. You got hints of the everyday from them. The same daily cycles, of play, work, drying clothes, of residents sitting in balconies, drinking chai and reading their daily newspaper. Older building colonies leaked onto the street, and you could see their gardens. The newer developments seem more opaque. Today's luxury apartments have even taken their gardens into the sky, moved them ten stories up, above their stacked parking bays.

Nostalgia is a strong impulse, a yearning for simpler times. But it can be unfair to the ones who do not have. Mobility between classes is necessary, and the bigger the gaps, the harder it is for people to grow out of them. Sadly, progress in India is binary, off, on, then off again. Change only comes when things have gone too far, and often it is disruptive. Change which has come too late and at the expense of the mill workers, the craftspeople, the kirana (small retail) shops...

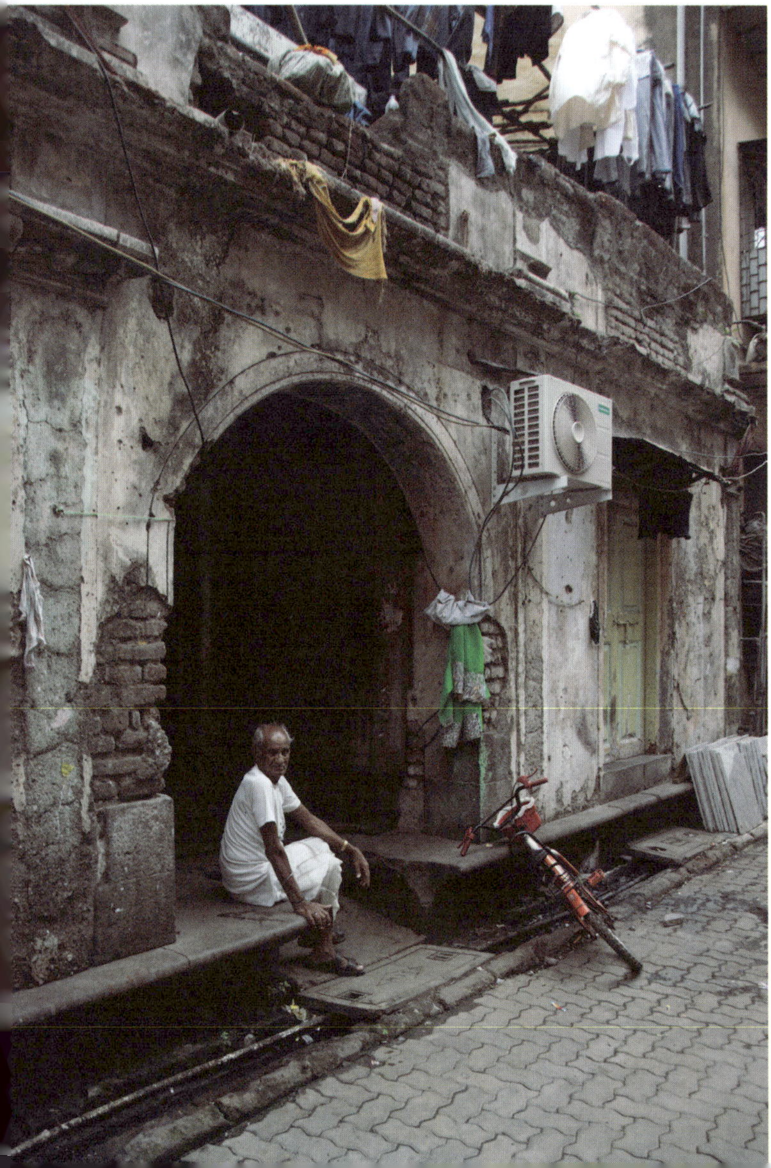

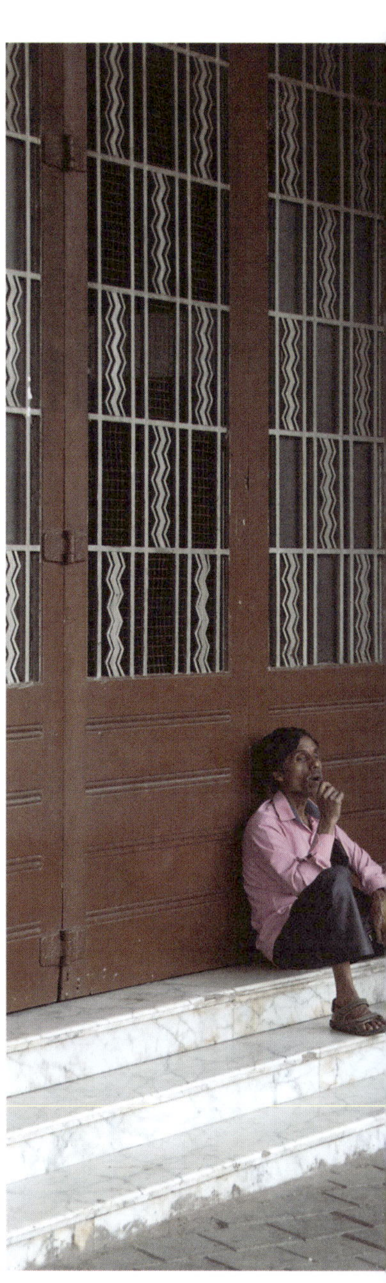

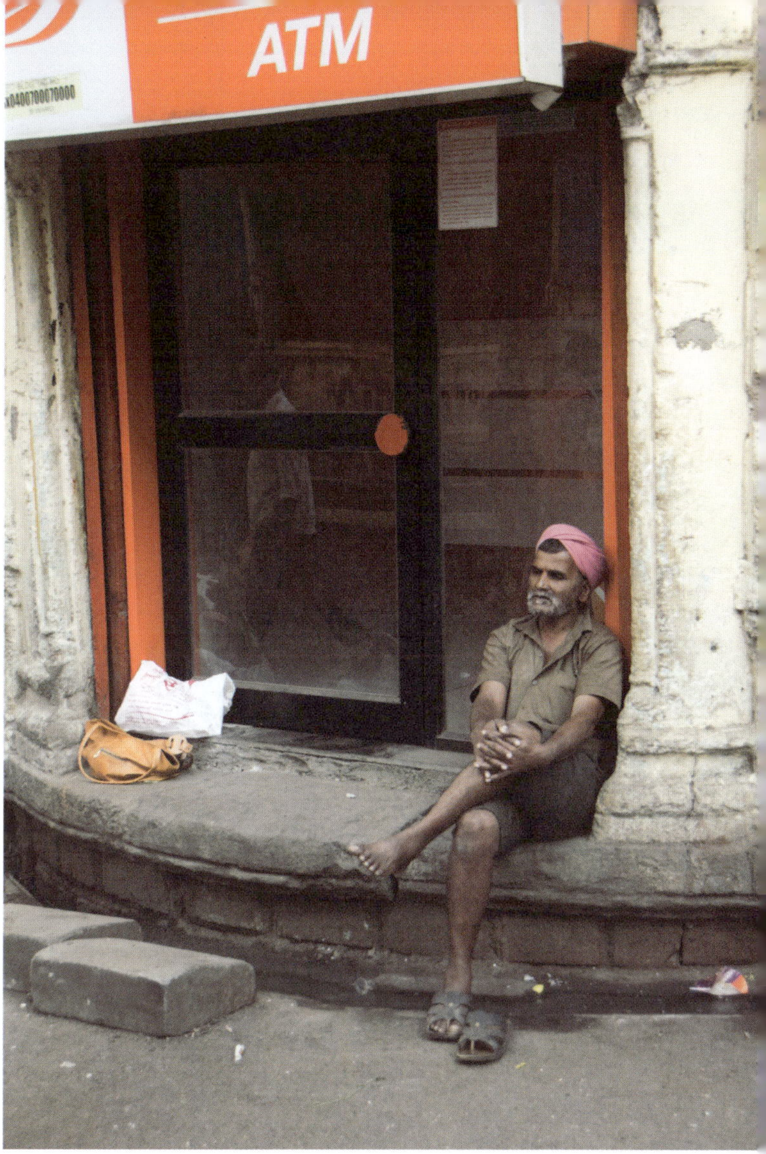

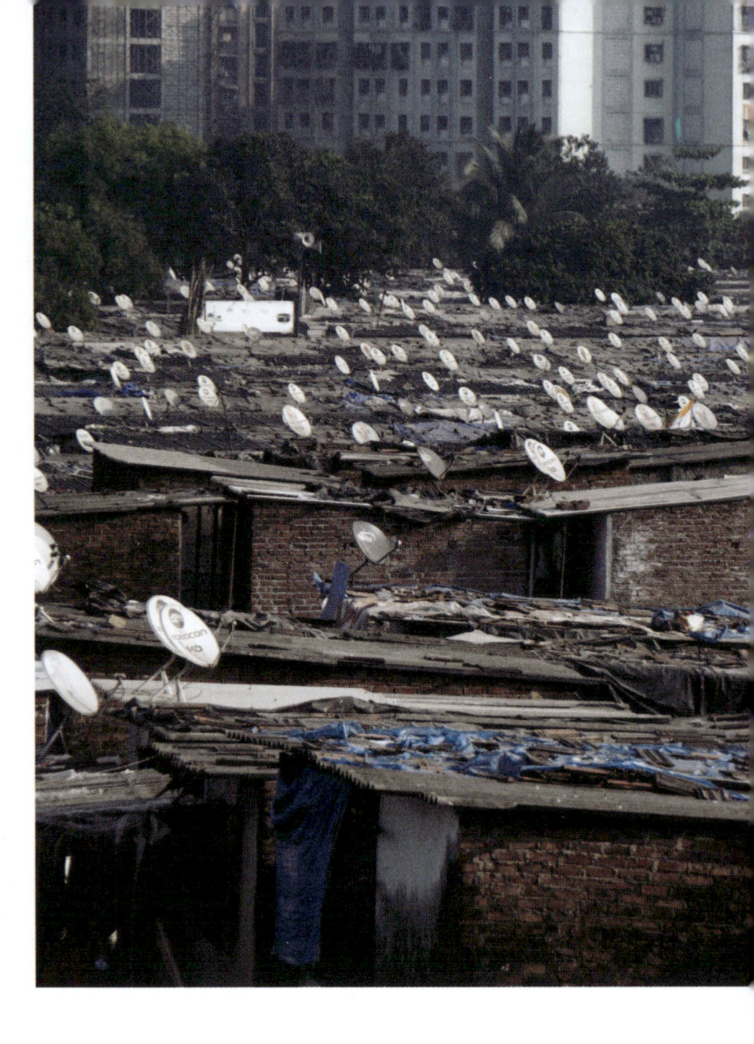

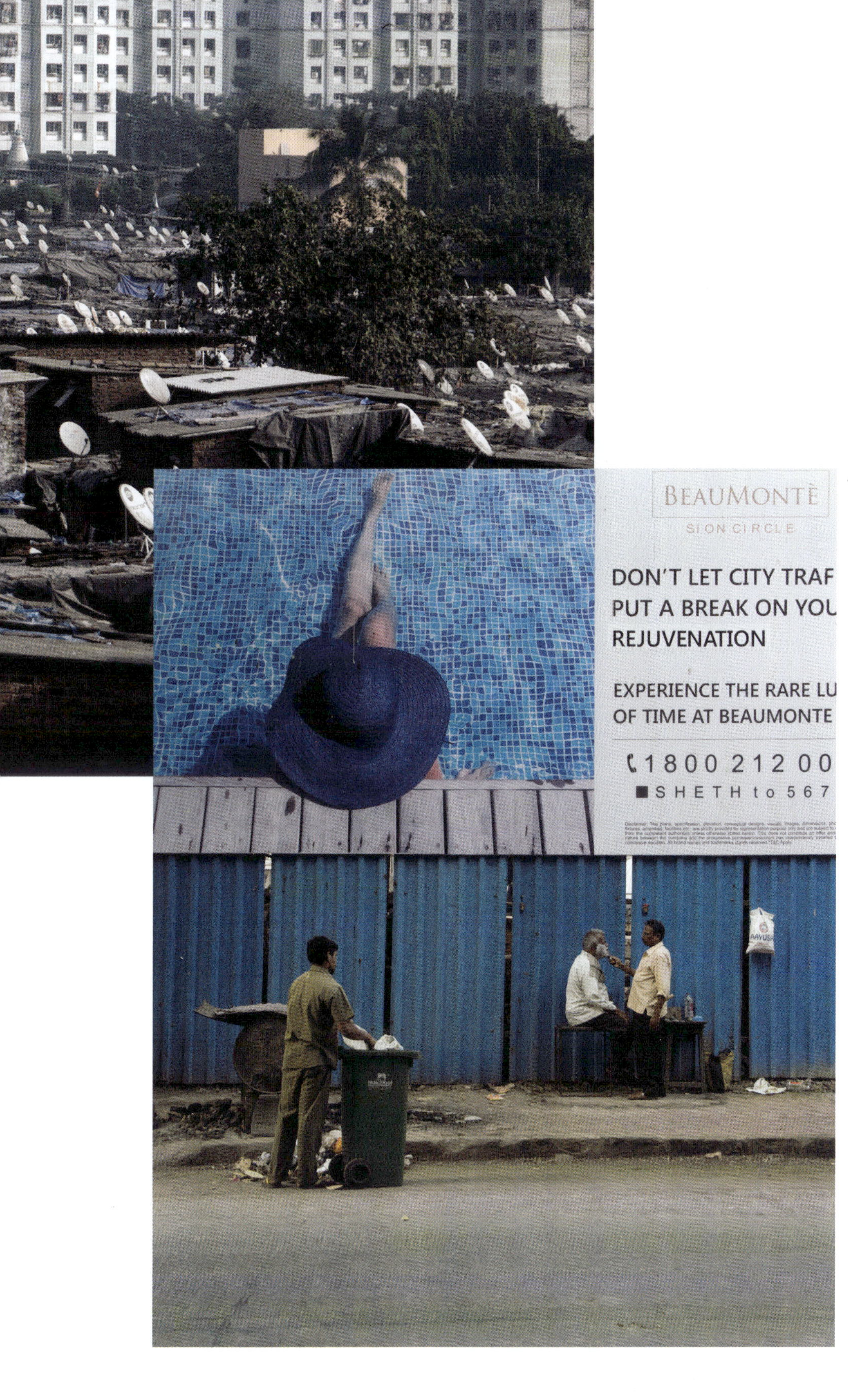
BeauMontè
SION CIRCLE
DON'T LET CITY TRAF
PUT A BREAK ON YOU
REJUVENATION
EXPERIENCE THE RARE LU
OF TIME AT BEAUMONTE
1800 212 00
SHETH to 567

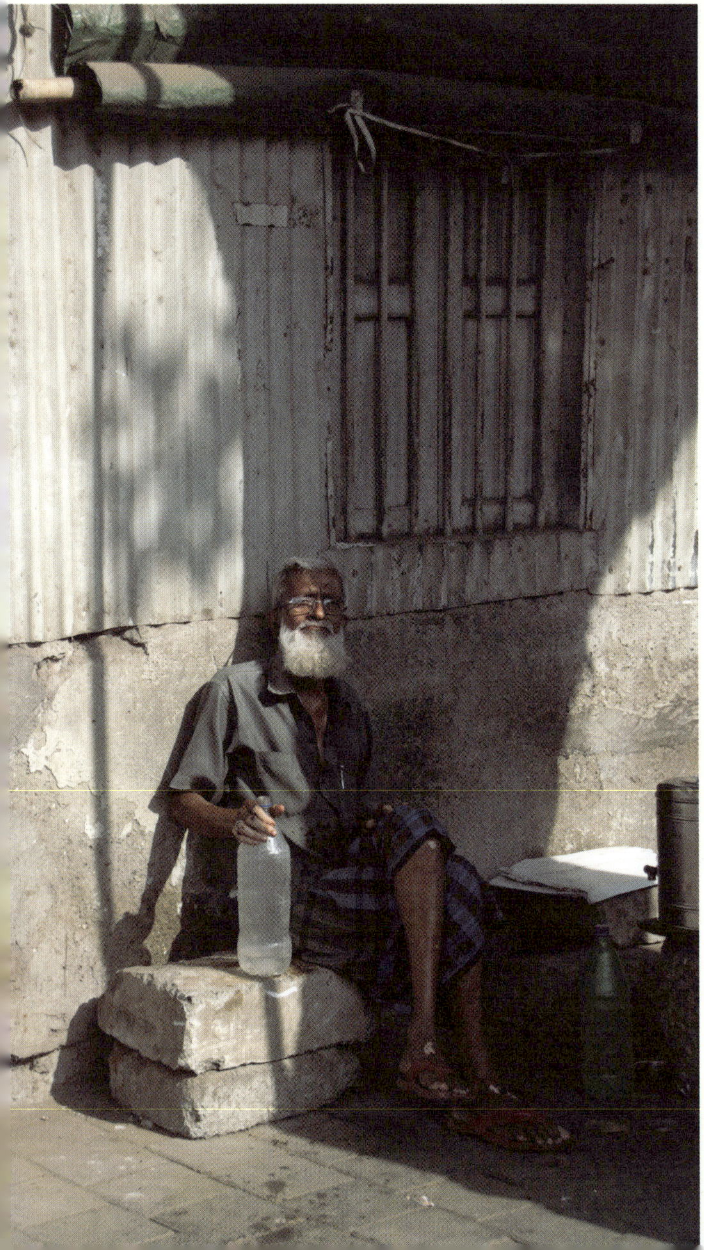

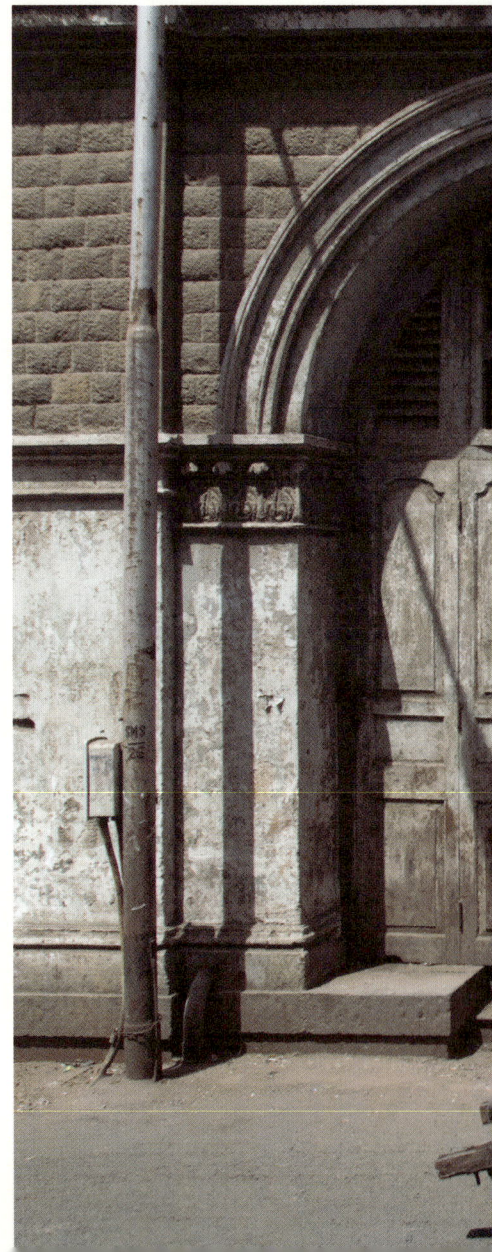

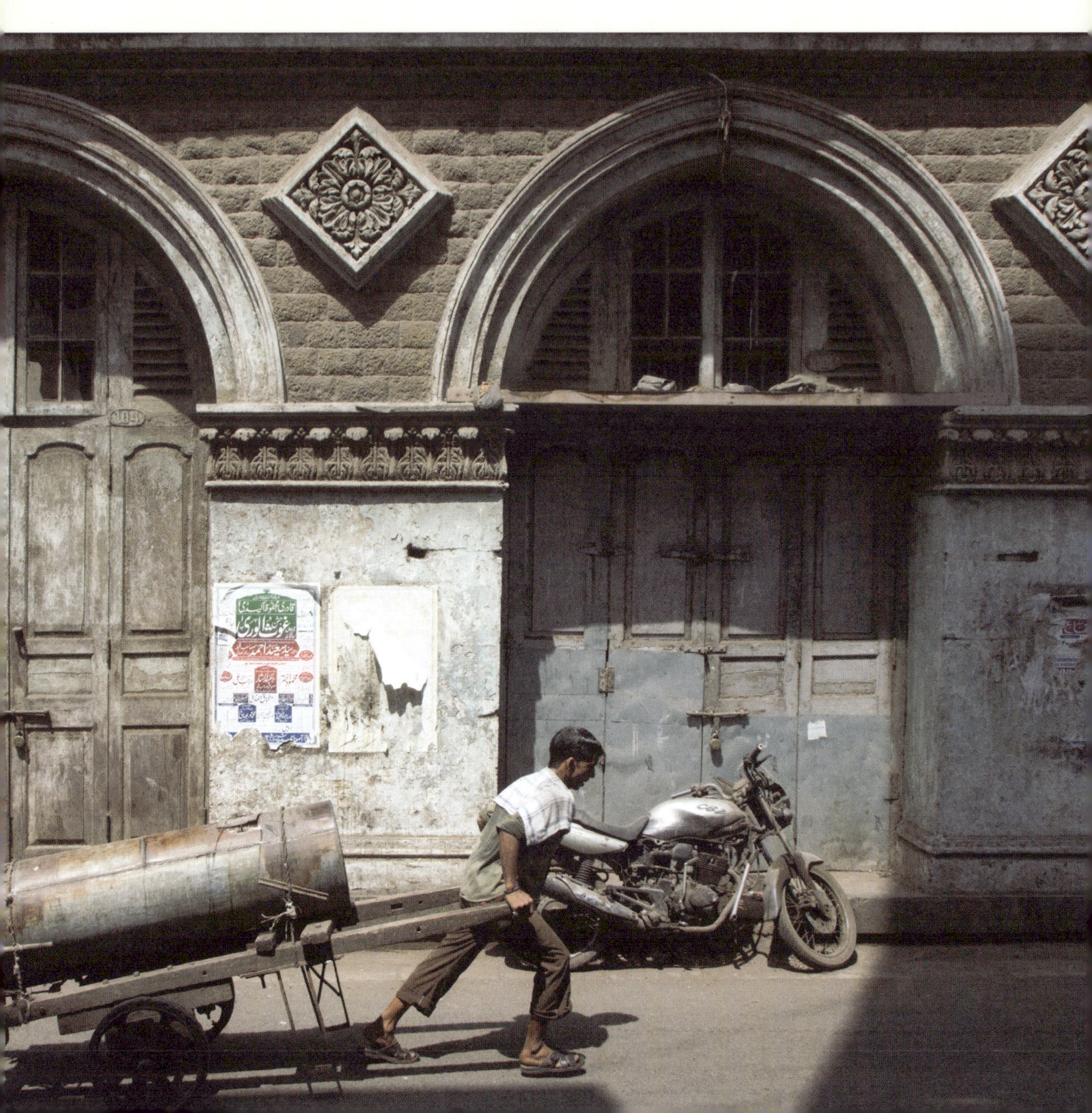

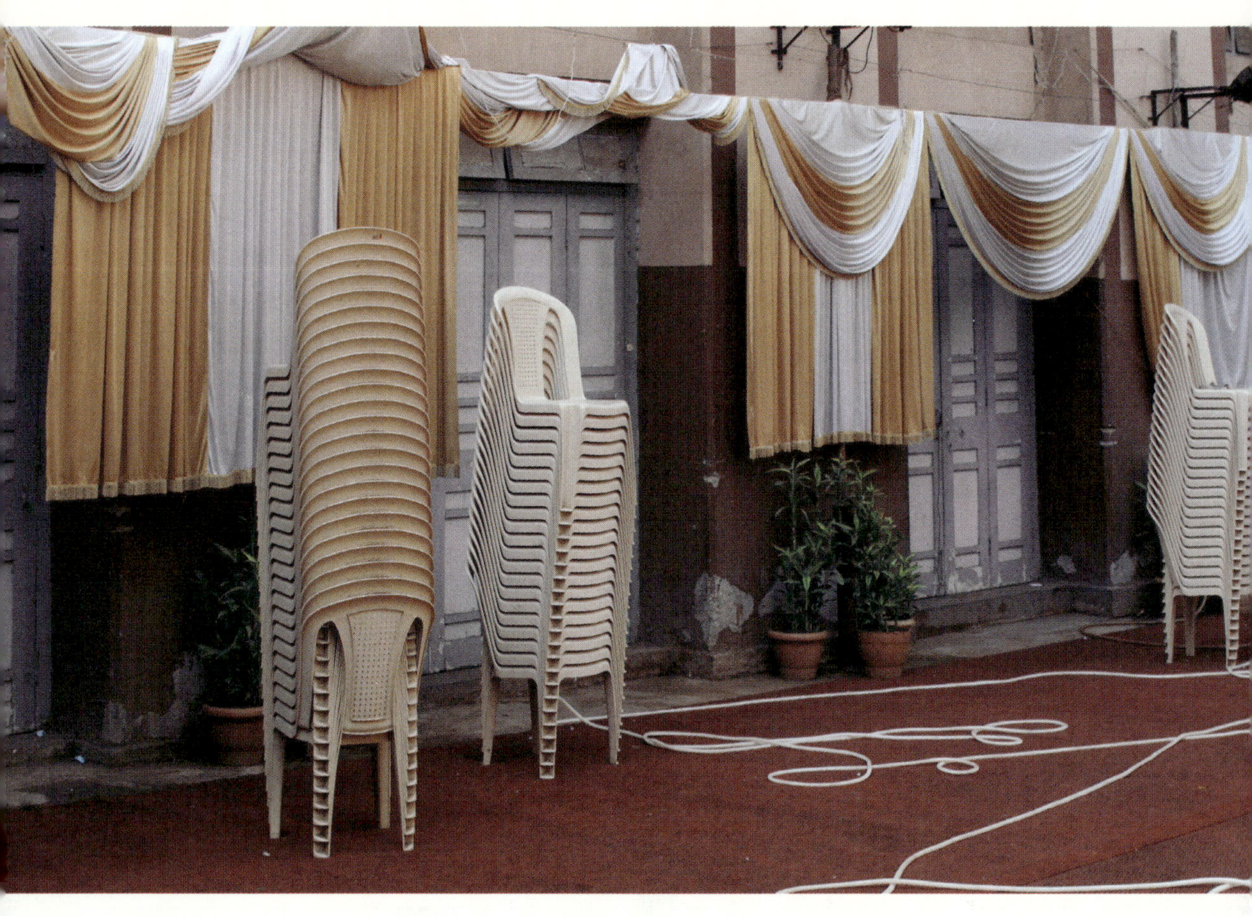

Masjid

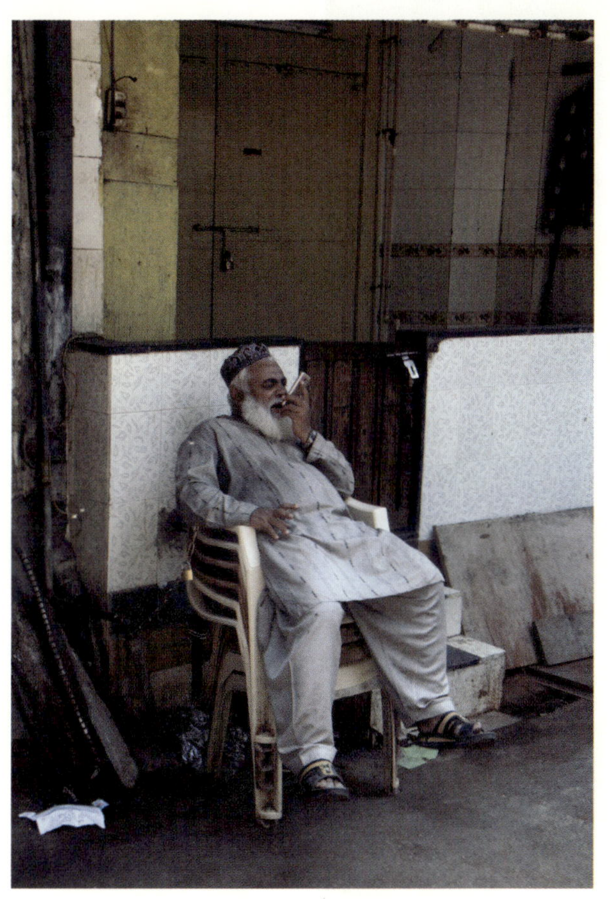

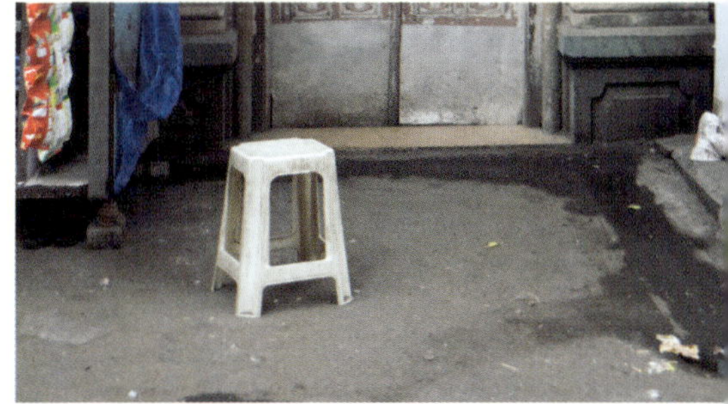

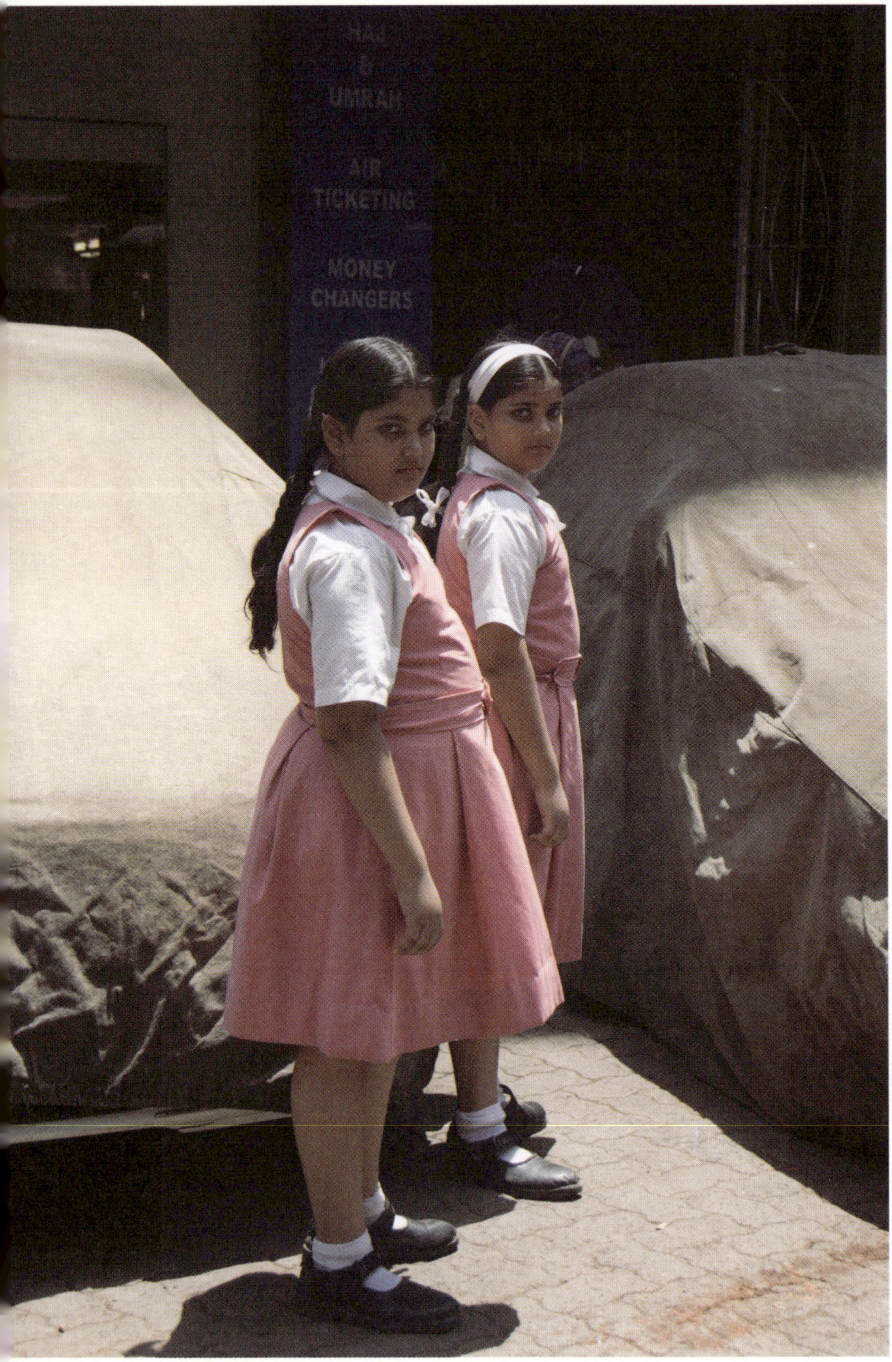

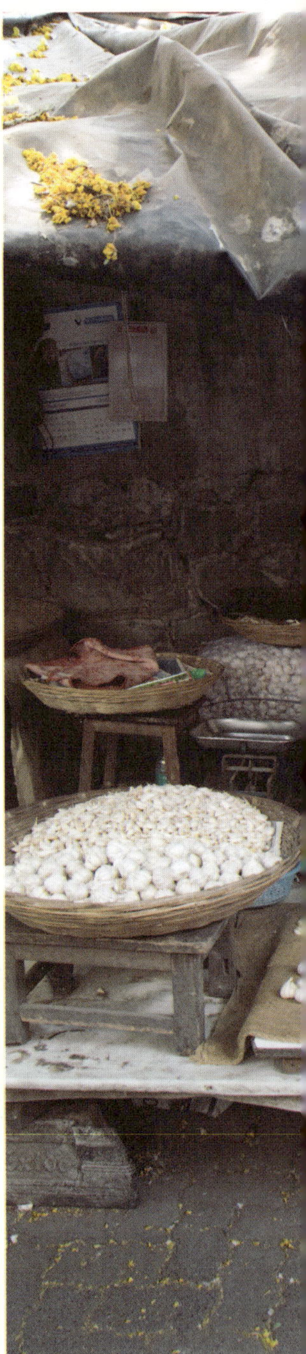

Masjid

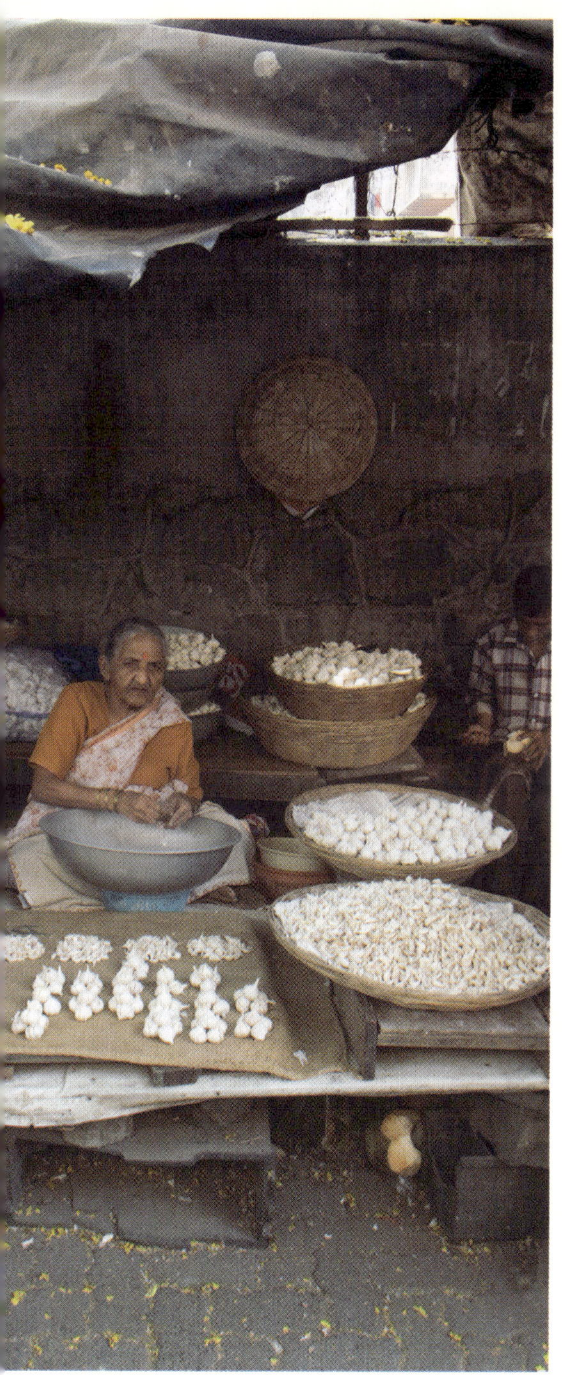

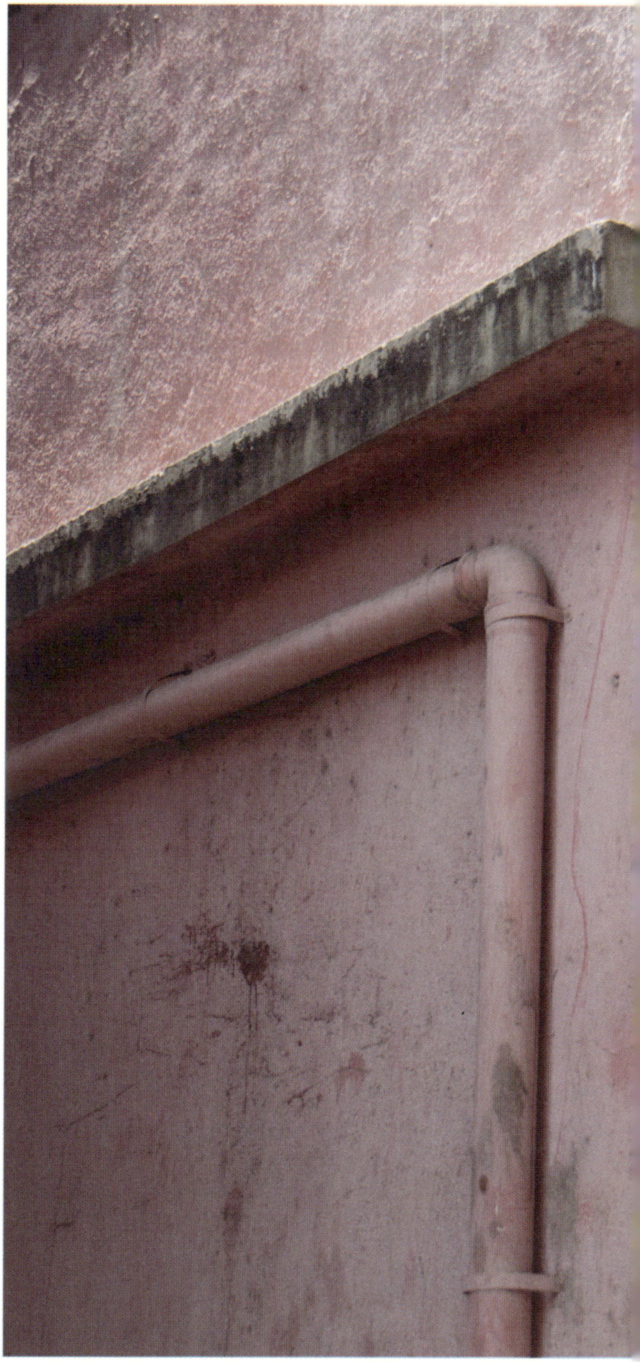

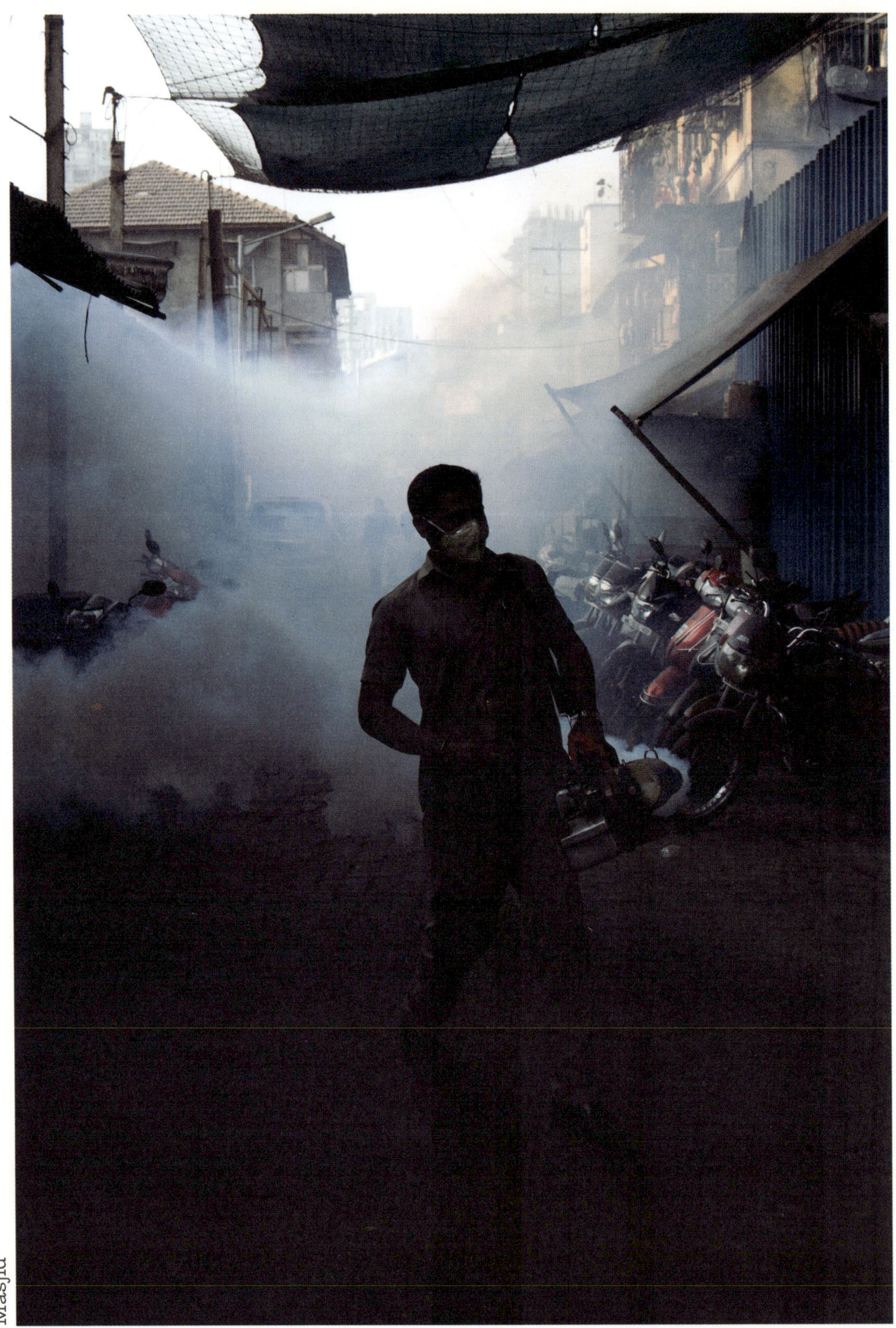

Masjid

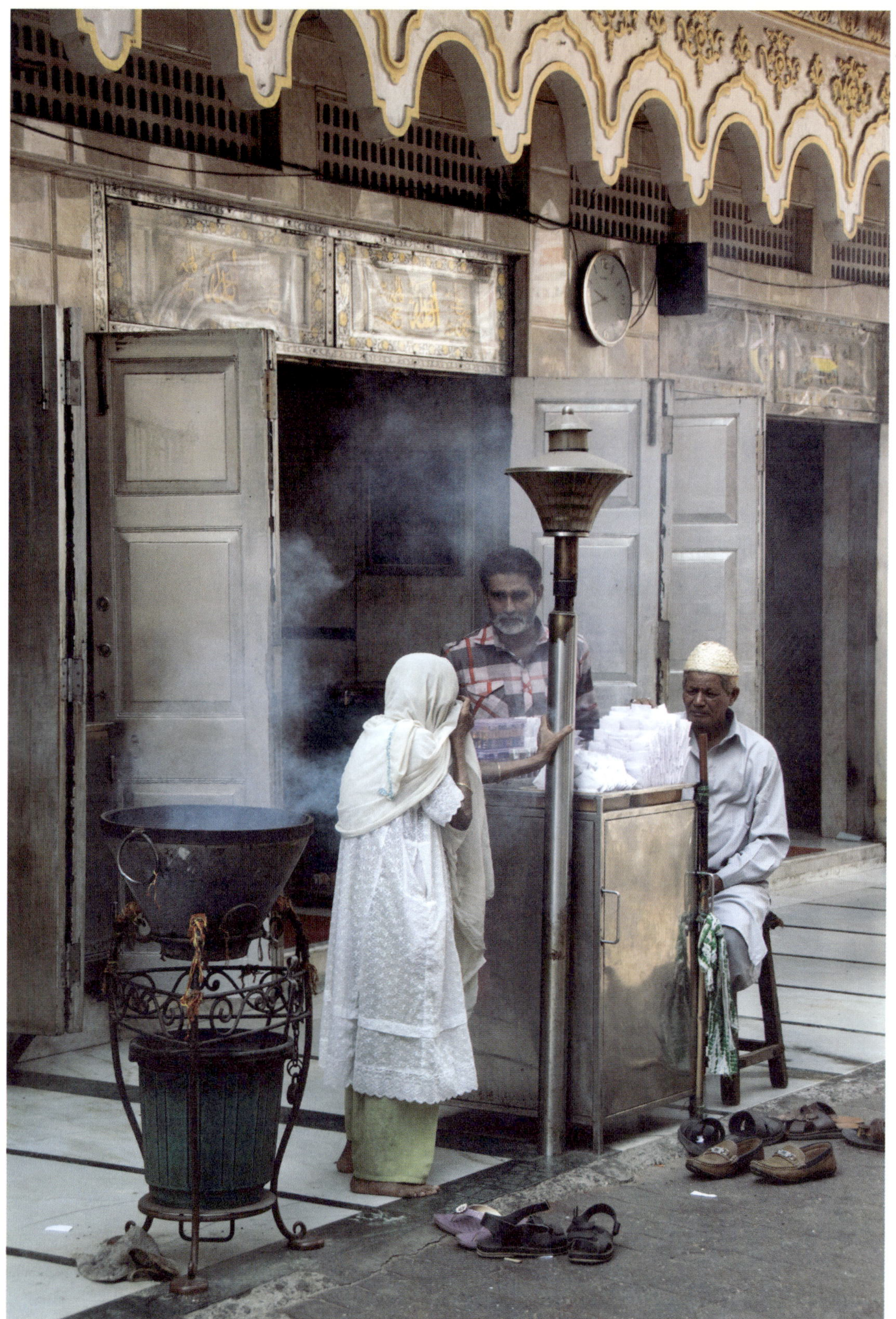

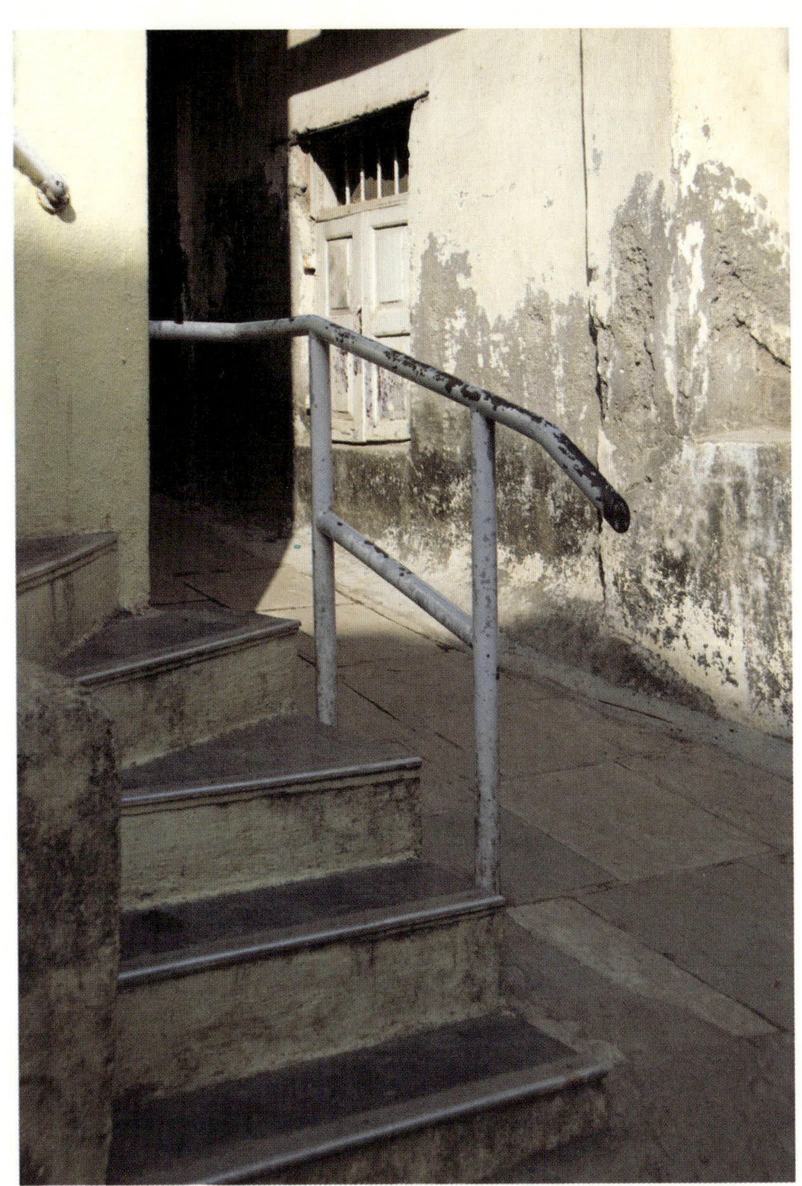

Byculla.

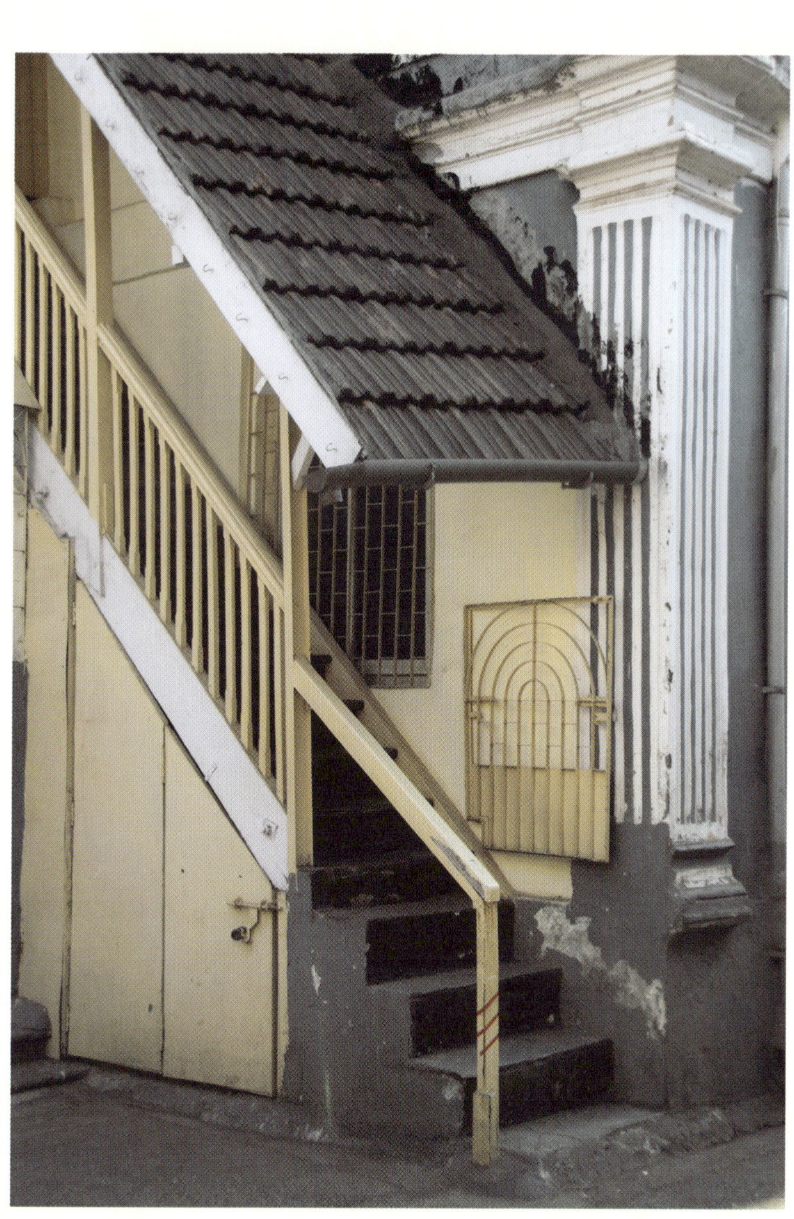

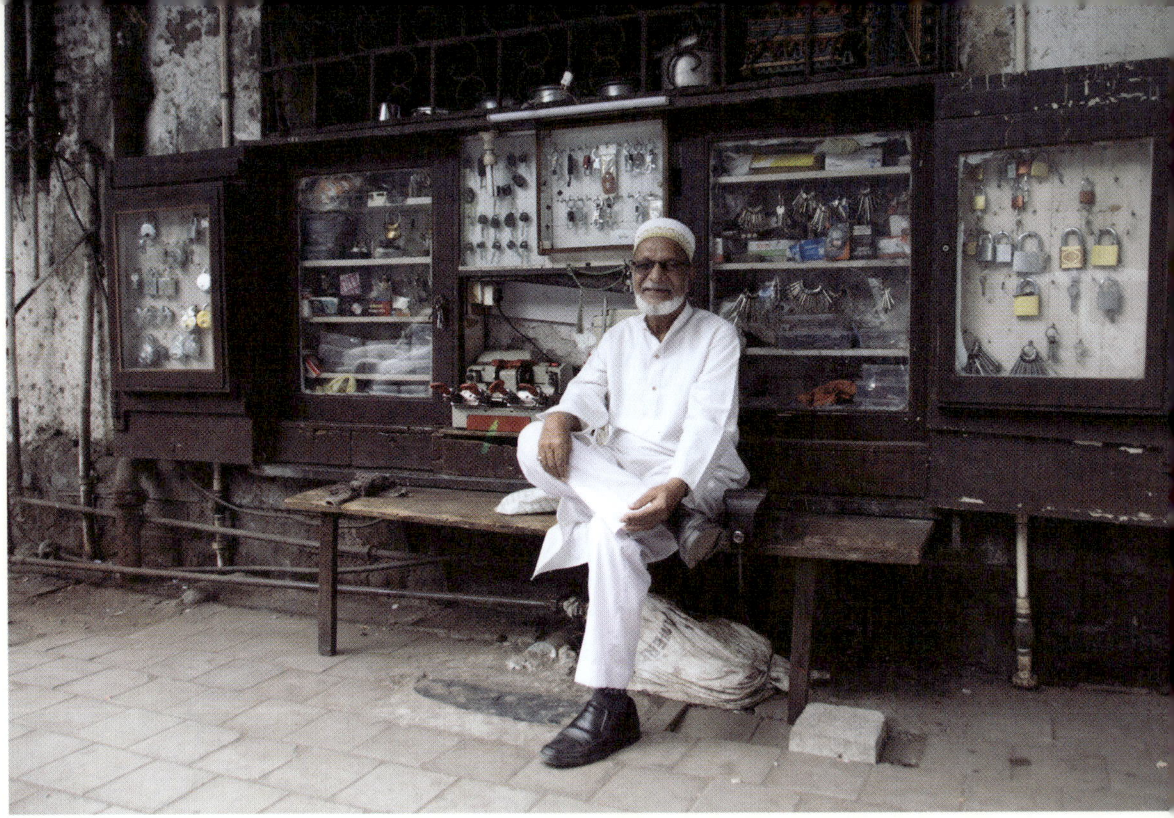

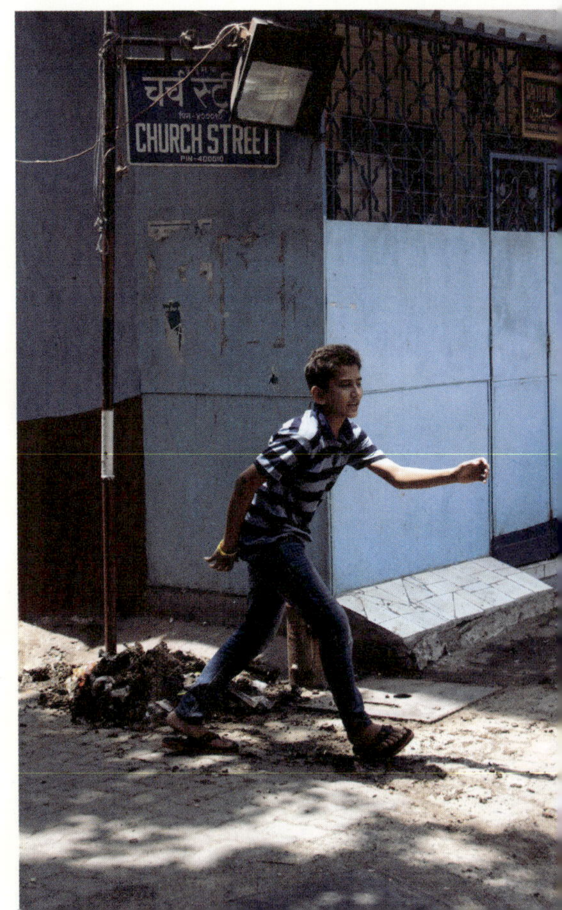

Byculla.

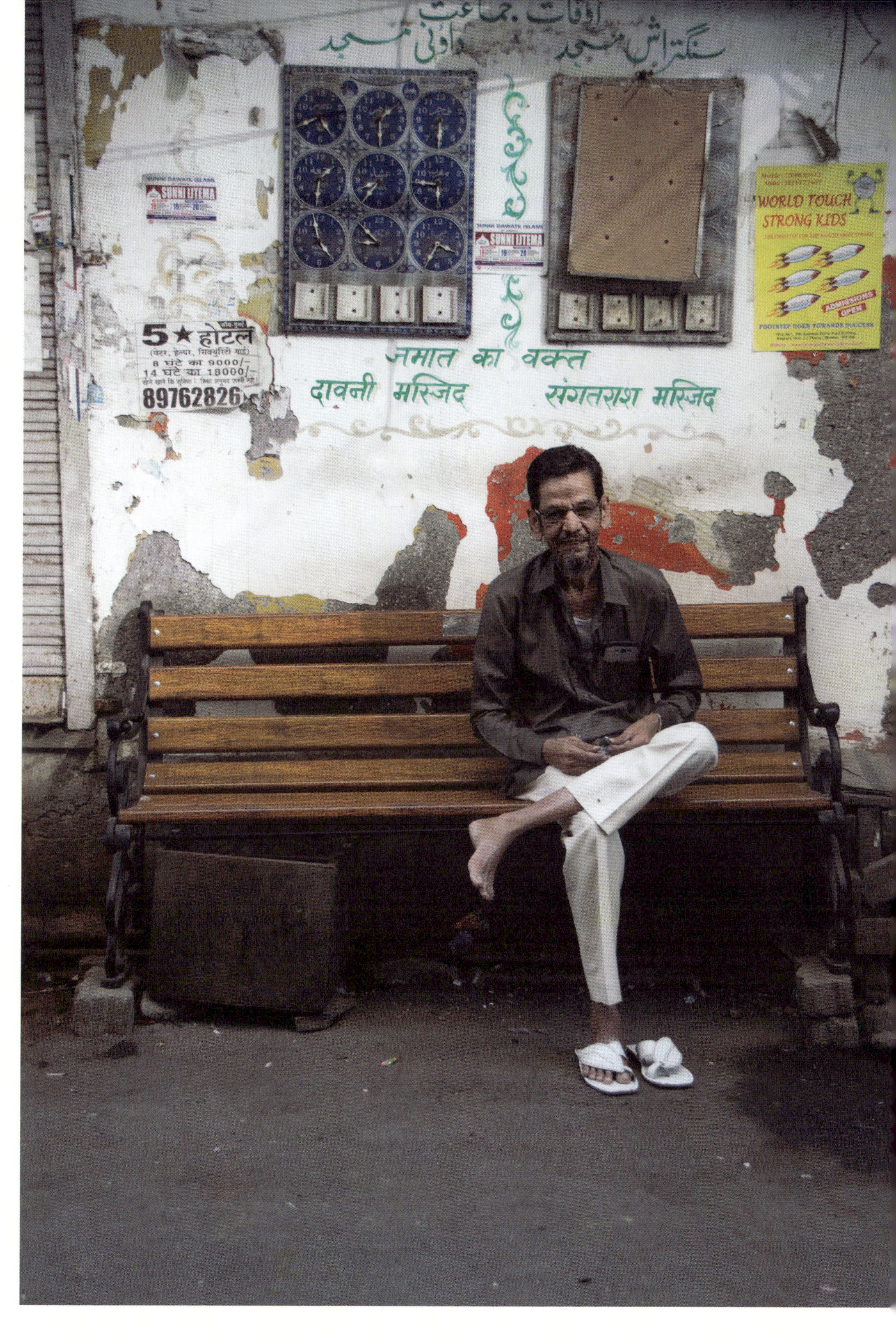
اوقات . جماعت
سنگتراش مسجد
داؤنی مسجد
SUNNI DAWATE ISLAMI
SUNNI IJTEMA
18 19 20
SUNNI DAWATE ISLAMI
SUNNI IJTEMA
18 19 20
Mobile : 72099 03513
Mobil : 98219 27465
WORLD TOUCH
STRONG KIDS
CELEBRATED FOR THE KIDS REASON STRONG
ADMISSIONS
OPEN
FOOTSTEP GOES TOWARDS SUCCESS
5 ★ होटल
(वेटर, हेल्पर, सिक्युरिटी गार्ड)
8 घंटे का 9000/-
14 घंटे का 13000/-
89762826
जमात का वक्त
दावनी मस्जिद   संगतराश मस्जिद

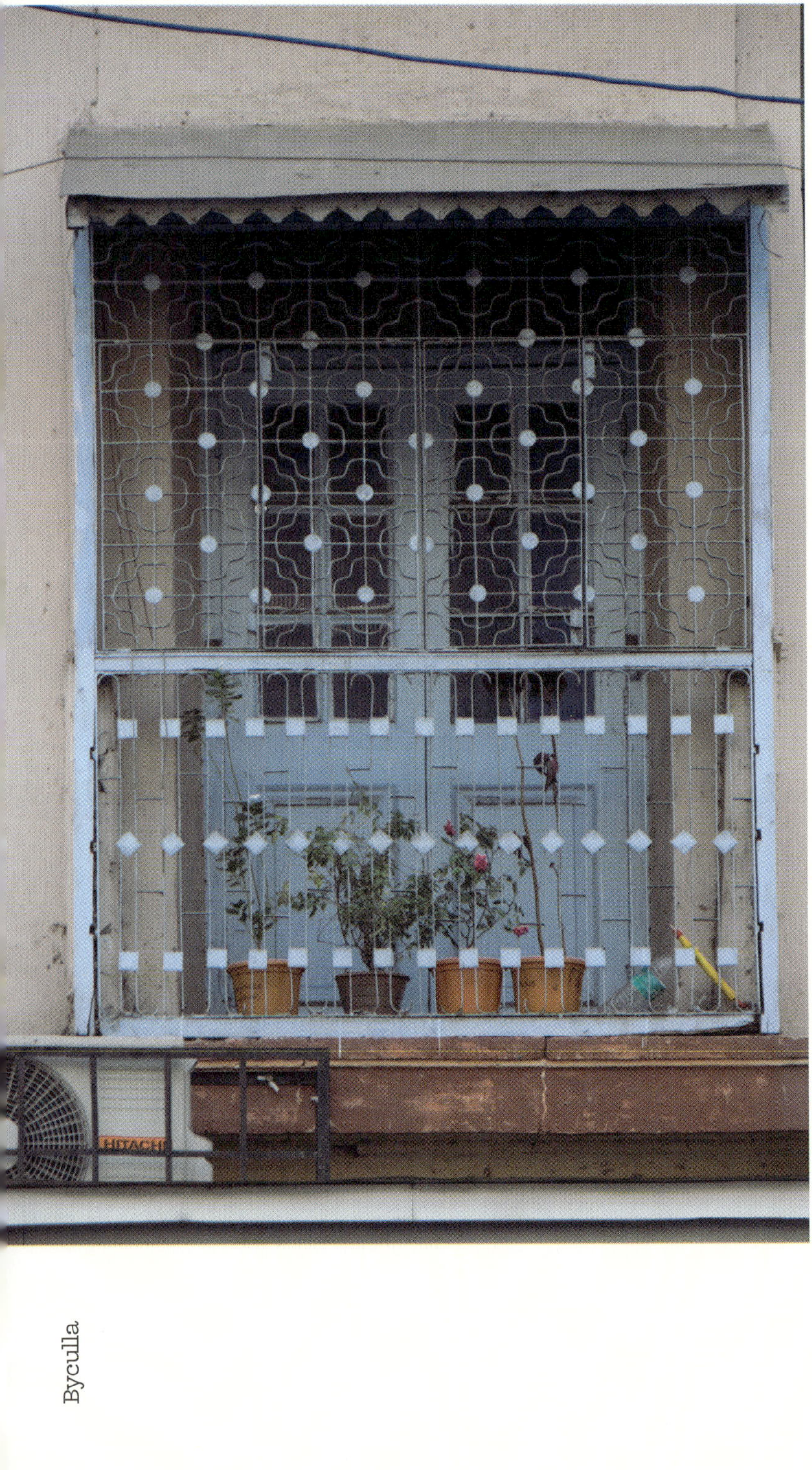

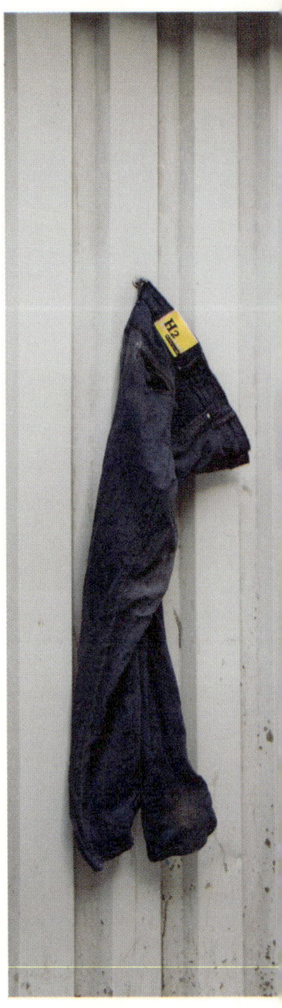

Byculla

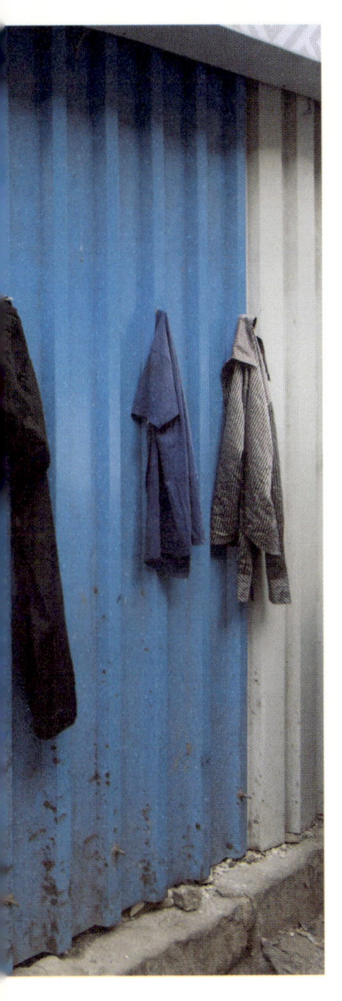

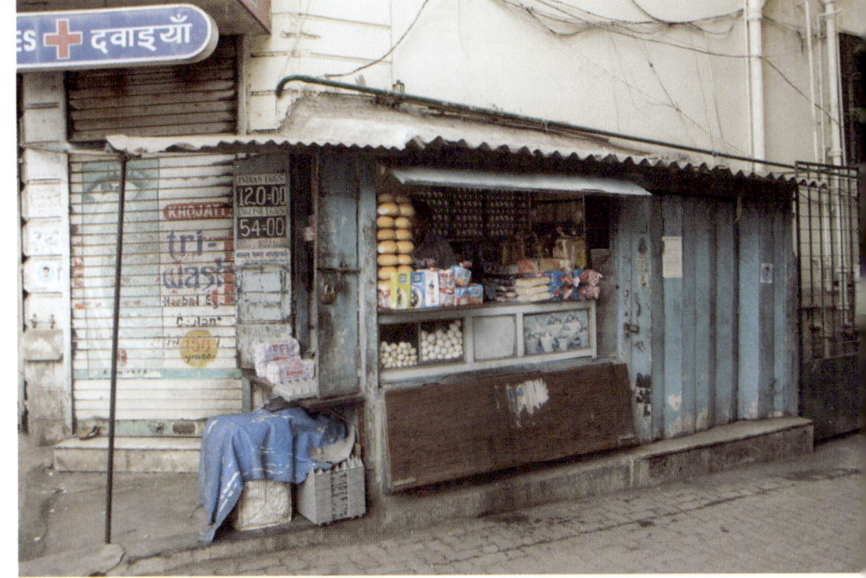
ES दवाइयाँ
KHOJATI
tri-
wash
Herbal
INDIAN EGGS
120-00
54-00

Warehouses Docks

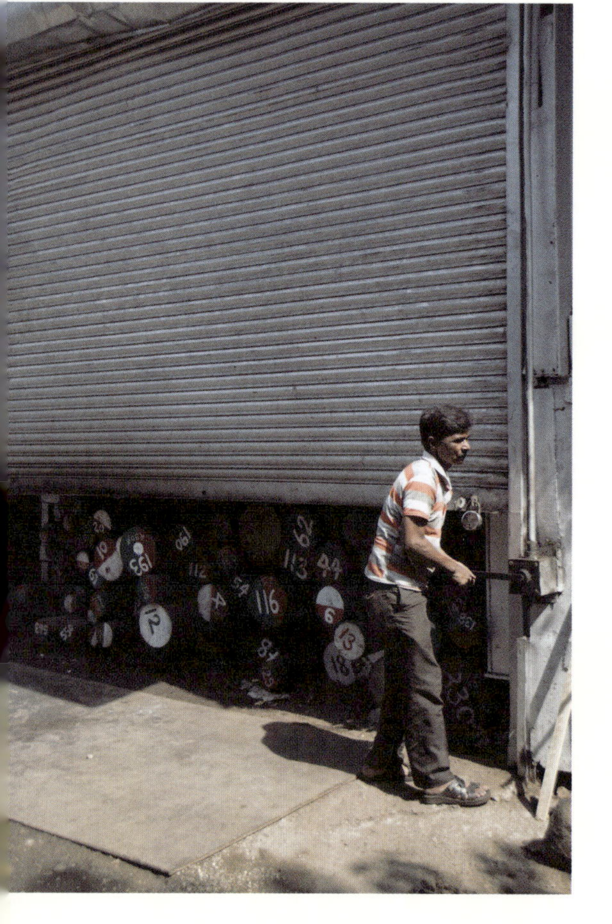

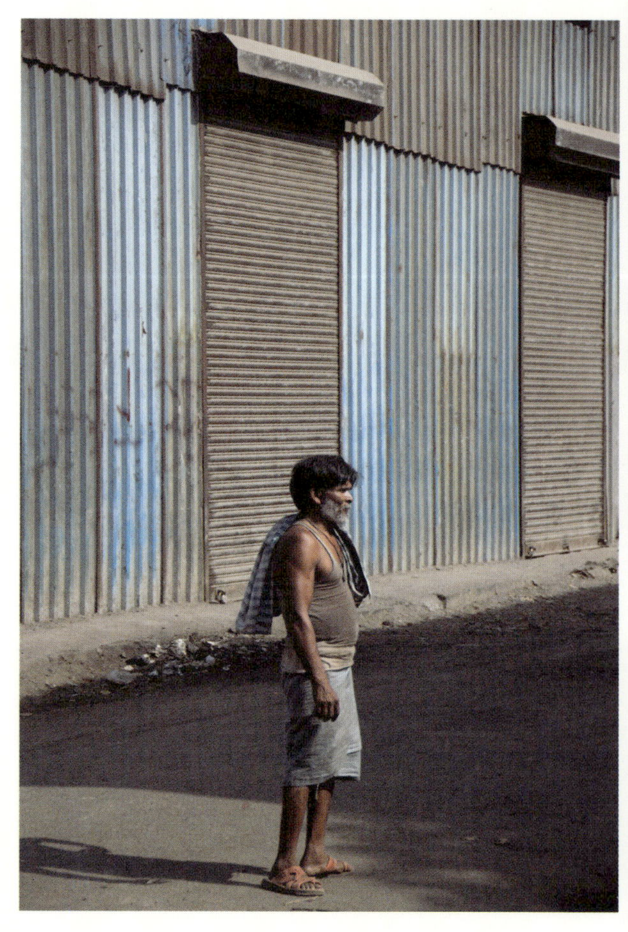

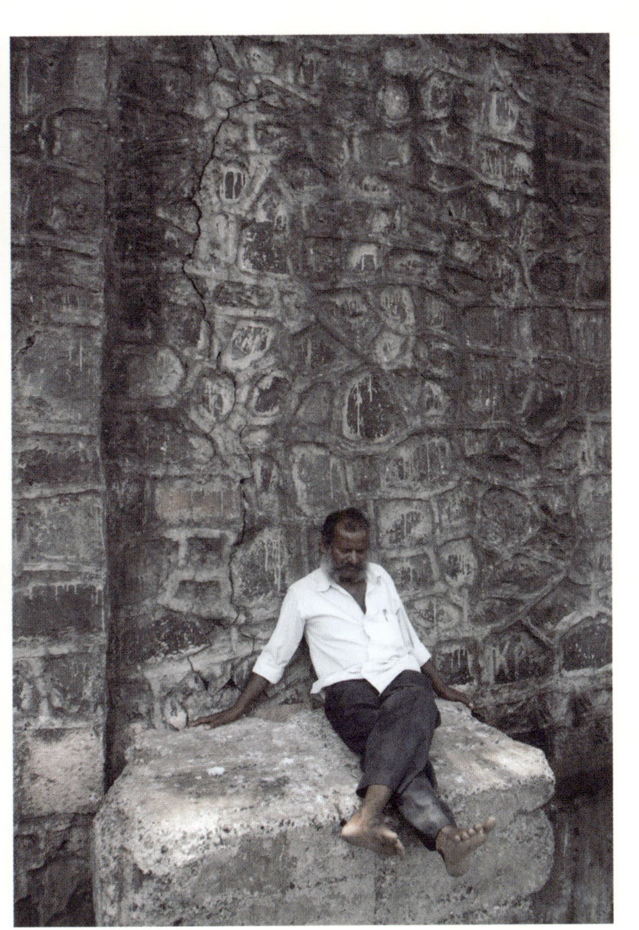

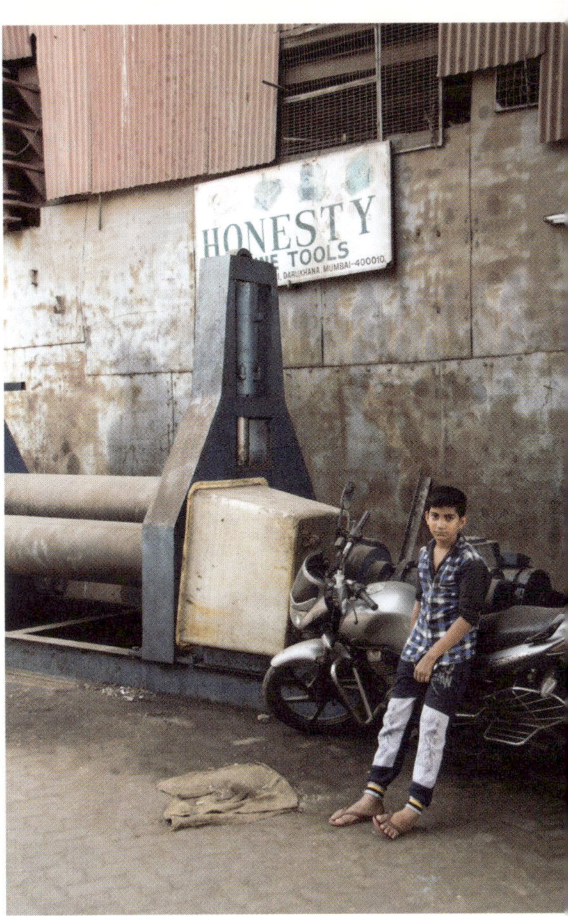

HONESTY
NE TOOLS
DARUKHANA, MUMBAI-400010.

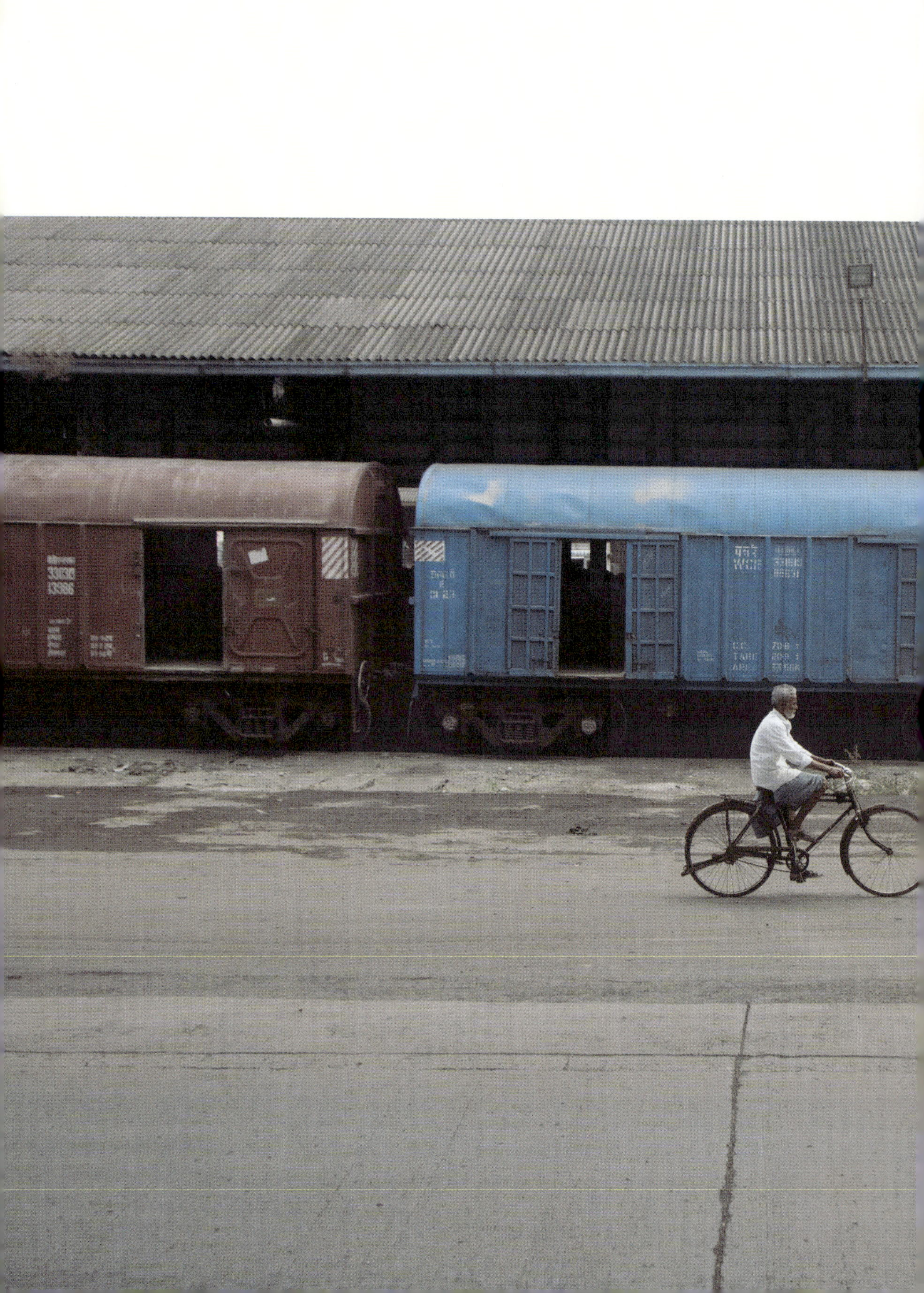

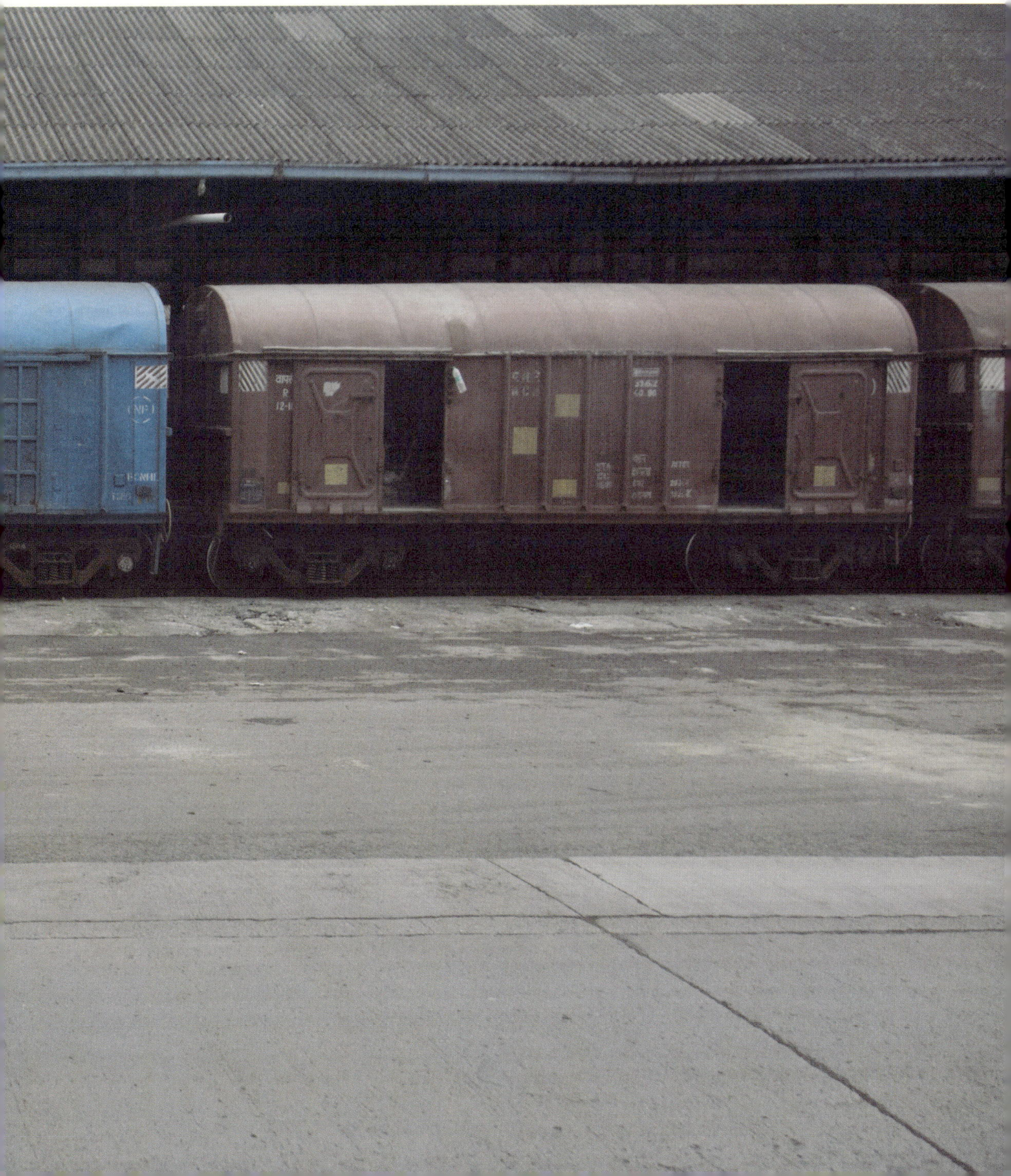

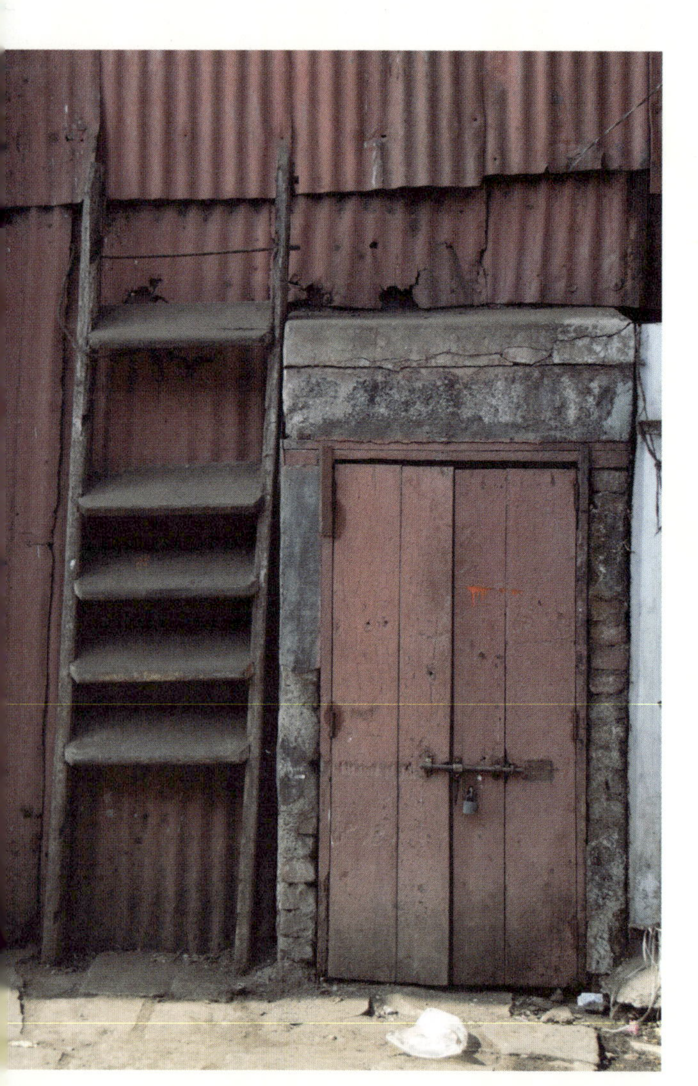
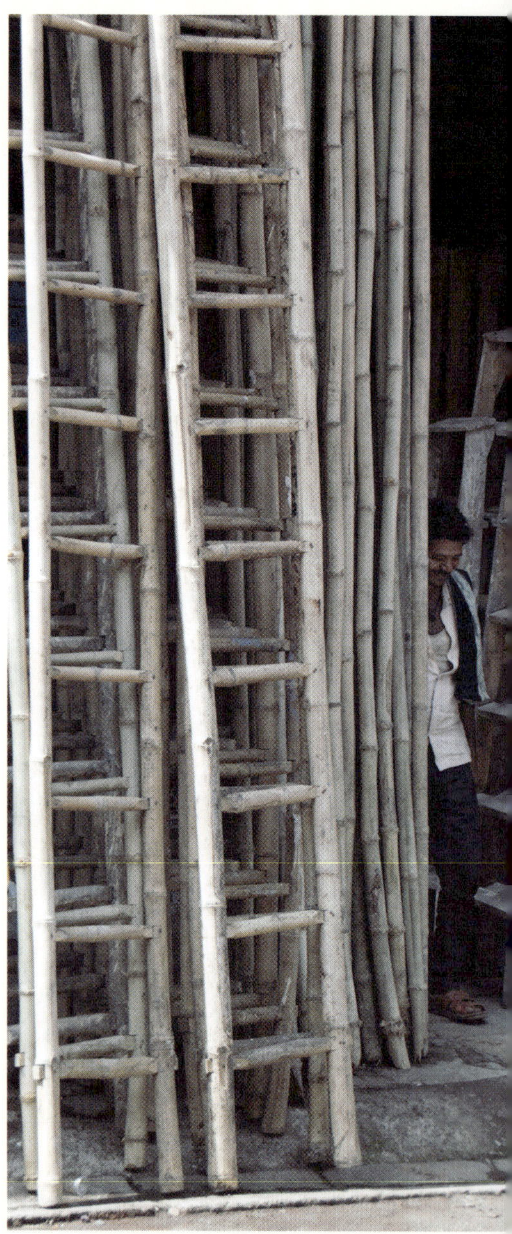

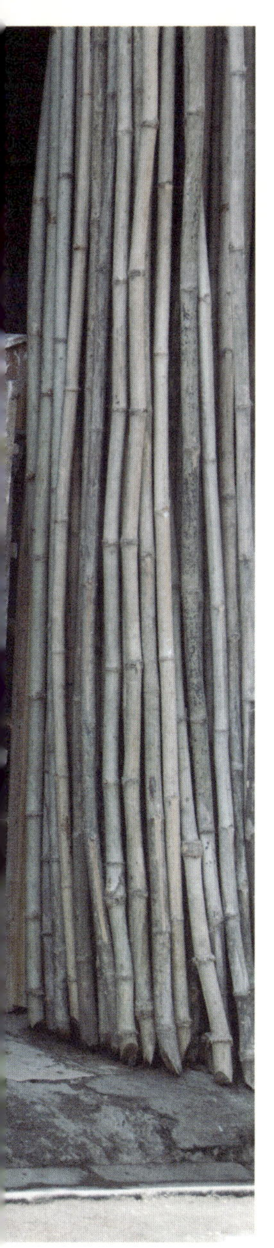

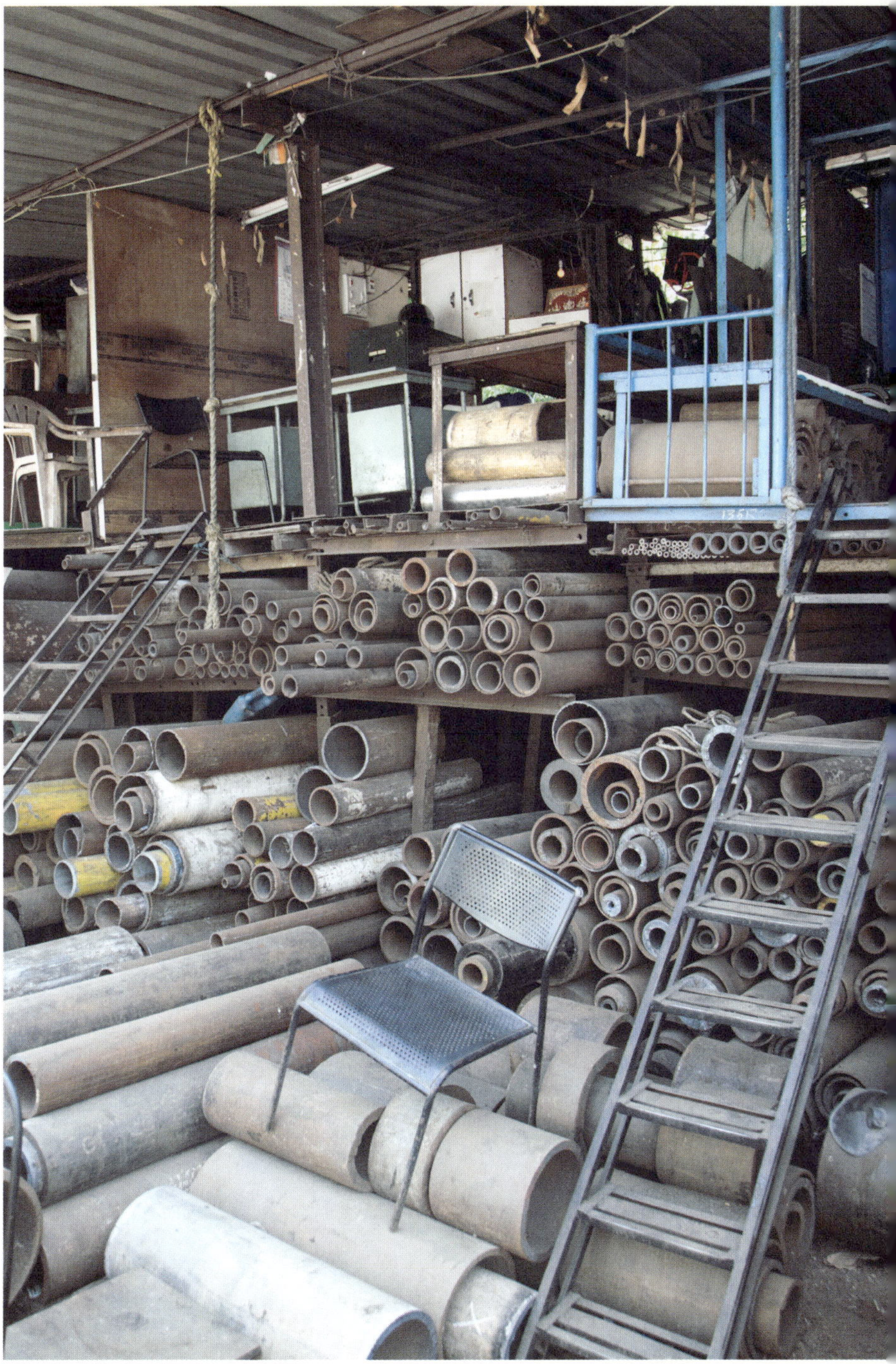

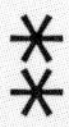

Parel

Post-independence, the people given the mandate to plan Mumbai
have had two significant opportunities to course-correct and fix
Mumbai's issues of congestion and livability. The first comprised
considerable reclamation efforts in various parts of the city – the
argument being that these new areas such as Nariman Point, Cuffe
Parade and Bandra Reclamation, which came up at different times,
would create new directions in development. Unfortunately, the
builder-politician nexus monopolised these endeavours and created
houses and offices for one class of people with no concern for the
community at large. This manipulation and control of the market
escalated prices and catalysed inequality.

The second missed opportunity came about when swathes
of land were made available, as Mumbai's many industrial mills,
stalled because of labour conflicts and a fast-changing business
environment, moved to the outskirts of Mumbai. If well-planned,
these pieces of land would have given Mumbai its badly needed open
spaces and affordable housing. Instead, the same builder-politician
nexus, in collusion with influential local union leaders associated
with the mills, and with vested interests, usurped these land parcels
to create luxury penthouse towers and 7-star hotels – leaving
pigeon-hole sized units built on a tenth of the remaining land for the
original mill workers, those very workers who built the businesses
that made the city of Bombay relevant.

This sort of gentrification has made Mumbai monotonal,
reducing its vibrancy and diversity. It has also added to the already
grotesque levels of inequality in the city, which in the long run will
prove unsustainable.

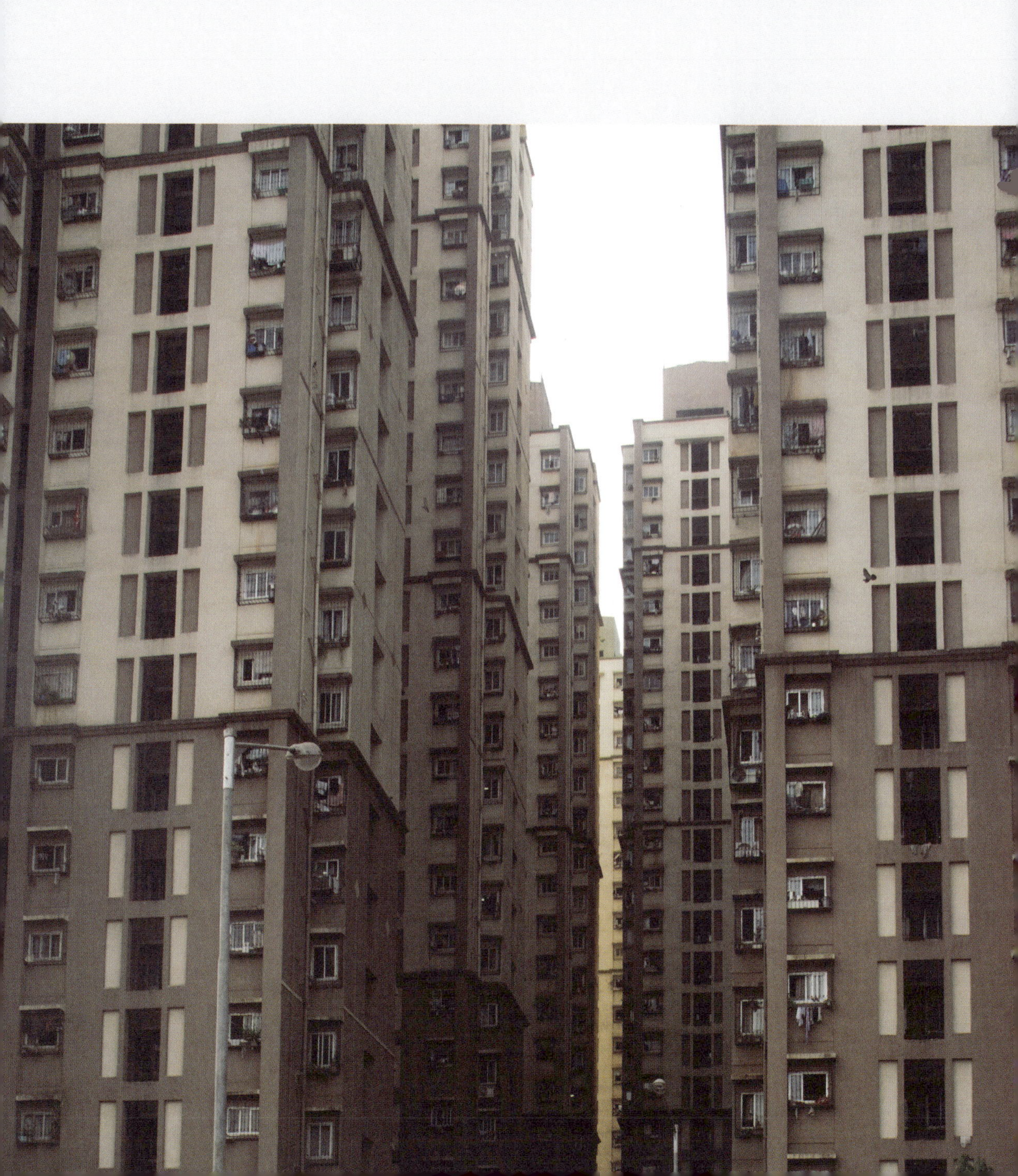

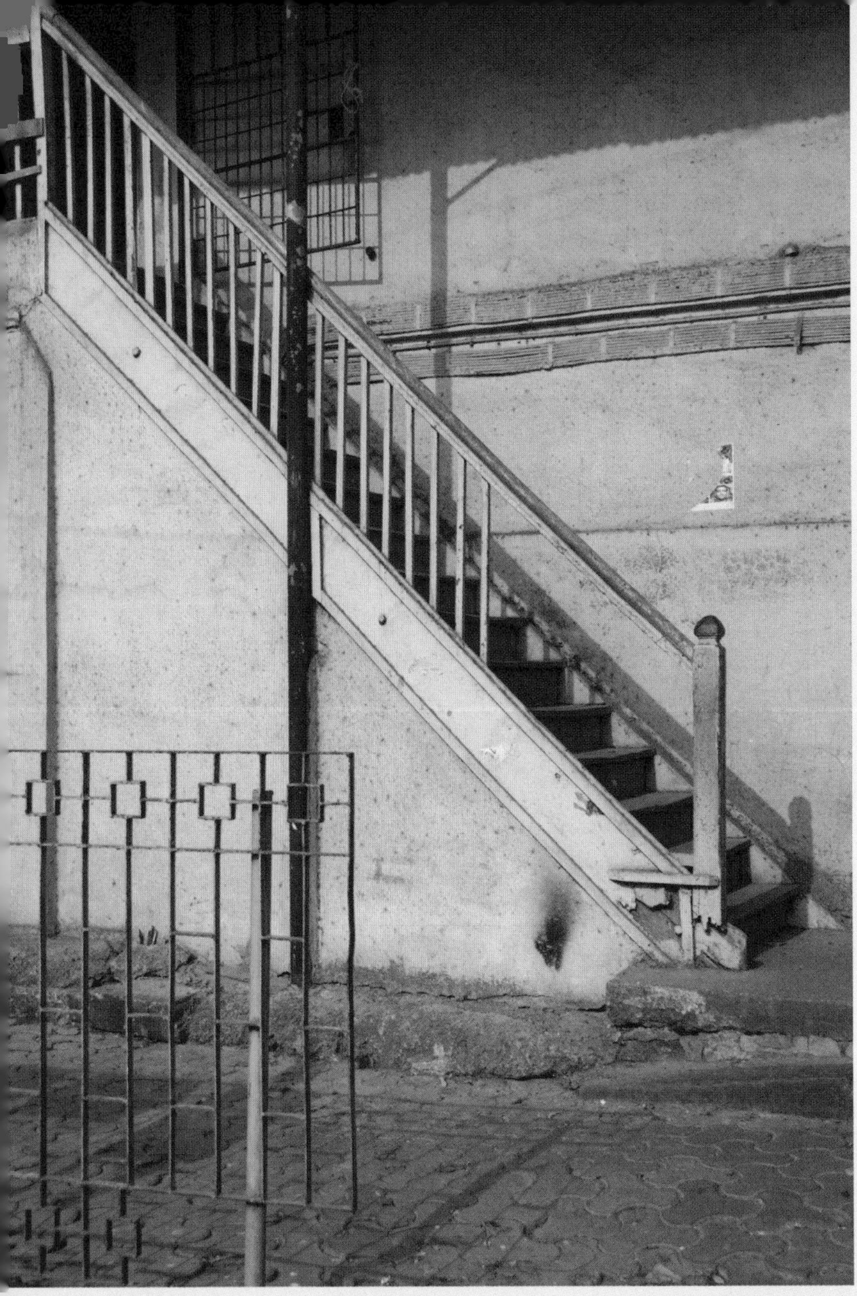

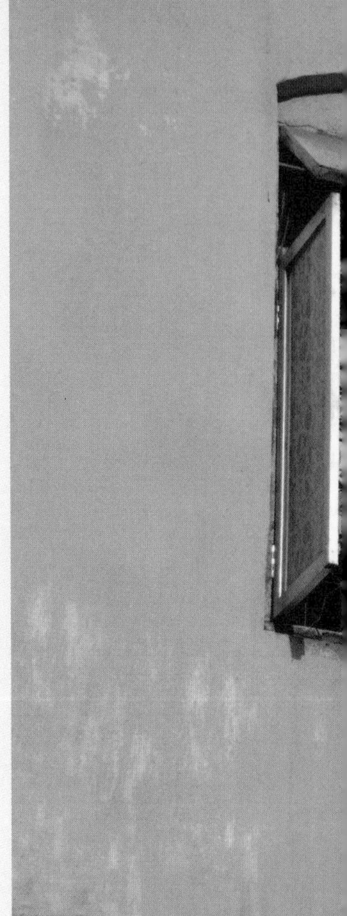
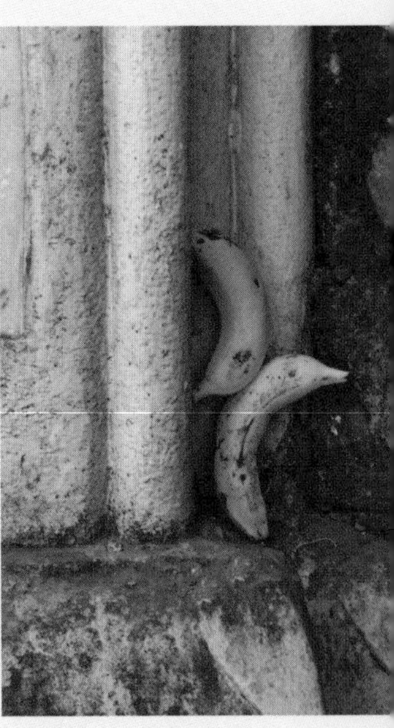

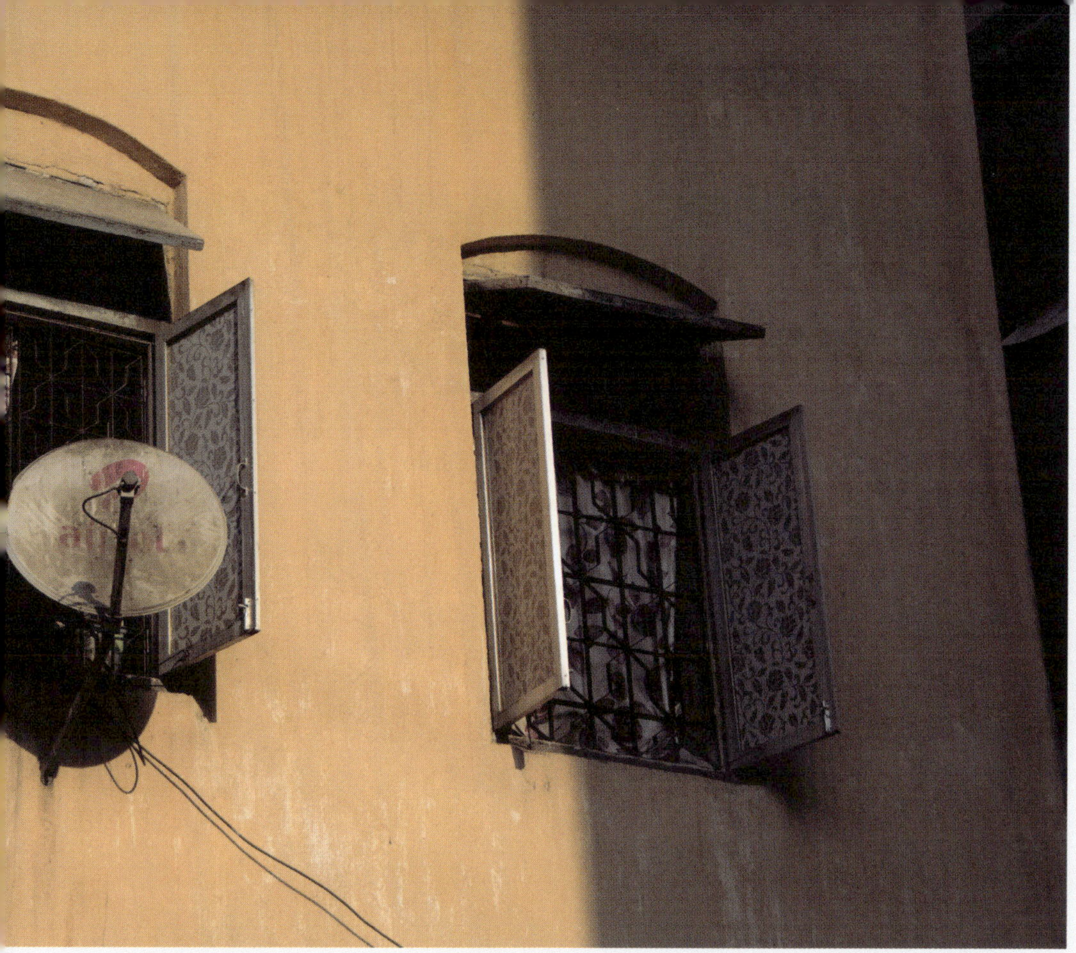

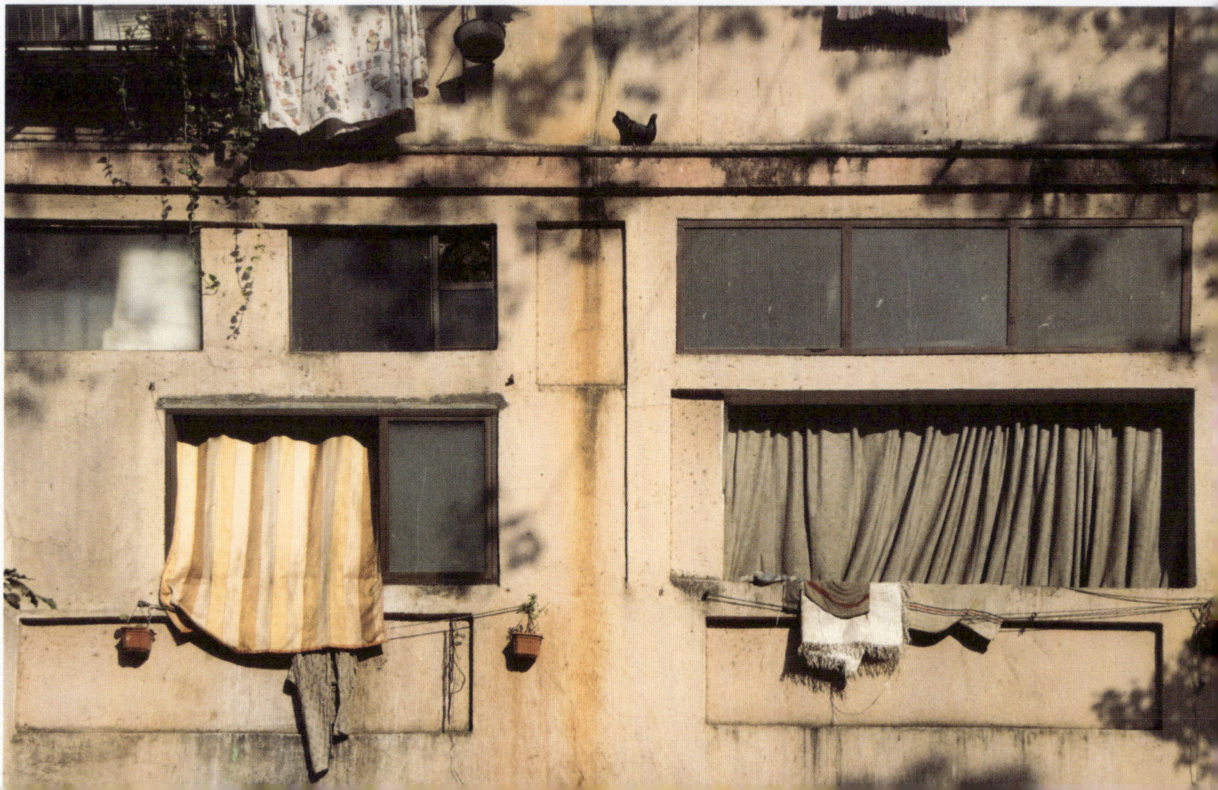

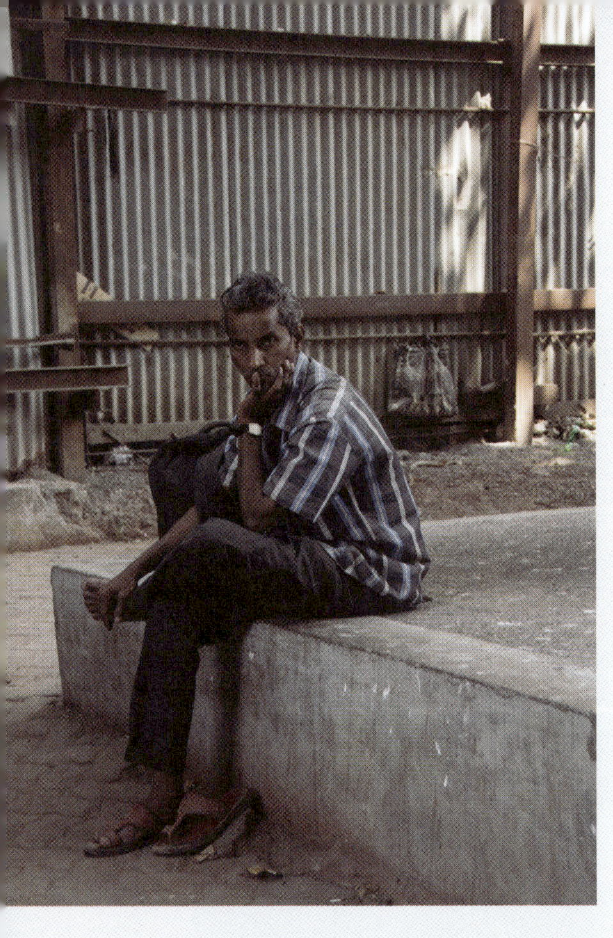

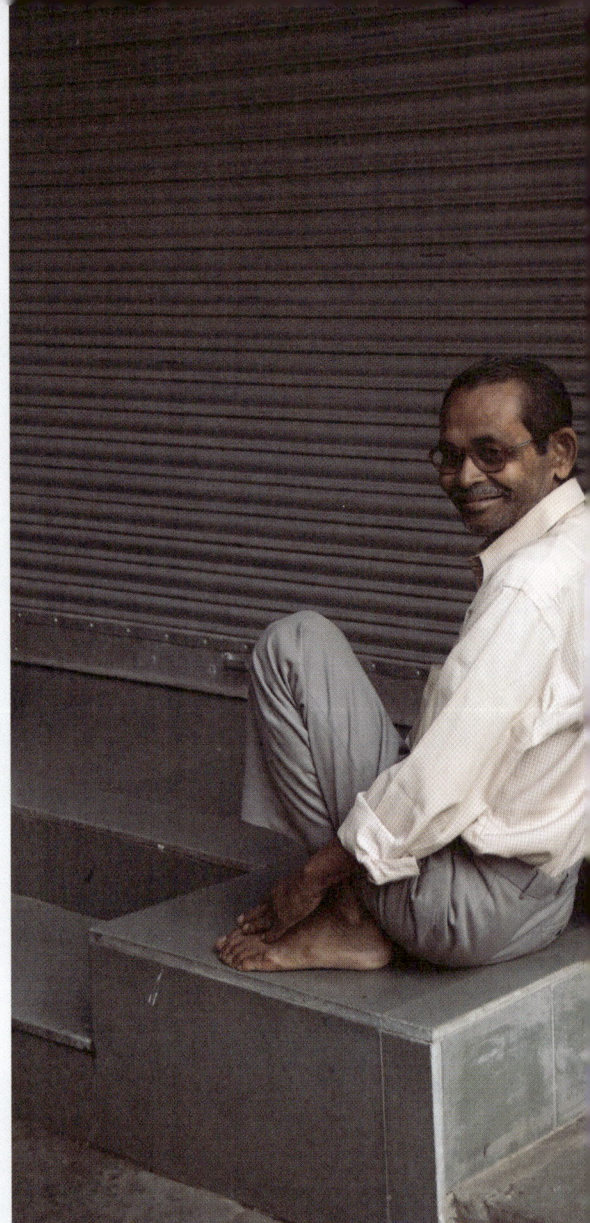

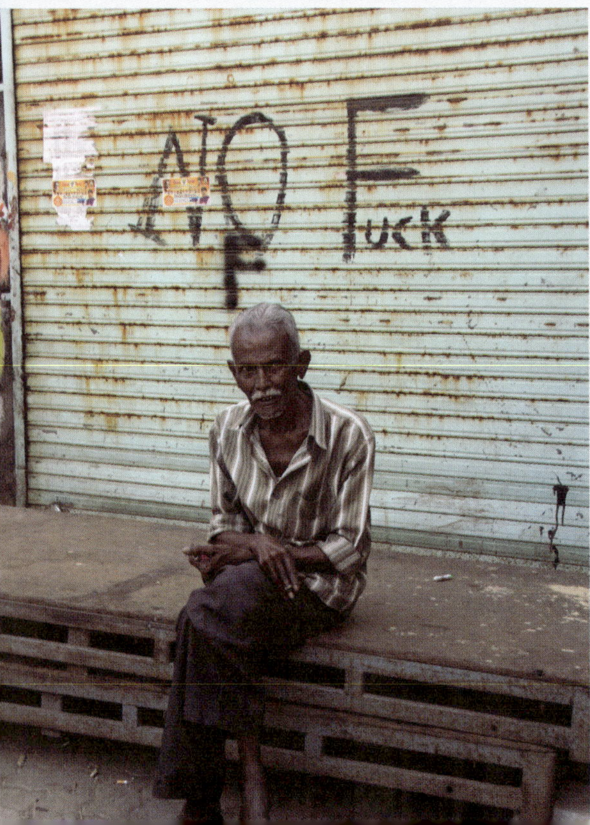
NO F
Fuck

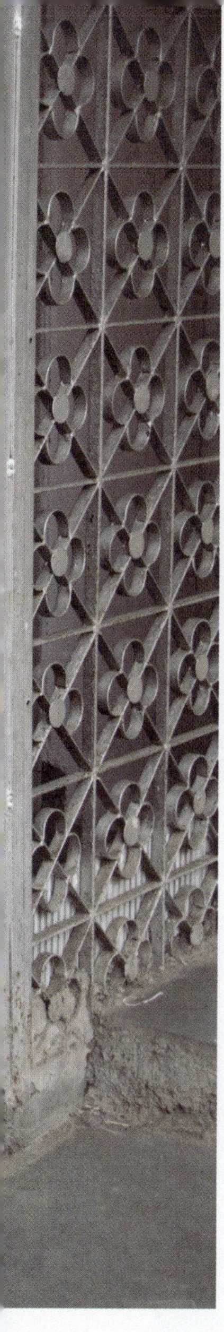
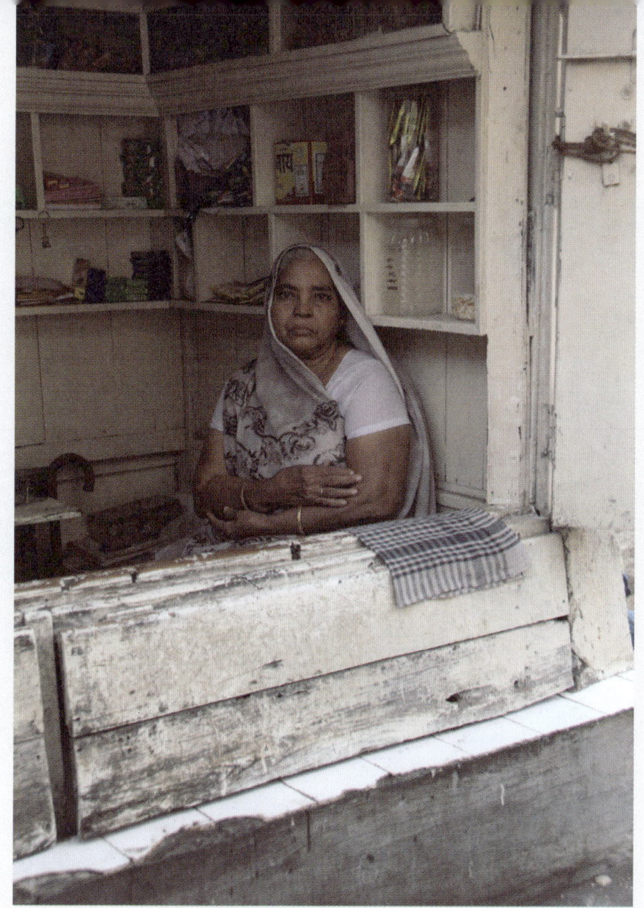
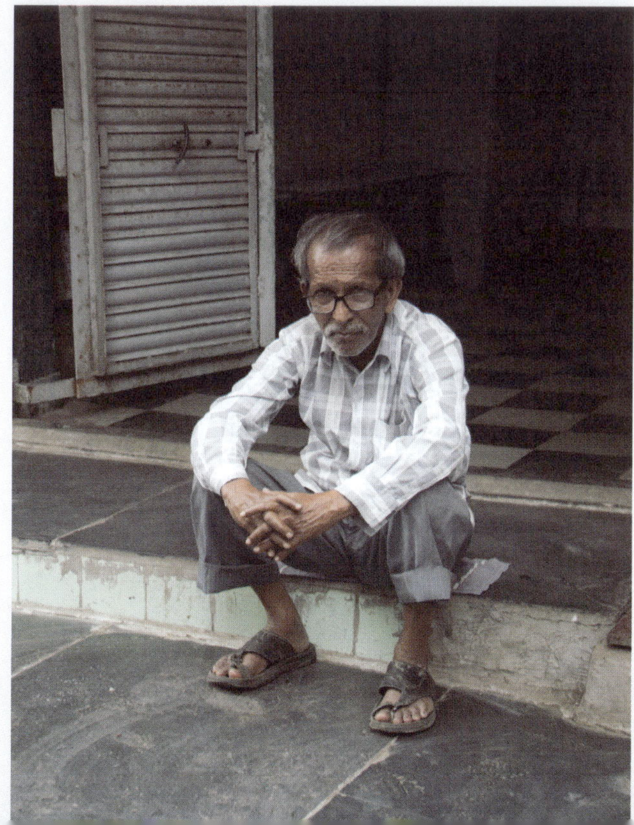

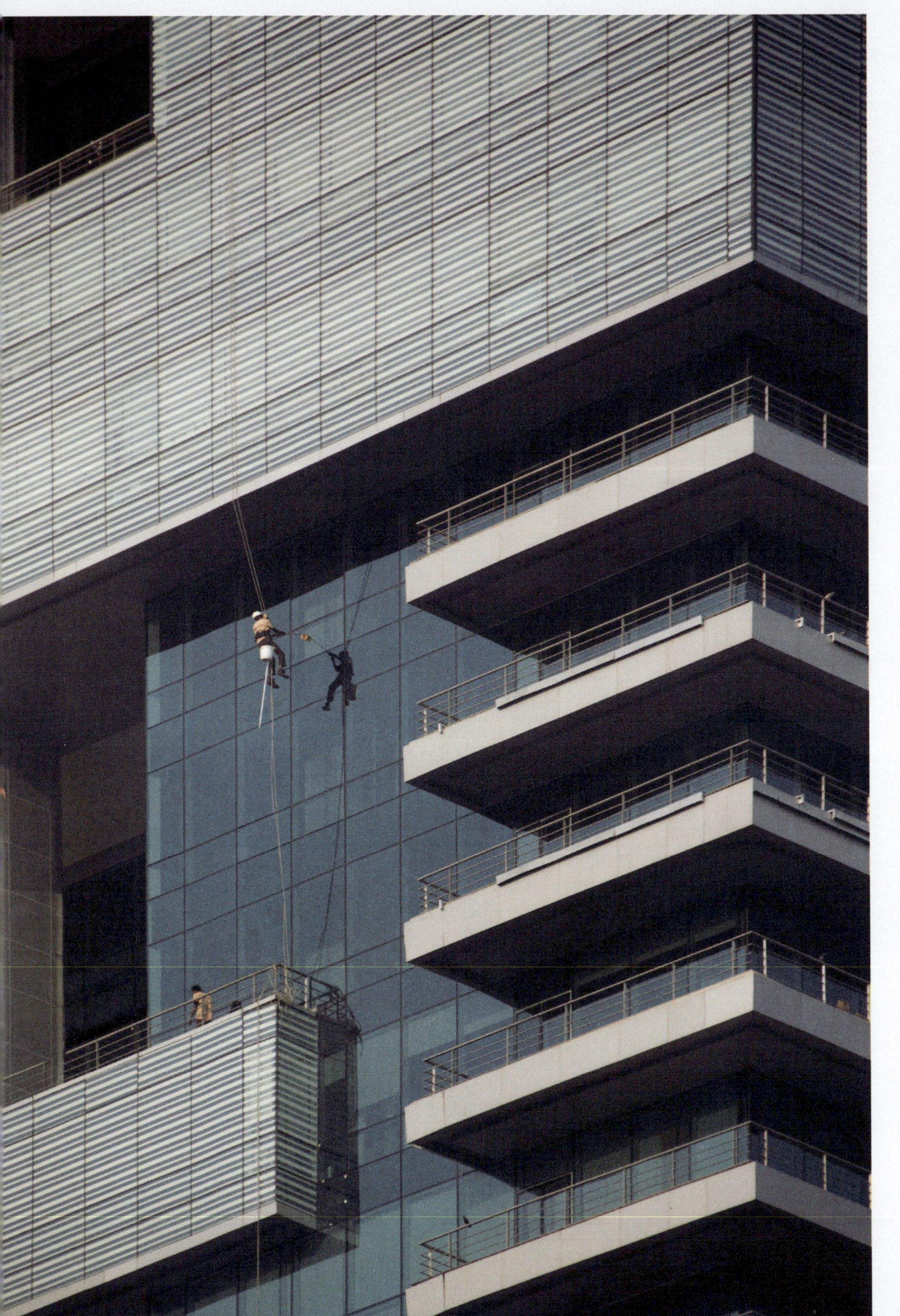

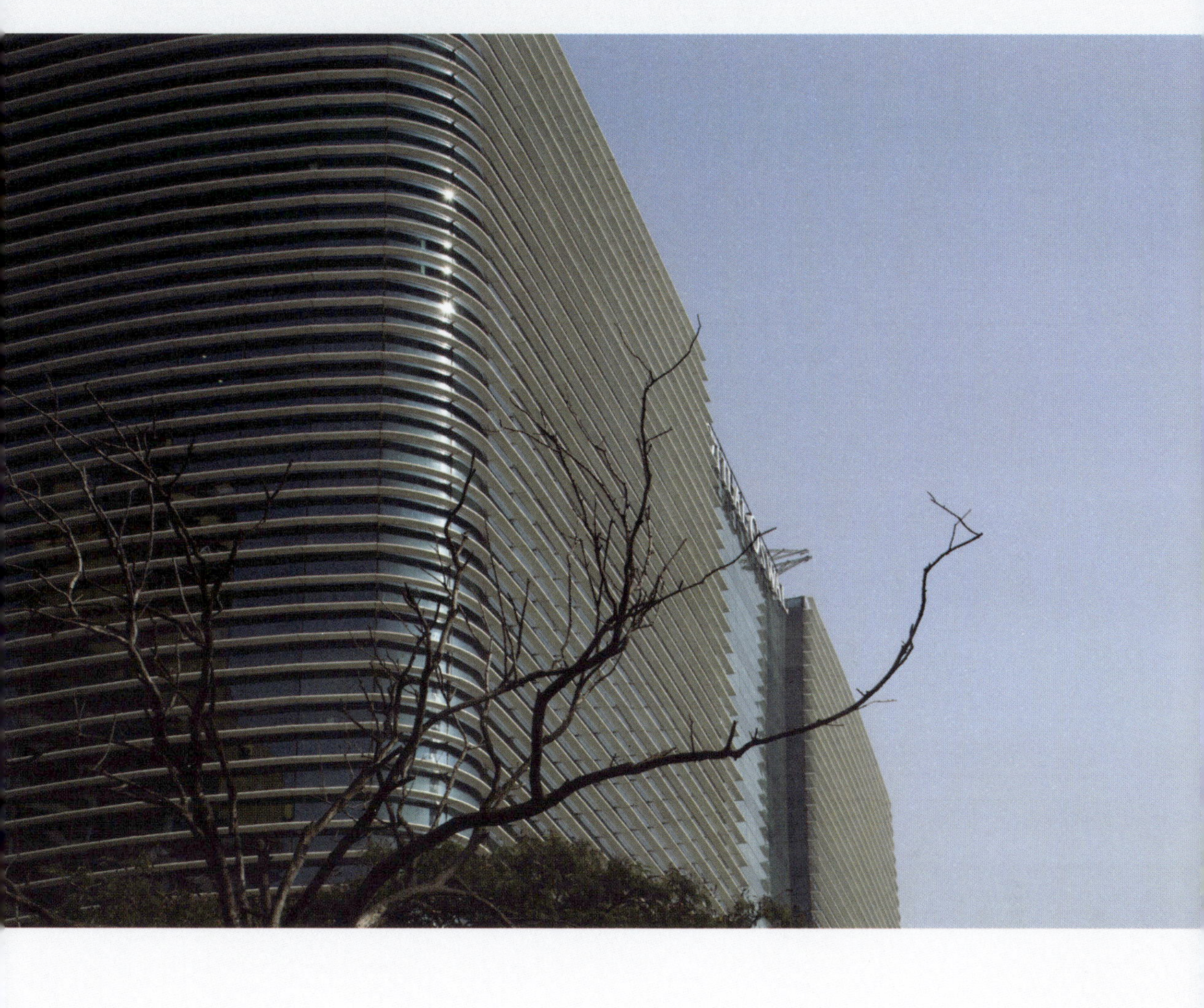

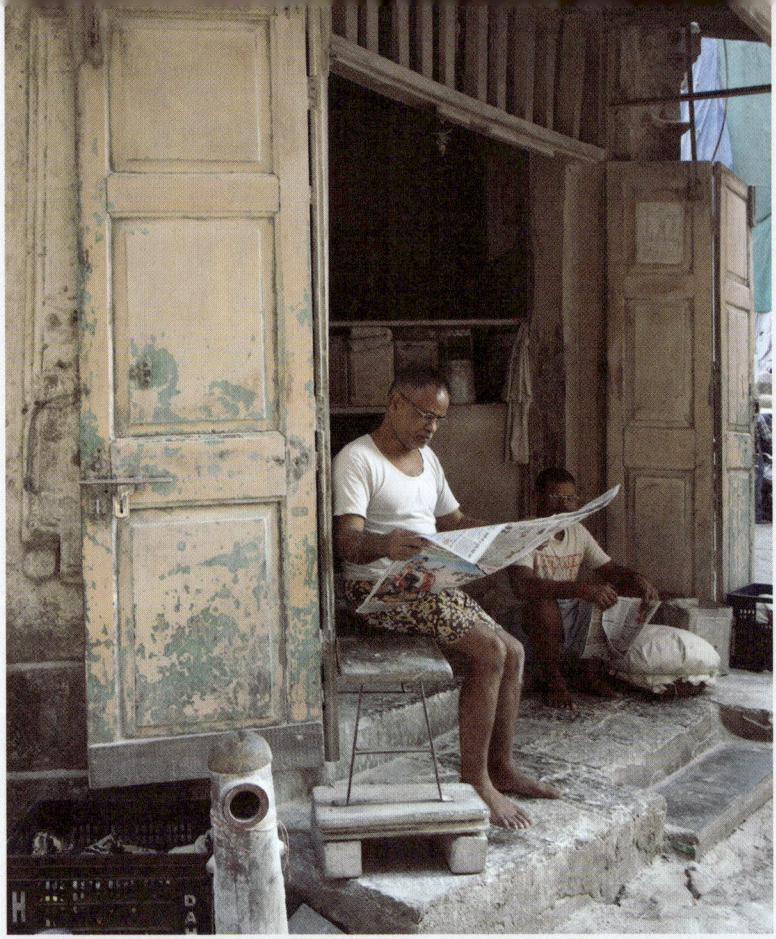

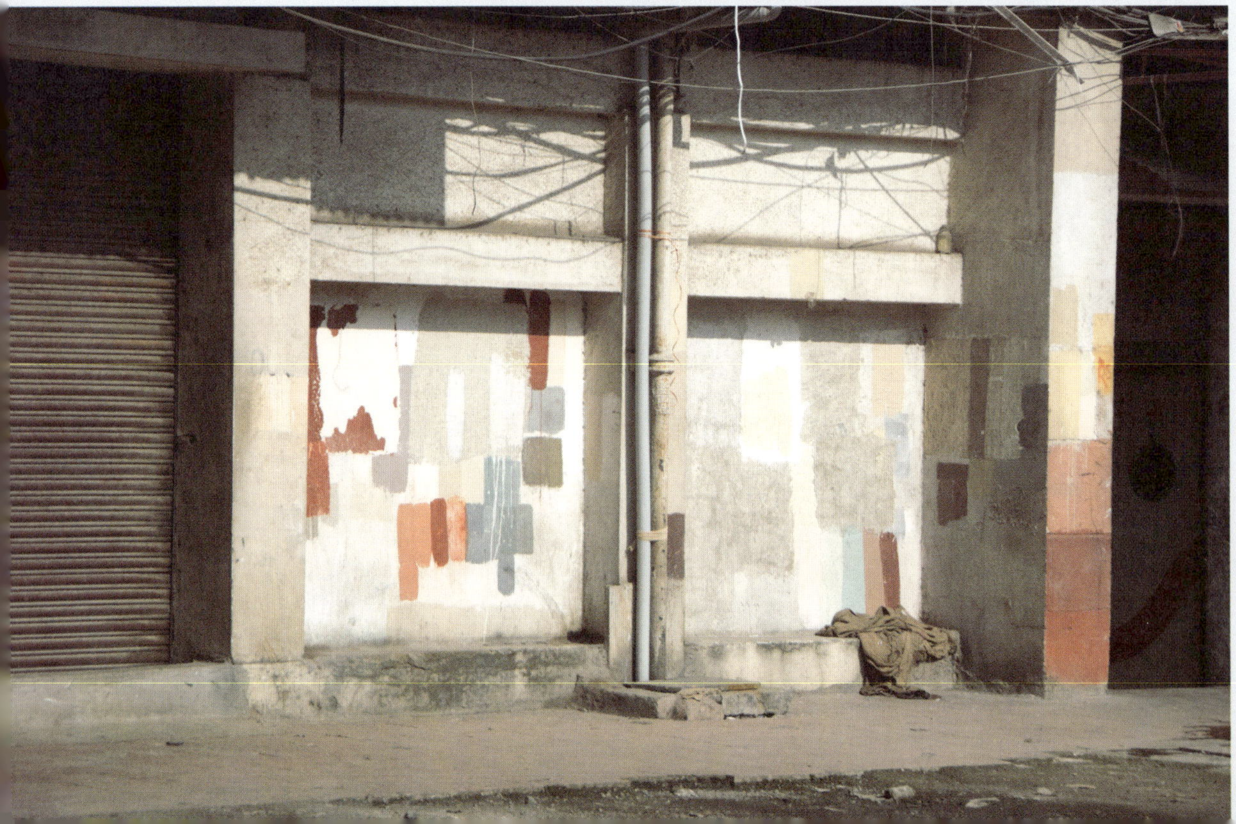

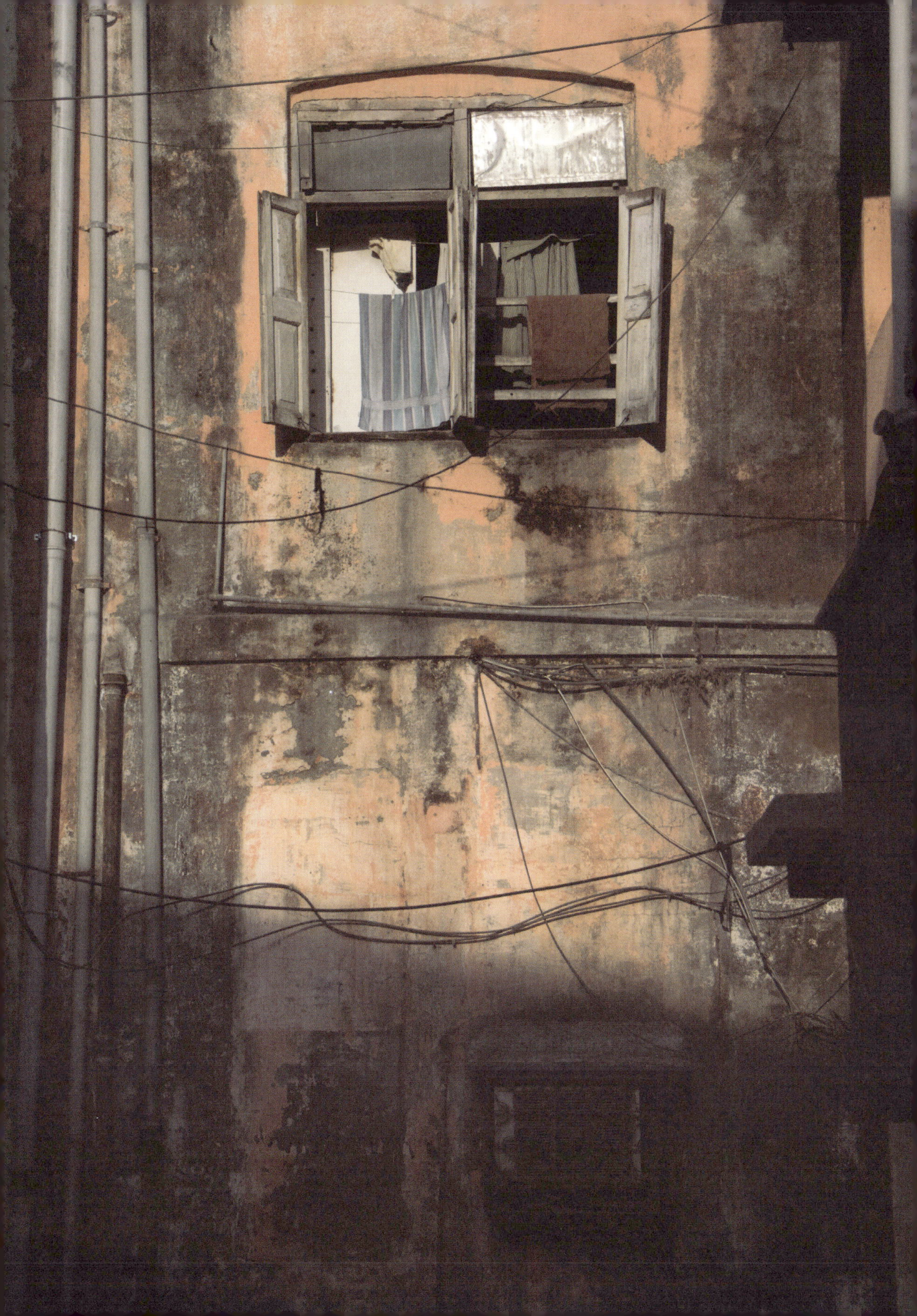

BUILT ON HOPE

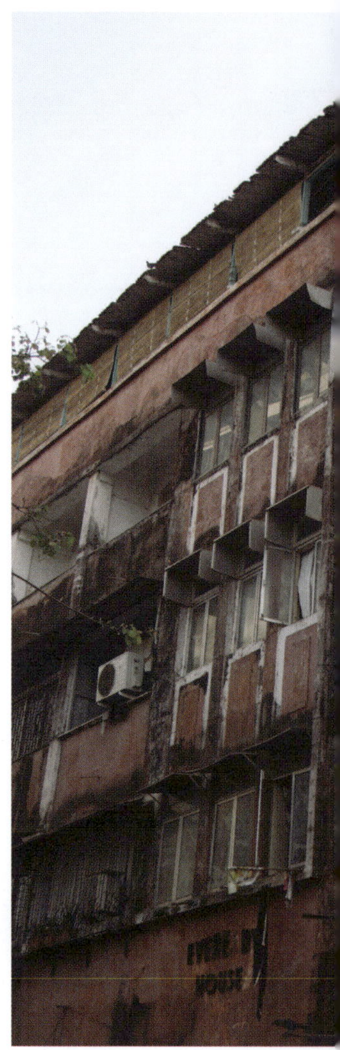

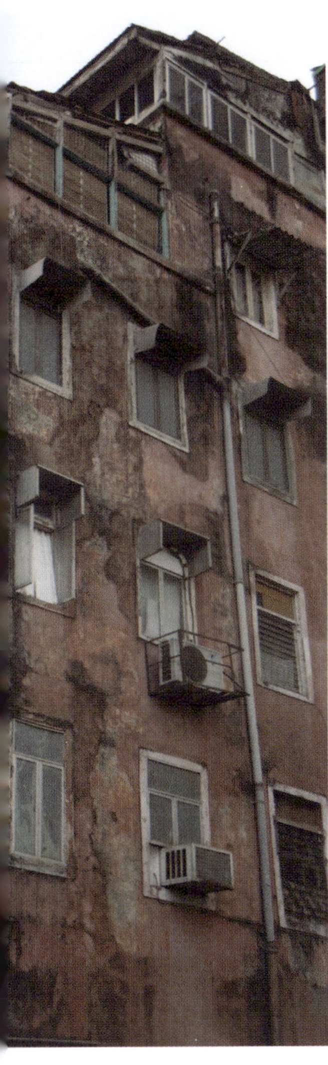

Writing the essays in this book has been hard for me,
as I am more of a visual person.

Nonetheless, Tara Books encouraged me to do so, convincing
me that it would help in the reading of the photographs.
While I was in the middle of writing, they nudged me to read
Dr. Ambedkar. Again, I was not sure. Throughout the series,
I had intentionally avoided pictures that were either religious
or political. I was looking to extract the city's identity using
subtler cues. Also, I didn't know much about Ambedkar or
his life. I knew more about Gandhi and considered him a
significant influence on my life. But on reading Ambedkar's
biography, I began to understand why things are the way they
are in India.

While Gandhi fought against Britain for India's freedom,
Ambedkar fought with Gandhi about what kind of liberty
India should have. Ambedkar tried to explain to Gandhi that
India had also to free itself from its internal problems, the
biggest being its caste system. For him, social and economic
infrastructure to correct these ills needed to be put in place

right from the beginning. Without these, many an Indian
would have a new nationality but not freedom. Gandhi hoped
that once free from the British, Indians would be able to rise
to his high moral compass and eradicate casteism through the
power of will. Ambedkar was sceptical, and he compared the
achievement of political freedom and democracy to building a
castle, but on a dung heap.

This last line resonated with me, and I found a direct
parallel between those words and what I saw on the streets
of Mumbai. Its flaws are evident, visceral even, its problems
immediate. But the chosen narrative to address these issues
is always one of aspiration, of dreams, fantasies. Let's not
look at our fundamental issues of inequality, congestion, lousy
infrastructure. Let's redevelop, let's build on top of our problems
and wish them away. The city was and continues to be a city
built entirely on hope.

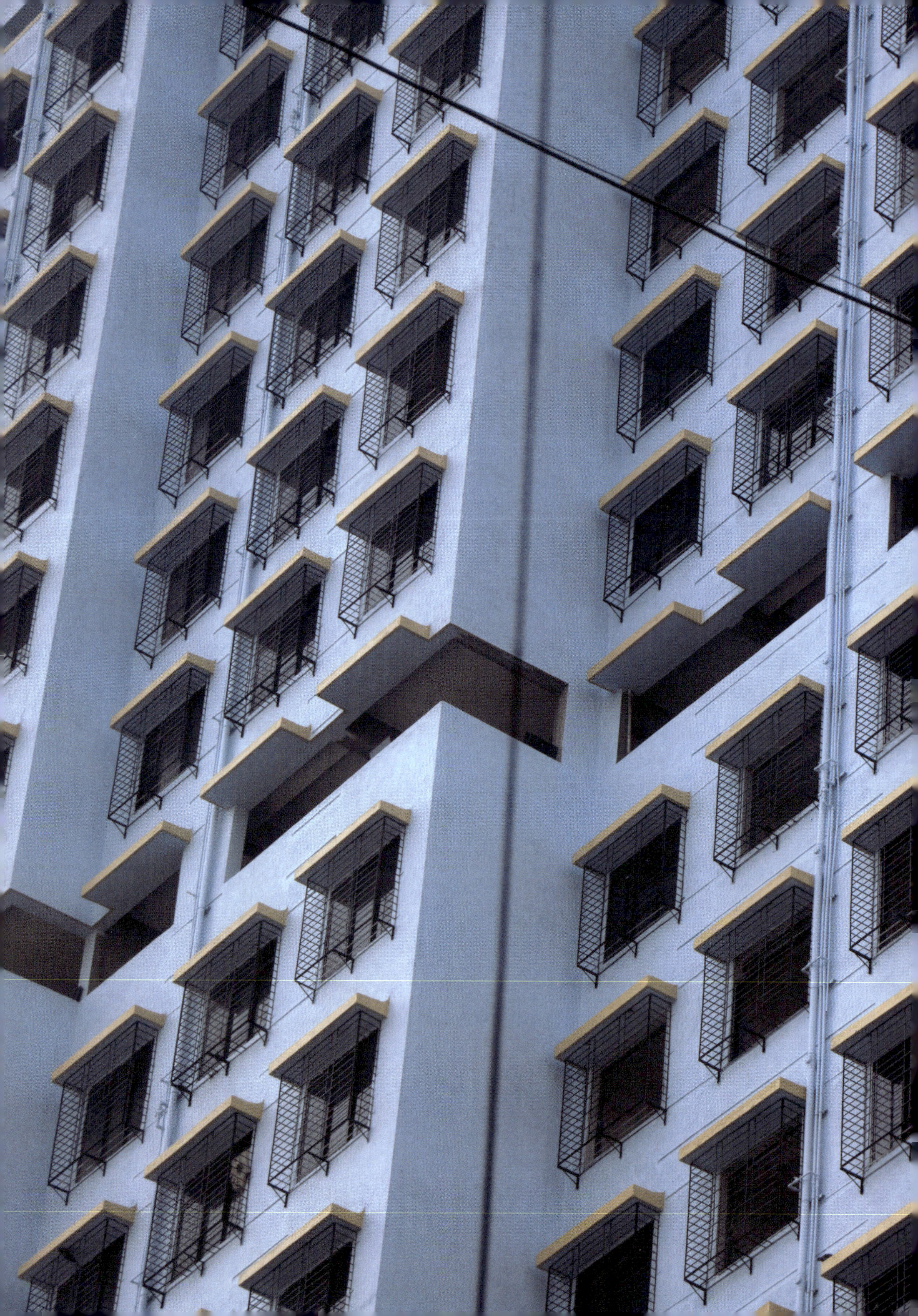

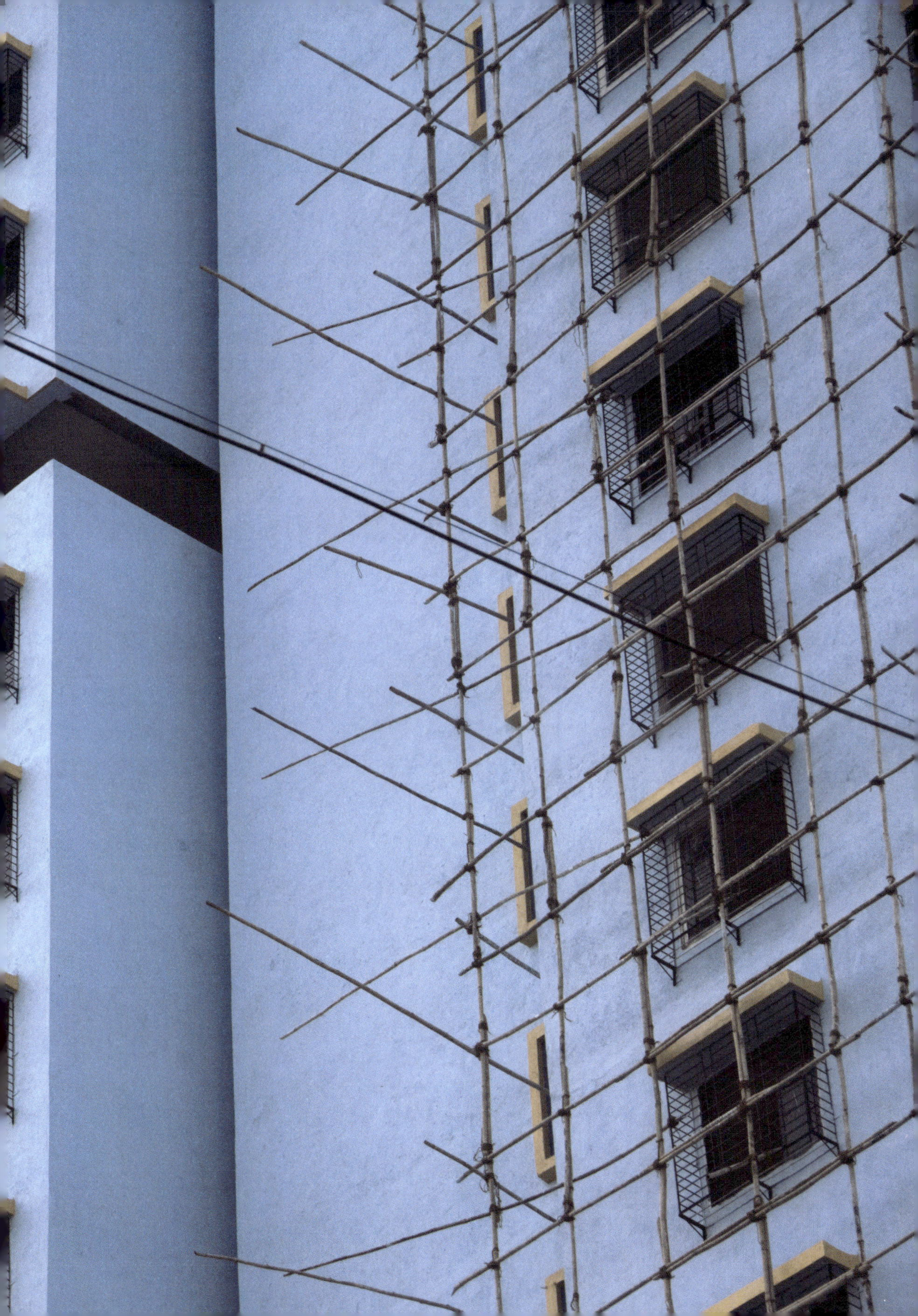

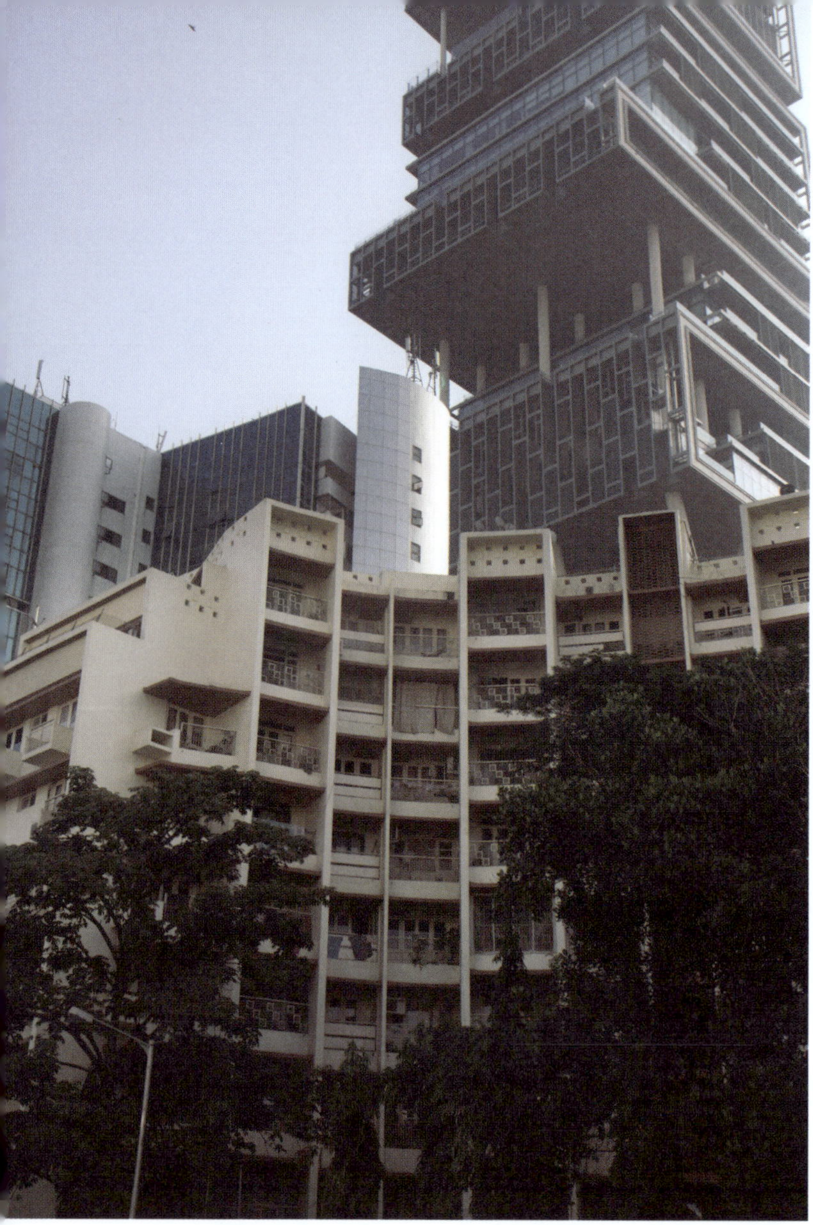

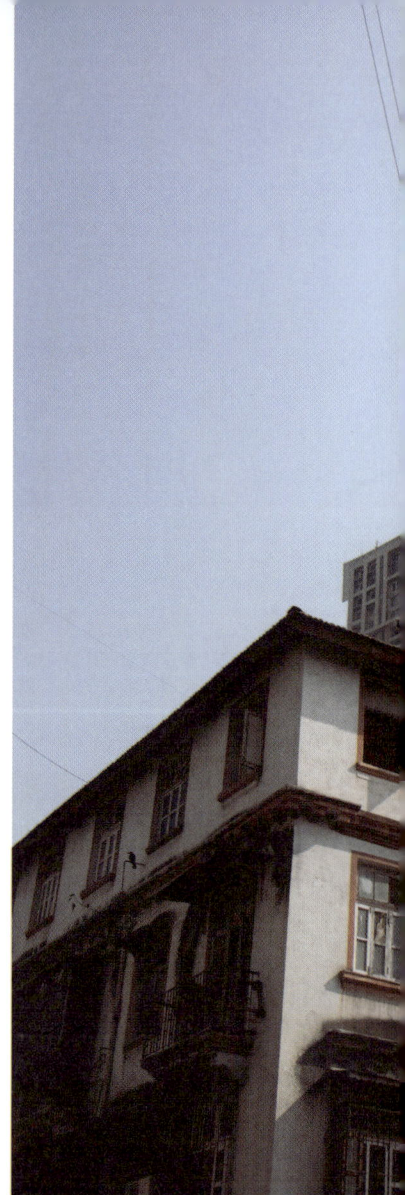

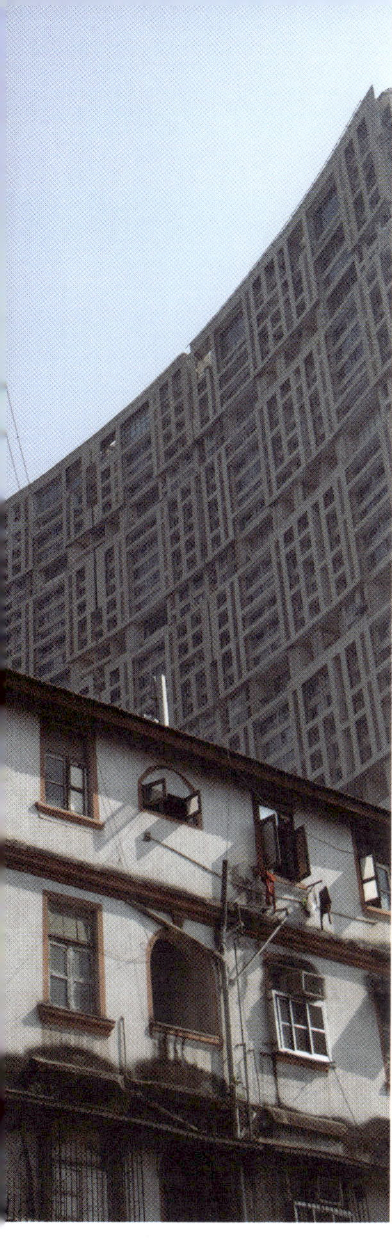

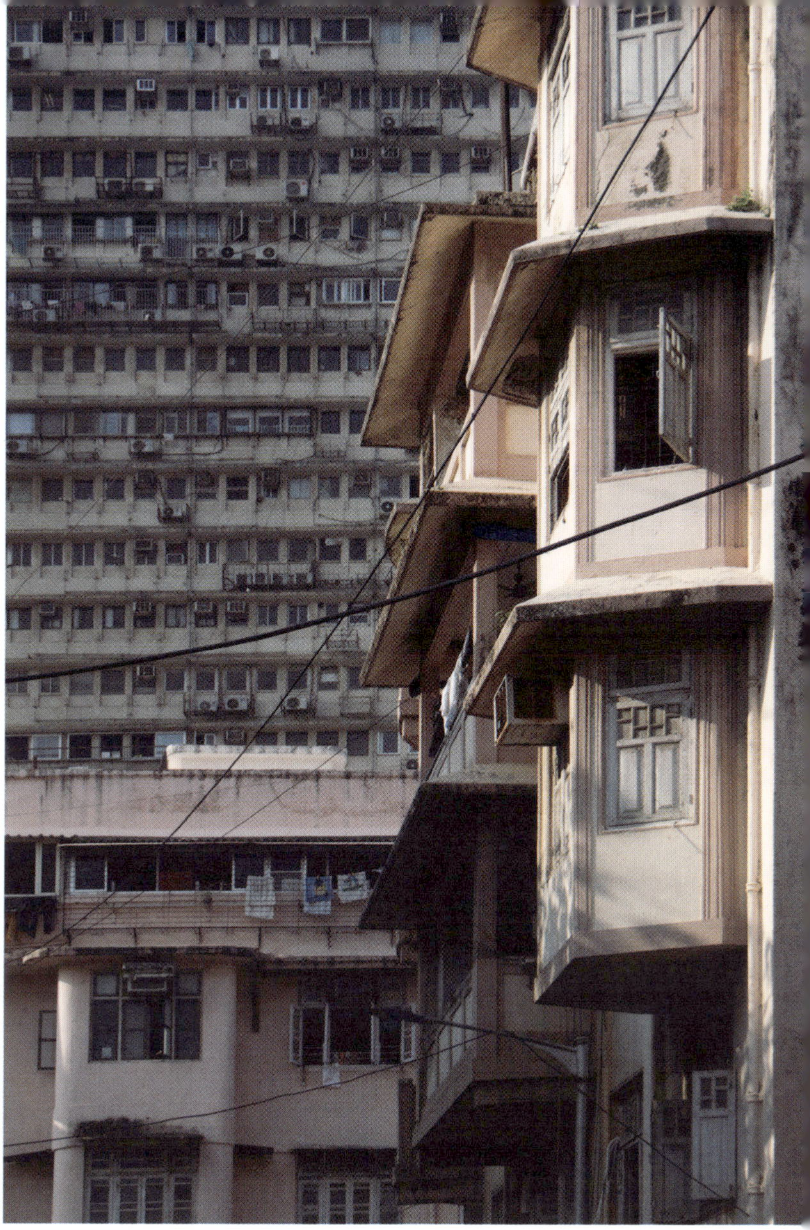

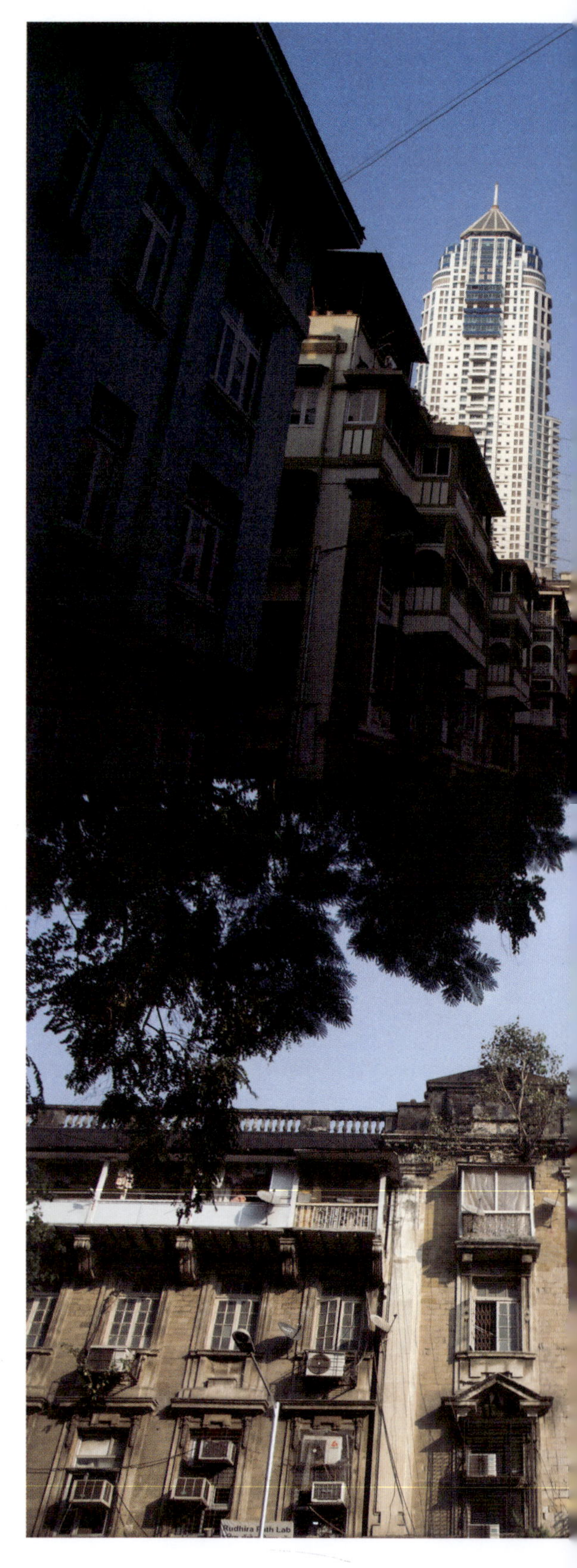

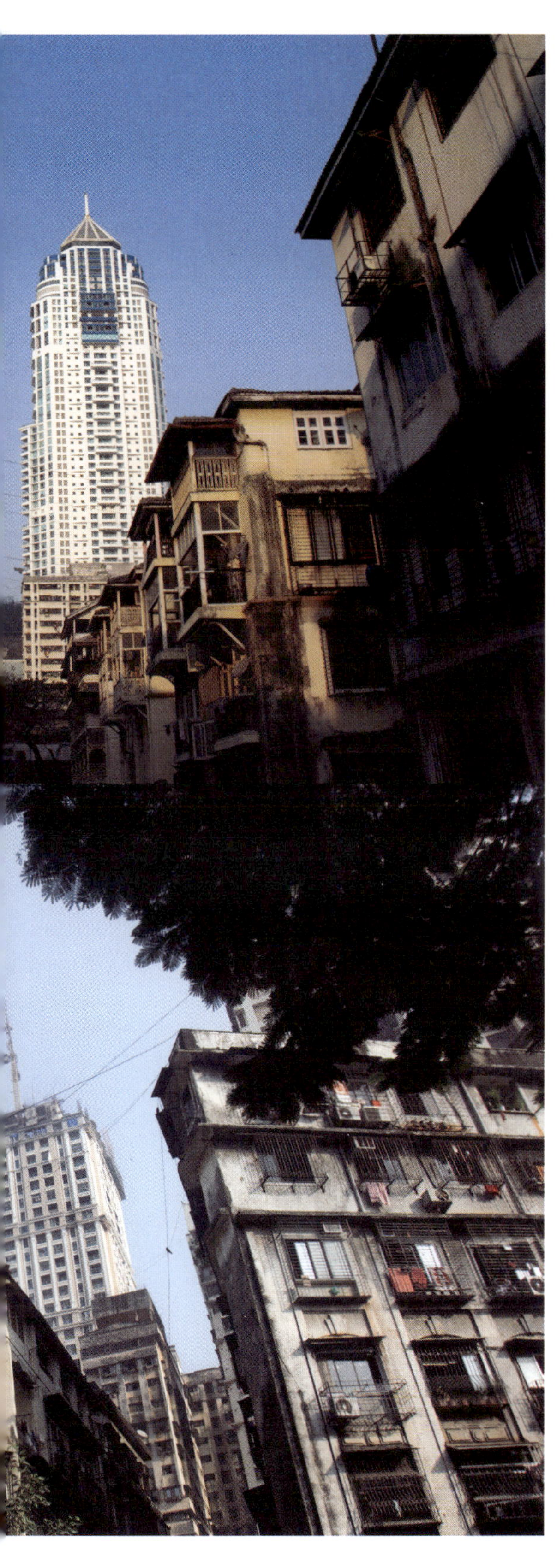

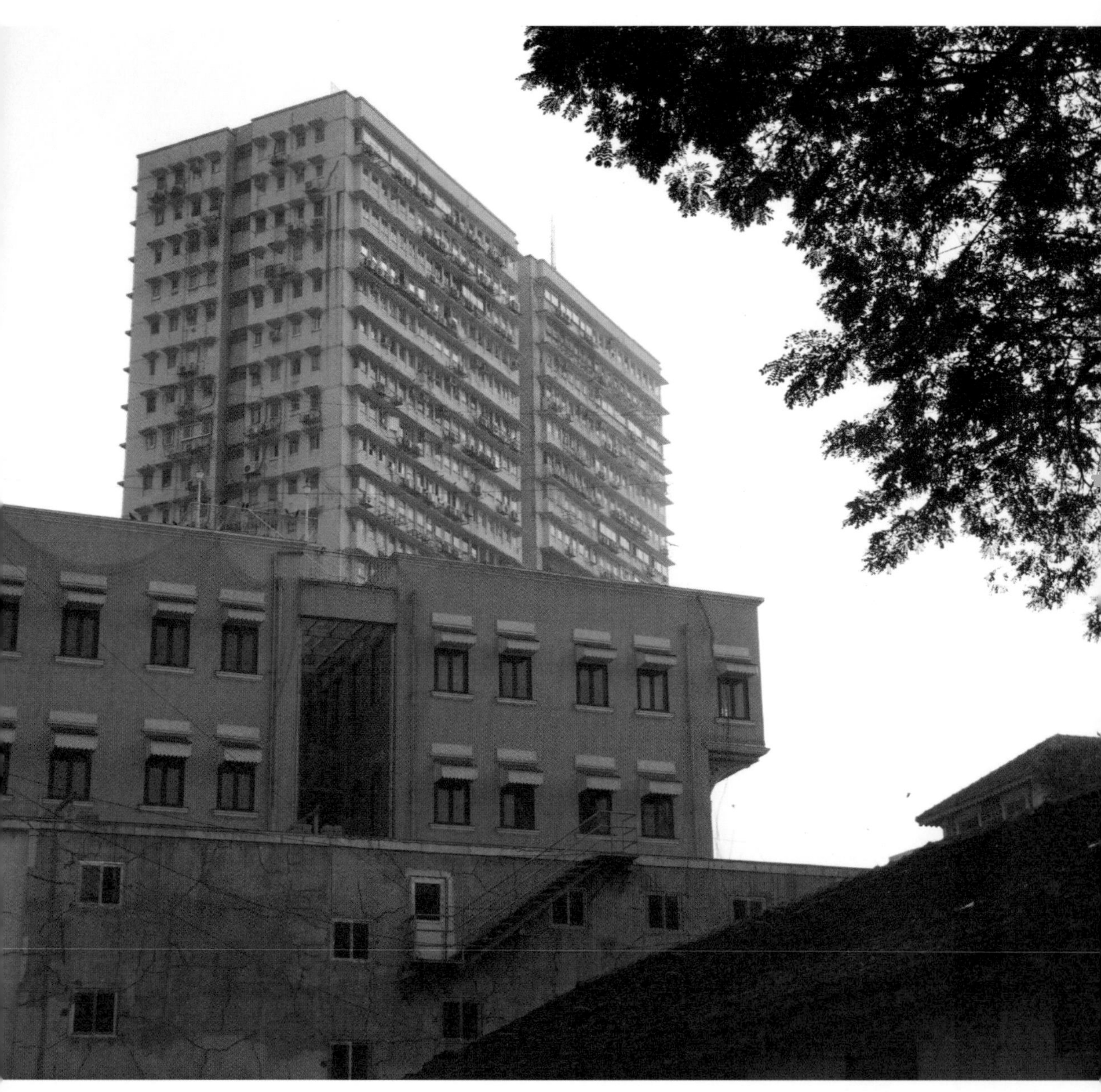

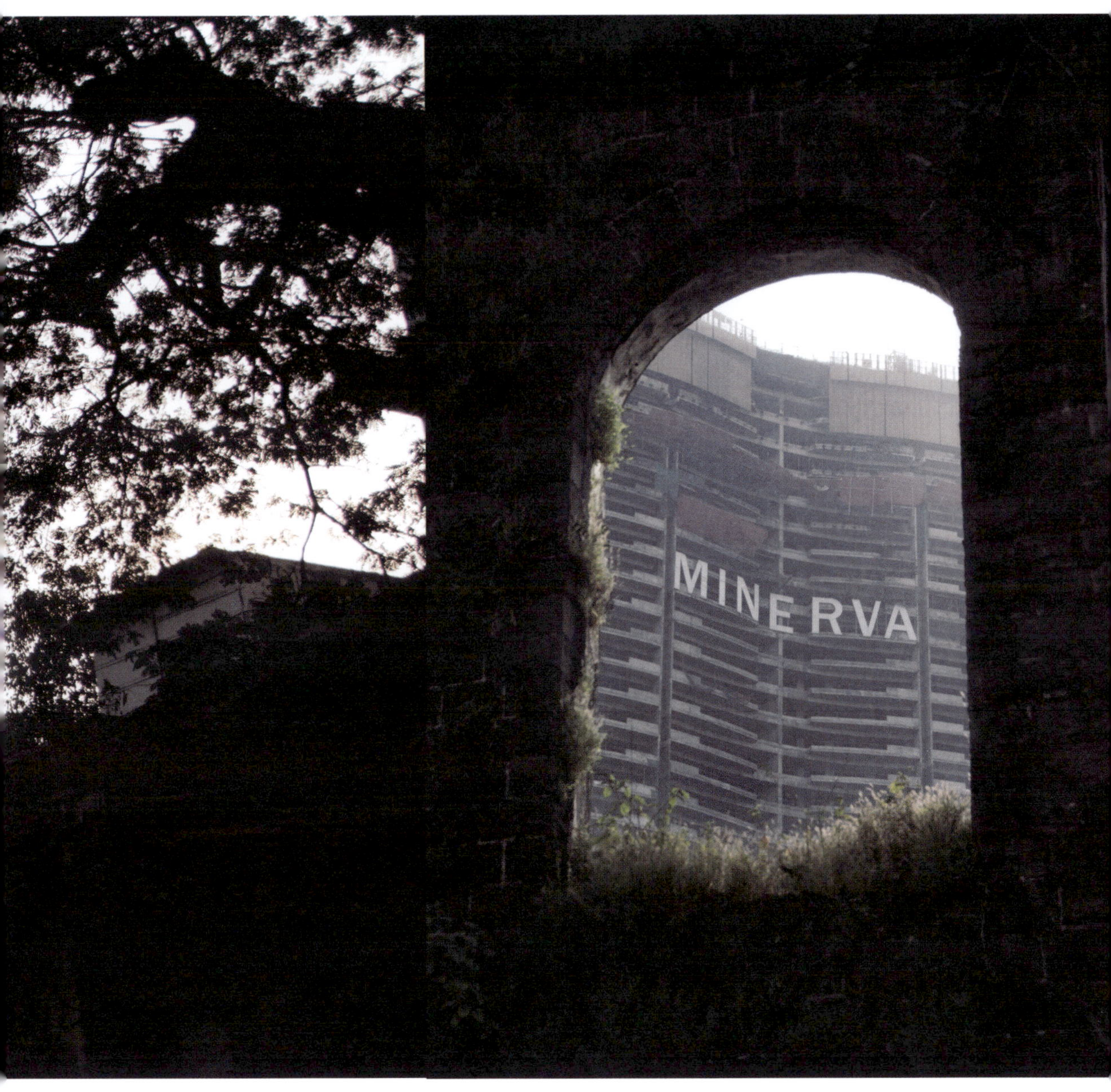
MINERVA

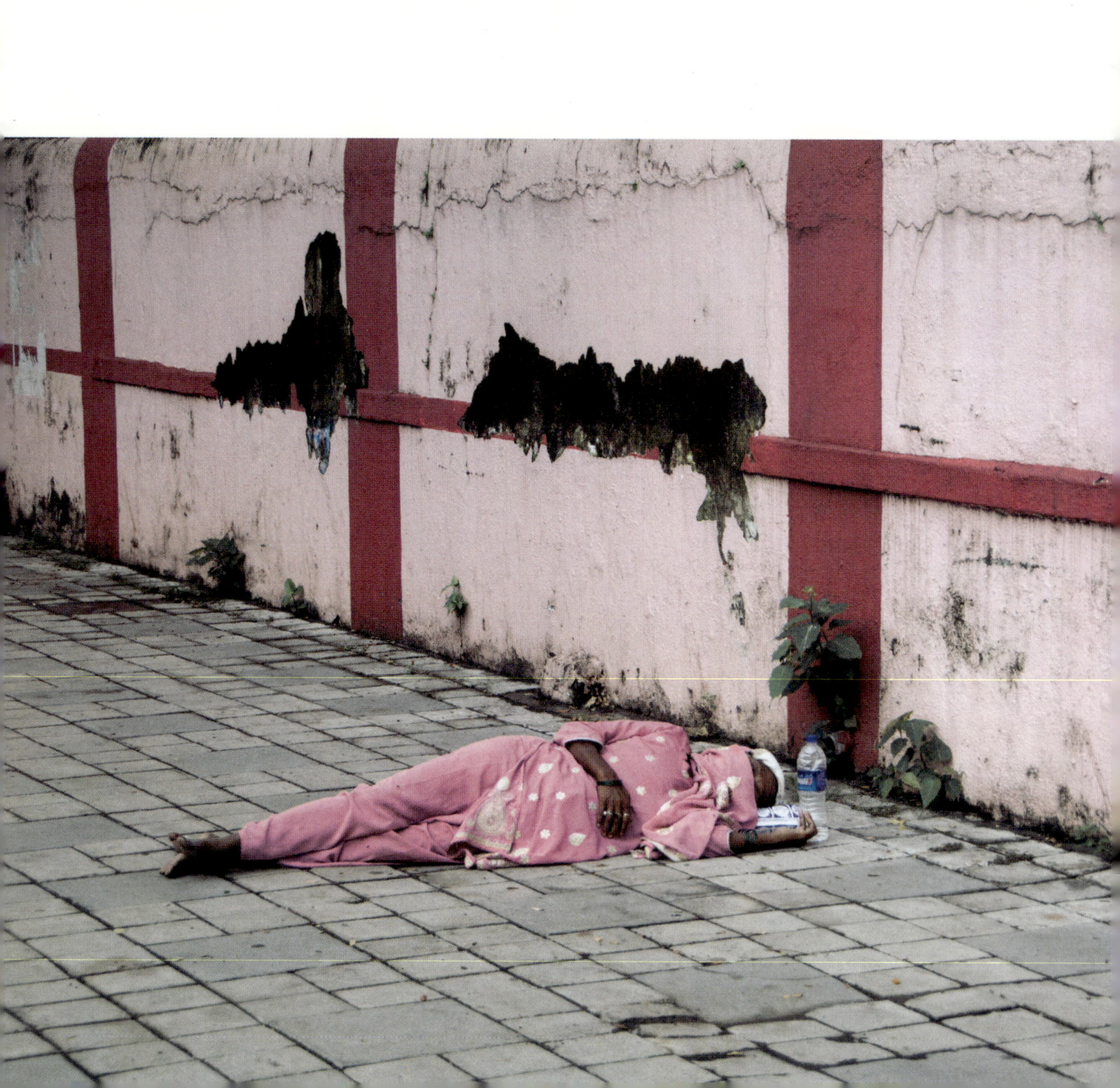

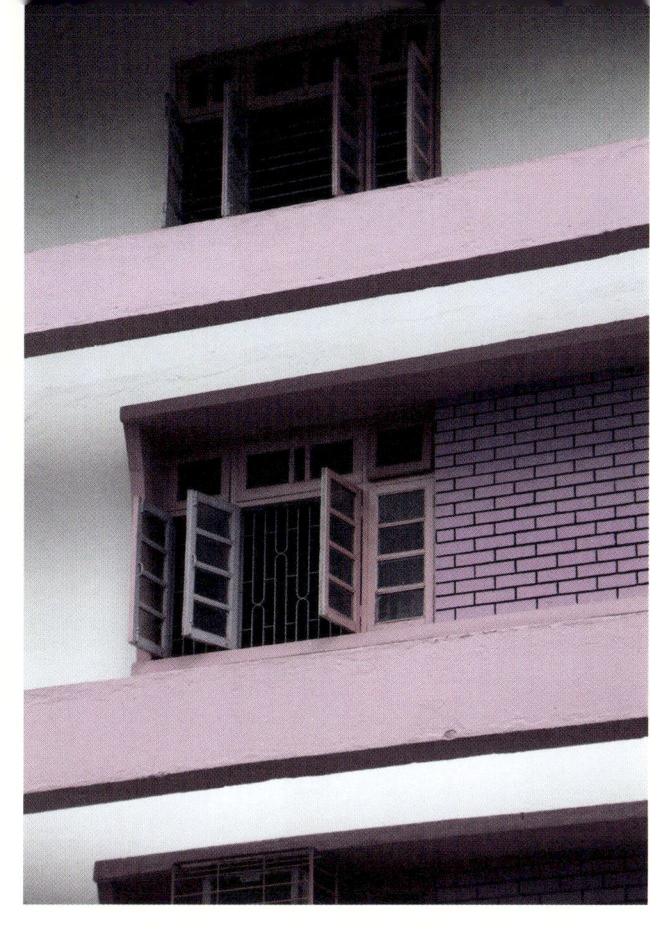
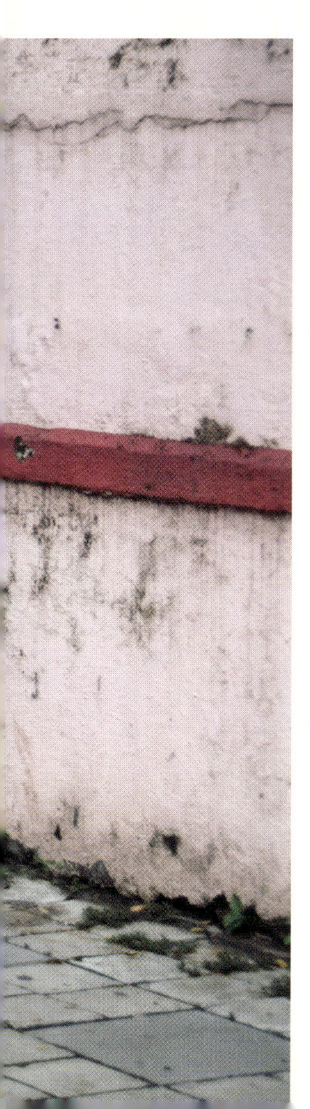

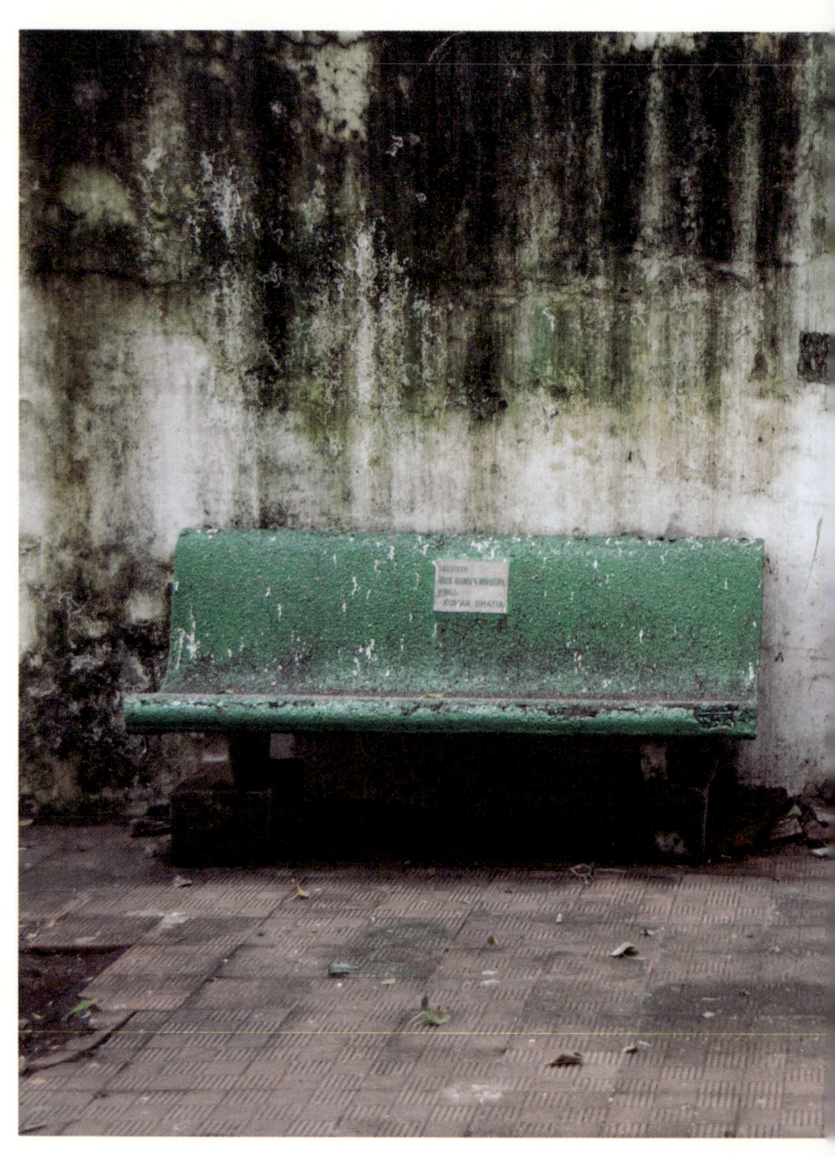

Sion

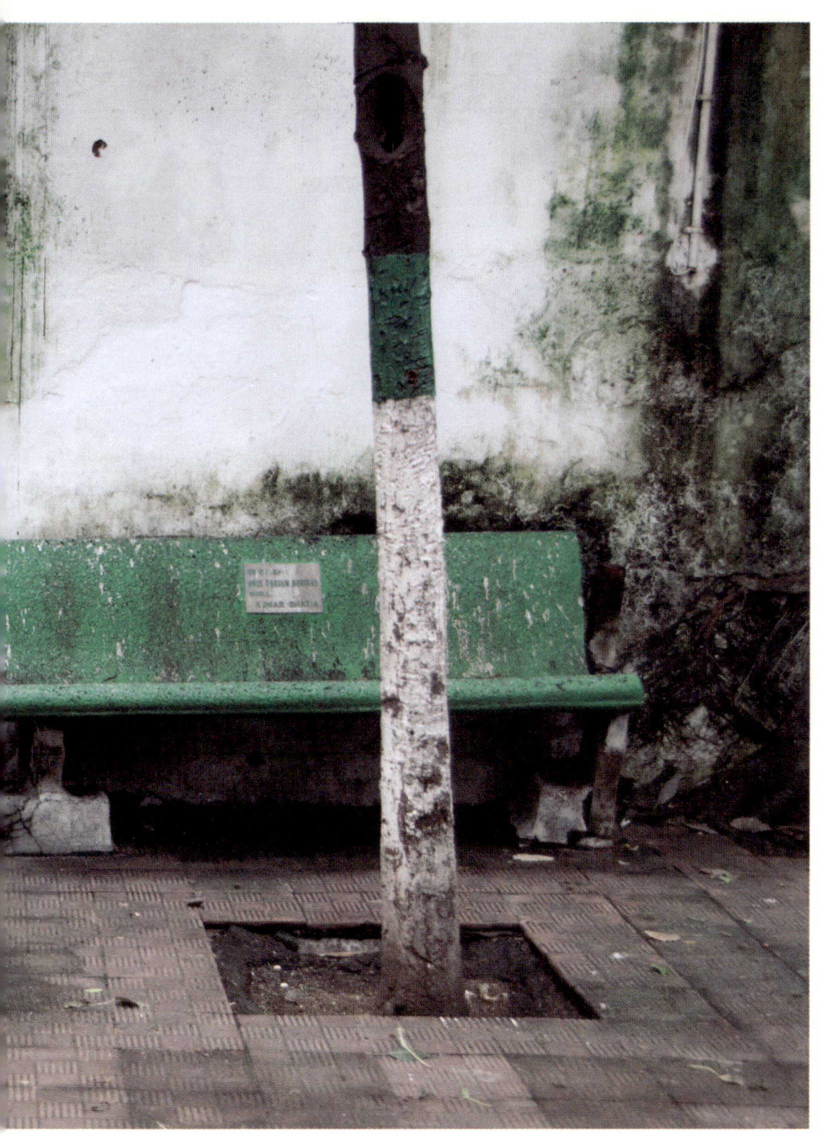

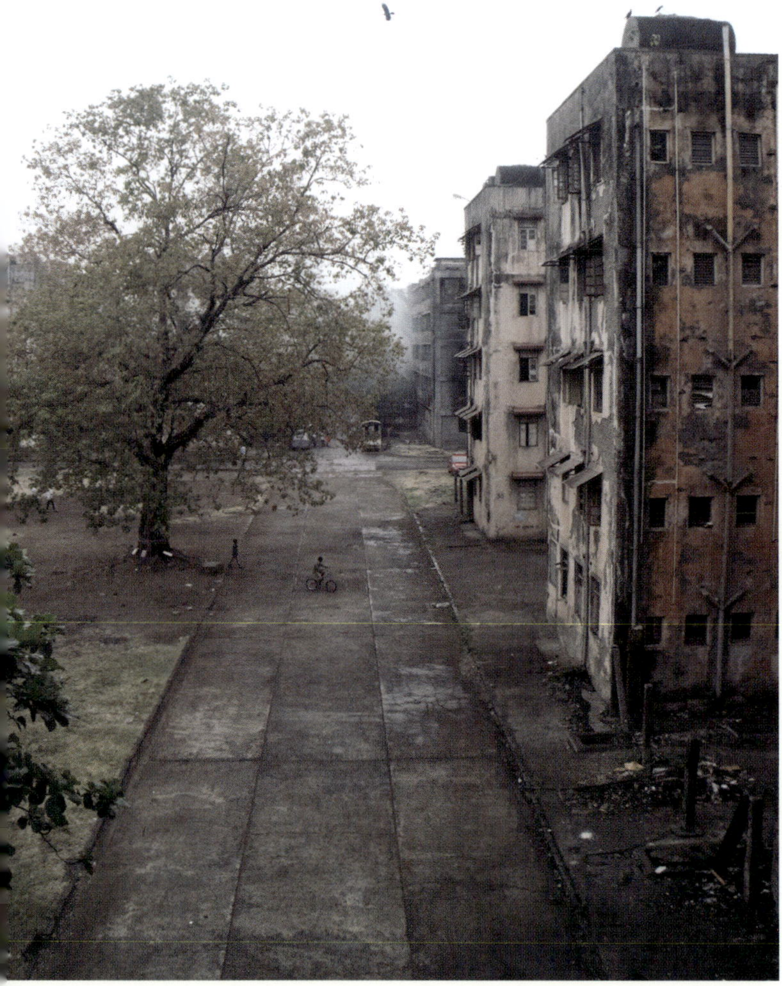

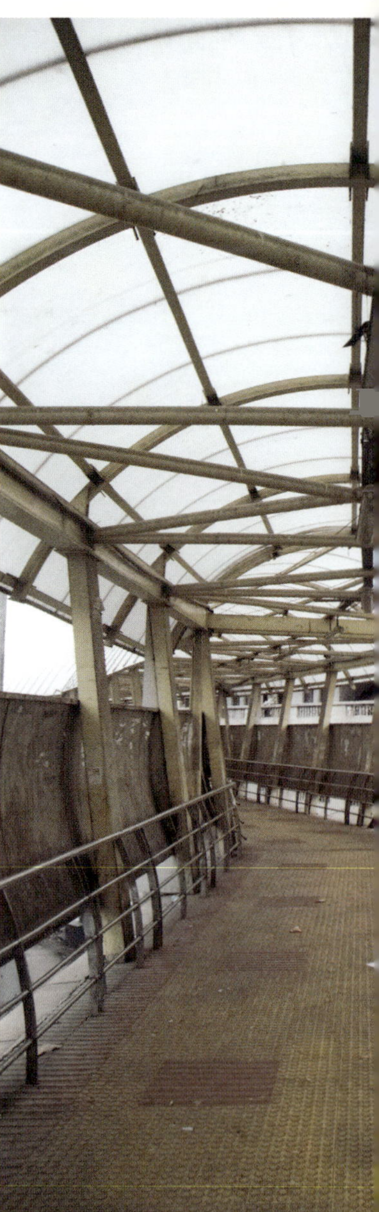

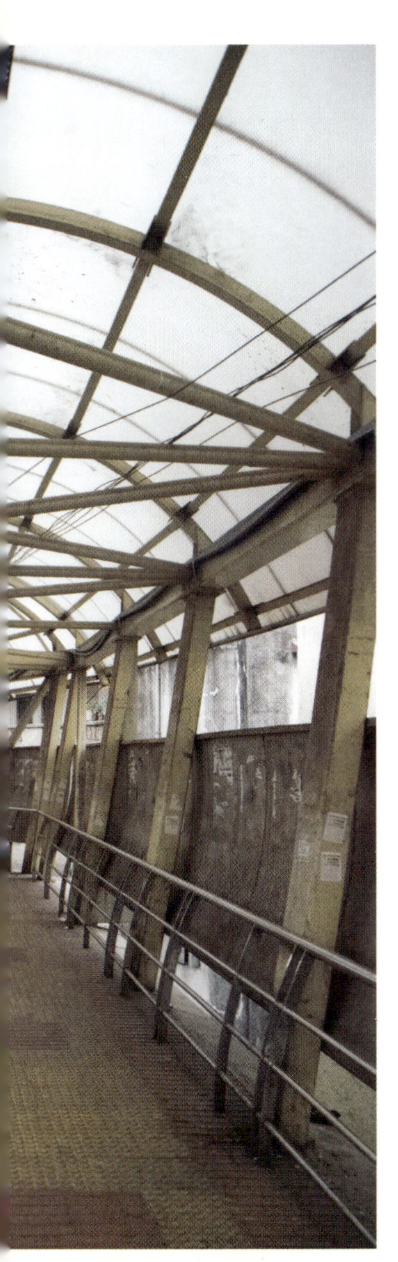

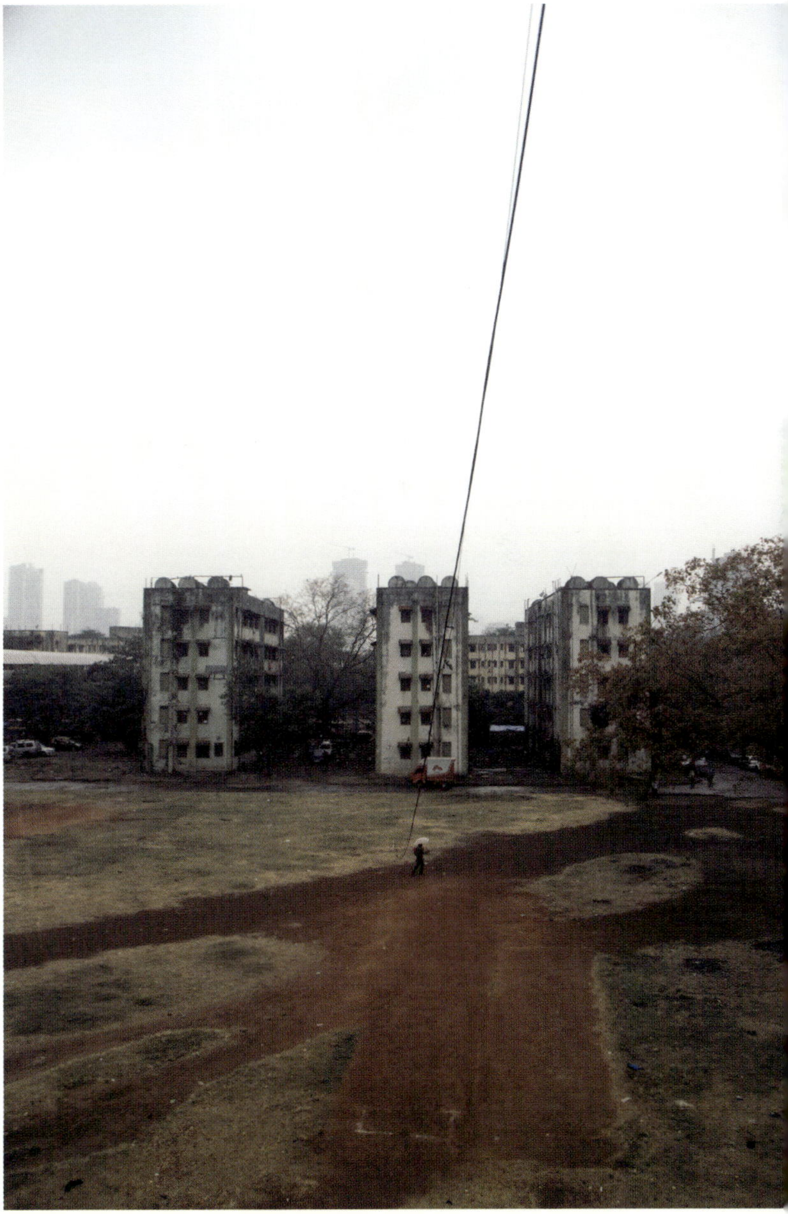

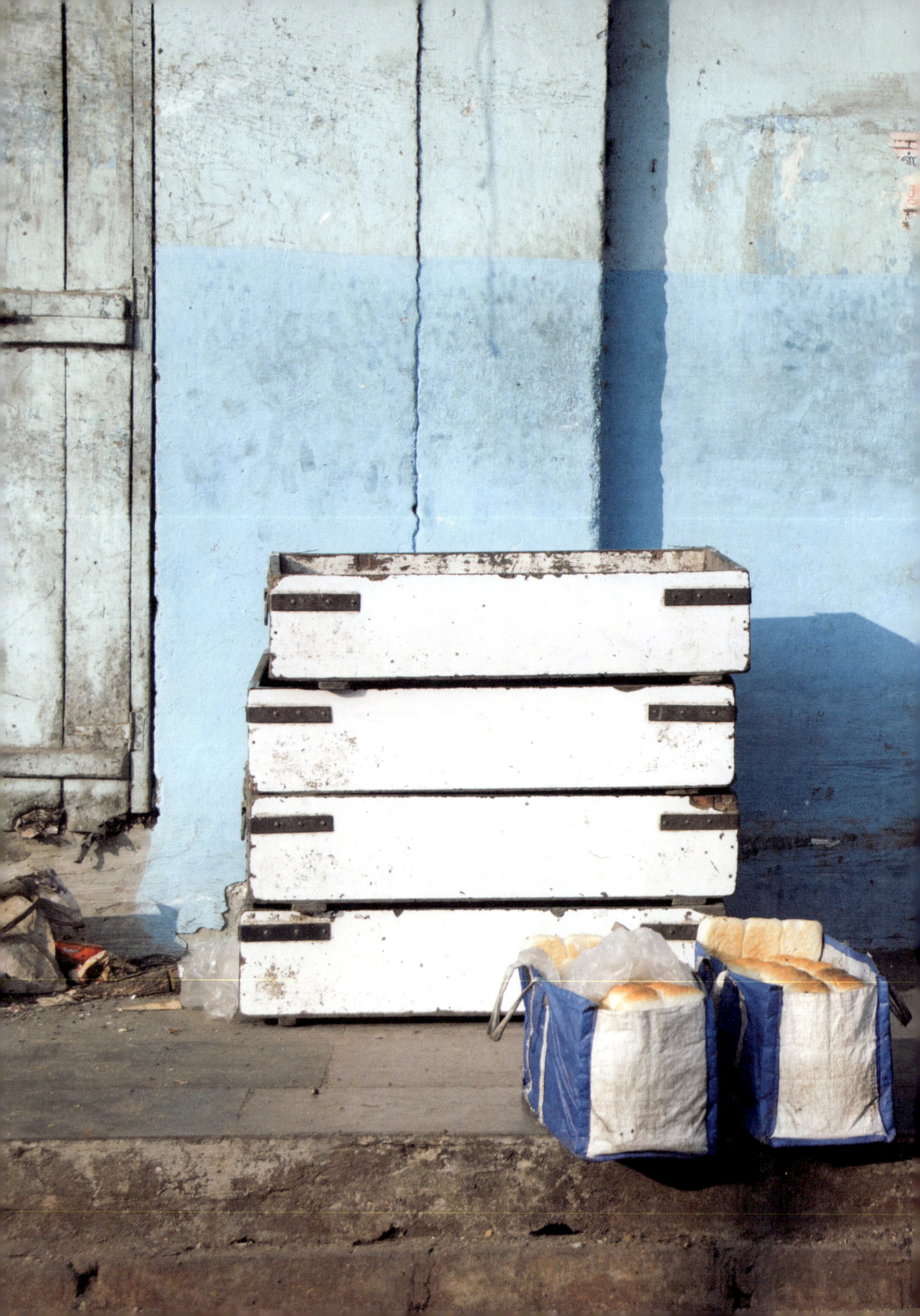

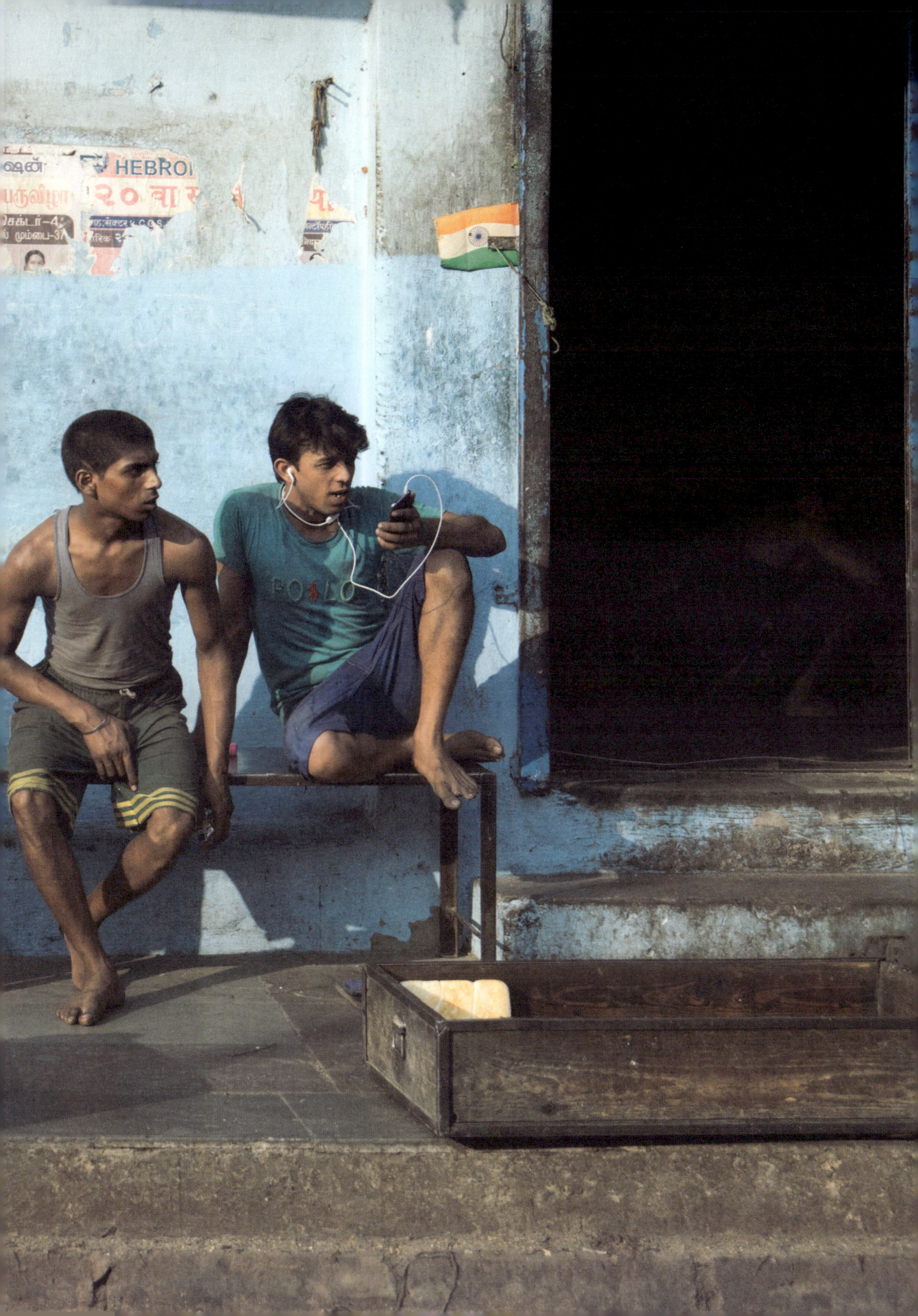
HEBRO

ENGINE ROOM

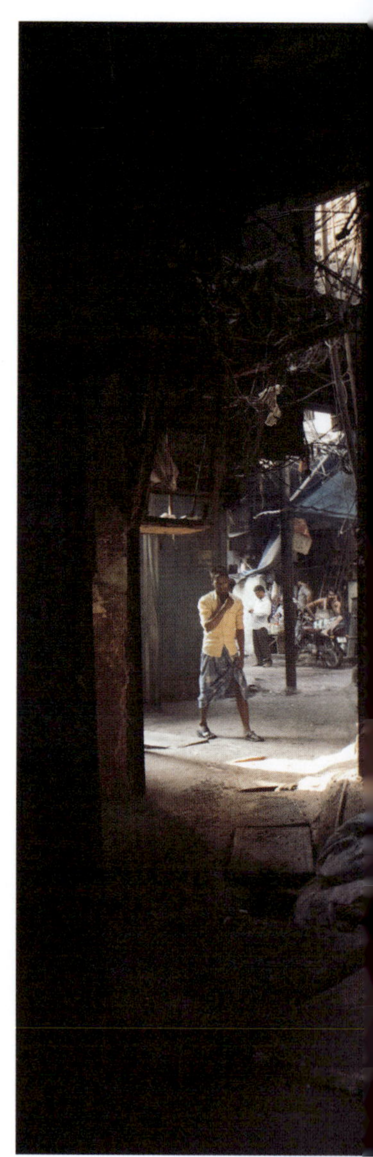

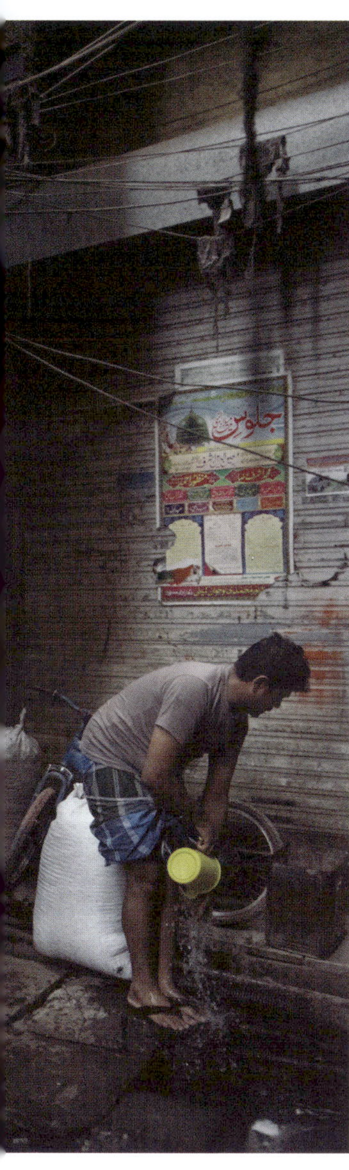

Almost all the photos you see in this book, I took early in the morning.

The last district of Mumbai I photographed was Dharavi. It was both by design and chance. Over the three years of walking the streets of the city, I did a sort of horseshoe shape around it, going south from my suburb Bandra to the city's southern tip, Colaba and then turning north to come back to Bandra. Mumbai has two local train lines that run pretty much north to south splitting most of the neighbourhoods into east and west versions of themselves.

I mapped my walks either side of these train lines, first doing the western part of an area and then doing the eastern half. I occasionally broke the pattern and changed things up, but mostly, I stuck to this discipline. So Dharavi naturally became the area I shot last. Another reason I waited for Dharavi was a mix of intrigue and intimidation. In my forty odd years in Mumbai, I had never been inside this neighbourhood, though I have driven past it many times.

Over the past few years, Dharavi has become somewhat of a global phenomenon – being the third largest slum in the world and easily one of the world's densest places. Danny Boyle shot an Oscar-winning Hollywood film here. Besides it is home to a counterculture, of local rappers and break-dancers. Inventive locals had started Dharavi tours bringing people from all over the world into its gallis. Looking in from the outside it was confusing to me. I had a genuine appreciation for the burst of creative energy coming from what seemed to be a tough place, but at the same time, a lot of it appeared opportunistic, an almost perverse exoticism of poverty. I wasn't sure how to approach it. I knew I had to go in there because I had set out to walk all of Mumbai, but I was conflicted.

Mumbai, I'd realised, is a consistently inconsistent city, with every part of it having everything, from high-rises, small industries, places of leisure, bastis, tree-lined streets to squalor. No single piece of Mumbai was one-toned, with every location throwing up a surprise or two. What I knew of Dharavi made it seem like it was one thing and it was a massive version of that one thing. I was therefore scared of going there, not because I feared for my safety, for I'd walked through others bastis in Mumbai without any untoward event. But I wanted to paint Mumbai in a good light, and it seemed that I could not go into Dharavi and claim 'all is well'.

So I left it to the end. When I did make it there, it was easily one of the more inspiring and fruitful sets of walks that I did. All is not well in Dharavi, nor is it in the rest of Mumbai, but the energy I felt in Dharavi left me encouraged. The first thing that hit me was that the day in Dharavi starts early. I would get there by 7.00 am, and it was already bursting with life. All the women were out, filling water into every type of vessel possible. Each household had a small-motorised pump to pull water to their outlet because the municipal pipes are so old that there is no water pressure.

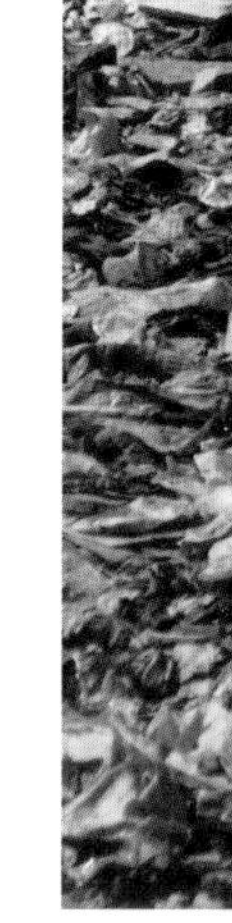

Everybody works in Dharavi, every member of every family or every other soul that lives there. Everyone does his or her part. While the women collect water to wash, bathe or to cook, the men are walking the kids to the local Balwadis (play schools). Within every block are small gallas (commercial units), big enough to fit no more than two people. These small commercial enterprises provide essential services to the residents. Each block has its own laundry service, breakfast shop, grocery store, etc. Some more centrally located junctions are full of street food stalls cooking all varieties of breakfast, sweet, savoury, spicy. Everything is fried in super hot oil, eliminating any chance of someone catching a bug. All of this is up and running first thing in the morning, much before the rest of Mumbai that comes to life, a good two to three hours later.

After completing their chores, the people of Dharavi set out to work in the rest of the city. If they are not commuting to other parts, then they are working in one of the many small-scale industries within Dharavi. Dharavi has a potter community; it is a hub for manufacturing leather goods; there are several tailoring units; material manufacturers, wholesale shops and a whole area full of units set up to recycle every possible spare part and all kinds of waste. It's the engine room of Mumbai, and therefore, as I've extrapolated before, of India. It is not one-toned at all, it's multifaceted. It's diverse, every Indian ethnic community is represented, and either lives or works in Dharavi.

Being super congested, some parts can get pitch dark. The inner bylanes are very thin and the makeshift houses on either side are stacked up to four storeys high. In here, even during the brightest part of the day, no light seeps in. But in here too life continues. I heard one fruit vendor selling kiwi, another selling pasta, and these are exotic items for India, not readily available even in the more posh parts of Mumbai. I saw municipal workers doing rounds collecting garbage. I saw an employee from the local power company taking meter readings so he could issue light bills. If you were to look at the mess of hanging wires, pipes, the lack of visibility and the sparse room to manoeuvre, you'd think how any lighting arrangement could possibly work. But it clearly does, insane as it might appear.

Successive governments have put out several master plans for the redevelopment of Dharavi, they have executed pilot schemes, but I don't think any of them have worked. So far the builder-government-local goon nexus has had a more significant say, applying the same default model of building social housing tower blocks. These building blocks, though permanent, compared to temporary structures, have not improved the quality of life. Yes, the current habitat is not safe, or indeed habitable, but if you look at the ground level shanties versus living in the proposed tower blocks, there isn't a question in my mind what the locals would prefer.

There is a sense of community in the current village-like layout, there is accessibility, and the openness that creates safety in numbers. In small rooms, up in tower blocks, that sense of community is broken, and the natural access to essentials disrupted. Also, you cannot have local snack shops, dhobi gallas (laundries), vegetable vendors, and grocers on every floor. The smaller scale of the service providers today gives the residents many more options, differing lines of credit, for example, something that larger consolidated shops in central markets will not provide to the people who live their lives day to day. Now that might not appear ideal, and clearly there is a desperate need for change, but past plans have failed, and I feel again it is because of a lack of imagination and laziness to think of unique solutions for a unique problem.

Unlike in other parts of the city, in Dharavi, I had more interactions with the local people. Here I was in their space, and I didn't have the option of shooting from afar. They all wondered what I was doing and whether I was a surveyor or a journalist. By now, they are used to the attention and amused by curious eyes. On one of the days, I met this young woman, Meena. She seemed to be of South Indian descent and was cleaning up her little canteen. Three young girls were sitting opposite her unit when she enquired what I was doing. I told her I was doing a personal art project documenting Mumbai by walking its streets. She asked me to ensure that I said something good about Dharavi, for everyone had given Dharavi a lousy name for too long. She was proud of Dharavi, she was hopeful, but I don't think she was fooling herself as to who she was or where she was.

Like her, I am proud of my roots. Yes, I want change, but the change has to appreciate who we are, what we are, and how we got here. It has to take responsibility for our roles in the city's story and not just blame the past for the current state of affairs. It also cannot just start with a clean slate. Dharavi is essential, its location is vital, it either provides necessary services or the hands on the deck of the ship that is Mumbai. Mumbai has to appreciate that, yes, we have the third largest slum in the world, but without it, we wouldn't be the metropolis we are today.

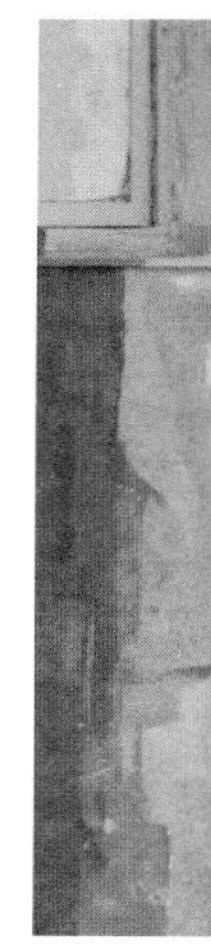

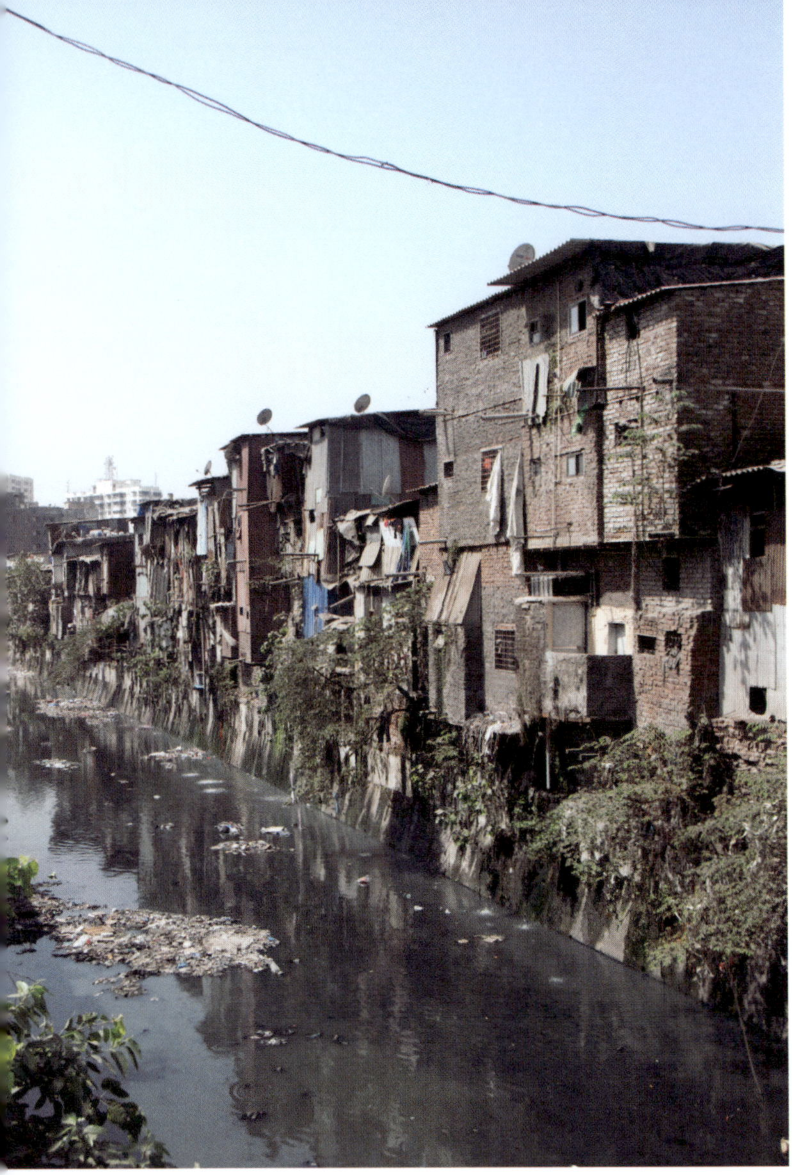

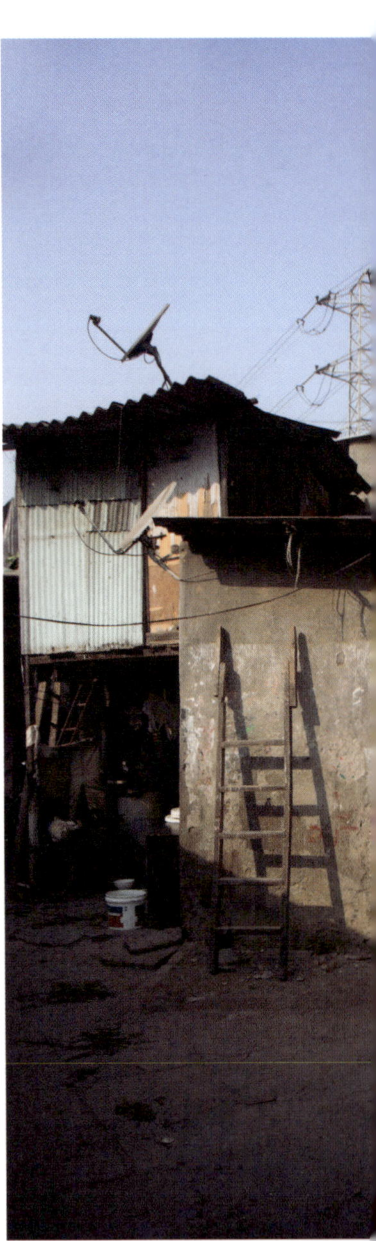

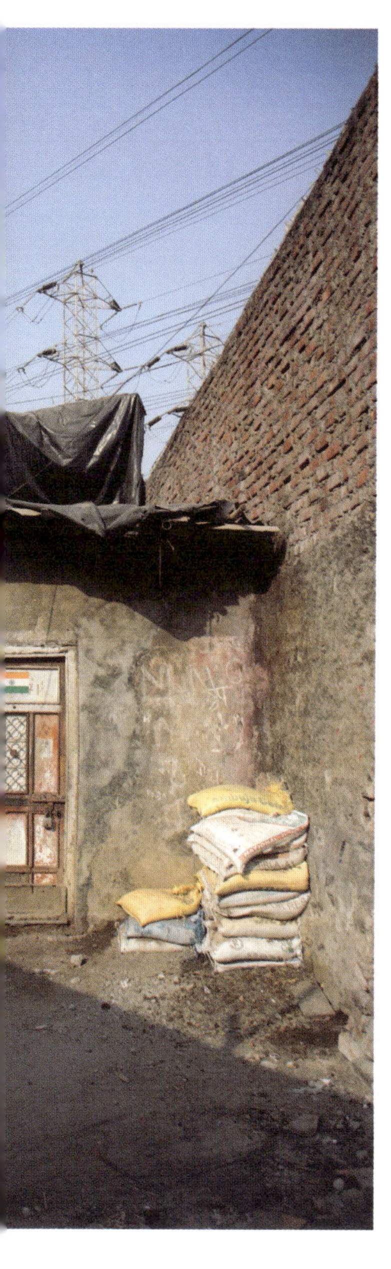

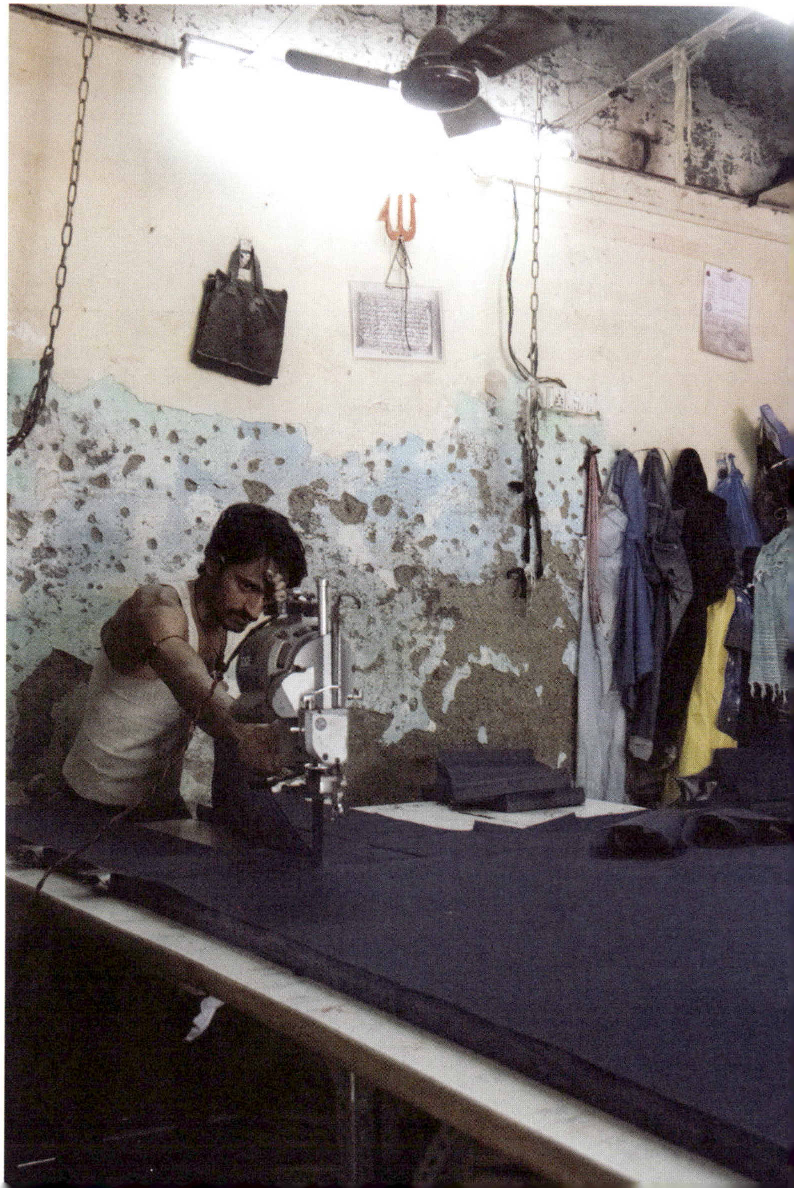

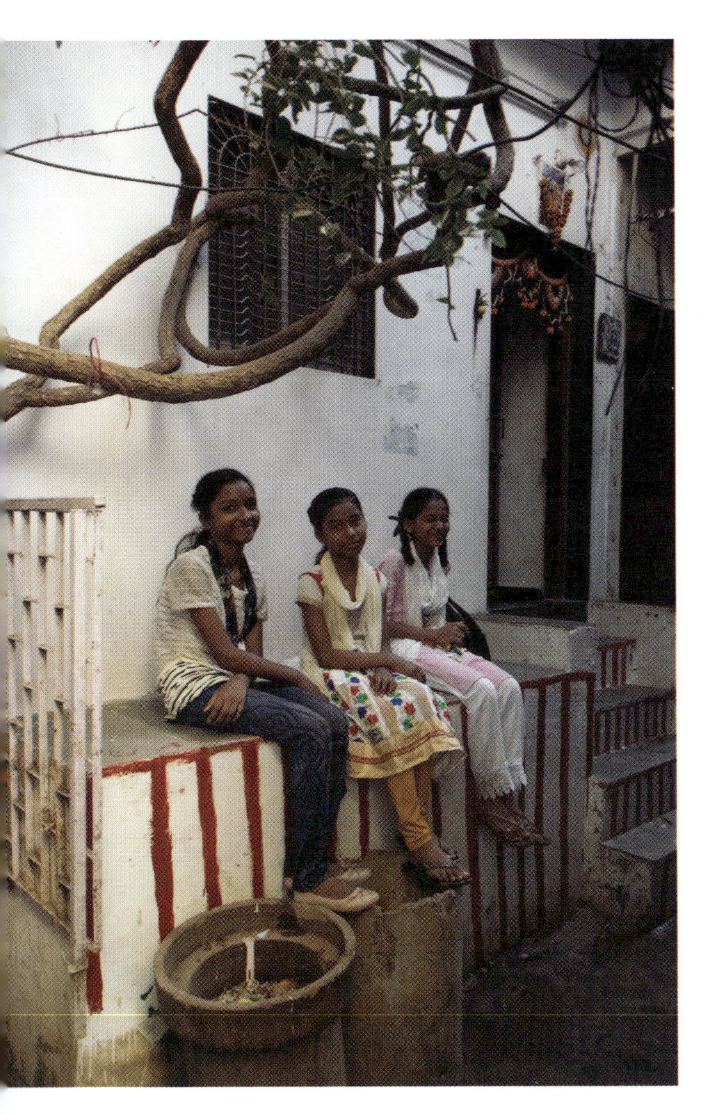

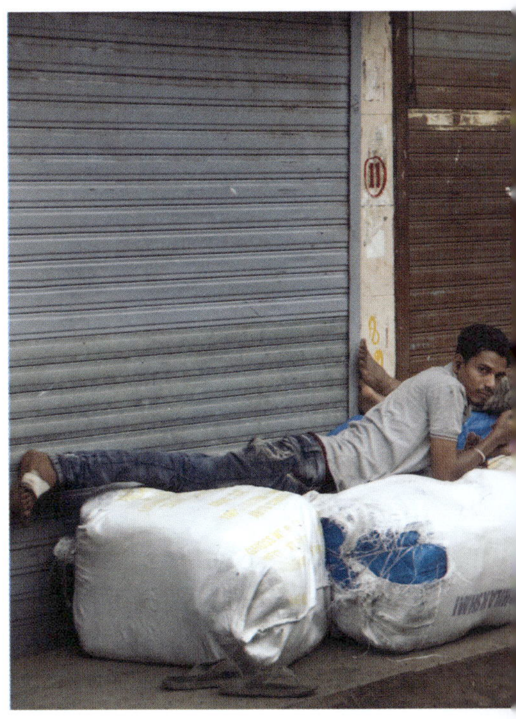

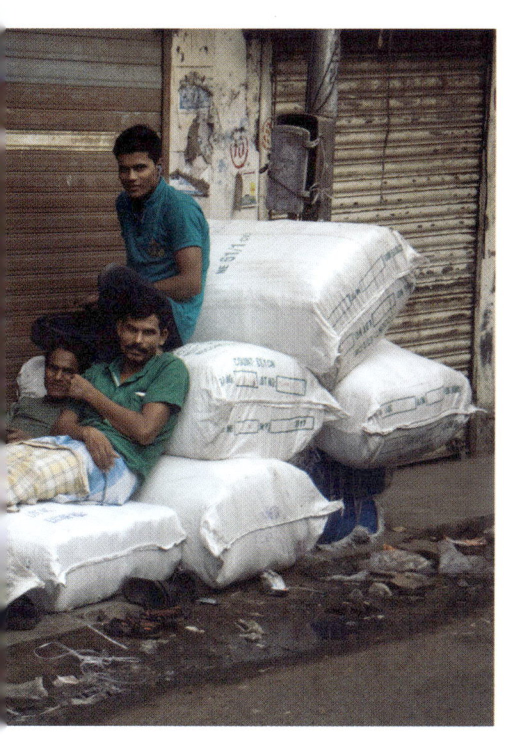

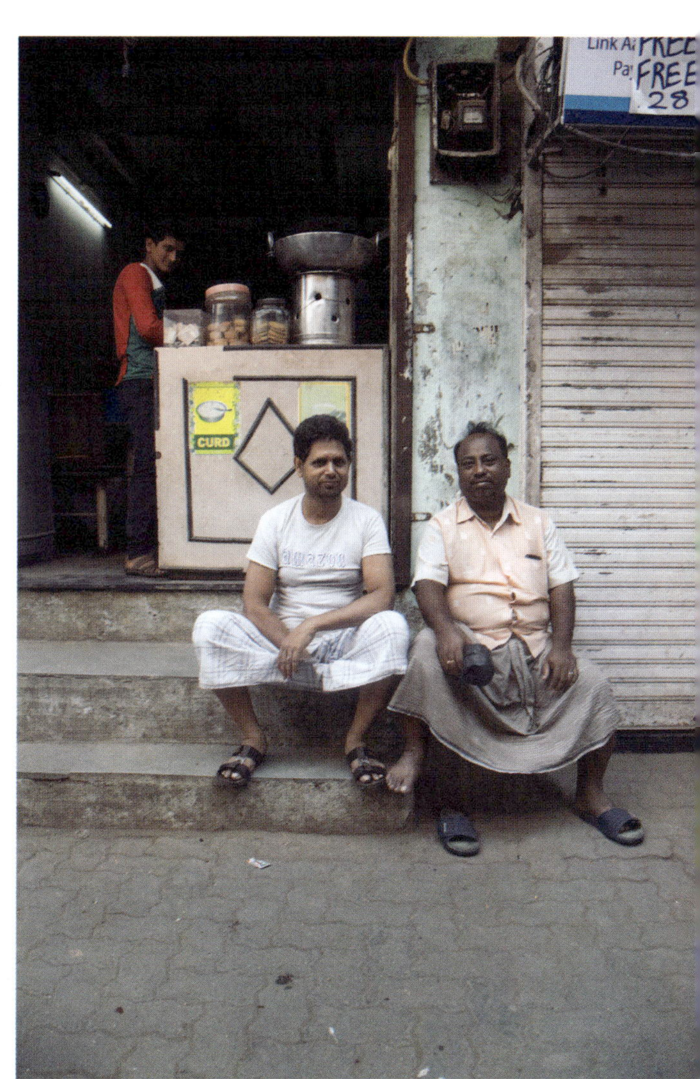

Link A
Pa
FREE
FREE
28
CURD

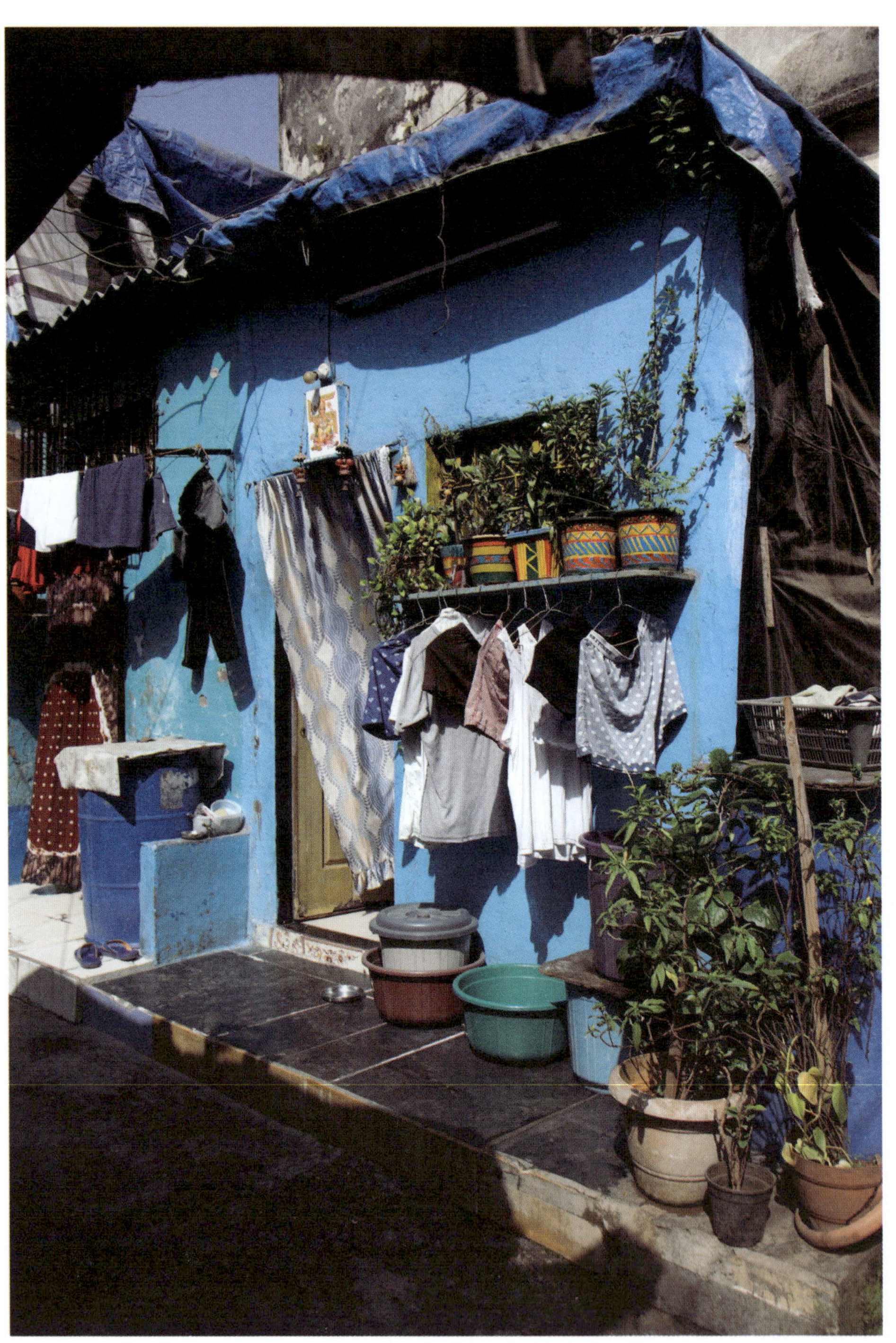

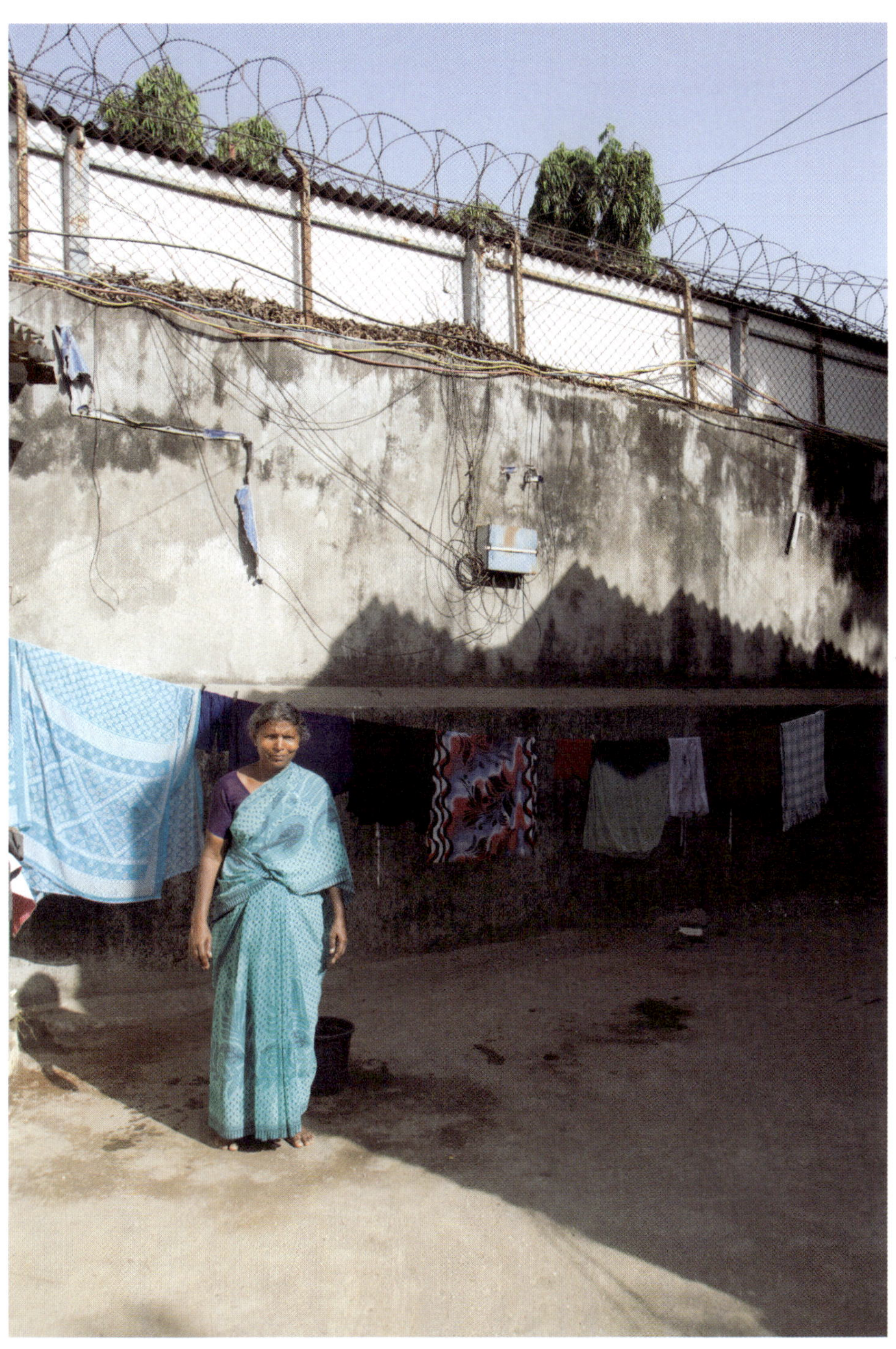

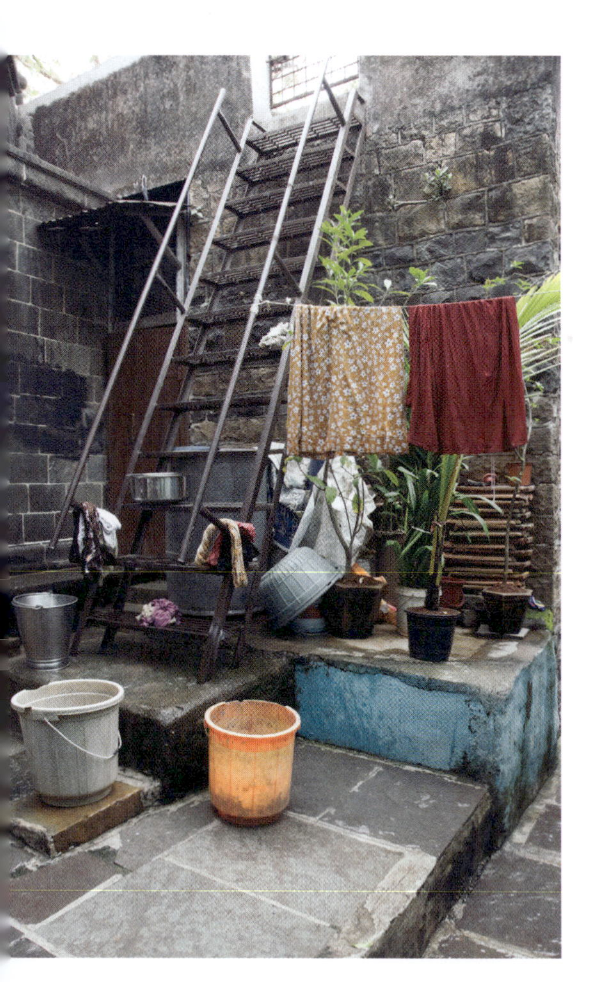

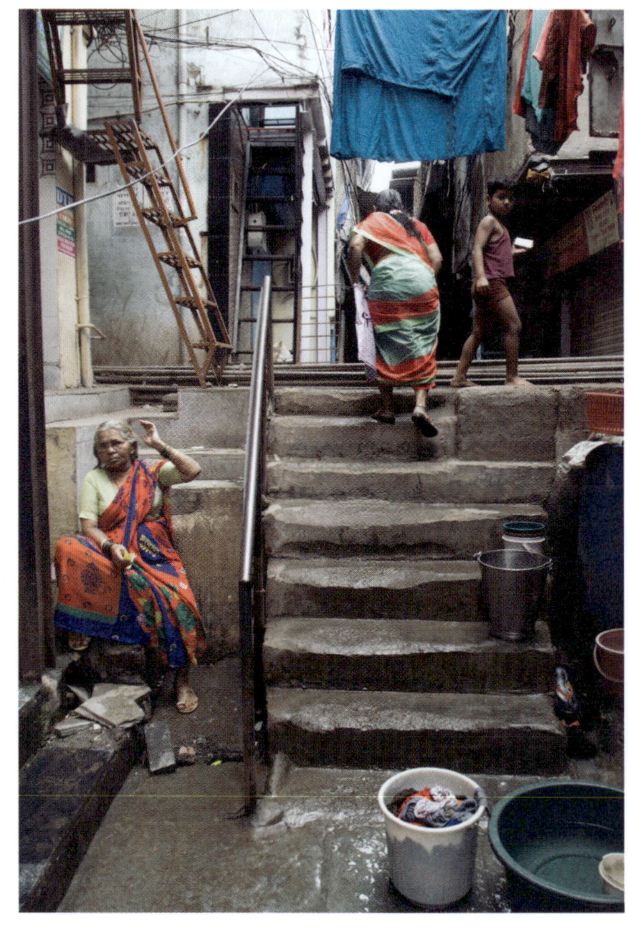

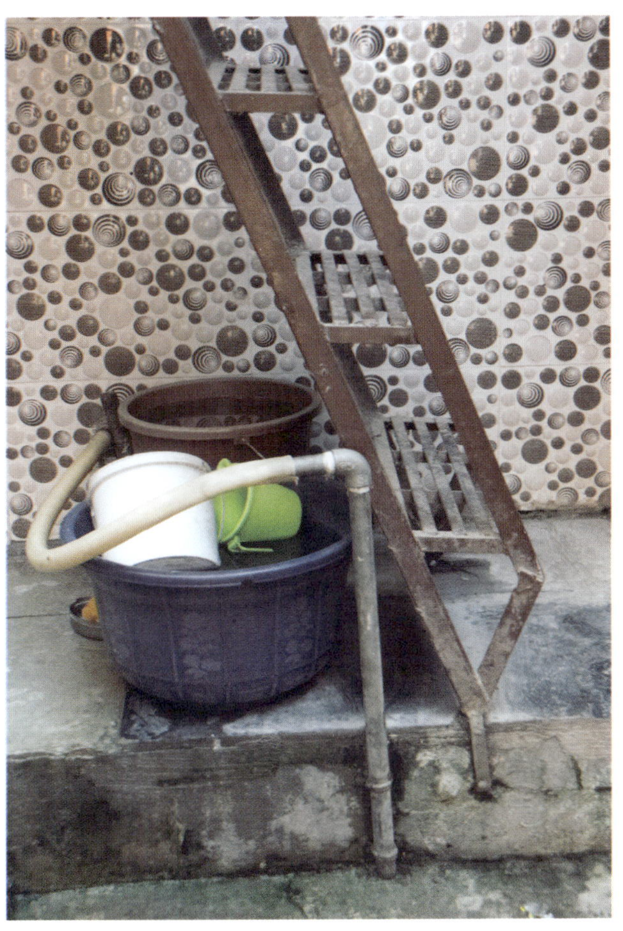

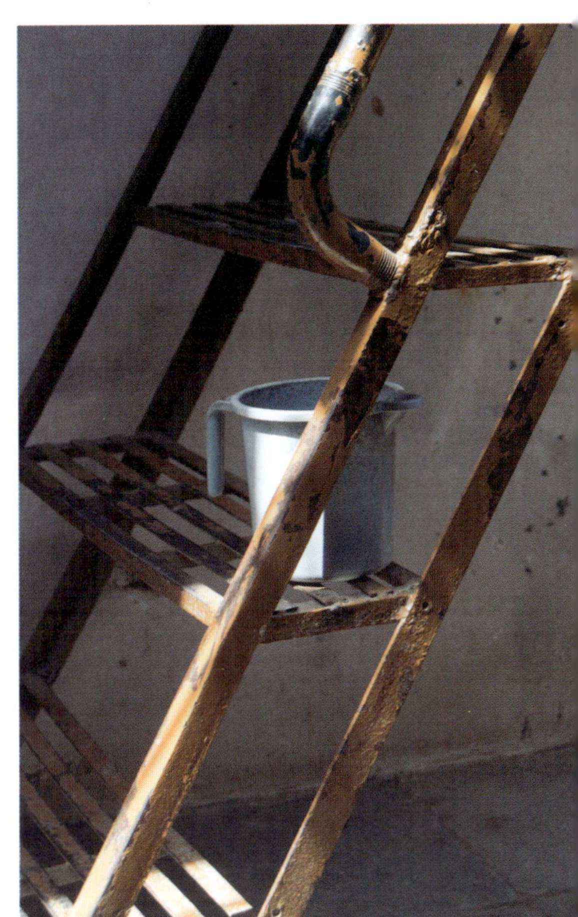

STILL BOMBAY

The city's contradictions have always been part of my creative discourse. Through my art, I've been trying to reconcile the two cities, the Bombay of everyone's dreams and the living, breathing Mumbai. While walking the whole city, I became acutely aware that directly or indirectly, I was connecting with all of Mumbai's twelve million people. Documenting their daily lives, photographing where they lived and worked humbled me: the sheer diversity of their stories, how different they were but how all of them on some level moved to the same rhythm, the rhythm that is Mumbai. The pictures made me think of the city in a much more nuanced way, with less judgment and more compassion.

The walks made me realise that I was living in a bubble, coming as I do, from a place of privilege. Mumbai within India is a bubble, and I lived in Bandra, which was like living in a bubble within a bubble. This conflict made me appreciate that everyone in this city is struggling, absurdly, even Ambani, with his giant calling card built on a dung heap and the millions who have to fight for a meal but have a satellite dish attached atop their makeshift roofs.

The photography tries to capture every kind of Mumbai, the black, the white and every other colour in-between – not looking for easy answers but trying to have a conversation. If in the city, the changes were more of a constant phenomenon, consistent, considered, and slower changes, with smoother transitions, then maybe we'd stop making the same mistakes again and again, and the gaps between the two cities would become smaller.

With the pictures – especially the colour-coordinated photos of the city's unassuming details, its architecture and its people – I was hoping to put some sort of skin back on the raw naked body that is Mumbai, and invoking nostalgia for a Bombay of my memories. What the city made me realise is that the idea of this city is not static. It is continually changing, continually appropriating the stories of its aspirants, adapting to their ways. Its name used to be Bombay, now it is Mumbai. Its form has changed regularly, it used to be seven islands, currently reclaimed into one landmass. Every day it grows, deeper inland, away from the sea and into the mainland. It is this flux, this energy, this openness that attracts people in numbers from all parts of Indian and now the world.

I was naïvely trying to tame the beast that is Mumbai, define it with a single idea or present it under a unique theme. While walking, I saw the city of my memories but also experienced the capital of a million dreams. On reflection, I find the city can be both, many Mumbais and still Bombay.

DESIGNER'S NOTE

When we first began our collaboration with Tara Books, they gave us
a choice to pick a book to design from among four proposals. We chose what
eventually became 'Still Bombay'. We were intrigued by what we saw: a set
of over 18,000 photographs of Mumbai clicked by artist and designer Mayur
Tekchandaney. He had turned his recovery from an accident into an elaborate
art project, photographing his city as he walked to heal himself. The project
grew organically: general observations led to more pointed photographs,
sometimes of specific details; the experience of seeing Bombay again, so to
speak, helped him articulate his new understanding with what he has known
all his life. Photographs led to writing whimsical essays.

When we worked our way through pictures and text we were not sure
what form this book ought to take: a photobook? A travelogue? An elaborate
zine? We felt the project had elements of all the above, and since we did not
have to conform to a set layout, we had scope for experimentation. Tara Books
also suggested that we participate in the project actively, and we were happy to
be more than a layout machine. As we saw it, this book warranted more than
a simple reading of pictures and we wanted to create a rich visual experience,
which captured Mayur's own organic and sometimes serendipitous visual journey
through his city.

Going through the large bank of photographs we noticed an everyman quality
to the photography — it had a pedestrian ambience, was observational and had
not set out to be aesthetically pleasing. It seemed to us that rather than the
individual picture, the relationship between photographs was far more important
and this, we thought, should guide our story-telling. Additionally, we wanted to
interpret Mayur's own experience of walking, observing and remembering. These
are abstract processes that don't follow a linear visual experience. For, as a walker,
you would notice the landscape as a whole at times, and at other times concentrate
on a small detail in a poster, missing even the building on which it is pasted.

We realised therefore that this book cannot be treated using a grid-like
format. Rather our layout design had to make room for image-making, with
each spread — a set of facing pages — featuring an image or related images
that made visual sense on their own, and also helped move the narrative.
Mayur's essays informed the image-making process that we embarked upon.
They were imaginative and whimsical, touching on various personal and civic
topics and presented a refreshing take on the maximum city. Our compositions
drew inspiration from various elements: movement, colour, texture, ambience
and story.

Our challenge here was to allow the images to communicate on their own,
and yet call attention to particular neighbourhoods and geographies, themes
and emotions. Conversations with Mayur and the Tara team helped address this
challenge — and Mayur pitched in more text, writing a set of short texts, which
could be read as extended captions. Some of these texts referenced particular
neighbourhoods, others were brief reflections on the city. He also grouped his
images into two sets: one, comprising photographs of specific places in the city,

and the other, of images that could be used to complement the essays and short texts. Our task was to assemble these various elements into a whole. As far as the essays were concerned, we did the following: each essay was prefaced by a spread, featuring the title in bold, a defining photograph and opening lines. This was followed by the rest of the text, framed by ambient and evocative photographic swatches and images that completed the sense of the essay. These images are neither illustrative nor do they reference particular sites or places in the city, rather they extend the meaning of the essay.

As for the short texts, which were not more than a paragraph long: we read them as interesting asides, rather loud thoughts on the city, in contrast to the leisurely tone of the essays. And here we had to distinguish texts that referenced places from those that were musings on the city. For the first, the choice of visuals was given, and for the second, we chose images that amplified the meanings of words. Texts accompanied by photos of places were placed against a light grey background and framed by a specific symbol, the Double Asterisk; while those that comprised ideas or musings were placed on a white background and framed by a Silicrow. These symbols have an archaic quality, which we thought went well with Mayur's sense of the city, as both old and new. In addition, they have been used in older texts, for much the same purpose, to help readers navigate varied levels of the narrative.

Our next challenge was to combine the photographs of particular places in the city, with the other two sections. We set these against a light beige background, with place names on either side of the spreads. These photographs are interspersed through the book, and follow the essays and short texts in what might appear a random manner, but which are actually directed by cues in the texts.

NOTE ON TYPOGRAPHY

The book's primary typeface is Valentin, a proportional typewriter typeface designed by Phillip Neumeyer (aka Rüdinger). We wanted a typeface that could become the visual personification of Mayur's voice, as much of the text feels candid and easy — almost conversational. We wanted a touch of nostalgia, with an easy, journal-like feeling throughout the text. Valentin suited perfectly, bringing a modern finish to a very familiar visual language (of typewriter type). Valentin is also proportional (as opposed to typewriter text's usual fixed-width quality) making readability much easier.

Valentin is paired with Chiswick Grotesk, designed by Paul Barnes (Commercial Type), for headlines. Chiswick is inspired by 18th century British sans serifs using the transitional model of John Baskerville as the foundation. We felt this was a perfect choice for a book about Bombay, with its colonial past existing in various forms even today.

NOVEMBER
Studio for Design & Typography

STILL BOMBAY
Copyright © 2021 Tara Books Pvt. Ltd.
For the text and photos: Mayur Tekchandaney

For this edition:
Tara Books Pvt. Ltd., India www.tarabooks.com and
Tara Publishing Ltd., UK www.tarabooks.com/uk

Design: November
Cover: Ragini Siruguri
Production: C. Arumugam

Printed in India by Canara Traders and Printers Pvt. Ltd., Chennai

ISBN 978-93-90037-01-8